RESIDENCE OF CHANDLER SPRAGUE, ESQ.

HISTORY

OF

NORTH BRIDGEWATER,

Plymouth County, Massachusetts,

FROM ITS FIRST SETTLEMENT TO THE PRESENT TIME,

WITH

FAMILY REGISTERS.

BY BRADFORD KINGMAN,

MEMBER OF THE NEW ENGLAND HISTORIC GENEALOGICAL SOCIETY; CORRESPONDING MEMBER OF WIS-
CONSIN HISTORICAL SOCIETY; ESSEX INSTITUTE, SALEM; WEYMOUTH HISTORICAL SOCIETY;
PILGRIM SOCIETY, PLYMOUTH; BOSTONIAN SOCIETY; HISTORIAN AND COR-
RESPONDING SECRETARY OF THE KINGMAN MEMORIAL ASSOCIATION.

BOSTON:
PUBLISHED BY THE AUTHOR.
1866.

– Notice –

The foxing, or discoloration with age, characteristic of old books, sometimes shows
through to some extent in reprints such as
this, especially when the foxing is very severe
in the original book. We feel that the contents of this book warrant its reissue despite
these blemishes, and hope you will agree and
read it with pleasure.

Entered, according to Act of Congress, in the year 1866, by

BRADFORD KINGMAN,

In the Clerk's Office of the District Court for the District of Massachusetts.

Facsimile Reprint

Published 1991 By
HERITAGE BOOKS, INC.
1540 Pointer Ridge Place, Bowie, Maryland 20716
(301)-390-7709

ISBN 1-55613-513-0

DEDICATION.

TO

The Descendants of the Early Settlers

OF

NORTH BRIDGEWATER,

WHEREVER RESIDING,

AND TO THE

Present Inhabitants of the Town,

THIS WORK IS MOST RESPECTFULLY DEDICATED

BY THE AUTHOR.

CONTENTS.

CHAP. I. — HISTORY OF NORTH BRIDGEWATER.

Situation and Extent, 1; Topography, 1; Centre Village, 2; Campello, 2; Sprague's, or Factory Village, 3; North-West Bridgewater, 3; Rivers and Brooks, 4; Hills, 5; Natural History, 6; Geological Formation, 10.

CHAP. II. — FIRST SETTLEMENT.

Grant of Plantation, 11; Bridgewater purchased of the Indians, 12, 13; Division of the Town, 15; Petition of the North Precinct to be set off as a separate Town, 16; Charter for a Precinct, 18; First Meeting of the Same, 19.

CHAP. III. — ECCLESIASTICAL HISTORY.

Ministry of Rev. John Porter, 21; Rev. Asa Meech, 25; Rev. Daniel Huntington, 28; Rev. William Thompson, 34; Rev. Paul Couch, 38; Rev. Nathaniel B. Blanchard, 43; Rev. Edward L. Clark, 45.

CHAP. IV. — ECCLESIASTICAL HISTORY, CONTINUED.

Second Congregational Church, 47; New Jerusalem Church, 49; South Congregational Church, Campello, 54; First Methodist Episcopal Church, 65; First Baptist Church, 66; Porter Evangelical Church, 69; Catholic Church, 75; First Universalist Church, 77; Quakers, or Friends, 79; Second Methodist Episcopal Church, 80.

CHAP. V. — MEETING-HOUSES OF THE CONGREGATIONAL PARISH.

First Meeting-House in the North Parish, 84; Its Appearance, 84; Second House, 89; Description, 90; Sale of Pews, 90; First Bell, 94; Seating of Colored People, 95; Third Meeting-House, 98; Pewholders, 100; Clock, 102; First Stoves, 103; Erection of the Fourth Meeting-House in 1854, 103; Dedication, 106; Description of the House, 108; Sale of Pews, 109.

CHAP. VI. — EDUCATIONAL HISTORY.

Free Schools, 110; Their Origin, 110; School Committee of the North Parish, 115; Division of the Parish into Districts, 117; School Committee of the Town, 120; Annual Appropriations, 121, 122; School Districts of the Town, 124; Adelphian Academy, 129; North Bridgewater Academy, 131; High School, 123, 131; Private Schools, 132.

CHAP. VII. — BIOGRAPHICAL HISTORY.

List of Graduates of Colleges, 133; Students of Normal School, 134; Rev. John Porter, 134; Rev. Asa Meech, 137; Rev. Daniel Huntington, 137; Rev. James Thompson, 130; Rev. John Porter, Jr., 139; Rev. Huntington Porter, 140; Rev. Eliphalet Porter, D. D., 140; Rev. Thomas Crafts, 142; Rev. Asa Packard, 142; Rev. Hezekiah Packard, D. D., 146; Rev. Joshua Cushman, 154; Rev. Napthali Shaw, 157; Rev. Theophilus Packard, D. D., 159; Rev. Jonas Perkins, 161; Rev. Eliphalet P. Crafts, 162; Rev. Levi Packard, 163; Rev. Austin Cary, 165; Rev· Zachariah Howard, 169.

CHAP. VIII. — BIOGRAPHICAL HISTORY, CONCLUDED.

Clergymen.

Rev. William Thompson, 170; Rev. John Goldsbury, 170; Rev. Paul Couch, 170; Rev. Nathaniel B. Blanchard, 171; Rev. Edward L. Clark, 172; Rev. Warren Goddard, 172; Rev. Nathaniel Wales, 173; Rev. John F. Norton, 175; Rev. Charles L. Mills, 175; Rev. Samuel H. Lee, 175; Rev. Matthew Kingman, 175; Rev. Abel K. Packard, 175; Rev. John Dwight, 176; Rev. D. Temple Packard, 176; Rev. Charles W. Wood, 177; Rev. Lysander Dickerman, 177; Rev. Zenas P. Wild, 177; Rev. Azariah B. Wheeler, 178; Rev. T. B. McNulty, 76.

Physicians.

Dr. Philip Bryant, 179; Dr. Peter Bryant, 179; Dr. Luther Cary, 180; Dr. Issachar Snell, 180; Dr. Elisha Tillson, 181; Dr. Ziba Bass, 181; Dr. Nathan Perry, 182; Dr. Jonathan P. Crafts, 183; Dr. Abel W. Kingman, 184; Dr. James F. Richards, 184; Dr. Edgar E. Dean, 184; Dr. Horatio Bryant, 184; Dr. Thomas Stockbridge, 185; Dr. James Easton, 185; Dr. Nahum Smith, 185; Dr. E. R. Wade, 185; Dr. Henry Eddy, 185; Dr. James L. Hunt, 185; Dr. Silas L. Loomis, 186; Dr. L. F. C. Loomis, 186.

Lawyers.

Lucius Cary, Esq., 187; Eliab Whitman, Esq., 187; Jonathan White, Esq., 188; Jonas R. Perkins, Esq., 189; Austin Packard, Esq., 189; Daniel Howard, Esq., 190; Lucius Kingman, Esq., 190; Caleb Howard, Esq., 190; Melville Hayward, Esq., 190; Ellis W. Morton, Esq., 191; Bradford Kingman, Esq., 191.

Miscellaneous.

Thomas J. Snow, 192; Frederic Crafts, Esq., 193; Deacon Heman Packard, 193; Augustus T. Jones, A. M., 194; Heman P. Deforest, 194; S. D. Hunt, 195.

CHAP. IX. — OFFICIAL HISTORY.

List of Selectmen of the Town, 197; Town Clerks, 198; Treasurers, 198; Moderators, 198; Representatives, 199; Senators, 199; Councillors, 199; Engineers of Fire Department, 199; Justices of the Peace, 199; Coroners, 200; Notary Publics, 200; Deputy Sheriffs, 200; Lists of Colonels, Lt.-Colonels, Majors, Captains, and other Military Officers, 201, 202; Votes for Governor from 1821 to 1865; Moderators of the Annual Parish Meetings, 205; Selectmen, Clerks, Treasurers, and Committee of the North Parish, 206, 207.

CHAP. X. — STATISTICAL HISTORY.

Population of the North Parish in 1764, 1790, 1810, 1820, 1830, 1840, 1850, 1855, 1860, 1865, 210, 211; Parish Rates in 1744, 211; List of Polls in the North Parish in 1770, 212; Owners of, and Valuation of Dwelling-Houses in 1798, 214; Industrial Table for 1837, 216; Valuation in 1840, 1850, 1860, 217, 218; Industrial Tables for 1845 and 1855, 219, 220, 221; Number of Persons engaged in various Trades in 1855, 223; Manufacturing Statistics for 1865, 224; Agricultural Statistics for 1865, 224.

CHAP. XI. — THE OLD FRENCH, AND FRENCH AND INDIAN WARS.

Capture of Louisburg, 225; Treaty at Aix-La-Chapelle, 225; War Renewed in 1754, 226; Attack on Nova Scotia by the Colonies, 226; Crown Point, 226; Niagara, 226; List of Men in the Crown Point Expedition, 226; Captain Simeon Cary's Company, 227; Captain Josiah Dunbar's Company, 227; Expedition against Canada, 227; Captain Lemuel Dunbar's Company, 228; Same at Crown Point, 228.

CHAP. XII. — THE REVOLUTIONARY WAR.

Controversy between England and America, 228; Acts of Trade, 228; Sugar Act, 228; Stamp Act, 230; Tea destroyed in Boston Harbor, 230; Boston Port Bill, 231; Preparations for War, 231; Minute Men, 231; Company marched on Lexington Alarm, 232; List of Persons in the various Companies in the Service during the War, 232; Shay's Rebellion, 243; List of Soldiers called into the Service to quell the same at Taunton, 244.

CHAP. XIII. — WAR OF 1812.

Impressment of Seamen, 243; Embargo, 246; War declared by the President, 246; Calls for Troops from Militia, 247; Pay Roll of Company from North Bridgewater stationed at Plymouth.

CHAP. XIV. — THE REBELLION OF 1861.

Election of 1860, 249; State of the Country at the Commencement of the Rebellion, 249; Steamer "Star of the West," 250; Secession of South Carolina, 250; Firing upon Fort Sumter, 250; Call for Seventy-five Thousand Volunteers for Three Months, 250; Company F, Twelfth Massachusetts Regiment, 251; North Bridgewater Brass Band, 254; Changes and Casualties in the Twelfth Regiment, 255; Call for more Troops, 259; Company I, First Massachusetts Cavalry, 260; List of Changes and Casualties in the Same, 265; Companies and Regiments in which Soldiers have been in the Service, 267; List of Changes, Promotions, Deaths, etc., during the Rebellion, 285; Narrative of the Twelfth Massachusetts Regiment, 289.

CHAP. XV. — MILITIA HISTORY.

First Militia Company, 292; Officers, 292; Military Division of the Parish, 292; North and South Companies, 292; Plymouth County Brigade, 293; First Cavalry Company, 1787, North Bridgewater Dragoon Company, 1853, Militia Districts, 295; Active and Reserve Companies, 295; District Number Sixty, 296; District Number Sixty-one, 296.

CHAP. XVI. — MISCELLANEOUS HISTORY.

Public Roads, 298; Streets, 300; Turnpike, 302; Railroads, 303; Stages, 304; Post-Offices, 306; Postmasters, 306; Town Maps, 307; Newspapers, 307; Publications by North Bridgewater People, 309; Libraries, 313; North Bridgewater Library Association, 314.

CHAP. XVII. — MISCELLANEOUS HISTORY, CONTINUED.

Indians, 315; Slavery, 317; Colored Persons, 318; Temperance, 319; Sinclair Band of Hope, 324; North Star Division, No. 88, Fraternal Lodge, No. 24, 325; Old Colony Temperance Union, 325; Sabbath Schools, 325; Music, 327; Band, 330; Thespian Society, 330; Union Musical Association, 331; Bank, 331; Savings-Bank, 332; Fire Department, 333; Fire Engines, 334.

CHAP. XVIII. — MISCELLANEOUS HISTORY, CONCLUDED.

Burying Grounds, 338; Melrose Cemetery, 340; Hearse, 341; Town Pound, 342; Lock-Up, 344; Poor, 344; Warning out of Town, 345; Town House, 346; Telegraph, 347; North Bridgewater Gas Light Company, 348; Franklin Debating Association, 348; Pi Beta Society, 348; Library Association, 349; Agricultural Library Association, 349; Soldiers' Aid Society, 350; Freedmen's Relief Association, 351; Industrial Association, 351; Philomathian Association, 352; Massasoit Lodge of I. O. of O. F., No. 69, 352; Paul Revere Lodge of Freemasons, 352; Fires, 353; Casualties and Miscellaneous Events, 357.

CHAP. XIX. — EARLY HABITS AND CUSTOMS.

Social Life, 366; Parties, 366; Spinning Matches, 366; Flax Raising, 367; Process of Manufacture, 367; Dress of Men and Women, 368; Amusements, 369; Raisings, 369; Style of Architecture, 370; Use of Cranes, 370; Tinder-Boxes, 371; Food, 371; Drinks, 372; Well-Sweep, 373; Rising and Retiring Early, 373; Attendance on Church Worship, 373.

CHAP. XX. — MISCELLANEOUS HISTORY.

Mills, 375; Manufactures, 377; Bridgewater Manufacturing Company, 377; Tanners, 380; Blacksmiths, 381; Shoe Tool Manufacturers, 382; Public-Houses, 385; Traders, 386; Tailors, 390; Hatters, 392; Bakers, 392; Saddlers, 393; Wheelwrights, 394; Coopers, 394; Clocks, 395; Watchmakers and Jewellers, 395; Drugs and Medicines, 395; Furniture Manufacturers, 396; Carpenters, 397; Painters, 397; Masons, 398; Tin-Plate and Sheet-Iron Workers, 398; Dentists, 399; Blacking Manufacturers, 399; Boot and Shoe Manufacturing, 399; List of Patents Granted to the North Bridgewater People, 410.

CHAP. XXI. — PRECINCT CONTROVERSY AND INCORPORATION OF THE TOWN.

Petition of the North Parish (Asa Howard and others) to be Incorporated into a Town, 417; Remonstrance of Gideon Howard and others, 420; Remonstrance of Eliab Whitman and others, 422; Petition in Aid of Asa Howard and others for an Act of Incorporation, 423; Remonstrance of Daniel Howard, Esq., as Agent for the Town of Bridgewater, 424; Vote of the Town, 426; Petition of Jesse Packard and others in Aid of Asa Howard's Petition, 427; The Act of Incorporation as passed June 15, 1821, 428; First Town Meeting, 429.

PREFACE.

THE present volume is submitted to the approval and criticism of the public, after many years of laborious toil and research, with the desire that it may add something to preceding history.

It was not undertaken for want of other employment, or for pecuniary profit, but has been a severe tax upon the author's time, as well as purse. The work was commenced about twelve years since, without any reference to its publication, but merely for the gratification of a natural curiosity which must arise in the mind of any one who extends his thoughts beyond the people and scenes immediately around him. None but those who have prepared a work of this kind can have any idea of the amount of labor and time required in its execution.

The author has devoted nearly all of his leisure time during the past eight years in examining the records of the town, as well as of the adjoining towns, also the Parish, Probate, and State records, and the ponderous volumes in the State Archives, beside the Registry of Deeds in several counties, muster rolls at the State House, to say nothing of the large number of town, church, and family histories that have been published, public addresses, sermons, orations, documents, plans, maps, etc.

Many an hour has been spent in deciphering the almost unintelligible records of early times. Days and even weeks have been devoted to a careful examination of files of newspapers or other publications, also in copying inscriptions on gravestones and monuments.

The matter here embodied consists of a mass of facts, items, and figures, many of them gathered from a correspondence of upwards of twelve hundred letters, as well as by a personal consultation with the people of the town.

During the winter of 1860, while the author was engaged in copying and examining the early records at the State House, Hon. Edward Southworth,

Jr., then a member of the House of Representatives, from North Bridge-water, first suggested the propriety of publishing the items which had been collected.   After much reflection, and consultation with several of the leading people of the town, sufficient encouragement was offered by those interested in such work, and it was commenced.

It was originally intended to publish a work of three hundred pages, but that was soon found to be too small to attain anything like completeness, and it has been increasing in size till it has reached upwards of seven hundred pages.

The only historical work ever published in the town was that of Moses Cary, issued in 1824, which was an account of some of the early families.

The next work was that of Hon. Nahum Mitchell, of East Bridgewater, which included the early families in the town of North Bridgewater, and was published in 1840.   These works, which contained but little beside genealogical accounts of families, have been a great assistance to the author in arranging the early families in the town, and to them he is indebted for many early items.

In the arrangement of the historical portion of the work, it was thought best to classify the subjects, instead of presenting them in the form of An-nals, while the family tables are arranged in alphabetical order by names.

It was intended to bring the Family Register down to the present time, and it is as full as could be made with the facilities at hand.   If anything is lacking, or inserted in the wrong place, members of families recorded here and their friends must take a part of the blame ; for if, in many instances more attention had been paid to letters of inquiry concerning their records, this department would have been more complete than it now is.   However imperfect this part of the work may be, the author feels a consciousness of having exerted all his skill, care, and pains to make it correct, and thinks it will compare favorably with other works of the same kind. There are no doubt many errors in the book, for among such a mass of names, dates, etc., it is hardly to be expected to be free from them.   He has, however, endeavored to collect his material from reliable sources.

To the author the work has been a labor of love, rather than with any view to pecuniary profit, and if he has succeeded in rescuing from oblivion any facts that otherwise might have been lost, he will feel rewarded for his painstaking.

There is an extended Table of Contents in the first part of the volume, which exhibits at a glance the leading subjects in each chapter ; and at the end of the volume will be found a General Index, prepared in the most care-ful manner, by the Rev. John A. Vinton, of South Boston, whose reputation as a writer and compiler of Genealogical History needs no better recommendation than his Vinton and Giles Memorials.

The map of the town was engraved, at great expense, from a drawing by Otis F. Clapp, engineer and surveyor, to whom the author owes his thanks for the excellent manner in which the work has been done. It was drawn from a map published by the town in 1853, with the recent changes and additions in the streets and roads to the present time.

The portraits inserted in the work are copies of photographs and paintings, have been prepared with much expense and care, and are considered very good likenesses.

Most of the church views were obtained by subscription, and were generally paid for by the different societies. Several of the cuts were inserted at the author's expense.

The work has been carefully printed by Messrs. Innes & Niles, to whom the author would express his thanks for the faithful manner in which their part of the work has been executed.

Among the many who have kindly lent the author their assistance during the progress of the work, he would especially mention the late Silvanus Packard, Esq., of Boston, from whom he received the liberal donation of one hundred dollars to assist in the publication of a history of his native town.

Special acknowledgments are due to Hon. Edward Southworth, Jr., Chandler Sprague, Esq., Bela Keith, Esq., and Capt. John W. Kingman for the many words of encouragement, and their prompt response to calls for material aid in the publication of this work, and whose kindness will ever be remembered.

From Samuel G. Drake, Esq., the able historian of Boston, Rev. Henry M. Dexter, D. D., John H. Sheppard, Esq., librarian of the New England Genealogical-Historic Society, Boston, Rev. Samuel C. Jackson, State Librarian, he has received much assistance in collecting information.

From Lewis Holmes, Esq., the obliging town clerk of Bridgewater, he has received many personal favors, which will ever be remembered with pleasure.

From Augustus T. Jones, Esq., editor and publisher of the " North Bridgewater Gazette," and Henry Howard, Esq., parish clerk, he has received many favors in the loan of public records and documents.

To William B. Trask, John Ward Dean, and William B. Towne, Esqrs., of Boston, William Allen, Esq., of East Bridgewater, Ebenezer Alden, M. D., of Randolph, and others who have aided the author in the contribution of items, in reply to many inquiries both by letter and verbally, he renders his hearty thanks.

In 1862, a circular was issued to all those residing at a distance who would be likely to feel an interest in having a good work, requesting any information that they might be able to give. At the same time a large number of letters were written to various persons concerning their records. From many the author received prompt, full, and satisfactory replies, while many others took no notice whatever of the same.

In 1864, a circular was issued, soliciting subscriptions for this work, promising to publish a list of such as subscribed at the end of the volume. In accordance with that agreement, the list may be found with the names as stated.

In closing, the author has only to add, that, should this work meet the expectations of the citizens of the town, increase their interest and attachment for things that are past, bring to mind those who have gone before them, and serve to keep alive the interest in historical and genealogical matters, then he will feel that his time and the expense incurred has not been spent in vain.

Bradford Kingman

BROOKLINE, August 1, 1866.

HISTORY OF NORTH BRIDGEWATER.

CHAPTER I.

HISTORY OF NORTH BRIDGEWATER.

Situation and Extent.—Topography.—Centre Village.—Campello.—"Sprague's" or Factory Village. — North-West Bridgewater. — Rivers, Brooks, Hills. — Natural History. — Geological Formation.

NORTH BRIDGEWATER is a town in the north-west part of Plymouth County, — bordering on Bristol County on the west, and Norfolk County on the north, — and is situated between 42°, 03′ and 42°, 08′ north latitude, and between 70°, 57′ and 71°, 04′ west longitude ; and is bounded on the north by Randolph and Stoughton, on the east by Abington and East Bridgewater, on the south by West Bridgewater, on the west by Easton. It is twenty miles south from Boston, thirty miles north-east from Providence, twenty-five miles north-west from Plymouth, sixteen miles south-east from Dedham, fifteen miles north-east from Taunton, and is five and a half miles in length from east to west, and five miles in width from north to south, and contains about thirteen thousand acres, and is about four and a half miles square, — has a total length of sixty-seven miles of public roads.

There are four villages in the town, — the " Centre," " Campello," " Sprague's or Factory Village," and the " West Shares," or " North-West Bridgewater." The Centre is a

large and growing place, containing a large number of stores,
manufactories; seven churches, the pride of the town; schools
of different grades; one academy; bank, savings bank, post-
office, hotel, and railroad depot; the best of fire departments,
and telegraph communication with Boston, and stations on
the line of railroad.   The stores of this place are of the
usual variety found in all large places, — being of the highest
order, — and the facilities for trade are not surpassed by any
in the county.   It is the emporium of trade for the surrounding towns, extending fifteen to eighteen miles.   There
is the best of dry-goods, furnishing and clothing, grocery and
hardware, furniture and crockery-ware stores to be found in
any country town; and it may truly be called a "live" place.

The next in importance is a neat and pleasantly located
village, about one and a half miles south from the centre of
the town, and formerly known as "Plain Village," now *Campello.**   It has always been noted for its extensive manufacturing establishments of boots, shoes, cabinet furniture, and
musical instruments; and the thrift and industry of her citizens may be clearly seen in the neat and tidy appearance of
the small cottages scattered throughout the limits of the
same.   The growth of this place was materially checked in
May, 1853, by one of the most destructive fires that ever
occurred in the town, if not in the county (a full account
of which appears in another part of this work), and from
the effects of which it has never fully recovered.   There
is, however, a large amount of business done in the shoe
trade; several large establishments being engaged in manufacturing goods for foreign markets, the owners or proprietors of which have stores for the sale of goods in Pearl

---

* *Campello.*   This name was first suggested to the citizens of Plain Village at
the time of the establishment of the post-office in February, 1850, on account
of the name of Plain Village being often confounded with other places spelled
nearly the same.   It was proposed by Rev. D. Huntington, and unanimously
adopted by the people as a proper one, — it signifying a small plain.

VIEW OF NORTH BRIDGEWATER IN 1838.

BIRTHPLACE OF BRADFORD KINGMAN (Campello).

street, Boston; one manufactory of musical instruments, one large variety store, two smaller grocery stores, post-office, railroad depot near to the village, rendering it a desirable place for business purposes or for a private residence. The main street runs the entire length of the village, north and south, with graceful elms on either side. There are three schools in the place and one church.*

"Sprague's or Factory Village" is another small and beautifully located cluster of houses and manufacturing establishments, about three-fourths of a mile east of the Centre Village, on the road leading to Abington. There is a large manufactory of last and boot trees in this place, with water and steam power, owned and conducted by Chandler Sprague, Esq., to whom the citizens of that portion of the town owe their success for the enterprising manner in which he has rendered the place attractive. Within a few years, he has erected a large and convenient building for his use, in which are conducted several branches of manufacturing; also a beautiful residence, situated but a short distance from the factory; also a store, where is kept the usual variety found in country stores. In this place is a neat and roomy school-house, with a bell, erected within a very few years; a sawmill, and three shoe manufactories, beside smaller establishments for the manufacture of shoe tools.

The next we have is the "West Shares," or "North-West Bridgewater," a prominent height of land from which magnificent views may be had. It is the highest portion of land to be found in the four Bridgewaters. On the north, we have a view of Blue Hills of Milton, and on the west we have a picturesque view of the Western Hills; and no place can excel it for its lovely scenery and its healthful locality. The land is of a good quality, and the people in this portion of the town are mostly farmers. In immediate proximity to

* Orthodox Congregational.

this place is one Methodist Church, school, post-office, and store; and is situated at about equal distance from Stoughton and North Bridgewater Villages.

RIVERS AND BROOKS.

This town is well watered by brooks and streams, — only one large enough to be called a river, and that of small size. Most of these have had mills erected upon them. The most prominent of these is the Salisbury River, which rises in the town of Stoughton, running southerly one-half mile west of the Centre Village, till it crosses Belmont Street, a short distance below the mill known as the Caleb Howard Mill, when it turns and runs east till it meets *Trout Brook.*

This brook also rises in the southerly part of Stoughton, and runs south about a half mile east of the middle of the town till it meets Salisbury Brook, near " Sprague's " Works. At this point, the two are joined, and run in a southerly direction, a short distance east of Campello Village, into the town of East Bridgewater.

Beaver Brook is another stream, rising in Weymouth; runs in a southerly direction, and forming a boundary line between Abington and North Bridgewater, till it enters East Bridgewater. Another river rises in Easton, and runs through the south-west part of the town into West Bridgewater, and is called Cowsett Brook.

Mike's Brook rises in the north-east part of the town, and runs south-westerly, and empties into Trout Brook, and is a very small stream.

West Meadow Brook rises north of the residence of Caleb Phillips, near Pleasant Street, and runs in a southerly direction into West Bridgewater, near Henry Jackson's.

Another small stream rises in the south part of Stoughton and north part of North Bridgewater, and near George W. Hunt's; running south-easterly, it empties into Salisbury Brook, near Galen Packard's mill.

Also, a small stream rises near the residence of the late Deacon Silvanus French, and, running south, enters West Bridgewater east of the late residence of Nahum Hayward, and empties into Salisbury River.

Although the streams in this town are small, there has been, at various times, considerable manufacturing done by water-power. There are no ponds in town, of any size, excepting those made by flowing meadows for mill privileges; the largest in town being that at " Sprague's Works; " next, at " Howard's Mills," and one at " Tilden's Corner." There is about a thousand acres in the town covered by water; the balance is well divided into woodland, pasturing, and mowing; and there is no town in the county where there is less unproductive or unimproved land than in this town. There are over four thousand acres of good woodland, and over eleven hundred acres of land tilled, exclusive of orcharding; over fifteen hundred acres of good upland mowing land, about eighty acres of orcharding, about six hundred acres of fresh meadow, about three thousand acres of pasture land.

HILLS.

Of the town of North Bridgewater, we may say that its surface is comparatively level, with but a few hills. Beside those already mentioned, there are some elevated spots here and there; prominent among which is *Cary Hill*, situated in the north-east part of the town, overlooking the village on the south, gently sloping in either direction, from the top of which we may get pure air and fine views in an autumn day. When the leaves are turned into rich drapery, it is worth while to ride to this place for the prospect that may be had. It is of very easy access by good roads; and the wonder is, that it is not more generally selected as a place of residence by those wishing a healthy and retired locality. The land in the immediate vicinity is good, well adapted to tillage, produces fine crops with little labor.

Prospect Hill is another high and pleasant spot of land, very desirable for building purposes, and but a short distance from the village in a north-west direction, and west of the late Captain Asa Jones's residence.

Ridge Hill is a rough and rocky pasture, running from near the residence of Freeman Holmes, in the south part of the town, northerly for about one mile, and has been much celebrated for its plentiful crops of huckleberries and blackberries.

Stone-House Hill is situated on the boundary line between North Bridgewater and Easton, a short distance west of the manufactory of H. T. Marshall, at "Tilden's Corner." At this place is an old cave, made in the solid stone ledge, and is said to have been used by the Indians as a dwelling. The cave may now be seen as formerly used. It is situated on the old road leading to Easton.

NATURAL HISTORY.

To the true votary of science, everything in Nature presents a lovely aspect. "To him, there are books in the running streams, sermons in stones, good in everything."

> "There is a pleasure in the pathless woods;
> There is society where none intrudes."

Every town has its natural history, and every mile of its surface, with its hills and plains, its rivers, ponds, rocks, and trees, — all have a charm that clusters around the home of childhood. The forests of North Bridgewater consist of red, white, and sugar maple (although the latter is scarce, it is occasionally found); white, red, and black ash; the tremulous poplar and verdant hemlock; the tall spruce, much used in building; white ash, used for carriage-work, scythes, and rake-handles, for hoops, sieve-rims, and boxes, and a superior wood for oars. Sassafras was in early times quite plenty, valuable only for medicinal purposes. Chestnut is not abundant. White oak is used for carriages, red oak for

CAVE ON STONE HOUSE HILL.

George H. Fullerton, Esq., has written a Pastoral Poem, entitled "Ruth," a highly interesting volume of 200 pages, the scene of which is laid at this place.

casks, the bark of which is used for tanning; hickory affording plenty of good shellbarks.

Butternut is not common, — here and there a tree. White pine is tolerably plenty; although it has been, of late, much cut for fuel and building purposes. Pitch pine is quite plenty, — good only for fuel, being knotty and pitchy; red cedar, used for rail-fences and pencil-woods, also very useful for linings to chests, as a protection from moths; red beech, used for plane-woods, last, and boot-tree forms. Tall and graceful elms rejoice the eye in every direction. In the early settlement of the town, large quantities of ship-timber of oak and chestnut were carried from the town to the sea-shore towns of Weymouth, Scituate, and Duxbury. Among those who did a large trade in that line were Messrs. Abel and Eliphalet Kingman, and, later, Edwin H. Kingman. Of late years, a ready market is found at home for all the wood cut, where formerly large lots were either carried to Boston and the seaport towns, or made into charcoal, and then sent to Boston. Since the railroads have been built, wood has been much used on the locomotives, and has made it scarce at times; but, if we take a look about the town, we shall find "a few more left of the same sort."

Fruit-Trees. — Of this kind of tree, not so great a variety is found as in many places; although the writer is happy in believing that there is an increasing interest being felt in this most important of agricultural pursuits, — that of raising fruit. The most common fruit is the apple. There is a fair assortment of them in the town; and the new orchards con-tain choice varieties, while the old and wild orchards have given way to the woodman's axe. Now, the apple is a staple article of consumption, the consumers being more numerous than the producers; and people are looking more to the cul-tivation of all kinds than ever before. Choice varieties are engrafted upon the stumps of old trees; and were it not for the borers that eat the roots, canker-worms and caterpillars that eat the leaves and branches, we might look with delight upon as fine orchards as could be found in any place. These pests have destroyed the orchards, as grasshoppers have the nice fields of grass; and the ways and means of ridding the orchards of these plagues is not yet fully understood. Next to the apple comes the pear-tree, which does not appear to thrive as well in this town as in many others, the land not being well adapted for this kind of fruit, though, of late, many have been successful, and raised choice kinds.

Peaches are raised to a very limited extent, the climate not being adapted for the successful cultivation of this variety. The trees are said to be short-lived, and do not flourish.

Cherries do very well; and much is being done in this kind of small fruit, many varieties being cultivated. Of the native shrubs, we find the town has the usual variety, — such as the blueberry and huckleberry, — that affords employment for the boys and girls in a pleasant afternoon, and a source of pleasure to older persons, furnishing an agreeable repast when eaten with milk. Then we find the raspberry, goose-berry, and thimbleberry. Of the raspberries, there are the red and white, that grow wild, and are cultivated in gardens. Gooseberries, of late years, have become an article of much use, many new varieties having been introduced, the best of which is the English variety, that grow as large as shellbarks. Then we have the currant, an exceedingly useful article of culture, and easily raised, valuable for wine or table use. Of these we have also several varieties, — red, white, and black. Then comes that highly esteemed and valuable luxury, — "a dish of ripe strawberries, smothered in cream." These are found in many places growing wild in the pastures; and, although they are sweet and delicious, they are found so scarce, that not much account is made of them. The culti-vated fruit of this kind is a favorite dish, of which there is a

great variety, among which are the " Hovey's Seedlings,"
" Early Virginia," and " Boston Pine." These are fast becoming an article of cultivation as much as the potato or
corn, and large amounts are cultivated in the gardens and
fields of this town. The first that were raised for market, to
any extent, were those by Mr. B. F. Lawton, of the West
Shares. Since then, several have raised them with profit,
and sent them to market. Of late, the most successful, or
doing the most in that line, are Ira Copeland, in the Factory
Village, and C. H. Packard, of Campello.

> " Wife, into the garden, and set me a plot
> With strawberry-roots of the best to be got;
> Such growing abroad among thorns in the wood,
> Well chosen and picked, prove excellent and good."   TUSSER.

The birds common in this locality are the quail, partridge,
snipe, woodpecker, woodcock, sparrow, thrush, robin, blue-
bird, bobolink, wren, pewee, lark, king-bird, blue-jay, black-
bird, chickadee, martin, barn, and bank swallow, cat-bird,
cuckoo, humming-bird, kingfisher, whip-poor-will, owl, hawk,
crow, bats. Wild geese occasionally light on the small ponds
in the outskirts of the town.

> " What songs with those of birds can vie,
> From the goldfinch that on high
> Swings its wee hammock in the sky ? "   CANNING.

Among the different kinds of fish that abound in our
streams may be found the trout, pickerel, sucker, shiner,
minnow, hornpout, eels, perch. Herrings, in early days, used
to run up the rivers, but, of late, are seldom found.

The early forests in town had their share of vexatious animals that were common in this part of the country; as
wolves, wild-cat. Foxes have become shy of company.
Skunk, musquosh, and mink have been severely hunted.
Woodchucks, rabbits, and squirrels of different kinds. Rac-
coons, that damaged the cornfields, have almost disappeared.

Moles and meadow-mice are found in the fields, and often do
much damage, gnawing bark off of trees in winter.

But the worst enemy the early settlers had to contend
with among the beast kind was the wolf, which troubled the
infant settlements exceedingly ; so much, that shepherds
were appointed over the flocks by day, and put in folds at
night, and securely guarded ; and, even after the town became quite thickly settled, these pests would make night
hideous by their howling around the farms. Rewards were
offered by the town for their heads, and wolf-traps were
common in all parts of the town.

The geological formation of this town is similar to many
other towns in Plymouth County. The hills, meadows, large
plains and intervales, deep swamps and rocky pastures, furnish food for almost all kinds of grass, trees, and shrubs. Of
the rocky portions of the town, we find sienite, or composition of feldspar, quartz, and hornblende. Says Dr. Hitchcock
in his survey through the State, —

" The most elegant variety of porphyritic sienite that I have met with
in the State occurs in North Bridgewater and Abington, and in other parts
of Plymouth County. Its base consists of quartz and feldspar, with an
abundance of epidote, disseminated, and in veins. This rock, if polished,
would form, it seems to me, the most ornamental stone in the State. The
feldspar, crystal, that constitutes it a porphyry, are of a flesh color. There
is a dark-colored mineral diffused throughout the mass, which may be hornblende or mica."

Where mica is found plenty in the composition, it is sometimes called sienite granite.

Large quantities of peat have been cut in the meadows of
the town in past times, and is now being used as a fuel
which is of an excellent quality.

Large quantities of iron-ore have been found in the western
and other sections of the town, and some has been manufactured into iron. It is not, however, plenty now, and the
business of making it into iron ceased several years since.

CHAPTER II.

FIRST SETTLEMENT.

Grant of Plantation. — Bridgewater purchased of the Indians. — Division of the Town. — Petition of the North Precinct to be set off a separate Town. — Charter for a Precinct. — First Meeting of the same

TO give a clear account of the early settlement of the town of North Bridgewater, it will be necessary to give some account of the origin of the town, its connection with and its identity with the parent town of Bridgewater, and a brief account of its having been set off from Duxbury, and the purchase of the Indians. The ancient town of Bridgewater — then comprising what is now North, East, West, and South Bridgewater, or Bridgewater proper — was formerly a plantation granted to Duxbury, in 1645, as a compensation for the loss of territory they had sustained in the setting apart of Marshfield from them in the year 1640. The grant was in the following language : —

" The inhabitants of the town of Duxbury are granted a competent proportion of lands about Saughtuchquett (Satucket), towards the west, for a plantation for them, and to have it four miles every way from the place where they shall set up their centre ; provided it intrench not upon Winnytuckquett, formerly granted to Plymouth. And we have nominated Capt. Miles Standish, Mr. John Alden, George Soule, Constant Southworth, John Rogers, and William Brett, to be feofees in trust for the equal dividing and laying forth the said lands to the inhabitants."

How these lands were divided, or what should entitle any one to a share, no record appears to show. Gov. Hinckley, in his confirmatory deed, says that the "inhabitants agreed among themselves." There were fifty-four proprietors, — each of whom held one share, — the names of whom are as follows : William Bradford, William Merrick, John Bradford, Abraham Pierce, John Rogers, George Partridge, John Starr, Mr. William Collier, Christopher Wadsworth, Edward Hall, Nicholas Robbins, Thomas Hayward, Mr. Ralph Partridge, Nathaniel Willis, John Willis, Thomas Bonney, Mr. Miles Standish, Love Brewster, John Paybody, William Paybody, Francis Sprague, William Bassett, John Washburn, John Washburn, Jr., John Ames, Thomas Gannett, William Brett, Edmund Hunt, William Clarke, William Ford, Mr. Constant Southworth, John Cary, Edmund Weston, Samuel Tompkins, Edmund Chandler, Moses Simmons, John Irish, Philip Delano, Arthur Harris, Mr. John Alden, John Forbes, Samuel Nash, Abraham Sampson, George Soule, Experience Mitchell, Henry Howland, Henry Sampson, John Brown, John Howard, Francis West, William Tubbs, James Lendall, Samuel Eaton, Solomon Leonard. To these shares were afterward added two more shares, — one to Rev. James Keith, of Scotland, their first minister; and the other to Deacon Samuel Edson, of Salem, who erected the first mill in the town, — making fifty-six shares.

This grant was considered as little more than an authority or right to purchase it of the natives. For this purpose, Capt. Miles Standish, Samuel Nash, and Constant Southworth, were appointed a committee to make the purchase; which they did, as appears by the following instruments : —

WITNESS THESE PRESENTS, that I, Ousamequin, Sachem of the Country of Poconocket, have given, granted, enfeofed, and sold unto Miles Standish of Duxbury, Samuel Nash and Constant Southworth of Duxbury aforesaid, in behalf of all the townsmen of Duxbury aforesaid, a tract of land usually called Satucket, extending in the length and breadth thereof as followeth : that is to say, from the wear at Satucket seven miles due east, and from the said wear seven miles due west, and from the said wear seven miles due north, and from the said wear seven miles due south ; the which tract the said Ousamequin hath given, granted, enfeofed, and sold unto the said Miles Standish, Samuel Nash, and Constant Southworth, in the behalf of all the townsmen of Duxbury, as aforesaid, with all the immunities, privileges, and profits whatsoever belonging to the said tract of land, with all and singular all woods, underwoods, lands, meadows, rivers, brooks, rivulets, &c., to have and to hold, to the said Miles Standish, Samuel Nash, and Constant Southworth, in behalf of all the townsmen of the town of Duxbury, to them and their heirs forever. In witness whereof, I, the said Ousamequin, have hereunto set my hand this 23ᵈ of March, 1649.

JOHN BRADFORD,
WILLIAM OTWAY, *alias* PARKER,

Witness the mark of 🖋 OUSAMEQUIN.

In consideration of the aforesaid bargain and sale, we, the said Miles Standish, Samuel Nash, and Constant Southworth, do bind ourselves to pay unto the said Ousamequin, for and in consideration of the said tract of land, as followeth : —

> 7 coats, a yard and a half in a coat.
> 9 hatchets.
> 8 hoes.
> 20 knives.
> 4 moose-skins.
> 10 yards and a half of cotton.

MILES STANDISH,
SAMUEL NASH,
CONSTANT SOUTHWORTH.

This contract is said to have been made on what was called " Sachem's Rock," in East Bridgewater, a little south of Whitman's Mills, and near the house of the late David Kingman.

This Ousamequin, sometimes called Ossamequin, was no other than Massasoit himself, who, in the latter part of his life, had adopted that name. The deed written by Capt. Miles Standish, one of the original planters of the Colony, and signed with the mark of the Sachem, is still in existence. When the old Sachem was called upon to execute his deed, he endeavored to make it as sure as possible. For that purpose, he affixed a mark in the shape of a 🏹.

Thus we have seen that the original town of Bridgewater, comprising the territory now known as North, East, West, and South Bridgewater, was purchased by Capt. Miles Standish and others for the trifling sum of seven coats, nine hatchets, eight hoes, twenty knives, four moose-skins, and ten and a

half yards of cotton; the whole not amounting to thirty dollars in value.

This town was the first interior settlement in the old
Colony. The grant of the plantation, as we have seen, was
in 1645, and the settlement made in 1650. The first settlers
had a house-lot of six acres each on the town river, and the
place was called Nuckatest, or Nuncketetest. The first lots
were taken up at West Bridgewater; first houses built and
the first improvements made there. The settlement was
compact, — the house-lots being contiguous, — with a view
for mutual protection and aid against the Indians; and, as a
further protection from the natives, they erected a stockade
or garrison on the south side of the river, and fortified many
of their dwellings. It is said that not more than one-third
of the original fifty-six proprietors ever removed and became
inhabitants of their new settlement. From this original
home, the settlers scattered into other portions of the town,
extending their dwellings first into the south part of the
town, toward Nippenicket Pond, on the road to Taunton,
whither they were in the habit of going either to mill or to
trade; and we are told they frequently went to that place
on foot, with the grists on their backs, a distance of several
miles.

The last settled part of the town was the north, which was
not till after 1700; no permanent settlement being made in
what was called the North Parish till after that time, and the
settlers were mostly from the West Parish, now called West
Bridgewater.

The plantation remained to Duxbury until June, 1656,
when it was incorporated into a distinct and separate town
in the following concise language : —

" ORDERED, That henceforth Duxborrow New Plantation bee allowed to
bee a tounshipe of ytselfe, destinct from Duxborrow, and to bee called by
the name of Bridgewater. *Provided* that all publicke rates bee borne by
them with Duxborrow upon equally proportions."

The court settled the rates to be paid by the proprietors as follows: —

" The town of Bridgewater is to bear one part of three with Duxbury, of their proportion of the country rates for the officers' wages and other public charges."

Previous to the incorporation of the town, the plantation had been called Bridgewater; but, of the origin of the name, we have nothing authentic, except a matter of fancy for a town in England of that name; and, from the time of its settlement, the town has maintained a strong position in the history of the country.

The town continued a united and harmonious whole until 1715. when a petition was sent to General Court to be set off into a separate parish or precinct; the petitioners representing. themselves as inhabitants of the easterly part of Bridgewater. A committee of two in the Council, and three of the House, was appointed to examine into the matter; who attended to their duties, and reported in favor of granting their request; which was accepted, and an act of incorporation passed June 1, 1716, with this condition: —

" That the whole town stand obliged to an honorable maintenance of the Rev. James Keith, their present aged minister, if he should outlive his powers and capacities of discharging the office and duty of their minister."

The new parish was called the South, and the old one the North, Precinct, which then included the West and what is now North Bridgewater. In 1723, that part of the old North Precinct now known as East Bridgewater, then known as the West Parish, was set off, and constituted a precinct called the East Parish, in Dec. 14, 1723; and May 31, 1738, fifty-five individuals, belonging in the old North Parish, sent a petition to the General Court, asking to be set off into a separate township; which petition was so far granted as to allow them the powers and privileges usually allowed to

parishes.   The following is a copy of petition and the act of
incorporation : —

To His Excellency Jonathan Belcher, Esqʳ ., Captⁱⁿ General and Governour
in Chief in and over his Majesties Province of the Massachusetts Bay, in
New England, and to the Honourable his Majesties Council and House of
Representatives in Generil Court Assembled at Boston, on the 31ˢᵗ of
May, 1738, the Petition of us, the Subscribers, Inhabitants of the Town
of Bridgewater, Consisting Chiefly of the North part of the west precinct, and two Familys of the East precinct, in sᵈ Town, —

Humbly Sheweth :

That, when the meeting house was lately bult In the West precinct, the
Inhabitants of the North part of sᵈ West precinct Cheerfully Consented to,
and Did their proportionable part In, building of sᵈ meeting House where
it Now stands, tho very Remote from the Petitioners, and at such a Distance
from them so as but few of their Families Ever Could, without Great Difficulty, attend the Publick Worship of God there ; but, Notwithstanding,
thay were Willing to Do the utmost of their power and ability to Promote
the Worship of God their, In hopes when thay ware able to have it Nearer
to them ; and, by the Providence of God, thay are Greatly Increased In
Numbers and Something In Estates, So that they look upon themselves
Capable of Bulding a Meeting House, and Sittling a Minister, and uphold-
ing the publick Worship of God among themselves, and are in hopes that
the Best part of the Town and West precinct have no Just Cause to object
against it, Since we have been so helpful, and Done to the utmost of our
power in Sittling the minister and Bulding the New Meeting House, In sᵈ
West precinct, and we are willing and Desirous that what we then Did
s'ould be left to that precinct, who are now able of themselves, under their
priesent good and Growing Circumstances, to maintain the Public Worship
of God ther without us, as will appear by the Valuation of their Estates
herewith Exhibited, which the more Emboldens us to petition this Honourable Court to Set us off a Distinct and Separate Township, by the following
metes and Bounds, which Includes not only the North part of Bridgewater,
but a small Tract of land and a few of the Inhabitants of the town of
Stoughton, which suitable accomodites them as well as us, viz. : Beginning
at a white oak tree standing on the North west part of Jonathan Packard's
field, on the Easterly side of the Countrey Road, and from thence East and
West till It meets with Easton Line, and East till it meets with the East
precinct Line, and then North on sᵈ Line Half one mile, and then North
East till it meet with Beaver Brook ; then by said Brook to the Colony
Line, So called ; then Westerly by sᵈ Line to a Beach tree which is the
Easterly Corner Bounds of Stoughton ; then on the Line between Brantrey
and Stoughton to Capt. Curtis' Land ; then Westerly to Salisbery plain
River ; then southerly by sᵈ Rever to the Colony Line ; then Westerly by
sᵈ Line to Easton Line ; and then South By sᵈ Line first mentioned. We

having In time past once and again petitioned this Honourable Court for Relief in the premises, but it so happened that this Honoured Court Did not then Grant the prayer of our petition in full, But Nevertheless, according to our Desier, Sent a Committee to view and Consider our circumstances, whose report (we humbley Conceve) was somthing Different from What we prayed for in our petition, and the matter falling through, in as much as it happened that his Excellency the Governour Did not then sign what the Honoured Court acted on said report, and we remaining under our Difficulties and unrelieved, But yet taking encouragement from what was acted on s^d report by the Honoured Court, and also from what was acted by our town in general, at a Town meeting Legally Called and Notified to that purposee, on the 15th of February Last, In which We had the major vote for our being set off a Distinct Township, and, that we might not be under Difficulties In Bulding an House and Settling a Minister all at once, have erected and Inclosed a good House for the publicke Worship of God Where it may Best accomodate us all. We Do therfore think it our duty once more humbly to Renew our Petition that We may be set off a Township as Before herein prayed for, and we Humble beg leave here to say, that what we now offer in Respect of our being So Set off is Sincerity for the promoting the Worship of God and Religion In the Puriety of it among us.

Wherefore we pray your Excellency and Honours would be pleased to here our Request and Grant our petition, and as we in Duty Bound Shall Ever pray.

Robert Howard,	Henry Kingman,	Joshua Warren,
John Johnson,	John Wormall,	Constant Southworth,
John Kingman, 2^d,	James Packard,	Seth Packard,
David Packard,	John Kingman, 3^d,	Samuel Brett,
Charles Snell,	Walter Downie,	John Allen,
Charles Cushman,	David Packard, Jr.,	John Dixon,
Nathaniel Hammond,	James Berret,	William Packard,
Theoplis Curtis,	Benjamin Edson,	Abiah Keith,
William Curtis,	Charles Bestwick,	Isaac Fuller,
Ashley Curtis,	John Packard,	Joseph Richards,
Edward Curtis,	Michael Langford,	Thomas Buck,
David Hill,	Ephrim Willis,	Isaac Kingman,
William Frinch, Jr.,	Jacob Allen,	Zacheus Packard,
James Hewett,	Joseph Pettengall,	Abijah Hill,
Daniel Howard,	Abiel Packard,	Daniel Field, Jr.,
Hugh McCormick,	Akerman Pettingall,	Timothy Keith, Jr.,
Nathan Keith,	Zachriah Cary,	Zachry Snell,
Solomon Packard,	John Pratt,	
William Frinch,	Timothy Keith.	

In the House of Representatives, June 14, 1738.

Read and ordered that the petitioners sarve the West Precinct in the town of Bridgewater, and also the town of Stoughton, with a Copy of the petition, that thay show Cause (If any they have), on the first Thursday of the setting of the Court, why the prayer thereof should not be granted; **and** the petition is referred, the meantime, for Consideration.

Sent up for Concurance.

J. QUINCY, *Spkr.*

IN COUNCIL, June 15, 1738.

Read and concurrid.

J. WILLIARD, *Secretary.*

16th Consented to.   J. BELCHER.

IN COUNCIL, Dec. 1, 1738.

Read again, togather with the answer of the West Precinct, In the town of Bridgewater, and other papers In the Case; and, the parties being admitted before the Bord, were fully Heard, in their pleas and allegations, thereon; all which being considered, —

ORDERED, That the prayer of the petition be so far granted as that all the land, with the inhabitants thereon living, half a mile to the northward of an east and west line, from the white oak at Jonathan Packard's corner, togather with David Packard, Solomon Packard, and Jacob Allen, inhabitants of the east side of the river, their families and estates, be set off and constituted a distinct and separate parish, and be invested with the poures privileges, and immunitys that all other precincts or parishes wethin this Province do or by law ought to Injoy.

Sent down for concurrence.   SIMON FROST, *Deputy Secretary.*

IN THE HOUSE OF REPRESENTATIVES, Dec. 2, 1738.

Read and Concurrid.

J. QUINCY, *Spkr.*

January 3. — Consented to.

J. BELCHER.

A true copy.   Examined.

SIMON FROST, *Deputy Secretary.*

This is a true Copy of an etisted copy examined By me.

ROBERT HOWARD, *Parish Clerk.*

NOTIFICATION OF FIRST MEETING.

Pursuant to a warrant directed to me from Samuel Pool, one of His Majiistise Justices of the Pees for the County of Plymouth, these are therfore to notify the freeholders and other inhabitants of the North Precinct, in Bridgewater, to assemble and meet together at the meeting-house in said North Precinct, in Bridgewater, on Monday, the fifth day of February Next, at one of the clock in the afternoon, then and there to Elect and chouse all precinct officers that shall be needful for the present year to be chosen. Dated at Bridgewater, Jan. the 19th, 1738–9.

ABIEL PACKARD.

Titicut Parish was formed from the southwest part of the South Parish, with a part of Middleboro', Feb. 4, 1743. This place consisted of forty-eight families, forty-one houses, two hundred and sixty-two inhabitants, in 1764; and, in 1810, it had a population of three hundred and eighteen.

The first meeting held in the North Parish, after the grant of the petition to become a separate parish, was held Feb. 5, 1739, for the purpose of organization and choosing the necessary officers, as appears by the following record: —

feb the 5th year 1738–9

" The North Precinct In Bridgewater Being Legally Notifyed meet to Gather at the place and time of Day Spessefied In the Notification and the meeting was setteled by the Chose of Timothy Keith, Moderator of sᵈ meeting & Robert Haward was chosen Clark of sᵈ meeting, and the Moderator by the voice of the precinct ajorned the meeting Half one Houre to the house of John Johnson and Robert Haward was precinct Clark for the present year, and sworn to the faithfull Discharge of his Offise, and Timothy Keith, David Packard, & Daniel Howard, ware Chosen, precinct Commettee, and It was further put to vote whether the precinct would Chuse any more precinct Offisers and it was voted In the Negetive "

Timothy Keith,
Moderator,

ROBERT HAWARD } Precinct Clark.
1739.

CHAPTER III.

ECCLESIASTICAL HISTORY.

Ministry of Rev. John Porter, Rev. Asa Meech, Rev. Daniel Huntington, Rev. William Thompson, Rev. Paul Couch, Rev. Nathaniel B. Blanchard, Rev. Edward L. Clark.

IN nearly all the early New England towns, the history of the church is a history of the town; and among the first things sought after, was the establishment of the gospel ministry among them. The prayer of the petitioners having been granted so far as to set them off into a separate parish, the next thing was, to see whom they could get to preach to them. For this purpose, a meeting was held, Oct. 8, 1739, "to see if the precinct would vote to have preaching three months this winter seson." It being voted in the affirmative, David Packard, John Kingman, and Abiel Packard, were chosen a committee "to Geat a minister to preach to us three months this winter seson." And the committee were also requested "to apply to Mr. Porter, Mr. Howard, or Ephrim Keith," to supply the pulpit for three months.

Monday, March 24, 1740, "it was put to vote to see whether the precinct would vote to have Mr. Porter preach to them three months." "Voted in affirmative." "Samuel Kingman, David Packard, and Timothy Keith, were chosen a committee to go to Mr. Porter to see whether he would suply the pulpet for the three months." What the result of their interview was with him does not appear on record. We judge, however, that an invitation to settle as a permanent preacher was more agreeable, as a meeting was called soon after, on the 21st of April, by the same committee, "to see if the sd precinct can agree to give Mr. John Porter a Call to be an orDained minister of the gospel for sd precinct; also to see what Grattess the precinct will agree to give said Mr. Porter, for Incouragement for to Settell among us; also what we can agree to pay unto Mr. Porter as a yearly salary."

At this meeting, it was "voted to Give Mr. John Porter a Call to be their minister;" also, "voted to Give him two hundred pounds as a Grattess for Incuragement to settell among us, and give him one Hundred and ten pounds per year, as a yearly salary, During the time he shall be our minister."

The committee appointed "to discorse with Mr. Porter upon the above mentioned premises" were Samuel Kingman, David Packard, Timothy Keith, Daniel Howard, and Samuel West.

Aug. 4, 1740, "voted one Hundred pounds additional money as Grattess, making Three Hundred pounds, beside an addition of five pounds per year for four years, and then ten pounds per year for five years, and then to stand at one Hundred and Eighty pounds per year; to be paid in yearly, in any passable money, at the Reat of silver at Twenty Eight Shillings per ounce; and so his salary to Rise and fall, as the price of silver Doth, Durind the time that he shall be our minister."

Aug. 25, 1740, "voted to chuse Samuel Kingman, David Packard, and James Packard, a committee to Give Mr. Porter a Call in behalf of the precinct;" also voted that the 18th of September should be kept as a day of fasting and prayer, before the ordaining of Mr. John Porter.

The call, as presented to Mr. Porter, is as follows, together with his acceptance of the same: —

MR. PORTER: Since it hath pleased God to favor us with your labors amongst us for several months past, it has been to our general acceptance:

and we have unanimously agreed to give you a call to take the pastoral charge of us, and hope that the same God who has made your labors so satisfactory to us will incline your heart to accept, convincing you that it is a call from him as well as us ; and, withall, we promise to make It our prayer to the Great God for you that he should furnish you with all ministerial gifts and graces for the work of the ministry and edifying of the body of Christ among us, and that we will ever honor and obey you when you shall become ours in the Lord.   These are therfore to certify you, that at a meeting legally warned, the precinct did, by a full and clear vote, give you a call to the ministry among us ; and for your further encouragement, did vote 300 Pounds for a settlement ; and for the pursuant year, one hundred and ten pounds for your salary ; and then to advance five pounds pr. year, four years, and then ten pounds pr. year five years, and then to stand yearly at one hundred and Eighty pounds per year, to be paid in yearly, in any passable money, at the rate of silver at 28 shillings pr. ounce ; and so your salary to rise and fall, as the price of silver doth, during the time you shall be our minister.

Dated at Bridgewater,   SAMUEL KINGMAN,
 North Precinct,   DAVID KEITH,
Aug. the 25th, 1740.   JAMES PACKARD,
 Precinct Committee to give Mr. Porter a call In behalf of the precinct.

ANSWER,

To be communicated to the North Precinct in Bridgewater, given the 25th of Aug., 1740.

BRETHREN AND FRIENDS : Inasmuch as it has pleased the Sovereign God, who has all hearts in his hand, and can turn them as the rivers of water are turned, so to incline and Unite you of this Place as to give me an invitation to settle among you in the work of the gospel ministry, though unworthy yet, Apprehending it to be the call of Christ, whose I am, and whom I ought to serve, I accept your call, and I trust I do it with due and becoming reverence and cheerfulness.

Brethren and Friends : Further I desire to express all due gratitude to you for your love and respect shown me in the various instances of it, and I pray God to continue it ; and you yet to manifest it in every regard, and as the gospel requires and acknowledge that those that preach the gospel, should live of the gospel ; so I shall expect an handsome and honorable maintenance from you so long as I shall sojourn among you as your pastor. But, above all, I shall expect and request you to be constant, earnest, and incessant at the throne of grace for me, that God would give me grace to serve him cheerfully and faithfully, in the great and difficult work I am now about to engage in, that so I may finish my corse with joy, and, in the day of Christ's appearing and kingdom, may have many of you of my charge as a seal of my ministry, that so then together we may receive a crown of glory which shall never fade away.

  I subscribe myself yours to serve in the Lord,
           JOHN PORTER.

Agreeably to the above call and acceptance, the Rev. Mr. Porter was ordained as pastor of the Fourth Church in Bridgewater, Oct. 15, 1740. *

The following is the covenant which the church adopted as the basis of their union : —

We whose names are underwritten, the most of whom have been members of the first church of Christ in Bridgewater, having now, as we conceive, a call from God to embody a distinct church by ourselves, according to gospel order, and as our particular circumstances require ; do, upon this solemn occasion, think it our duty, and therefore agree, to renew the covenant which our fathers made, both with God and with one another, under a humbling sense of our violations of past covenant engagements, adding hearty prayers that our past sins may be forgiven, and that we may have the help of the Holy Spirit, to enable us to keep that covenant with God, wherein we solemnly engage, as follows : 1st. That we will take the Lord Jehovah to be our God, by a free choice of him, a firm dependence on him, and satisfaction in him, as our chief good, renouncing all other interest whatever. 2d. That we will cleave to the Holy Scriptures as our only rule of faith and obedience. 3d. That we will acknowledge our Lord Jesus Christ in his threefold office, as our Prophet, Priest, and King ; particularly in his kingly government ; that all his laws and ordinances may be upheld by us in the purity and power of them ; that an able and faithful ministry be encouraged and continued among us ; that in all the administrations of the house of God, we will have a due regard to the power of office belonging to the ministry, and the privileges belonging to the brethren, as to judgment and consent. That we will endeavor faithfully to observe the rules of purity, in respect to the visible qualifications of those we admit to communion with us, that the table of the Lord be not polluted, — that they be such as have a competent understanding of the mysteries of Godliness, and of a well-ordered conversation, and who, upon examination, hold forth repentance from dead works, and faith in our Lord Jesus Christ. We will conscientiously observe the rules of discipline which Christ hath prescribed, that the temple of God be not defiled ; will see that church censure be faithfully dispensed to such as are full communicants, and to the children of the covenant. The adult in church relation (though not yet admitted to full communion), walking orderly, and waiting upon God to prepare them for the full enjoyment of him in all his ordinances, shall (at their desire) have the initiating seal of baptism administered to their children, and they themselves shall be encouraged and excited to follow the Lord in all the ways of his appointment ; and when they offer themselves to join with the church, shall be examined respecting their proficiency, under the means,

* David Packard provided for the ordination, for which he had twenty-nine pounds and ten shillings.

and hold forth such evidences of the grace of God as may be required to make their communion comfortable. 4th. We will walk in Love one toward another, endeavoring to keep the unity of the Spirit in the bond of Peace, that there be no schism or rent in the body of Christ.

5th. In all difficult cases, we will apply to neighboring ministers and churches of Christ for counsel.

6th. We will walk with God in our houses with a perfect heart, duly attending on family worship and government, in the faithful discharge of relative duties, endeavoring that true religion may be propagated to posterity, that our God may be our children's God after us. 7th. We will bear our testimony against the growing sins of the times, and of this place ; and it shall be our endeavor, that the work of reformation in all parts of it be carried on among us. 8th. As we have opportunity, we will seek the good of one another, and so the good of all men, both with respect to spirituals and temporals. 9th. It shall be our endeavor to stand complete in all the will of God, — to cleave to the Lord and one another through all adversity. All this we do sincerely and solemnly engage in the sight of God, men, and angels, in a humble dependence of faith upon the merits of our Lord Jesus Christ, for our acceptance with God, and on the power of his spirit and grace to work all our works in us and for us ; and, finally, to perfect all that concerns us to the praise of his glory. Adopted, Sept. 18th, 1740.

1. Timothy Keith,
2. David Packard,
3. James Packard,
4. Zacheus Packard,
5. Samuel West,
6. Abiel Packard,
7. John Kingman,
8. Joshua Warren,
9. Seth Packard,
10. Caleb Phillips,
11. Isaac Fuller,
12. Zachariah Cary,
13. John Johnson,
14. Nathaniel Hammond,
15. Hannah Keith,
16. Hannah Packard,
17. Jemima Packard,
18. Mercy Packard,
19. Lydia Packard,
20. Sarah Packard,
21. Rebecca Kingman,
22. Jane Warren,
23. Mercy Packard,
24. Hannah Phillips,
25. Sarah Fuller.

Rev. Mr. Porter was a man of very respectable talent, distinguished for his prudence, fidelity, exemplary life, and holy conversation. The great doctrines of the gospel were prominent in all his preaching; and a crucified Redeemer was a theme on which he delighted to dwell with peculiar earnestness, interest, and satisfaction. He continued to preach to this society for sixty years, when, feeling weary with many years of service in the vineyard of the Lord,

and feeling the infirmities of age creeping upon him, he
called for aid to assist him in his ministerial labors. To this
claim the church and society readily assented, as appears by
the following vote : April 21, 1800, " Voted, To chuse a
committee of seven to look up sum suitable Person or Persons to assist Rev. Mr. Porter." Capt. Jesse Perkins, Dea.
David Edson, Daniel Cary, Moses Cary, Daniel Howard,
Esq., Dea. Eliphalet Packard, Lt. Caleb Howard, were chosen
as said committee. This committee found a man in the person of Asa Meech, who preached to them as a candidate
until, at a meeting held Aug. 18, 1800, " Voted, that thursday the twenty-Eighth day of August be held as a day of
Fasting and prayer for directions in settling a colleague
with Mr. Porter, and also to apply to Mr. W. Reed, and Mr.
Gurney to preach on that occasion."

Also, " Voted that the parish committee request Mr.
Meech to supply the pulpit further."

MINISTRY OF REV. ASA MEECH.

Sept. 1, 1800, " Voted to give Rev. Asa Meech a call."
Also, " Voted to choose a committee of seven to Report a
plan for the settlement of Mr. Meech, which consisted of the
following persons: Capt. Jesse Perkins, Matthew Kingman,
Deacon E. Packard, Capt. Abel Kingman, Capt. William
French, Ichabod Howard, Lieut. Caleb Howard," who subsequently reported a plan as follows; namely, "That he be our
minister until two thirds of the legal voters of the parish are
dissatisfied with him, and then to be dismissed by giving him
a years notice. Also he having the same privilege to leave
the people when he thinks proper he giving them a years
notice." Also, "that the Said parish pay him four Hundred
Dollars for the first five years; and after the expiration of the
five first years, Three Hundred and thirty four dollars a year,

so long as he continues our minister." The above Report was accepted, and it was " Voted the above committee present Mr. A. Meech with the call of the parish to the work of the ministry," which is as follows: —

To MR. ASA MEECH, Candidate for the Sacred ministry now residing in this place.

SIR, Whereas our aged and beloved pastor has requested the settlement of an assistant with him in the work of the Sacred Ministry. And as we are very desirous of a continuance of the regular Administration of Gospel ordinances among us — And having experience of your good abilities as a Gospel Preacher and such good evidence of your good moral character as gives us great satisfaction, Therefore we the members of the fourth church and congregation of the Christian Society in Bridgewater do hereby invite you with a Solemn call to Settle with us as a colleague pastor with the Rev. John Porter. That you may be more particularly informed of the doings of the Parish in this, a committee consisting of the following named gentlemen, viz. Captain Jesse Perkins, Matthew Kingman, Lieut. Caleb Howard, Dea. E. Packard, Capt. Abel Kingman, Capt. Wm. French, Ichabod Howard, will wait on you with the vote of the parish respecting the encouragement they offer you, as an inducement to Settle with us in the Sacred Ministry, and give you such other information as you may desire. Your answer is requested as soon as may be consistent with a full deliberation on so solemn and such an important subject.

DANIEL CARY, *Parish Clerk.*

The North Church in Bridgewater met this day [Sept. 29, 1800], and proceeded to hear the answer of Rev. Asa Meech.

BRIDGEWATER, Sept. 23, 1800.

To THE FOURTH CHURCH AND CONGREGATION of the Christian Society in Bridgewater. Whereas you have given me an invitation and Solemn call to settle with you in the Gospel Ministry as a Colleague Pastor with the Rev. John Porter, Having looked to God by prayer for his most gracious direction and having consulted my friends and fathers in the ministry, And after mature deliberation on the Subject, I trust and hope that a door is opened in divine providence for my usefulness in this place. This is therefore to manifest my acceptance of your call and my willingness to be employed in performing the important office and duties of the Christian ministry among you so long as God shall open the way by harmonizing our minds and give me grace wisdom and strength. And while I commit all to the great head of the Church may Grace, mercy, and peace be multiplied, to us abundantly from God our father and the Lord Jesus Christ.

ASA MEECH.

Sept. 29, 1800, " Voted that the ordination of Rev. Asa Meech be on the fifteenth day of October next." *

Mr. Meech † was ordained as a colleague pastor with Mr. Porter, Oct. 15, 1800, and continued to preach till the death of Mr. Porter, which took place March 12, 1802, in the eighty-seventh year of his age, and sixty-second of his ministry. He continued his labors after the death of Mr. Porter, until, early in 1811, he was requested to resign, and was dismissed by an Ecclesiastical Council for that purpose. His farewell sermon was preached Dec. 1, 1811.

His ordination sermon was preached by Rev. Lemuel Tyler, A. M., Pastor of the first church in Preston, Mass., from text, Titus i. 9 : " Holding fast the faithful word, as he hath been taught, that he may be able by sound doctrine, both to exhort and to convince the gainsayers." Which was a very able discourse upon the necessity of gospel ministrations, the qualifications of ministers, or what gospel ministers should do to promote, and must do to secure, peace and promote good order in the church; also on the doctrine of election, justification, and revelation, and

---

* At this meeting a committee of three were chosen to make provision for the Council ; namely, Capt. Jesse Perkins, Daniel Cary, and Capt. Howard Cary, who were provided for by Mr. Daniel Cary, at an expense of $165.58.

† Rev. Asa Meech was son of Thomas Meech, born in Boston, April 20, 1775. He was not a college-educated man, but in 1807 received an honorary degree f. om Brown University. He was approved as a candidate for the ministry by the New London County Association, in May, 1799, was ordained at North Bridgewater, Oct. 15, 1800, and dismissed in 1811; from thence he removed to Canterbury, Conn., and was installed Oct. 28, 1812, where he remained till the spring of 1822, preaching his farewell sermon May 5th. Here his ministry was not only useful in increasing the number of the church, but by establishing its faith and order. Towards the close of his pastorate, however, a feeling of personal opposition arose which rendered his removal expedient. He emigrated to Canada, where he purchased a farm near Hull, and employed himself thenceforth in its cultivation, preaching at times, as opportunity was offered. He died Feb. 22, 1849, at the age of seventy-four. He had published three sermons, — one of which was that on leaving Canterbury.

He married (1st) Mary DeWitt of Norwich, April 29, 1802, (2d), Maria DeWitt Nov., 1809, (3d), Margaret Dockstader, Nov. 7, 1822, and had by the three wives twenty-one children, the survivors of whom now reside in Canada.

the divinity of the Holy Ghost. He then goes on, giving a short exhortation to the pastor, and then to the people. *

MINISTRY OF REV. DANIEL HUNTINGTON.

For a third time this society were called to settle a pastor. Their next minister was Rev. Daniel Huntington, who came from New London, Conn., to North Bridgewater, early in the spring of 1812; and after preaching a few weeks, received a unanimous call to become their pastor. The following are some of the votes passed at the legal meetings of the society : —

At a meeting held Dec. 23, 1811, it was "Voted that thursday the 19th day of December be kept a Day of fasting and prayer for Divine Direction to a parson to settle with us — in the work of the ministry, and that the parish committee apply to Dr John Reed, Rev Mr Strong, and Rev Mr Sheldon to assist, and that the committee provide for them."

March 23, 1812, "Voted to choose a Committee of Seven men to procure a candidate or candidates to supply the pulpit, and made choice of Gideon Howard Esq, Howard Cary Esq, Dea Ichabod Howard, Abel Kingman Esq, Dea David Edson, Caleb Howard Esq, and Capt Zachariah Gurney."

A meeting was held July 13, 1812, "To see if the Parish are united in Mr Daniel Huntington as a preacher of the Gospell," it was "voted unanimously in favor of Mr Daniel Huntington," "and to use means to procure him to supply the pulpit preparatory to a settlement." "Voted that the Committee already chosen to perform that Duty use their discretion either to apply personally or by letter."

August 17, 1812, "Voted to Join with the church to give Mr Huntington a Call, to settle with us in the work of the Sacred Ministry"; also "Voted to offer him Seven Hundred

* Both of the above sermons were printed and circulated.

Dollars as settlement and Seven Hundred dollars as an annual salary, or Seven Hundred and fifty Dollars, to be paid annually so long as he remain our minister." Captain Jesse Perkins, Dea. David Edson, Dea. Ichabod Howard, Caleb Howard, Esq., Howard Cary, Esq., Joseph Silvester, Esq., Abel Kingman, Esq., were chosen a committee to wait upon Mr. Huntington, and make him the above offer, which was in the following words: —

To MR. DANIEL HUNTINGTON, Candidate for the Sacred Ministry :

SIR, Whereas the Grate head of the Church in his wise and Righteous Providence has seen fit that this church and Society should be Destitute of a pastor, we are desirous to have the regular administration of gospel ordinances restored to us, and having had so much Experience of your good abilities as a gospel preacher, am induced to hope that your labors may be blest among us. We, therefore, members of the fourth church and congregation in Bridgewater, do hereby give you solemn call to settle with us, and take upon you the sacred office of pastor according to the regular mode practised in our churches. That you may be more particularly informed of the doings of the parish, a committee, consisting of the following gentlemen, viz. : Capt Jesse Perkins, Dea David Edson, Dea Ichabod Howard, Caleb Howard, Esq, Howard Cary, Esq, Joseph Sylvester, Esq, Abel Kingman, Esq, will wait upon you with the votes of the parish relative to the encouragement they offer you as an inducement to settle with us in the sacred ministry, and give you such other information as you may desire. Your answer is requested as soon as may be consistent with a full deliberation on so solemn and important a Subject.

Signed by order and in behalf of said Parish.

JESSE PERKINS, Parish Clerk.   MOSES CARY, Moderator

Bridgewater, Aug. 17, 1812.

ANSWER.

To THE MEMBERS of the fourth Church
    and Society in Bridgewater :   Sept 14, 1812.

BRETHREN AND FRIENDS : Having taken into serious and prayerful consideration the invitation Which you have given me to settle among you in the Gospel ministry, together with the offer which accompanies it, viewing almost unanimous expression of your wish and the pecuniary· provision which evinces its sincerity, as indicative of the will of our divine Master, who in his providence has brought us together, I have thought it my duty to accede to your proposal, and hold myself in readiness to take upon me the sacred offices of your pastor according to the regular order of church, whenever it shall please the great head of the church, by the laying on of hands by the Presbytery, to put me in trust with the Gospel. With Regard to choice of compensation which was left me by your note, I would inform you that the first offer, viz.: Seven Hundred as a settlement, and Seven Hundred as an annual salary is prefered and accepted.

Yet before the question of my settlement among you is fully concluded, suffer me to present to you a few requests, Which I believe it cannot be incompatible with your interest to grant, and, *First*. It is my wish that for the words " until it is needful to procure another minister in his room," which is annexed as a limitation to your offer of a salary, the following may be substituted : " During his ministry among us," as the latter expression, it is thought, will more safely guard against future misunderstanding. *Second*. I have to request, for the same purpose, that my letter addressed through the hands of Silas Packard, Esq., to the Church and Society, on subjects connected with my proposed settlement, may be put on record, that I may not be excluded from the society of my friends and relatives, who reside at some distance, nor be debarred such recreations as is necessary to health. I must request the privilege of exemption from parochial duty for three weeks annually. Shall these requests be granted ?

Brethren and Friends, I shall cheerfully give myself to the work of the ministry among you, confidently hoping that you will receive me in brotherly love, and constantly exercise towards me that christian tenderness and candor, for which delicacy and responsibility of my situation will so loudly call above all, trusting that you will not cease to supplicate the God of all grace and consolation that he would bless our connection and make it a source of our mutual and everlasting joy.

Your Brother and Servant in Christ,

DANIEL HUNTINGTON.

North Parish, Sept. 14, 1812. " Voted that the ordination be on the last Wednesday in October, accordingly the Council met on the Twenty Eighth Day of October, consisting of

> Rev. Zedekiah Sanger, D. D., of South Bridgewater,
> Rev. John Reed, D. D.,   " West   "
> Rev. James Flint, D. D.,   " East   "
> Rev. Daniel Thomas, of Abington,
> Rev. Jacob Norton, of Weymouth,
> Rev. Thomas T. Richmond, of Stoughton,
> Rev. Luther Sheldon, D. D., of Easton,
> Rev. Jonathan Strong, D. D., of Randolph,
> Rev. Edward D. Griffin, D. D., of Boston,
> Rev. Joshua Huntington, of Boston,
> Rev. Abel McEwen, of New London, Conn., together

with their delegates," and he was duly installed as pastor of the "Fourth Church in Bridgewater." Rev. Mr. McEwen preached the Sermon, from the text Nehemiah vi. 3 : " I am doing a great work, so that I cannot come down ; why should the work cease whilst I leave it, and come down to you ? " Rev. Dr. Griffin offered the ordaining prayer. Rev. Dr. Sanger gave the charge. Rev. Mr. Huntington, of Boston, a Brother of the pastor-elect, then pastor of the " Old South Church " in Boston, extended the right hand of fellowship. Of the success of Rev. D. Huntington's labors among this church and society, we may say that, at the time of his settlement, the parish was just recovering from the effects of an unhappy division. This recovery, of course, was gradual; and the first three years may be considered as occupied in wearing out the prejudices and jealousies thus excited, so that the ordinary means of grace could be profitably used. During this period of time, the ways of Zion mourned. In 1812, but one was received into the church on profession, and one in 1813. In 1814, three ; in 1815, one ; and then came one of God's times to favor Zion. In 1816, seventy-eight were added to the church ; * and in 1817, ten more were added as the fruits of the same harvest. During the whole time he remained with this people, a period of twenty-one years, there were received into the church two hundred and fifty-three members ; previous to 1820, there were one hundred and six members admitted. The years 1830, 1831, and 1832 were distinguished by an unusual interest in this church and neighboring churches. During those years, eighty-six were added.

And, as a consequence of too frequent services in his own and neighboring churches, the health of the pastor

* A full and interesting account of this revival was published by Rev. Mr. Huntington, in the " Boston Recorder," June 10, 1817.

gradually failed, and he was obliged to resign his pastoral labors, which he did by a letter, which was read to the congregation by Rev. Dr. Hitchcock, of Randolph, March 10, 1833, and calling a meeting, on the 19th of the same month, to act upon the request.   Agreeably to the notification, the church met, and Eliphalet Kingman chosen to preside. After prayer by Rev. Mr. Huntington, the subject of the request of the pastor was considered, and after careful inquiry concerning the necessity of the measure proposed, it was "Voted, unanimously, that although we most sincerely regret the necessity of the Measure proposed, yet we feel constrained by a sense of Duty to our pastor, and to the cause which both he and we profess to love, to comply with his request;" also made choice of Dea. Silvanus French, Dr. Nathan Perry, and Heman Packard, a committee to represent the church before the Council, which consisted of

Rev. Luther Sheldon, D. D., First Church in Easton,
Rev. Richard S. Storrs, First Church in Braintree,
Rev. Melancthon G. Wheeler, First Church in Abington,
Rev. Calvin Hitchcock, First Church in Randolph.

This Council convened at the house of the pastor, March 27, 1833.   Rev. R. S. Storrs, *moderator ;* Rev. Calvin Hitchcock, *scribe.*   Afterward adjourned to Col. Edward Southworth's Hall, where a communication was read, presented from the church and society, in which it was declared that it was with great reluctance they consented to his dismission, and as an expression for the pastor's ill health, "Voted that he be requested to accept of a liberal donation."

The Council, after mature deliberation, voted "That in view of all the circumstances of the case before them, they are constrained, with much reluctance, to express their con, currence with the parties in reference to the dismission of Rev. Daniel Huntington, and do consider his pastoral and ministerial Relation as regularly dissolved, according to Ecclesiastical order," and state that

The providence of God, that has so clearly indicated this result, is deeply mysterious. When we reflect on the uninterrupted harmony of feeling, and the entire cordiality of the intercourse and co-operation of the pastor and the flock for more than twenty years, and add to this the fact of a constantly strengthening attachment, down to the present time, and also the remembrance of the unusual amount of blessing with which the relation now dissolved has been attended, We are constrained to pause in silent wonder, and then exclaim, "Even so, Father, for so it seemeth good in thy sight." In pronouncing the relation dissolved, we feel we are but declaring the will of Heaven; and most deeply do we sympathize with Each of the parties in this mutual trial. To the dearly beloved brother, with whom we have so long walked to the house of God in company, and so often taken sweet council, we give a parting hand, with emotions that cannot be uttered. We know him, — we love him; we shall never forget him nor his toils, nor his sorrows, nor his joys, nor his paternal sympathies, nor his rich success in the cause of the redeemer; and most affectionately do we commend him as a faithful brother, and able minister of the new testament, a strenuous defender of the faith once delivered to the Saints, and an indefatigable laborer in the vineyard of the Lord. Our prayers will go up to God without ceasing, that he may be fully restored to the services of the Sanctuary, and become the Spiritual father and guide of other hundreds in some other portion of our Zion; and that he may long live, and everywhere enjoy the same hallowed confidence, and full esteem of his brethren, which have been inspired by his uniform course of conduct, in the sphere of action from which he now departs in obedience to the call of Heaven. The brethren of the church and the members of this society will accept the assurance of strong sympathy and unimpaired affection on the part of this council. There is no root of bitterness that has sprung up in an evil hour; it is no diminution of your love; it is no spirit of envy or covetousness that has brought you into your present state of trial. The hand of the almighty afflicts you; and will you not say, shall we receive good at the hand of the Lord, and shall we not receive evil? We know, beloved brethren, that hearts are ready to break, and that you sorrow most of all, lest you should see the face of your beloved pastor no more. But while we cannot chide your tears, nor wonder that you are ready to inquire, Why, Lord? We are bound to say to you, fear not. The same God who gave you the treasure in which you have so long rejoiced still lives, and listens to the sighs and prayers of his people; go to him, and he will sustain and direct and bless you still. The friends of your pastor will be your friends; his brethren will be your brethren; his God will be your God. Live in Love, cherish unity of spirit, and preserve it ever in the bonds of peace. As your sorrows are mutual, so shall be your consolations. As your day is, your strength shall be. And hereafter, when the Son of man shall appear in the clouds of heaven, may you, with your beloved and faithful pastor, and your children of many generations, stand before him, and hear from his lips the blessing, Well done, good and faithful servant; enter ye into the joy of your lord.

RICHARD S. STORRS, Moderator.

A true copy :   CALVIN HITCHCOCK, Scribe

  HEMAN PACKARD, Clerk.

MINISTRY OF REV. WILLIAM THOMPSON.

Again, after the lapse of twenty-one years, is this Society called upon to fill a vacancy in their pulpit, caused by the dismission of Rev. D. Huntington.*   March 19, 1833, " Voted to choose a committee of five, to supply with preaching," and Darius Littlefield, Heman Packard, Capt. Jeremiah Beals, Lieut. Ephraim Cole, and Dea. Silvanus French, were chosen said committee.

June 13th, 1833.   At a meeting of the Parish, held this day, "Voted to give Rev. William Thompson a call to settle with them as their pastor.   Mr. Thompson, however, wishing for time to consider the matter, gave his decision July 24, accepting the invitation of the Society; and they " Voted to have the ordination Sept. 18, 1833." †

Accordingly, an Ecclesiastical Council was held at the house of Silas Packard, Esq., Sept. 17, at nine o'clock, A. M., for the purpose of ordaining Mr. Thompson, which consisted of the following : —

Rev. Joel H. Lindsey, of Park St.· Church, Boston ;

                         Zachariah Gurney, Delegate.

Rev. Calvin Hitchcock, D. D., West Randolph ;

                         Ezekiel French, Delegate.

Rev. David Brigham, East Randolph ;

                         Ezra Thayer, Delegate ;

---

* Rev. D. Huntington removed to New London, Conn., and engaged in teaching a private school of young ladies, preaching only occasionally, where he remainep till called to settle at Campello, Mass., Jan. 1, 1840.

† Afterwards changed to the seventeenth.

Rev. Baalis Sanford, Union Church, E. and W. Bridgewater;
> Samuel Rider, Delegate.

Rev. Ebenezer Gay, Trinitarian Church, Bridgewater;
> Isaac Fobes, Delegate.

Rev. Luther Sheldon, Easton ;
> Giles Randall, Delegate.

Rev. John Codman, Dorchester;
> Dea. Charles Howe, Delegate.

Rev. Daniel Huntington, New London, Conn. (former pastor).

The Council proceeded to examine the papers as laid before them, and receiving testimonials of Mr. Thompson's church standing and theological studies, with his approbation to preach the gospel, and examining him as to his views and acquaintance with experimental religion, and becoming fully satisfied with them, it was " voted unanimously to proceed to ordain him."

The following was the order of exercises : —

1. Voluntary, by the Choir ; 2. Anthem ; 3. Introductory Prayer, by Rev. Ebenezer Gay, of Bridgewater; 4. Hymn :

> " There is a stream, whose gentle flow ; "

5. Sermon by Rev. Joel H. Lindsey, of Park Street Church, Boston, text, 2 Cor. ii. 16, " And who is sufficient for these things?" 6. Ordaining Prayer, by Rev. Calvin Hitchcock, D. D., of Randolph ; 7. Hymn, tune " Old Hundred : " —

> 1 Great Lord of angels, we adore,
>> The grace that builds thy courts below ;
>> And through ten thousand sons of light,
>> Stops to regard what mortals do.
>
> 2 Amidst the wastes of time and death,
>> Successive pastors thou dost raise,
>> Thy charge to keep, thy house to guide,
>> And form a people for thy praise.
>
> 3 At length, dismissed from feeble clay,
>> Thy servants join th' angelic band ;
>> With them, through distant worlds they fly ;
>> With them before thy presence stand.

4 Oh, glorious hope ! oh, blest employ !
   Sweet lenitive of grief and care !
When shall we reach those radiant courts,
   And all their joy and honor share ?

5 Yet while these labors we pursue,
   Thus distant from thy heavenly throne,
Give us a zeal and love like theirs,
   And half their heaven shall here be known.

8. Charge to Pastor, by Rev. Daniel Huntington; 9. Right Hand of Fellowship, by Rev. Baalis Sanford, of East Bridgewater; 10. Address to the Church and Society, by Rev. Daniel Huntington; 11. Anthem,

" Let us, with a joyful mind; '

12. Concluding Prayer, by Rev. David Brigham, of East Randolph; 13. Doxology,

" Praise God, from whom all blessings flow; "

14. Benediction, by the Pastor.

The day was unusually pleasant, and the exercises very interesting and satisfactory to all present.

Mr. Thompson continued with this people but a short time, owing to a pressing call from a new Theological Seminary at East Windsor, Conn., which he received in September, 1834, and which, after one refusal, and another urgent call, he was led to accept, and where he now labors as " Professor of Biblical Literature," at East Windsor, Conn. The Council, called for advice in relation to the request of Rev. Mr. Thompson for dismission, convened at the house of Silas Packard, Esq., Sept. 4, 1834, and consisted of the following persons : —

Those chosen by the Pastor were, —

Rev. John Codman, D. D., of Dorchester; Rev. Daniel Dana, D. D., of Newburyport, Mass.; Rev. George W. Blagden, D. D., of Salem Street Church, Boston; Rev. Elisha Fisk, of Wrentham, Mass.; Rev. Lyman Matthews, of Braintree.

Those appointed by the Church and Society were, —
Rev. Warren Fay, D. D., of Charlestown, Mass.; Rev. S. Gile, of Milton; Rev. Jacob Ide, of Medway, Mass.; Rev. Sylvester Holmes, of New Bedford, Mass.; Rev. Erastus Maltby, of Taunton, Mass.

The claims of the Seminary were strongly urged by Rev. Dr. Tyler, president of the institution, in behalf of the trustees; and the claims of the society and church were represented by Rev. Calvin Hitchcock, D. D., of Randolph, in a very able manner. The Council, after considerable discussion and deliberation, "voted that the relation between Rev. William Thompson and the Church be dissolved." The society held a meeting Sept. 5, 1834, and "voted to accept of the report of the Council," which is as follows : —

The removal of settled pastors from their charges, endangers in a high degree the best interests of the churches, and is not to be encouraged except where circumstances seem clearly and imperiously to demand it. Such circumstances in the present, interesting state of the world, when so much is doing for the cause of Christ, must be expected to occur. And when they do, are to be met with a spirit of expanded benevolence, both by churches, and their pastors ; especially should this be the case, when the Theological Seminaries of our land call upon us, for those, who, by talent, experience, acquisitions, and more than all, by practical piety, are needed to instruct those who are to be under shepherds of the flocks of the Redeemer. In yielding up their pastors to such claims when clearly and affectionately presented, the churches emphatically give, and have given to them again in full measure, pressed down and running over. When other pastors sent forth by the instrumentality of him who was once their own, becoming willing and efficient workmen, in many parts of the Lord's vineyard, such is the call now made upon this beloved church by one of these institutions, and the council would affectionately suggest that in considering this call, it is important that the church should contemplate the relations to the vital interests of the whole of Zion sustained by such seminaries, and reflect also upon the fact that as they are dependent in a great measure on such institutions for faithful workmen, who shall go forth and reap the harvest of the world now white for their entrance, it becomes them to cherish toward them no common interest, but to be ready to sustain them by their most earnest endeavors ; especially should this be the case when it is remembered that the instructors in these seminaries, since they are to teach those who are to be future pastors, should be previously taught themselves, in the field of practical labor, and must therefore generally come from our churches. Impressed with such sentiments, this council do advise this church to acquiesce in the late decision of their beloved pastor, and resign him to what he believes to be the call of the great Head of the church.

Some of the council desire it to be stated that they have come to this decision without deciding on the merits of the Theological Institute of Connecticut, but solely on the ground of Mr. Thompson's strong conviction of duty, and would express their opinion that but for such a conviction now publicly and clearly expressed, he might still be more useful in this present sphere of labor. The council recommend that the adoption of this result should be understood by the church, and society, as dissolving the connection between them and their beloved pastor ; and in announcing this result they wish to express their strong sympathy in the self-denial the contemplated separation must cost them, and to assure them of their fervent prayers in their behalf. To this people, it may be difficult to resign a pastor to whom their attachment is so strong, and in whom confidence is so entire. This trial seems to be aggravated by dissolving this happy relation so soon after it had been formed. All this the council most deeply feel, yet we confide in God to sustain and guide you in this day of your affliction. And here our confidence in your future course and prospects is greatly strengthened by a recollection of your unanimity in the changes through which you have passed. while we commend you to the great Head of the church, we fervently pray that you may remain of one mind, and soon be perfectly united in another pastor, who shall guide you, and your children, to that rest where the pain of separation shall be known no more.

JOHN CODMAN, Moderator.
ERASTUS MALTBY, Scribe.

A true copy of the original result.

ERASTUS MALTBY, Scribe.

MINISTRY OF REV. PAUL COUCH.

AT a meeting of the Society held July 20, 1835, it was " *voted* to unite with the Church in giving Rev. Paul Couch * a Call to settle with us in the ministry, not one dissenting vote." Also " Voted that we offer the Rev. Mr. Couch an annual Salary of Seven Hundred and fifty dollars, and also a Gift of One Hundred and fifty dollars."

August 9th. Chose a committee of five to confer with Mr. Couch, and agree upon a council. Capt. Jeremiah Beals,

* Rev. Paul Couch was born in Newburyport, 1803 ; graduated at Dartmouth College, 1823, Andover Theological Seminary, 1826; was ordained at West Newbury, Mass., March, 1827, Bethlehem, Conn., 1829, where he preached till he came to this town, in 1834.

Eliphalet Kingman, Esq., Jesse Perkins, Esq., Nahum Perkins, and Dea. Sylvanus French were selected for that purpose, who agreed upon the following persons: —

Rev. Ebenezer Gay, Trinitarian Church, Bridgewater;
Cornelius Holmes, Delegate.

Rev. Baalis Sanford, Union Church, E. and W. Bridgewater;
Dea. John Soule, Delegate.

Rev. James W. Ward, First Church in Abington;
Richard Vining, Delegate.

Rev. Calvin Hitchcock, West Randolph;
Ezekiel French, Delegate.

Rev. David Brigham, East Randolph;
Thaddeus French, Delegate.

Rev. Erastus Maltby, Trinitarian, Taunton;
George B. Atwood, Delegate.

Rev. John Codman, Second Congregational Church, Dorchester;
Dea. Charles Howe, Delegate.

Rev. David Sanford, Dorchester.
Rev. Samuel Gile, D. D., Milton.
Rev. Jonas Perkins, D. D., Braintree.
Rev. Daniel Huntington, New London, Conn. (former Pastor).
Rev. Luther Sheldon, D. D., First Church, Easton;
Caleb Pratt, Delegate.

Wednesday, Oct. 7, 1835, being the day agreed upon for
his installation, Col. Nathan Jones, Captain Jeremiah Beals,
and Jesse Perkins were chosen a committee to make arrangements for that day.

The following was the order of exercises: —

1. Voluntary, by the Choir; 2. Anthem, by Haydn, —

" Wake the song of Jubilee; "

3. Introductory Prayer, by Rev. Erastus Maltby; 4. Original
Hymn, by their former pastor, Rev. D. Huntington: —

1 Herald of our Saviour God,
Welcome, welcome, in his name!
Sound his wondrous grace abroad;
All his boundless love proclaim.

2 Sinners renewed — lost — defiled,
  Shall the joyful news receive :
Cleansed, restored, and reconciled, —
  Bless his holy name, and live.

3 To each bruised and bleeding heart,
  Gilead's healing balm apply ;
Hope to trembling souls impart ;
  Wipe the tear from sorrow's eye.

4 Through Emanuel's favored land,
  Sound the trump of Jubilee !
Bid the prison-doors expand ;
  Hail the ransomed captives free.

5. Sermon, by Rev. John Codman, D. D. ; 6. Consecrating
Prayer, by Rev. Jonas Perkins, D. D. ; 7. Original Hymn, by
Rev. D. Huntington :

1 Ascended Saviour, thee we praise ;
  For all thy truth and kindness shown,
Accept the honors that we raise,
  And smile upon us from thy throne.

2 Yea, from that glorious throne come down ;
  Here with thy Church vouchsafe to stay ;
And let thy constant presence crown
  The joys of this auspicious day !

3 Still let our faith expect and prove
  Th' exhaustless bounty of thy hand ;
And while we taste thy richest love,
  Our heart with gratitude expand.

4 A double portion of thy grace
  On this thy messenger bestow ;
And 'neath the shining of thy face,
  Let his with heavenly lustre glow.

5 Grant him these num'rous souls to bear,
  As trophies of his faithful love, —
Seals of his high commission here, —
  Gems in his crown of joy above.

6 Then to thy great and holy name,
  Pastor and flock, through endless days,
Thy truth and mercy shall proclaim,
  In rapt'rous songs of grateful praise.

8. Charge to the Pastor, by Rev. Samuel Gile, of Milton;
9. Right Hand of Fellowship, by Rev. Baalis Sanford; 10.
Address to the Church and Society, by Rev. Calvin Hitchcock; 11. Anthem, by Mozart: —

"Hallelujah, Amen." *

12. Concluding Prayer, by Rev. Ebenezer Gay; 13. Benediction, by Rev. Paul Couch.

Rev. Mr. Couch continued to preach the gospel to this
people in all its simplicity, and with marked ability, freedom,
and candor, — such as had its desired effect upon the community in which he moved, — till May 8, 1859, when he asked
to be relieved from his pastoral labors, which request was
granted, July 1, 1859, and the estimation in which he was
held by his people may be seen in the following resolutions
which were passed by the church, at a meeting held on that
day :—

Resolved, that while in view of the circumstances set forth by our pastor in his communication as the reasons which, in his opinion, render it expedient that he go away, and which have induced him to request his release from
his pastoral charge over this church and society and people, we have, at a
previous meeting, reluctantly recorded our assent to his request. And we
esteem it a duty which we owe to ourselves, and to him, to say, that in taking this step we defer to his judgment, and consult his express wishes, and
are not led to it by any disaffection on our part.

We still appreciate those traits in his character which, manifested among
us, won for him our affection and regard, and we will cheerfully bear testimony, unitedly, to that high mental culture, that maturity of judgment,
that sincerity, earnestness, and fearlessness, in declaring from the pulpit the
counsels of God ; that ready sympathy with the afflicted and sorrowful
among his people, and that love and known consistency of his daily life with
his office as minister of Christ, which have constrained us always to esteem
with respect and reverence his teachings, and to submit with love and
confidence to his guidance ; and when in the prospect of a speedy separation,
all these things are vividly brought to mind, concerning our beloved pastor,

* The music on this occasion was conducted by Thomas J. Gurney, and was of
the highest order; and the other exercises were gratifying to a large an l attentive
audience.

6

it is not without painful misgivings that we consent to the sundering of those ties which, for the period of twenty-four years, bound him to this church and people.

Resolved, if such separation takes place, we tender our pastor assurances of our wishes and our prayers for his welfare, wherever he may be called to labor, and express the hope that his labors here may prove to him as he goes, and to us who remain, not only a present memory, but, by the grace of God, a means and a pledge of a happy reunion of church and pastor in a better world.

With a view to the dismission of Mr. Couch, an ecclesiastical council was called for the purpose of hearing and acting upon the request of their pastor for a dissolution of his connection with the church and society, which meeting was held July 19, 1859. The council was as follows : —

Rev. Richard S. Storrs, D. D., of Braintree ; Elisha French, Delegate.
Rev. Jonas Perkins, D. D., of Braintree ; Levi W. Hobart, Delegate.
Rev. Charles W. Wood, of Campello ; Josiah W. Kingman, Delegate.
Rev. Ezekiel Russell, D. D., of East Randolph ; John Adams, Delegate.

After hearing the statement of the pastor requesting his dismission, and the statements of the church and society, who very reluctantly yielded their assent, the council voted,—

That in view of all the circumstances, the strong convictions and preference of the pastor, and the assent, though reluctant, of the church and society, it is expedient that the ministerial and pastoral relation of the Rev. Paul Couch to the First Church and Society in North Bridgewater, be dissolved, the dissolution to take effect, or the relation to terminate, the first day of August, 1859.

In coming to this result the council cannot withhold the expression of their deep regret that a connection, that has so long existed, been so auspicious to both pastor and people, sealed by effusions of the Eternal Spirit, cemented by mutual affection and esteem, and so productive of permanent good to the cause of truth and the honor of Christ in the world, should be thus sundered. Deeming themselves incompetent to judge of the validity of all the reasons for the course pursued, and trusting much to the sound discretion and judgment of the parties themselves, this council still in view of all the circumstances seem constrained to acquiesce in what seems to be the leadings of Providence. This council deeply regret the separation from one, whose urbanity, large experience, and Christian kindness and wisdom have ever done so much to enlighten, and cheer ministerial intercourse in all its connections. They therefore commend the Rev. Paul Couch to the churches of Christ, as one rich in ministerial experience, able, gifted, faithful, and beloved, with no blemish on either his Christian or ministerial reputation. This council also commend this dear church for the sacrifice they have made for the cause of truth, and the prosperity of the kingdom of Christ in this place. They commend them for the affection and kindness they have shown to their pastor, their deference to his wishes, their provision for his wants. They would urge them, also, to a settlement of the gospel ministry among themselves as soon as circumstances will allow it, and to a perseverance in the cause hitherto pursued.

They finally deeply sympathize with them in their separation from a pastor that has been so long and so justly respected and beloved, and commend them in their disappointment, to the care of the Shepherd of Israel.

RICHARD S. STORRS, Moderator.
EZEKIEL RUSSELL, Scribe.

A true copy of the doings of the council.

E. RUSSELL, Scribe.

North Bridgewater, July 19, 1859.

Rev. Mr. Couch preached his farewell discourse, July 31, 1859.*

MINISTRY OF REV. NATHANIEL B. BLANCHARD.

Immediately after the dismission of Rev. Mr. Couch, an invitation was given to Rev. N. B. Blanchard,† a native of Abington, Mass., who had been preaching for three years at Plymouth, to supply their pulpit for one year, commencing the first Sabbath in August, 1859. After this term had expired, they had become so attached to him as a preacher, and finding him to be a man of ability, he received a call June 12, 1861, to settle with them as their pastor; which

---

* On Monday evening following, a large number of the society and friends came together in the vestibule of the church, for the purpose of presenting him and his family tokens of their regard to them. A gold watch and one hundred dollars in money were presented to Mr. Couch, a silver goblet and a set of spoons to Mrs. Couch, and a splendid guitar to their daughter, Miss Harriet E. Couch, who had sung in their choir for many years.

From North Bridgewater, Rev. Mr. Couch removed to North Cambridge, Mass., where he received an invitation to preach. Here, also, the people had taken possession of the house he was to occupy, by stocking it well with a year's supply of provisions.

† Rev. Nathaniel B. Blanchard was born in Abington, Mass., July 26, 1827; graduated at Amherst College in 1853; completed his theological course at Bangor Theological Seminary in 1855; ordained to the Christian ministry at Edgartown, July 15, 1856; preached three years in the Pilgrim Church, Plymouth, Mass.

call he accepted, August 4, 1861, and was installed Sept.
18, 1861.   The Council consisted of Rev. T. Stowe, of
New Bedford, Rev. Henry B. Hooker, D. D., of Boston;
Rev. Jonas Perkins, D. D., of Braintree ; Rev. H. D.
Walker, of Abington; Rev. Charles L. Mills, of the Porter
Church in N. Bridgewater; Rev. Stephen G. Dodd, of
East Randolph; Rev. James P. Terry, of South Weymouth.
After the business meeting, and examination of the papers
of the pastor-elect, the council proceeded to the ser-
vices of installation, commencing at one and a half o'clock,
P. M., with the following order of exercises: 1. Volun-
tary ;   2. Reading of the Scriptures and Prayer, by Rev.
Mr. Stowe; 3. Hymn ; 4. Sermon, by Rev. Dr. Hooker,
D. D. ; 5. Installing Prayer, by Rev. Jonas Perkins, D. D. ;
6. Anthem ;   7. Charge to the Pastor, by Rev. H. D.
Walker; 8. Right Hand of Fellowship, by Rev. Charles L.
Mills; 9. Charge to the People, by Rev. S. G. Dodd ; 10.
Prayer, by Rev. J. P. Terry ; 11. Hymn ; 12. Benediction, by the Pastor.   The sermon on this occasion is said
to have been an able and interesting exposition of the
relations of the gospel of Christ to the human conscience,
and the other services were of an interesting nature.   Mr.
Blanchard continued his labors of love to this people until the month of August, 1862, when, his health failing, he
relinquished his labors for a season to travel, that he might
recover.   He was on his way to Plymouth, N. H., stopping
at Concord, N. H.; became worse, and there died, August 7,
1862.   His remains were brought to his church, where funeral services were attended by Rev. H. D. Walker, of East
Abington, August 9th; and afterwards his body was taken
to Edgartown for burial.

     At a meeting of the church, held soon after the funeral,
the following resolutions were passed, expressive of their
feelings at his decease: —

Whereas Almighty God, by his inscrutable Providence, has removed from us our beloved pastor, Rev. Nathaniel B. Blanchard, by death, —

Resolved, That we are deeply sensible of the great loss we have sustained by being deprived of his instructive, faithful, earnest, and zealous ministrations; that we received him as a man after God's own heart; that we loved him as our pastor and our friend ; and we would honor his memory as that of one endeared to us by the most holy associations.

Resolved, That in all the civil and social relations, while he sustained the dignity of his profession and sacred office, Mr. B., by the grace and urbanity of his demeanor, won the respect and affectionate regard of all the members of the community in which he moved.

Resolved, That we heartily sympathize with his family in this the sad hour of their bereavement.

Resolved, That the foregoing resolutions be published in the "North Bridgewater Gazette," and also that a copy of the same be sent to the widow of the deceased.

HENRY HOWARD, Clerk.

MINISTRY OF REV. EDWARD L. CLARK.

After the decease of Rev. Mr. Blanchard, the pulpit was supplied by various ministers, among whom was Mr. Clark. At a meeting of the "First Congregational Church," held April 11, 1863, it was unanimously voted to give Mr. Edward L. Clark * a call to become their pastor; which call he accepted, and was ordained Sept. 22, 1863. After a careful examination of the papers that had passed between Mr. Clark and the church and society, and finding them satisfactory, the council proceeded to examine the candidate, closely interrogating him in regard to his religious experience, and becoming fully satisfied, "voted to proceed to the services of installation," which were in the following order : —

1. Introductory Prayer, by Rev. Charles W. Wood, of

* Rev. Edward L. Clark, was born in Nashua, N. H., Feb. 3, 1838 ; fitted for college at Phillips Academy, Andover, Mass.; graduated at Brown University, Providence, R. I., 1858 ; spent one year travelling through Egypt, Palestine, and other ancient places in the Holy Land; studied theology at Andover Theological Seminary; graduated 1862; was ordained as chaplain of the 12th Regiment Massachusetts Volunteers, with whom he remained one year; afterward settled as pastor of the First Congregational Church in North Bridgewater, Sept. 22, 1863.

Campello; 2. Reading of the Scriptures, by Rev. Ebenezer Douglas, Bridgewater; 3. Singing 518th Hymn of the Psalmist; 4. Sermon, by Rev. A. L. Stone, of Park Street Church, Boston; 5. Anthem, by the Choir; 6th. Installing Prayer, by Rev. Jonas Perkins, D. D., of Braintree; 7. Charge to the Pastor, by Rev. J. Lewis Diman, of Brookline, Mass.; 8. Right Hand of Fellowship, by Rev. Samuel H. Lee, of the Porter Church; 9. Address to the People, by Rev. Paul Couch, of Jewett City, Conn. (their former pastor); 10. Concluding Prayer, by Rev. D. Temple Packard, of Somerville, Mass.; 11. Singing 117th Psalm; 12. Benediction, by the Pastor.

CHAPTER IV.

ECCLESIASTICAL HISTORY—CONTINUED.

Second Congregational Church.—New Jerusalem Church.—South Congregational Church, Campello.—First Methodist Episcopal Church.—First Baptist Church.—Porter Evangelical Church.—Catholic Church.—First Universalist Church.—Quakers, or Friends.—Second Methodist Episcopal Church.

SECOND CONGREGATIONAL SOCIETY.

DURING the year 1824, many of the members of the " First Congregational Church," under the pastoral care of Rev. Daniel Huntington, becoming dissatisfied with the views of their pastor, and entertaining different views of Christian doctrines, especially on the doctrine of the Trinity, the native character of man, divinity and atonement of Christ, regeneration, and other kindred views of the gospel, petitioned the General Court to be incorporated into a separate society, which petition was granted in the following words, which we copy verbatim:—

Be it enacted by the Senate and House of Representatives in General Court Assembled and by the authority of the Same.

That

Abiel Kingman,	Zeba Thayer,	John Field,
Micah Packard,	Sihon Packard Jr.	Zophar Field,
David Cobb Jr.	Apollas Howard,	Austin Howard,
Nathan Hayward,	Welcome Howard,	Josiah W. Curtis,
Gideon Howard,	Caleb Howard Jr.	Richmond Carr,
David Packard,	Azor Packard,	Otis Howard,
Marcus Shaw,	Simeon Dunbar,	David Edson 3d,
Jesse Packard,	Nathaniel H. Cross,	Luke P. Lincoln,
John Battles,	Joseph S. Packard,	Thomas Reynolds,
Hiram Atherton,	Joseph D. Snell,	Azel Reynolds,
Nahum J. Smith,	Zenas Packard Jr.	Oliver Snell,
Newton Shaw,	Stillman Willis,	Isaac Snell,
Anthony S. Allen,	Silas Snow,	Jeremiah Snell,

Edwin Keith,	Silas Snow Jr.	James J. Sanders,
Washburn Packard,	John Curtis,	Daniel Bryant,
Asa Brett,	Hosea Packard,	Ara Battles,
Hervey Hersey,	Asa Shaw,	Abijah Childs,
Samuel Thayer,	Samuel Packard,	Thomas White,
Samuel Howard,	William Curtis Jr.	Thomas White Jr.
Eliphalet Thayer,	Isaac Packard,	Arza Leonard,
Oliver Snell Jr.	Isaac Richards,	John White,

With their families and estates, together with such others as may hereafter associate with them, and their successors, be, and they are hereby incorporated into a Society by the name of the " Second Congregational Society " in the town of North Bridgewater, with all the Powers, privileges, and immunities which other religious societies in this Commonwealth are by law entitled to, and may purchase, receive by gift, or otherwise real estate to the value of which, Shall not exceed the sum of Eight Thousand Dollars.

passed June 18, 1825.

Soon after this, a lot of land was purchased of Micah Faxon for a church. This was located on a rising spot of ground, south of the present public house, and near "Kingman's Brick Block." A house was erected, which was dedicated August 9, 1826, with appropriate services, as follows : Introductory Prayer and Reading of the Scriptures, by Rev. John Pierpont, of Boston; Dedicatory Prayer, by Rev. Eliphalet Porter, D. D., of Roxbury, Mass.; Sermon, by Rev. Benjamin Huntoon, of Providence, R. I., from the text, Acts xxiv. 14: " But this I confess unto thee, that after the way which they call heresy, so worship I the God of my fathers, believing all things which are written in the law, and in the prophets;" Concluding Prayer, by Rev. James Kendall, D. D., of Plymouth; Benediction, by Rev. Richard M. Hodges, of Bridgewater.

Rev. John Goldsbury,* of Warwick, Mass., received an invitation to become their pastor, and his accepting of the same,

* Rev. John Goldsbury was born in Warwick, Mass., Feb. 11, 1795; fitted for college at different schools and academies, and under private instruction ; graduated at Brown University in 1820 ; commenced the study of divinity at Harvard College in 1821, under Professors Ware, Norton, and Willard ; taught in Taunton Academy several years ; was ordained in North Bridgewater, Wednesday, June 6, 1827, where he remained till Sept 4, 1831 ; now resides in Warwick, Mass.

NEW JERUSALEM CHURCH (First Edifice).
Erected 1835.

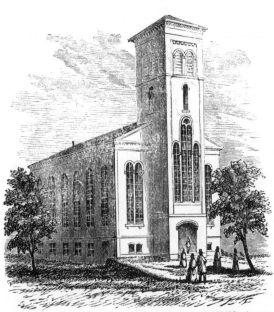

NEW JERUSALEM CHURCH (Second Edifice).
Erected 1856.

he was ordained Wednesday, June 6, 1827, with the following services: —

1. Introductory Prayer and Reading of the Scriptures, by Rev. J. P. B. Storer, of Walpole, Mass.; 2. Sermon, by Rev. Luther Hamilton, of Taunton, Mass.; 3. Ordaining Prayer, by Rev. John Reed, D. D., of West Bridgewater, Mass.; 4. Charge to the Pastor, by Rev. Eliphalet Porter, D. D., of Roxbury, Mass.; 5. Right Hand of Fellowship, by Rev. Ezra S. Gannett, D. D., of Boston; 6. Address to the People, by Rev. John Pierpont, of Boston; 7. Concluding Prayer, by Rev. Henry Edes, D. D., of Providence, R. I. The pleasantness of the day and the deep interest in the occasion, caused the house to be thronged. The sermon was from text, John xviii. 37: "To this end was I born, and for this cause came I into the world, that I should bear witness unto the truth."

The sermon on that occasion was exceedingly interesting and very judicious, dwelling at some length on the simplicity of the truth which the Christian teacher is required to inculcate. Among the many things noticed were the difficulties of a Christian ministry, — the indifference to truth prevalent in the world, — the prejudices of opinion that hinder the reception of truth, — and the disposition among men to mystify and obscure the plainest principles. The charge to the pastor, by Rev. Dr. Porter, was listened to with peculiar interest, from his filial allusion to one under whose ministry many of this society had formerly sat: — (Rev. John Porter, father of Rev. Eliphalet Porter, D. D., of Roxbury, Mass.)

NEW JERUSALEM CHURCH.

THE knowledge of the "New Church" doctrines were introduced into this part of the country by the Rev. Holland Weeks, of Abington, Mass., who was dismissed from his

7

society in that town about the year 1820, for having be-come a believer in them, which circumstance created no small excitement at the time, and was the means of indu-cing some others to look into the subject, and to become believers themselves. The first society of receivers of the doctrines in this place was formed in 1827, and consisted of ten members; namely, Sidney Perkins, Nathaniel B. Har-low, William French, Martin Beal, Jabez Field, John Field, of North Bridgewater, Isaiah Noyes, Daniel Noyes, Elisha Faxon, and Austin Cobb, of Abington. In 1828, the number had increased to twenty. During that year, a hall was fitted up in the house of Jabez Field, to hold public meetings. Rev. Eleazer Smith preached for them once a month, from 1827 to 1831, and afterwards every Sabbath, till 1834. In 1831, the hall owned by Major Nathan Hayward was occu-pied by the society for meetings, and, still later, the build-ing previously used by the Second Congregational Society, or better known as the "Unitarian meeting-house." Also, the hall over the hotel then kept by Edward E. Bennett. In 1832, the society petitioned the legislature for an act of incorporation as a religious society, which was granted, as may be seen by the following act, dated March 3, 1832, and styled —

THE FIRST SOCIETY OF THE NEW JERUSALEM CHURCH IN NORTH BRIDGE-WATER.

Be it enacted by the Senate and House of Representatives in General Court Assembled, and by authority of the Same,

That Jabez Field, Lucius Field, James A. Tolman, Ruel Richmond, Robert Stoddard, Nahum Smith, Rufus Dorr, Orville Handy, Winslow B. Cushman, James Humphrey, Wm. French, Ephraim Howard, Josiah Pack-ard, Charles Howard, Nathaniel B. Harlow, Lyman Clark, Sidney Perkins, Eleazer Smith, John Field, Sanford Brett, Samuel Howard, Marcus Shaw, William Faxon, John Ide, and Arnold Hunt, together with those who have associated, or may hereafter associate with them, or their Successors, for the purpose of public worship, be, and they hereby are incorporated into a religious Society by the name of the " *First Society* of the *New Jerusalem*

Church'' in the town of North Bridgewater, with all the powers and privileges and subject to all the duties and liabilities of Parishes, according to the Constitution and Laws of this Commonwealth.

" Be it further enacted,'' That the said Society shall be capable in Law to purchase, hold, and dispose of any estate, either real or personal, not exceeding the Sum of Twenty Thousand Dollars, for the Support of public Worship and for other lawful Parochial purposes.

The first meeting held under the provisions of the above acts was held April 5, 1832, at the house of Jabez Field, at which William French was chosen moderator ; Lyman Clark, clerk and treasurer : Jabez Field, collector ; John Field, Nathaniel B. Harlow, and Marcus Shaw, prudential committee. In August, 1834, Rev. Haskell M. Carll was invited to preach to the society, which he continued to do about three years. On the 7th of December, 1834, he organized a church in the society. Soon after, in September, 1835, the building of the first house of worship in the town, of that denomination, was commenced, and was dedicated on Saturday, January 16, 1836. There were present at the dedication Rev. H. M. Carll, the pastor of the society ; Rev. Thomas Worcester, of Boston ; Rev. Adonis Howard, of East Bridgewater. The dedicatory service was read by Rev. Mr. Carll. Sermon, by Rev. T. Worcester ; Reading of the Word, by Rev. Adonis Howard. Mr. Carll left the society in the fall of 1837, and Rev. Warren Goddard,* the present pastor, commenced preaching for them October 14, 1838 ; and January of the next year, 1839, an invitation was extended to him to settle with them as their pastor. This call he accepted, and he was ordained the 19th of September, 1839. The following are the

* Rev. Warren Goddard was born in Portsmouth, N. H., Sept. 2, 1800. Fitted for college at Portsmouth Academy ; graduated at Harvard University, Aug., 1818; studied theology with Rev. T. M. Harris, of Dorchester, Mass.; afterward pursued the study of law with Hon. John Reed, of Yarmouth, Mass.; admitted to the bar, in Barnstable County, Mass.; practised law two years in Barnstable, and one in Boston, in connection with Professor Parsons ; installed at N. Bridgewater in 1839.

DOCTRINES OF CHARITY AND FAITH.

1. That God is one in essence, and in person, that from love towards men, he assumed humanity and glorified it, and that he thus became God with us, the Saviour and Redeemer Jesus Christ.

2. That the word is divine Truth proceeding from the Lord; that it was written by inspiration, and is adapted to all the various states of Angels and men, and that thus it is the divine Medium by which men are consociated with Angels and by which men and Angels are conjoined with the lord.

3. That the Lord alone is the Source of Genuine life, the precepts of which are the ten Commandments; that these precepts are to be obeyed by man as of himself, with the acknowledgment that the will and power to do them are of the Lord alone. And thus that men are regenerated and Saved by the Lord, by means of a life according to his precepts.

The first house of worship was fifty-eight feet in length, forty feet in width, and twenty feet high; spire sixty-five feet high; painted white, with green blinds. The interior contained fifty-two pews, beside a neat, plain pulpit, and a small choir-gallery. The building was situated on land purchased of Sidney Perkins, the building and land costing about three thousand dollars.

This society worshipped in the old house above described until the dedication of another house, which had been built to suit the wants of the growing society, and which took place January 22, 1857. The services commenced about ten o'clock in the forenoon, and were conducted by the pastor, Rev. Mr. Goddard, and were of a deeply impressive character, well fitted to bring the hearer into a state receptive of his love who desires our offerings, "to the end that he may more abundantly enrich us with spiritual blessings." The weather was such on that day, so very severe, that but few, comparatively, were present, and those mostly from the people of the town. The services were reading of the Psalm 122, followed by a chanting from an appropriate selection (No. 80, Psalm 84). After which Psalm 132 and others were read responsively by both pastor and people the people of the society standing, mostly in front of the desk, and responding as an act on their part of offering up the house to the worship and service of the Lord. The music was not only appropriate, but well performed. After the exercises were over, a collation was partaken of in the hall below by nearly all who had been present, including many from the neighboring societies, and a very pleasant season of social interview closed the exercises of the day.

Description of the New Church Temple.

This church is situated on a spacious lot of ground, bordered with trees of considerable size, fronting the west. The dimensions of the main building are seventy-nine by fifty-six feet. It is built in the Italian style, with a plain, square tower at the west (front) end, eighty-eight feet in height and twenty-two feet square, projecting ten and a half feet forward from the main building. The entrance in front is by a wide double door into the vestibule, from which there is an ascent by eleven easy steps into side entries, or lobbies, from which one enters the body of the church. This measures sixty-one by forty-five feet, and contains one hundred and two pews, all on the main floor, there being no side galleries. They are arranged in semi-circular order, without doors, cushioned, and covered with crimson damask. The floor is handsomely carpeted, and walls and ceiling elegantly painted in fresco. On the east side is a projection of four feet deep by thirty-two wide, a space for the Tabernacle, a repository for the word in the centre, and for a small private room each side of it. The tabernacle consists of an ark of fine cabinet work, overhung with crimson curtains. Over it is the inscription, in large letters, "Behold the Tabernacle of God is with man." To the right of it, but standing out in front, on the edge of the platform, is the pulpit, which is of octagonal form and, like the tabernacle, of black walnut. The communion-table stands at the left side. The organ-loft is within the body of the tower, oppo-

site the pulpit, having in front a small gallery for the singers, elevated about eight feet above the pew-floor. There is
a basement of brick, affording space for a hall under the
whole main building, to which there is an entrance from the
vestibule within, and also by doors from without, at the
northwest and southwest corners. The superstructure is
of wood, colored in imitation of freestone. The house is
provided with a good-toned organ, of suitable size and capacity, manufactured by George Stevens, Esq.*

SOUTH CONGREGATIONAL CHURCH.

This church was composed of members who belonged
to the First Congregational Church, in the Centre Village,
under the pastoral care of Rev. Paul Couch. The people
in the southerly portion of the town having become quite
numerous, and the inconvenience of attending constantly
upon public worship at such a distance (one and a half
miles) was such that a new and more convenient means
was thought of. Hence, after much consultation and many
meetings, thirty-four persons petitioned to a Justice of the
Peace to call a meeting for the purpose of organizing them
into a new society. The following persons were the original members : —

Ziba Keith, Benjamin Keith, Azor Packard, Thomas Pack-
ard, Charles Keith, Jason Keith, Vinal Lyon, Isaac K. French,
Cary Howard, Oliver Jackson, Nahum Hayward, Pardon
Keith, Jonathan Snell, Abijah Holmes, Calvin Hatch, John
W. Snell, Albert Hunt, Sylvanus French, Davis Kingman,
Charles Williams, John Millett, Stafford Drake, Robert Pack-
ard, Jr., Aaron B. Drake, Stephen D. Soule, Ephraim Jack-
son, Abijah Thayer, Josiah Dunbar, Freeman Holmes, Fear-

* Martin Wales, Esq., of Stoughton, presented the society with two thousand
dollars toward paying the expense of building the new house. Chandler Sprague,
Lyman Clark, and George W. Bryant were building committee ; Jason Perkins,
contractor.

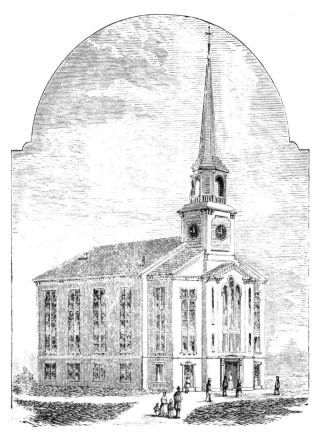

SOUTH CONGREGATIONAL CHURCH (Campello).
Second Edifice—Erected 1854.

ing W. Bent, Jonas Keith, Bela Keith, Josiah W. Kingman, Zina Hayward. Agreeable to the petition above referred to, Hon. Jesse Perkins, Esq., issued a warrant calling a meeting, to be held at the house of Bela Keith, Esq., December 3, 1836, at one o'clock, P. M.: when the following officers were chosen: Josiah W. Kingman, *moderator;* Jason Keith, *clerk;* Charles Keith, *treasurer;* Azor Packard, Ziba Keith, Charles Keith, *parish committee.*

The first step taken toward erecting a house of worship was to obtain a spot of land upon which to build. For this purpose, Isaac Keith gave the society the lot now owned and occupied by them, on the corner of South and Main streets, Campello, on condition that they pay him the interest on the sum of Two Hundred and Fifty Dollars, Annually, until the decease of Mr. Keith and wife, then to become the property of the society.

The first house of worship was built by subscription, and cost $4,307.37, of which sum three thousand dollars only was subscribed. The house was built under the direction of Bela Keith, Esq., as master-builder, in 1836, who paid the balance ($1,307.37) over the subscription. The frame was raised July 4th, 1836, was a plain, substantial building, sixty feet in length, forty-three feet in width, and twenty-one feet posts, with a spire eighty-five feet in height, and a bell weighing 1032 pounds, manufactured by George Holbrook, of East Medway, Mass. The house had sixty pews,* besides the choir gallery. The basement was used as a vestry for evening meetings. The society having been duly organized, and a house of worship erected, it was thought best to form a new church among themselves. For this purpose the following persons made application to be dismissed from the First Church, with suitable testimonials, to be formed into

---

* The pulpit was manufactured by Josiah W. Kingman, who also made the pew-arms and trimmings.

another church, and to use a similar creed as the one which they leave : Sylvanus French, Mercy E. Keith, Abigail Keith, Olive Jackson, Martha Keith, Charles Keith, Mehitable Keith, Ziba Keith, Polly Keith, Mary Keith, Sylvia Howard, Huldah Howard, Keziah Hayward, Charles Williams, Zilpha Hatch, Josiah W. Kingman, Joanna Packard, Robert Packard, Sarah Packard, Mary Packard, Josiah Dunbar, Sybil Dunbar, Anna Dunbar. This request was granted. A council was next called, for the purpose of organization, which met at the house of Josiah W. Kingman, Esq., on Tuesday, January 3d, 1837, at which time and place it took the name of the " South Congregational Church," in North Bridgewater. The following Articles of Faith and Covenant were adopted by them at that time :

CONFESSION OF FAITH AND COVENANT OF THE SOUTH CONGREGATIONAL CHURCH, NORTH BRIDGEWATER, MASS.

WE solemnly profess our unfeigned belief of the Holy Scriptures of the Old and New Testaments, as given by divine inspiration ; our acceptance of all the doctrines contained in them, and our submission to the whole will of God, therein revealed. Particularly, we profess to believe that the Lord Jehovah, the Father, the Son, and the Holy Ghost, is the one living and true God ; that the Lord Jesus Christ is the Son of God, essentially equal with the Father, and the only Saviour of men; that the Holy Ghost is also God, and that he is the only Sanctifier of those who believe in Christ to the salvation of their souls.

We believe that, in consequence of the fall of man from his primitive state of innocence, all the human race, while unregenerate, are destitute of holiness ; and therefore that a renovation of heart, during the present life, through sanctification of the Spirit of God, is necessary to fit mankind for union and communion with the visible Church of Christ on earth, and for admittance into the kingdom of heaven.

We believe, that in order to effect our deliverance from the bondage of corruption, and from the curse of the law, under which we all have fallen by transgression, the Eternal Word, who in the beginning was with God, and was God, was made flesh, and dwelt among men on earth ; uniting with his divinity the whole human nature (yet without sin) in the person of the Lord Jesus Christ. That this mysterious and adorable personage, having magnified and honored the divine law by his doctrine and example, at length died on the cross, the just for the unjust, that he might bring us to God :

and that it is through the efficacy of his propitiatory sacrifice alone, his people obtain the divine favor and blessing.

We believe that, having thus laid down his life, he took it again, being declared the Son of God with power, by the resurrection from the dead; and that he is now at the right hand of the Father, a prince and a Saviour, bestowing repentance and remission of sins, through the agency of the Holy Spirit attending the ministry of his word, on those whom the Father hath given him, in the everlasting covenant of redemption, as a seed to serve him.

We believe, that whosoever will may come and partake the blessings of this great salvation, as they are freely and sincerely offered in the Gospel; yet that none of our apostate race are, of themselves, disposed to forsake sin, and devote themselves to God, in heart and life; so that it rests with him, in the exercise of his sovereign wisdom and goodness, to have mercy on whom he will have mercy; making his Gospel effectual to their conviction and conversion, by the attendant energy of his Holy Spirit.

We believe that none who are thus made partakers of the heavenly calling shall be finally deprived of the grace which was given them in Christ Jesus before the world began; but that they shall all be kept by the power of God, through faith unto salvation.

We believe that the Lord Jesus Christ shall appear again at the last day, to judge the quick and dead; that he will then receive to mansions of eternal rest all who have truly believed and obeyed his Gospel; and sentence to everlasting destruction from his presence, and from the glory of his power, all who have died, or who shall then be found living in impenitence and unbelief.

COVENANT.

Humbly hoping that these truths have come, not only to our understanding, but to our hearts, "in power, and in the Holy Ghost, and in much assurance;" and that we have been enabled to receive them with that faith which purifies the heart, and works by love, and in the exercise of that repentance which is unto life, We do now solemnly avouch the Lord Jehovah to be our God; Jesus Christ, the Son of God, to be our Redeemer; and the Holy Spirit to be our Sanctifier.

Depending on divine grace for spiritual strength and comfort, we take the word of God as our only rule of faith and practice; avowing it to be our supreme desire and solemn determination to seek his glory, and his favor, in obedience to all his holy will. Accordingly, we engage to unite in maintaining and attending on the ministry of his word and ordinances, as he shall give us ability and opportunity, to be thereby edified in our holy faith. We submit ourselves, individually, to the brotherly watch and discipline of the community which we hereby form, and mutually engage to watch over, to exhort, to assist, comfort, and admonish each other in brotherly love, as our relation and circumstances may require.

The next thing to be done, after the formation of a church, was to find a man to preach to them. After hearing many candidates, at a meeting held January 9th, 1837, the Church and Society " voted to give Rev. Thomas Kidder a call to settle with them in the ministry, and to give him a salary of Five Hundred and Fifty Dollars per year." This call was not accepted. The next person that received a call was Rev. John Dwight, of Medway, Mass., to whom the Society offered Six Hundred Dollars as a yearly salary. This was accepted; and Josiah W. Kingman, Ziba Keith, Dea. Jacob Fuller, and Bela Keith were chosen a committee to make arrangements for his installation. The day being fixed for the ordination, a Council, consisting of the following persons, was called, to meet April 12, 1837, namely: Rev. Jacob Ide, of Medway, Mass.; Rev. Mr. Bennett, of Woburn; Rev. Paul Couch, of N. Bridgewater; Rev. Luther Sheldon, of Easton; Rev. Baalis Sanford, of East Bridgewater; Rev. James W. Ward, of Abington; Rev. Jonas Perkins, of Braintree; Rev. Calvin Hitchcock, of Randolph; Rev. Ebenezer Gay, of Bridgewater; Rev. Dr. Park, of Stoughton; and Rev. John Dwight* was duly ordained as their pastor.

Mr. Dwight labored with this people until March, 1839, when he was dismissed. Various preachers were heard from that time until November, when, at a meeting of the society, held November 19, 1839, it was " voted to unite with the church in giving Rev. Daniel Huntington, of New London, Conn., a call to become their pastor.

Josiah W. Kingman, Charles Keith and Dea. Sylvanus French were chosen a committee to confer with Rev. Mr.

---

* Rev. John Dwight was born in Shirley, Mass., Jan. 2d, 1810; fitted for college at Woburn Academy; taught school in Woburn two terms; graduated at Amherst College in 1835; studied theology with Rev. Jacob Ide, D. D., of West Medway, Mass.; licensed to preach by the Mendon Association in the early part of 1837; received a call to settle over the South Church in Campello, Mass., in 1837; was ordained April 12, 1837; dismissed in March, 1839; installed over the " Second Church " in Plymouth, Mass., July 18, 1841; dismissed in March, 1846; installed pastor of the church in North Wrentham, Mass., June 23, 1853; dismissed April 1, 1856. He married Sarah Ann Hastings, of Boston, April 14, 1837, and has six children, all of whom reside at North Wrentham, Mass.

Huntington, and offer him six hundred dollars salary; which offer being accepted, a council, consisting of Rev. Richard S. Storrs, D. D., of Braintree; Rev. Ebenezer Gay, of Bridgewater; Rev. Luther Sheldon, of Easton; Rev. Calvin Hitchcock, of Randolph; Rev. Jonas Perkins, of Braintree; Rev. Baalis Sanford, of East Bridgewater; Rev. Paul Couch, of North Bridgewater, was called for the purpose of installing him as their pastor, January 1, 1840. He continued to preach to this people till May, 1851, when Mr. Huntington, thinking the time had come for him to relinquish his labors, "that some one might fill his place whose influence might the more effectually call forth its resources, and more equallize the pecuniary liabilities," asked that a council be called to consider the question of his dismission, which was granted. A meeting of the church and society was held, and a strong opposition to his dismission being manifested, the council unanimously declared themselves "happy to find, in the light of all the documents before them, and the verbal assurances given them by the pastor on the one hand, and the committee of the church and society on the other, that there is no sufficient ground for such action as is indicated, by the letter missive, in the existing circumstances of the parties concerned;" and Mr. Huntington finally withdrew his resignation, and continued to supply the pulpit as before until the regular yearly meeting, April 18, 1853, when he was requested to resign his position. He therefore tendered his resignation to the church, at a meeting held May 2d, 1853, and asked for a council to be convened for the purpose of his dismission. The following persons composed the council: Rev. Richard S. Storrs, D. D., of Braintree; Rev. Jonas Perkins, of Braintree; Rev. James W. Ward, of Abington; Rev. David Brigham, of Bridgewater; Rev. Baalis Sanford, of East Bridgewater, who met May 11, 1853, when the relation between pastor

and people was dissolved. The council, after due deliberation, came to the following result: —

Doubtless sufficient reasons may exist for the dissolution of the pastoral
relation, independently of Providential calls to stations of increased responsibility, and of the summons to give account of one's stewardship at the tribu-
nal of God. The failure of health ; the loss of intellectual vigor, or moral
character on the part of the pastor; the unfriendliness of influential individuals ; the exhausted resources of church and congregation, or the long and
total suspension of divine influences, may indicate the expediency, not to
say the necessity, of terminating the connection between the pastor and his
flock. Even in cases like these, it is more than probable that, had patience
its perfect work, and were a more humble reliance on God maintained, the
plea of expediency or necessity would be nullified by the onward progress of
time. But in the case before the council to-day, neither failure of health,
loss of intellectual vigor nor moral character, — neither individual unfriendliness, exhausted resources, nor want of success in the ministry, is or can be
urged as the ground either of the tender or acceptance of the pastor's resignation ; his health never was better ; his character, in whatever aspect
viewed, has never stood higher, nor has he an acknowledged enemy within
the church or outside of it; and the congregation has been growing in wealth
ever since he came to it, while the church has doubled its numbers ; he
loves his people warmly, and with one consent they profess to reciprocate
his love. Such is the testimony both of those who wish the pastoral relation dissolved, and those who deprecate the means ; and yet, at their mutual request, this council is assembled to " advise and assist " in the question
of his dismission.

After previous advice, kindly given and received two years ago, but
now overlooked, and without any important change in the circumstances of
the parties, nothing remains to the council but, agreeably to the earnest
request of the pastor and the corresponding action of the church, without
the assignment of any satisfactory reasons on the part of the church, to declare the pastoral relation hitherto subsisting between Rev. D. Huntington
and the South Church in North Bridgewater to be dissolved by their mutual
agreement. While making this declaration, the council feel bound, by regard to the honor of the ministry and the sacredness of truth, to affirm of
the pastor, in accordance with the statements made to them, that for no
fault of his own is this dissolution accomplished. That having been long
tried and well known to all the pastors and churches of the region round
about, as a man of unblemished character, a Christian of deep experience,
a minister of uncommon talent, fidelity, and affectionateness, and a model
of meekness, self-denial and devotedness to the interests of Zion, he pos-
sesses our entire confidence and warmest love ; and he is hereby, most cordially and unreservedly commended to the fraternal regards of all ministers
and churches among whom his future lot shall be cast, as well as to the safe
conduct of " Him who dwelt in the bush," and led his people of old into the
promised land.

SOUTH CONGREGATIONAL CHURCH (Campello).
First Edifice—Erected 1836.

Destroyed by fire. May 24, 1853.

And most cordially do the council sympathize with those specially afflicted by the bereaving event of this day. Most deeply do they lament existing
trials, whether real or imaginary ; and most affectionately advise to a more
patient waiting on God in the future, and a firmer reliance on his almighty
arm in the support of the ministry of his appointment. And if he shall
give you another pastor hereafter, as we fervently hope and pray, may he
be equally a man of God's own heart as the man you lose to-day, and a
man whose instructions shall be as pure, whose life shall be as exemplary,
whose spirit shall be as affectionate, whose fidelity shall be as clear to all
men, and whose success shall be far more abundant in eradicating the love
of money, which is the root of all evil, in winning souls to Christ and filling
Heaven with hallelujahs to the Lamb that was slain ; and for this, may
your faith and love grow exceedingly, and your labors abound more and
more, till you shall be called to join the general assembly and church of the
first-born, whose names are written in heaven.

R. S. STORRS, Moderator.
J. W. WARD, Scribe.

A True Copy.

Attest : JAMES W. WARD.

On the twenty-third day of May, 1853, the people of this
part of the town were visited by one of the most disastrous
fires that ever occurred in the county, destroying several
buildings, among which was their house of worship. Now
there must be something done, — no pastor, no house in
which to hold their meetings. The people of that place,
however, did not long remain thus. A meeting of the parish was called June 1st, to see what should be done. At
this meeting, a committee of five were chosen to proceed
at once in the erection of a house; namely, Bela Keith,
Martin L. Keith, Cary Howard, Aaron B. Drake, Vinal Lyon,
with Josiah W. Kingman and Dr. Horatio Bryant as advising
committee. This committee set themselves immediately to
work, the result of which was the erection of the present
edifice, which is of wood, painted in imitation of freestone,
eighty-four feet long, fifty-six feet wide, with posts forty feet
high, and a spire one hundred and eighty-five feet high. *

* The spire of the church, as first erected, was blown down in the great snow-
storm of January, 1857. The present spire is one hundred and thirty-five feet
high. Rebuilt by W. R. Penniman, of South Braintree.

On entering the building, we find on the first floor one large
vestry, one small vestry, and a large, carpeted, well-fur-
nished room for the use of the "Ladies' Benevolent Society."
Ascending from the main entrance, on either side, a very
easy flight of steps, we find ourselves in a vestibule, from
which we ascend to the choir-gallery, or enter the auditory.
The interior aspect of this house is fine. The spacious
floor, well-arranged slips, neatly carpeted and upholstered,
the chaste and elegant pulpit, * and finely frescoed walls,
give the place an air of pleasantness, quite in contrast with
the churches of earlier days.

The original outlay in the construction of this house was
sixteen thousand dollars. It is built in the Romanesque
style of architecture, from plans drawn by Messrs. Towle &
Foster, of Boston. The builder was Mr. William Drake,
of Stoughton. The bell was cast at the foundry of Mr.
George Holbrook, of East Medway, Mass., and weighs
thirty-two hundred pounds. A marble-faced clock was presented to the society by Henry K. Keith, in 1854, which was
placed in front of the choir-gallery. B. F. Hayward, F. H.
Shiverick, and Samuel French were a committee appointed
to make arrangements for the ordination and dedication,
which took place September 21, 1854, with appropriate exercises.

Rev. D. Temple Packard,† a native of the town, and who

* The pulpit was made by Henry R. Haven, is of rosewood, and polished in the
highest style.

† Rev. D. Temple Packard was born in North Bridgewater, Mass., Aug. 24,
1824; received a common school education in his native town ; fitted for college
under the tutorship of Rev. Paul Couch, at the Adelphian Academy, No. Bridgewater, and Phillips Academy, Andover, Mass.; graduated at Amherst College,
August, 1850 ; taught high school at East Braintree, Mass., one year ; entered
Bangor Theological Seminary, Oct. 1851, and graduated Aug. 30, 1854. After receiving two other calls, he accepted the call of the South Church in North Bridgewater, where he was ordained Sept. 21, 1854; dismissed Oct. 1, 1856; from thence
he removed to the West, preaching at Rock Island, Ill., and Davenport, Iowa; returned to Massachusetts in 1858, and in June of that year, commenced preaching
for the " First Congregational Society in Somerville, Mass.; " installed as pastor
of that church and society, Sept. 21, 1860, where he continues to reside.

had just completed his theological course of study, was the first minister settled in the new house. He was invited to supply them during the building of the new church, by vote passed April 18, 1854. This he continued to do in " Salisbury Hall," till the new vestry was finished, when services were held there on the Sabbath, and May 22, 1854, the society " voted to give Rev. D. Temple Packard a call to settle with them in the ministry, and offer him 800 Dollars as his Salary," which call he accepted, and he was ordained as their pastor Thursday, September 21st, 1854. The services on that occasion were as follows : —

1. Reading of the Scriptures and Invocation, by Rev. Abel K. Packard, of Yarmouth, Mass.; 2. Introductory Prayer, by Rev. S. L. Rockwood, of Hanson; 3. Sermon, by Rev. Richard S. Storrs, D. D., of Braintree; 4. Ordaining Prayer, by Rev. Jonas Perkins, of Braintree; 5. Right Hand of Fellowship, by Rev. J. M. Manning, of Medford, Mass.; 6. Charge to the Pastor, by Rev. Paul Couch, of the First Church in North Bridgewater; 7. Address to the People, by Rev. Luther Sheldon, D. D., of Easton; 8. Concluding Prayer, by Rev. Ebenezer Gay, of Bridgewater; 9. Benediction, by the Pastor.

The following hymn was sung on that occasion : —

> We bid thee welcome in the name
>   Of Jesus, our exalted Head ;
> Come as a servant ; so he came,
>   And we receive thee in his stead.
>
> Come as a shepherd ; guard and keep
>   This fold from hell and earth and sin ;
> Nourish the lambs, and feed the sheep ;
>   The wounded heal, the lost bring in.
>
> Come as a watchman ; take thy stand
>   Upon thy tower amidst the sky ;
> And when the sword comes on the land,
>   Call us to fight, or warn to fly.

Come as an angel, hence to guide
 A band of pilgrims on their way ;
That safely walking at thy side,
 We fail not, faint not, turn, nor stray.

Come as a teacher sent from God,
 Charged his whole counsel to declare ;
Lift o'er our ranks the prophet's rod,
 While we uphold thy hands with prayer.

Come as a messenger of peace,
 Filled with the Spirit, fired with Love ;
Live to behold our large increase,
 And die to meet us ALL ABOVE.

Mr. Packard continued to preach to this people with abil-ity, earnestness, and eminent success, having large audiences, till September 25, 1856, when he tendered his resignation. A council was called at his request, which was held October 1, 1856, and the relation between pastor and people was dissolved, very much to the regret of the community.

The society were now without a pastor from October 1, 1856, to February 3, 1858, during which time various preachers were heard, and December 9, 1857, an invita-tion was extended to Rev. Charles W. Wood,* of Ashby, Mass., to become their pastor. This invitation he accepted. and he was duly installed by council, February 3, 1858, the exercises of the day consisting of Invocation and Reading of the Scriptures, by Rev. Frederick R. Abbe, of Abington ; Prayer, by Rev. Henry L. Edwards, of South Abington ; Sermon, by Professor Phelps, of Andover Theological Semi-nary ; Charge to the Pastor, by Rev. Charles L. Mills, of the Porter Church, North Bridgewater ; Right Hand of Fellow-ship, by Rev. Isaiah P. Thacher, of Middleboro' ; Address to

---

* Rev. Charles W. Wood was born in Middleboro', Mass., June 30, 1814 , fitted for college at Plainfield Academy, Conn., and Pierce Academy, Middle-boro', Mass.; graduated at Brown University, Providence, R. I., in 1834 ; grad-uated at Andover Theological Seminary in 1838 ; ordained at Ashby, Mass., Oct.. 1839 ; at Campello, Feb., 1858.

the People, by Rev. Horace D. Walker, of Abington. The day was exceedingly pleasant, and the exercises of a very pleasing kind. The sermon was an eloquent production, and the choir performed their part in an admirable manner.

FIRST METHODIST EPISCOPAL SOCIETY.

Previous to 1830, there was no regular organized society of this denomination in the town. During this year, Nathaniel Manley and one hundred and ten others, formed themselves into an association, with the following articles of agreement : * —

" Whereas, we the subscribers, being disposed to encourage and promote the public worship of God, in a way agreeable to the dictates of our own consciences, do hereby agree to form ourselves into a religious society by the name of the First Episcopal Methodist Society in North Bridgewater,' for the purpose of promoting, carrying on, and supporting the public worship of God, in conformity to an Act passed Feb. 16, 1824." Early in the month of April,† a committee, consisting of Isaac Packard, John Tilden, and Galen Manley, were chosen to procure land and erect a church. They purchased a lot of land of Micah Packard for the sum of $41.20, it being the lot where the house now stands. A house was erected, fifty-four feet long, twenty-one feet wide, twenty-two feet high, with a spire eighty feet high, and a bell weighing 1,060 lbs., made by George Holbrook, of Medway, Mass. The exterior appearance of the house is neat, painted white, with nine windows, and green blinds. The interior of the house is well furnished, containing fifty-eight pews, choir-gallery with seats ‡ for fifty persons. The floor is neatly carpeted, walls arched overhead. In 1855, a clock was put

---

* March 9, 1830.   † April 12, 1830.

‡ This is the only house that retains the elevated corner seats for colored people, which are in each corner of the choir-gallery.

9

up; and in 1857, a new and commodious pulpit was placed in the house. The instrumental music is a seraphine.

The house was built under the direction of Messrs. Isaac Hartwell, John Tilden, and Galen Manley, as building committee, and cost $3,000. Mr. John Peterson was master-carpenter. A parsonage-house was built in 1860. The following is a list of the clergymen who have supplied the pulpit of this society, and the years each has served: —

Rev. P. Crandall, 1834–5
  "   E. Bradley, 1835–6.
  "   D. Kilburn, 1836–7.
  "   S. Benton, 1837–8.
  "   C. Noble, 1838–9.
  "   L. Bates, 1840–41.
  "   A. Palmer, 1841–43.
  "   H. Mayo, 1843.
  "   L. Harlow, 1844.
  "   B. M. Walker, 1845.
  "   D. Stebbins, 1846–7.
  "   T. Spilsted, 1847–8.

Rev. G. W. Rogers, 1848–9.
  "   J. Livesey, 1849–50.
  "   John D. King, 1850–51.
  "   E. Blake, 1852–53.
  "   T. B. Gurney, 1853–54.
  "   A. B. Wheeler, 1855.
  "   J. B. Weeks, 1860–61.
  "   Israel Washburn, 1861.
  "   Charles A. Carter, 1862 to 1863.
  "   William A. Clapp.
  "   Alexander Anderson.

Bridgewater circuit was set apart from Stoughton and Easton July, 1832, at a conference held in Providence, Rhode Island.

FIRST BAPTIST CHURCH.

This church was constituted January 10th, 1850, and consisted of seventeen members, the names of which are as follows: Rev. James Andem, pastor; Emma A. Andem, Williams Alden, Persis Packard, Nathaniel Shepardson, Alpheus Alden, Priscilla C. Alden, Edmund R. Wade, Julia Ann Wade, Harriet Thayer, Joanna Packard, Olive T. Packard, Caroline F. Packard, Sally Hall, A. Amanda French, Frederick L. Trow, Jonas P. Jameson. Officers of the church: Rev. James Andem, pastor; Edward S. Packard, George F. Parish, *deacons;* Alpheus Alden, *clerk;* Edmund R. Wade, *treasurer;* Dea. Edward S. Packard, Dea. George F. Parish, Nathaniel Shepardson, F. L. Trow, *standing committee.*

Previous to the organization of this church in 1850, those members belonging in the town had met in a hall where they had preaching from February, 1849, Rev. Isaac Woodbury, of Haverhill, Mass. being the first preacher, who preached for four successive Sabbaths. The people were next supplied with transient ministers, mostly from the Newton Theological Institute, among whom was Rev. S. A. Thomas, of Dighton, who spent one of his vacations with them. Rev. James Andem, of Brookline, commenced to supply their pulpit for one year, from October, 1849. During the year 1850, the church had great encouragement to erect a house of worship, the numbers having already increased from seventeen members to fifty-seven, in the short space of one year. Its members consisted mostly of young persons, and not belonging to the most wealthy class, their perseverance in erecting and sustaining a church is all the more creditable.

A small but neat house of worship was erected by this society in September, 1850, fifty feet long, thirty-five feet wide, twenty feet high, without steeple or bell, costing about $2,500, and was dedicated January 22, 1851, with the following exercises: 1. Chant; 2. Invocation; 3. Hymn, written by the Pastor, Rev. James Andem. (Music by Isaac T. Packard).

> 1 Praise dwell on every tongue,
>   While Zion's courts we throng, —
>   Auspicious day !
>   Let every heart unite
>   To hail thy cheering light,
>   Chasing dark shades with bright
>   And heavenly ray.
>
> 2 The grace thy love bestows
>   Like streams in fulness flows,
>   Ancient of days !
>   Thou who on earth once dwelt,
>   Make thy pure presence felt
>   Where humbly we have knelt
>   In prayer and praise.

> 3 In this thy dwelling-place,
>   Let wisdom, truth, and grace
>   In worship blend.
>   These courts thy glory fill,
>   As dew on Hermon's hill,
>   Thy purer love distil,
>   And here descend.

4. Reading of the Scriptures; **5.** Introductory Prayer;
6. Hymn, written by Rev. James Andem : —

> 1 Great God, our Father and our Friend,
>   Before thy throne thy children bend ;
>   Let songs of praise before thee swell,
>   While in thy courts thy children dwell.

> 2 Great Source of truth, to thee, in prayer,
>   We give this house ; — make it thy care.
>   Here let thy saints, a goodly vine,
>   Nurtured by grace, be *wholly* thine.

> 3 Be thou their shield and thou their rock, —
>   Be Christ the shepherd of his flock, —
>   And hoary age and blooming youth
>   Here drink of living wells of truth.

> 4 From year to year loud anthems rise,
>   In sacred numbers to the skies ;
>   And prayer ascend from Zion's hill,
>   That heavenly grace may here distil.

> 5 Praise to thy name, through Christ thy Son,
>   Great God, for what thy love has done ; —
>   When praise on earth is still in death,
>   We'll praise thy name with nobler breath.

7. Sermon, by Rev. Pharcellus Church, D. D. ; **8.** Dedicatory
Prayer; **9.** Anthem; **10.** Benediction, by the Pastor.

The land on which this building stands is situated on the
west side of Montello Street, and was purchased of Mr. Sidney Perkins for the sum of three hundred dollars.

The second minister that was ordained was Rev. Richard
K. Ashley. The ordination was September 29, 1852, and
consisted of the following : —

PORTER EVANGELICAL CHURCH (Centre Village).
Erected 1850.

1. Voluntary, by the Choir; 2. Reading of Doings of Council; 3. Reading of Scriptures, and Introductory Prayer; 4. The Lord hath chosen Zion; 5. Ordination Sermon on that occasion was by Rev. J. Aldrich, of Middleboro', Mass.; 6. Anthem,

"How beautiful upon the mountains!"

7. Ordaining Prayer, by Rev. I. Smith, of East Stoughton; 8. Charge to the Pastor, by Rev. N. Colver, of South Abington; 9. Right Hand of Fellowship, by Rev. A. E. Battelle, of Marshfield; 10. Address to the People, by Rev. Thomas E. Keely, of Kingston, Mass.; 11. Hymn, —

"We bid thee welcome in the name;"*

12. Concluding Prayer; 13. Doxology, —

"Praise God, from whom all blessings flow;"

14. Benediction, by the Pastor.

The society now have no house of worship in which to meet, and no regular preaching. Their building was sold at auction, July 13, 1854, to Samuel S. Brett and Fearing W. Bent, and has been used as an armory for the "North Bridgewater Dragoons."

PORTER EVANGELICAL CHURCH.

This church was formed of members who withdrew from the "First Congregational Church in North Bridgewater" for the purpose of forming another church, it being deemed advisable that something should be done to awaken a new interest in the cause of truth, and to induce union of feeling and action in the support of the ordinances of the gospel, according to Orthodox Congregational usages and principles. After various meetings for consultation, it was voted unanimously, February 7th, 1850, "That we will take measures to form another Orthodox Congregational Church in this place,

* See hymn on page 63.

as soon as it may be deemed expedient." A committee was chosen to see how many would unite in the movement. This committee reported, February 12th, 1850, the names of seventy persons who were in favor of immediate action, and who were prepared to unite in the formation of another church. At this meeting it was agreed to lay the subject before the church at their next meeting, and take means to call a council immediately, for the purpose of formation, if they deemed it expedient. This was done at a meeting of the church held the day following (February 13th), and a committee was appointed by the church to call a council for that purpose. At a meeting of the church held February 19th, it was voted that they adopt the same Articles of Faith and Covenant * as those used by the First Church. Also voted, that the name of the new church shall be " The Porter Evangelical Church." A council was accordingly called, which met on the 6th day of March, 1850, and which organized the church in the evening of the same day, the public services consisting of 1. Introductory Prayer, by Rev. Luther Sheldon, D. D., of Easton ; 2. Reading of the Articles of Faith and Covenant, by the same ; 3. Consecrating Prayer, by Rev. David Brigham of Bridgewater ; 4. Fellowship of the Churches, by Rev. E. Porter Dyer, of Hingham ; 5. Address to the Church, by Rev. David Dyer, of Dorchester ; 6. Concluding Prayer, by Rev. Erastus Maltby, of Taunton. The church met Friday, March 8th, and "voted to establish public worship forthwith," and various committees were chosen to make such arrangements as seemed necessary for that purpose.

The first meeting for public worship was held in the hall of Tyler Cobb, on Sunday, March 10th, 1820. Rev. Joseph Merrill, of Dracut, Mass., preached on that day and the two succeeding Sabbaths.

* See Articles of Faith and Covenant of the South Church in Campello, they being the same.

The next minister was Rev. John F. Norton,* who came to the town April 6th, 1850, and preached five Sabbaths, when the church and society united in giving him a call to become their pastor, May 7th, which he accepted May 10th, 1850. His installation took place in the meeting-house of the First Church, June 5th, 1850. The following were the order of services on that occasion : —

1. Voluntary, by the Choir; 2. Reading Minutes of the Ecclesiastical Council; 3. Invocation and Reading of the Scriptures; 4. Anthem; 5. Introductory Prayer; 6. Hymn, —words and music composed for a similar occasion by Rev. D. Huntington, —

" Herald of our Saviour God ; "

7. Sermon, by Rev. A. C. Thompson, of Roxbury, Mass.; 8. Chant, —

" I will give you pastors according to mine own heart ; "

9. Installing Prayer, by Rev. Luther Sheldon, D. D., of Easton; 10. Charge to the Pastor, by Rev. Calvin Hitchcock, D. D., of Randolph; 11. Right Hand of Fellowship, by Rev. J. P. Terry, of South Weymouth; 12. Hymn, —

" How beautiful upon the mountains ! "

13. Address to the People, by Rev. D. Huntington, of the

* Rev. John F. Norton was born in Goshen, Litchfield County, Conn., September 8, 1809 ; entered Yale College in 1829 ; but his health failing, he left college during his junior year. He received the degree of A. M. from that institution, in 1848 ; studied theology at the Theological Seminary at East Windsor, Conn., where he graduated in 1837 ; travelled nearly a year in Northern and Western Europe ; was principal of academies in Goshen, Brooklyn, and Norfolk, Conn., for eight years ; was ordained pastor of church in Milton Parish, Litchfield, Conn., October 23, 1844 ; installed pastor of Porter Evangelical Church in North Bridgewater, Mass., June 5, 1850 ; dismissed at his request, December 4, 1851 ; installed pastor of the Evangelical Church in Athol, Mass., March 17, 1852 ; married, first, Harriet Frances Jenkins, of Falmouth, Mass., August 19, 1839, who died February 3, 1849 ; second marriage to Sophia W. Elliot, of Bridgeport, Conn., December 31, 1850 ; she died June 6, 1852. He then married Ann Maria Mann, of Stoughton, Mass., September 26, 1853 ; has one child living, Lewis Mills Norton, born December 26, 1855.

South Congregational Church, Campello; 14. Concluding Prayer; 15. Hymn, — by the congregation, — tune "Hamburg:" —

'Tis done — the important act is done ;
　　Heaven, earth, its solemn purport know ;
Its fruits, when time its race has run,
　　Shall through eternal ages flow.

The covenants of this sacred hour,
　　Great Shepherd of thy people, seal ;
Spirit of grace, diffuse thy power,
　　Our vows accept, thy might reveal.

Behold our guide, and deign to crown
　　His toils, O Lamb of God, with love ;
His lips inspire ;　each effort own ;
　　Breathe, dwell within him, heavenly Dove.

Behold his charge :　what wealth shall dare
　　With its most priceless worth to vie ?
Suns, systems, worlds, how mean they are,
　　Compared with souls that cannot die !

The sun may set in endless gloom,
　　The planets from their stations flee,
Creation fill oblivion's tomb ;
　　But souls can never cease to be.

Oh, when, before the judgment-seat,
　　The wicked quake in dread despair,
May we, all reverent at thy feet,
　　Pastor and flock, find mercy there.

16. Benediction.

Mr. Norton continued with this people until December 4th, 1851, when he was dismissed.

Rev. Charles L. Mills * was their next pastor, he being in-

---

* Rev. Charles L. Mills was born in Morristown, New Jersey, August 11, 1812 ; graduated at Yale College in 1835 ; studied theology at the Theological Seminary, Princeton, N. J. Mr. Mills preached in various places in the West, and about New England, for twelve years or more, and in 1852, was called to settle as pastor of the Porter Evangelical Church of North Bridgewater, where he remained till February, 1862. After a brief respite from pastoral labor, he received a call to settle at Wrentham, Mass., where he was ordained as pastor of the First Congregational Church, February 10, 1863. He married, first, Elizabeth, daughter of Dea. William Lyman, of Middletown, Conn. ; second, Rebecca, daughter of Dea. Peter Smith, of Andover, Mass.

stalled August 11th, 1852. 1. Invocation and Reading of the Scriptures, by Rev. Abel K. Packard, of Yarmouth, Mass. (now of Anoka, Minnesota); 2. Introductory Prayer, by Rev. J. P. Terry, of South Weymouth; 3. Sermon, by Rev. Richard S. Storrs, D. D., of Braintree; 4. Installing Prayer, by Rev. James W. Ward, of Abington; 5. Charge to the Pastor, by Rev. Luther Sheldon, D. D., of Easton; 6. Right Hand of Fellowship, by Rev. Daniel Butler, of Westboro', Mass.; 7. Hymn,—

> 1 He that goeth forth with weeping,
>   Bearing still the precious seed,
> Never tiring, never sleeping,
>   All his labor shall succeed.

> 2 Then will fall the rain of heaven,
>   Then the sun of mercy shine;
> Precious fruits will then be given,
>   Through an influence all divine.

> 3 Sow thy seed, be never weary,
>   Nor let fears thy mind employ;
> Be the prospect ne'er so dreary,
>   Thou mayst reap the fruits of joy.

> 4 Lo, the scene of verdure brightening,
>   See the rising grain appear;
> Look again! the fields are whitening;
>   Sure the harvest time is near.

8. Address to the People, by Rev. I. P. Langworthy, of Chelsea; 8. Concluding Prayer, by Rev. John F. Norton, of Athol (their former pastor); 10. Benediction, by the Pastor. Rev. Mr. Mills preached to this people until February 18th, 1862, when he was dismissed.

Their present pastor is Rev. Samuel H. Lee,* who was ordained September 17, 1862; the services being as follows: —

* Rev. Samuel H. Lee was born in Sprague, Conn., December 21, 1832; fitted for college at Williston Seminary, East Hampton, Mass.; entered Yale College, 1854; graduated in 1858; graduated at the Normal School, New Britain, Conn., 1852; was a teacher in the Normal School three years; studied theology at Yale

10

1. Invocation and Reading of the Scriptures, by Rev. E. Porter Dyer, of Hingham; 2. Introductory Prayer, by Rev. E. Douglas; 3. Sermon, by Rev. Edw. N. Kirk, D. D., of Boston; 4. Ordaining Prayer, by Rev. S. G. Dodd, of East Randolph; 5. Charge to the Pastor, by Rev. Richard S. Storrs, D. D., of Braintree; 6. Right Hand of Fellowship, by Rev. Charles W. Wood, of Campello; 7. Address to the People, by Rev. D. Temple Packard, of Somerville; 8. Concluding Prayer, by Rev. F. R. Abbe, of Abington; 9. Benediction, by the Pastor.

This ecclesiastical society was legally organized March 20th, 1850, and a committee, consisting of Simeon Leach, David Howard, and Edwin H. Kingman, were chosen to select a lot of land, and procure plans for a house, who were subsequently authorized to purchase a lot, and proceed with the building. The lot on which the edifice now stands was purchased of the late Silas Packard, Esq., for the sum of one thousand dollars, and contains about eighty-four square rods, having a front on Main Street of seven rods, with a depth of twelve rods. The house is situated between the residence of the late Silas Packard, Esq., and that of Franklin Ames, Esq., and but a short distance north of the First Church. The plans of this building were drawn by Messrs. Melvin and Young, of Boston, and the building is sixty feet wide, eighty-eight feet in length, with twenty feet posts, with a spire one hundred and seventy-five feet in height. The house has ninety pews on the main floor, beside the front seat, which is held free; has twenty-four pews in the side-galleries, with seats for sixty persons in the choir-gallery, in front of the organ. There is a large and commodious basement, finished into three rooms, the largest being used as a chapel, which is

Theological Seminary two years; received an invitation to settle as pastor of the Porter Evangelical Church in North Bridgewater in 1862, where he was ordained September 17, 1862.

ST. PATRICK'S CATHOLIC CHURCH (Centre Village).
Erected 1859.

forty-three feet by fifty-eight, and eleven feet high. Mr. Joseph Sanger, of Watertown, was the contractor, who furnished all the material (excepting foundation and brick work for the basement) for the sum of $7,937. The house was raised about the first of August, 1850, and so far completed that the chapel was first used for public worship Sunday, October 13th, 1850. The house was completed, and dedicated January 9th, 1851. The total cost of house, land, furniture, and organ, including interest on borrowed money, up to the time of selling the pews (January 10th, 1851), was $14,935. The amount obtained from the sale of pews was $12,500, beside other pews taken soon after the adjournment of the sale, making nearly enough to cover the entire cost to the society. Various donations were made to the society toward furnishing the house, amounting to four hundred and thirty-five dollars, from different individuals. The church and society paid two hundred dollars for a new collection of hymn-books for church and chapel use, making about $16,200 paid and pledged for future payment during the first year of its existence.

Number of members, at the time of organization of the church, was ninety-five.

Admissions to the church, during Rev. John F. Norton's settlement, fifteen by profession, fourteen by letter.

Admissions, during Rev. Charles L. Mills's settlement, one hundred and two by profession, forty by letter.

The amount of donations for objects of benevolence made by this church and society since their organization, amount to over $5,000.

CATHOLIC CHURCH.

Previous to the year 1856, the members of this church were attendant on church worship in private houses, and in

the various halls in the village, and were supplied by transient
clergymen.   During that year Rev. Thomas B. McNulty *
came to the town as a stated pastor, in connection with some
others in the immediate vicinity, the care of which devolved
upon him.   Here he soon succeeded in gathering a large
number of regular church worshippers; and during the same
year purchased a parcel of land for the sum of $5,225, situ-
ated on the west side of Main Street, near Wales's Corner, in
the south part of the village, and containing about three-
fourths of an acre, upon which he has caused a large and
splendid church edifice to be erected, one hundred and ten
feet long, fifty feet wide, built in the Romanesque style of
architecture.   The basement is built of Quincy granite.   The
principal story is of brick, trimmed with freestone.   The
tower and steeple is one hundred and eighty feet in height.
The auditory is furnished with one hundred and forty-six
slips, capable of holding seven hundred persons.   The altar
is at the west end of the building, and at the east or front end
is the choir-gallery.   The chancel window is made of stained
glass, with emblematic panes, representing the four evangel-
ists, *Matthew, Mark, Luke,* and *John.*   The house is furnished
with a magnificent organ, from the manufactory of E. & G. G.
Hook, of Boston.   Upon the side walls are displayed fourteen
pictures, representing different scenes in the Lord's passion,
painted at great expense in Italy.   The cost of the church
was $25,000, which together with the land cost about $30,000.
The architects were Messrs. Fuller & Ryder, of Boston.
Mr. Andrews, of Nashua, N. H., was the contractor.   The
preacher's pulpit, also the railing around the altar, was man-

* Rev. Thomas B. McNulty was born in Londonderry, Ireland; fitted for college at Londonderry Academy; graduated at Foyle College; studied philosophy
and theology at Irish College, Paris; was ordained June 6, 1846, at the Parish
Church of Sulpiece, by Monsieur Affre, Archbishop of Paris; came to America in
1853, and after preaching at Lowell, Salem, and other places, was appointed to
take charge of the Catholic Church in North Bridgewater and vicinity.

REV. T. B. McNULTY

ufactured by Messrs. Howard, Clark, & Co. In the south-west corner of the house is the sacristy, and in the northeast corner is a private room out of which is the entrance to the basement story. In point of durability and style of architect-ure, this house is not to be surpassed by any in the town. Its position is prominent, and makes a bold appearance upon the principal thoroughfare in town.

This church was dedicated Sunday, May 22, 1859; and al-though the weather was quite rainy, there was a large assem-bly present. The services were as follows: —

Bishop Fitzpatrick, of Boston, delivered the Sermon. High Mass was celebrated by Rev. Mr. Roach, of Randolph. Rev. Mr. Shahen, of Salem, officiated as Deacon. Rev. Mr. Tallon, of New Bedford, as Subdeacon. Rev. Mr. Haley, of Boston, was Master of Ceremonies, a number of other priests as-sisting. Rev. Mr. McElroy, of Boston, preached at Vespers. Singing was performed by a choir from Salem.

The number of attendants on church worship at this place is about two thousand.

FIRST UNIVERSALIST CHURCH AND SOCIETY.

This society was organized August 31, 1857, at which time Josiah V. Bisbee was chosen clerk, David F. Studley, treas-urer, Ellis Packard, O. O. Patten, Lorenzo D. Hervey, F. O. Howard, William H. Cooper, executive committee, Thaddeus E. Gifford, collector.

Previous to this time, this denomination had no regular preaching, and since its organization it has had transient preachers until the settlement of Rev. William A. Start.

The following persons composed the society at its forma-tion: Otis Hayward, Lorenzo D. Hervey, Ellis Packard, Da-vid Hall, David F. Studley, F. O. Howard, Amasa O. Glover, Marcus Holmes, Oren Bartlett, Thomas Swift, E. L. Thayer,

Jerome Thomas, F. A. Thayer, Luther Tower, Martin Packard, Isaac Harris, Waldo Field, Thaddeus E. Gifford, Edwin E. Pollard, John W. Hayward, A. B. Marston, Seth Leonard, Joseph E. Estes, Josiah V. Bisbee, O. O. Patten, Charles E. Tribou, Samuel F. Tribou, Elijah Tolman, C. G. Swift.

The society erected a neat and commodious house of worship on Elm Street, in the month of May, 1863. Its dimensions are sixty feet in length, thirty-eight in width, and contains sixty pews, capable of seating three hundred persons comfortably. The pews are of a circular form, with the seats nicely cushioned, floor carpeted, and in all respects, the house is complete. In the rear of the pulpit is the following inscription upon the wall, which is nicely frescoed: "Behold I bring you glad tidings of great joy, which shall be unto all people." Underneath this house is a capacious and convenient vestry.

The house was dedicated, with appropriate exercises, on Wednesday, May 20, 1863, commencing at 10 o'clock A. M., as follows: 1. Voluntary, by the Choir; 2. Prayer of Invocation, by Rev. E. Hewitt; 3. Reading of the Scriptures, by Rev. J. G. B. Heath; 4. Anthem, by the Choir; 5. Consecrating Prayer, by Rev. A. P. Cleverly; 6. Hymn; 7. Sermon, by Rev. A. A. Miner, of Boston; 8. Anthem; 9. Prayer, by Rev. H. Jewell; 10. Hymn; 11. Benediction. The sermon was from the text in Psalm xxii. 27, 28: "For the kingdom is the Lord's, and he is the governor among the nations." At the conclusion of these services, the friends were invited to a most generous repast in the vestry; and the society spared no pains or expense to secure temporal as well as spiritual comfort to their visitors. After a short intermission, the services of installing Rev. William A. Start as pastor of the church was commenced in the following order of exercises: 1. Anthem, by the Choir; 2. Invocation, by Rev. J. Eastwood, of Brighton; 3. Reading of the Scriptures, by Rev. M. R. Leonard, of South Dedham; 4. Hymn; 5. Sermon, by Rev. J. Crehore, of Abington, text, Eph. iv. 12, 13: "For the perfecting of the saints, for the work of the ministry, for the edifying of the body of Christ: till we all come in the unity of the faith, and of the knowledge of the Son of God, unto a perfect man, unto the measure of the stature of the fulness of Christ;"* 5. Hymn; 6. Installing Prayer, by Rev. G. H. Emerson, of Somerville; 7. Charge to the Pastor, by Rev. A. A. Miner, of Boston; 8. Right Hand of Fellowship, by Rev. James Eastwood, of Brighton; 9. Charge to the People, by Rev. A. P. Cleverly, of Boston; 10. Prayer; 11. Anthem; 12. Benediction, by the Pastor.

This society owe much of their success to the active, zealous, and persevering efforts of Rev. A. P. Cleverly and Rev. J. Crehore.

QUAKERS, OR FRIENDS.

There was an Association, or Society of Friends, in North Bridgewater, formed April 26, 1838, and consisted of twenty-five members, as appears by record, which is as follows: —

"We the undersigned hereby become members of a Society forming of this sect, called Quakers, and do hereby agree to subject ourselves to the rules and regulations which shall be adopted by said Society, in the town of North Bridgewater."

Michael O. Neil,	John R. Morrill,	William Ripley,
Nahum J. Smith,	M. B. Peirce,	Charles S. Johnson,
Cyrus Packard,	Jabez D. Lamson,	Jarvis D. Smith,
Jacob W. Crosby,	Ambrose Packard,	Thomas Batchelder,
Edward Southworth, Jr.,	Josiah Fuller,	Edwin W. Bosworth.
Daniel Guild,	John L. Skinner,	Noah Blodgett,
Charles L. Hathaway,	Apollos O. Howard,	Nathan Packard,
Roswell Richardson,	Reuben S. Webster,	Jeremiah Stetson, Jr.
John Leonard,		

At the request of Nahum J. Smith and twenty-four other

* The sermon was very timely and effective, as well as practical, showing fully the needs of a minister, his dependence on the people for support, the minister's relation to the sorrowing, the various relations of the people, and the sources of inspiration to his labor, and the awards as fruits of his toil.

members, a meeting was called by Hon. Jesse Perkins, Esq., a justice of the peace, which met at the hall of Col. Edward Southworth, April 30, 1838, at seven o'clock P. M., for the purpose of organization; at which time Edward Southworth, Jr., was chosen clerk, who took the oath of affirmation in the usual form; Jacob W. Crosby, Nahum J. Smith, John L. Skinner, were chosen overseers; Cyrus Packard, treasurer and collector, besides a committee to prepare a constitution and by-laws; — meeting then adjourned to May 8, 1838. The "meeting met according to adjournment, and after discussing various matters connected with the Society, adjourned to June 7," when they again came together for friendly conversation, and again adjourned *sine die.*

The above is the latest record to be found concerning this society, and it is presumed that the society did not flourish for any length of time. Many of the members mentioned above are living, from whom a reliable account can be had.

SECOND METHODIST EPISCOPAL CHURCH.

This church was formed in 1842, consisting of about thirty members, among whom were the following persons: —

Sanford Alden, Eliza G. Alden, Liberty Packard, Mary A. Packard, Israel Packard, Jr., Jane W. Packard, Cornelius H. Dunham, Lucia Dunham, Thaddeus Gifford, Abigail Gifford, Mary Edson, Fearing W. Bent, Mehitabel W. Bent, Jarvis D. Smith, Martha Smith.

The society first held meetings in Hayward's Hall, commencing March 2, 1842; afterward occupied the Unitarian Church till July 23, 1843, when they removed to the hall of Tyler Cobb.

Rev. O. G. Smith was their first pastor, who preached to them from the organization of the church till 1844. He was succeeded by Rev. Addison Childes, of the Providence Conference, who soon after closed his earthly labors, and the so-

FIRST METHODIST EPISCOPAL CHURCH (Northwest Bridgewater or West Shares). Erected 1830.

SECOND METHODIST EPISCOPAL CHURCH (Centre Village).
Erected 1853.

ciety employed Rev. H. C. Atwater, a graduate of Yale College, and at that time a teacher of the Adelphian Academy, till the close of the conference year, when he was admitted to the conference, and stationed there in 1845. During the same year, a plain but substantial house of worship was erected, costing $2,600, built by Messrs. Dunbar & Soule. Sanford Alden, Fearing W. Bent, Thomas Hathaway, Liberty Packard, Israel Packard, Jr., Cornelius H. Dunham, and Oliver D. Shepardson were appointed trustees.

Henry Smith was located for this church in 1846, and remained two years; Lemuel Harlow in 1848, but was not received. His place was filled by

1. Rev. Edward Otheman, in 1848.
2. Rev. J. B. Husted, in 1850.
3. Rev. John Livesey, Jr., 1851-2.
4. Rev. Azariah B. Wheeler, 1853.
5. Rev. Erastus Benton, 1854-5.
6. Rev. Andrew McKeown, 1856.
7. Rev. Robert McGonegal, 1857-8.
8. Rev. J. Cooper, 1859.
9. Rev. N. Bemis, 1860-61.
10. Rev. M. P. Alderman, 1862.
11. Rev. R. T. Ely, 1862-3.
12. Rev. F. A. Crafts, April, 1864.

The number of members in this church in 1864 is 174.

Officers of the church: Sanford Alden, Philip Reynolds, Elijah Gay, Darius C. Place, John Ellis, Edwin J. Benner, George R. Whitney, Thomas Hathaway, John Montgomery, trustees.

During the year 1853, this society erected a new and splendid church edifice, at an expense of $24,000. Barnabas Snow was the contractor and master-builder, Isaiah B. Young, of Boston, architect. The building is ninety-four feet long by sixty feet wide, with a tower one hundred and ten feet high, containing a bell weighing 1,827 pounds, from the foundry of Henry N. Hooper, of Boston, costing $665. The interior of the house is furnished with one hundred and ten pews and an elegant organ, manufactured by Mr. George Stevens, of Cambridge, Mass. A baptismal font of marble, was presented to the society by S. S. Green. Also, a beautiful Bible and hymn-book, presented by the " Young Gen-

11

tlemen's Charitable Association," connected with the church.

The corner-stone of this church was laid July 25, 1853, with appropriate ceremony, as follows: 1. Remarks, by Rev. A. B. Wheeler; 2. Reading of the Word, by Rev. Paul Couch; 3. Singing; 4. Prayer, by Rev. T. B. Gurney; 5. Benediction.

Previous to the benediction, occurred the ceremony of depositing a tin box in one of the corner foundations of the tower, which contained the following: —

Records of the Second Methodist Church in North Bridge-water; names of original and present members of the Second Conference; officers of the Sabbath-school; trustees of the church; building committee; architect and master-builder; pastors of the various churches in town; copies of order of exercises on the occasion; minutes of the Providence An-nual Conference; missionary report of the Methodist Epis-copal Church; Sabbath-school report; discipline of the Meth-odist Episcopal Church; copies of Zion's Herald, Church Ad-vocate and Journal, Missionary Advocate, Sabbath-School Advocate, North Bridgewater Gazette.

This house was dedicated to the worship of God, June 1, 1854, with the following order of exercises, commencing at 10 1-2 o'clock: —

1. Voluntary on the Organ; 2. Reading of the 84th Psalm, by Rev. George W. Stearns; 3. Voluntary, by the Choir; 4. Reading of the 964th Hymn of the Methodist Collection, by Rev. J. B. Gould; 5. Reading of Solomon's Prayer at the dedication of the temple, — 1 Kings viii., — by Rev. J. Ma-ther; 6. Dedicatory Prayer, by Rev. F. Upham; 7. Volun-tary, by the Choir; 8. Sermon, by Rev. Miner Raymond (Principal of Wilbraham Academy), text 1 Tim. i. 15: "This is a faithful saying, and worthy of all acceptation, that Christ Jesus came into the world to save sinners;" 9. Concluding Prayer, by Rev. I. J. P. Collyer; 10. Reading of the 970th Hymn, by Rev. W. T. Harlow.

The sermon was spoken of as a masterly exposition and defence of the cardinal doctrines of the gospel as taught by that denomination.

Pews were sold to the amount of $16,000 a short time after the dedication, and everything bade fair for a prosperous and useful society.

This church was blessed with a great revival in January, 1843, the result of which was, large numbers were added to the church, and a flourishing Sabbath-school organized.

The *Leaders* of this church, for 1864, are Philip Reynolds, Darius C. Place, John Montgomery, L. Simmons, V. R. Brown.

The *Stewards* are Sanford Alden, Isaac Jacoy, George M. Copeland, Stephen Mason, John Ellis, Gustavus Newman, Cyrus Jernegan, George R. Whitney.

CHAPTER V.

MEETING-HOUSES OF THE CONGREGATIONAL PARISH.

First Meeting-House in the North Parish. — Its Appearance. — Second House. — Description. — Sale of Pews. — First Bell. — Seating of Colored People. — Third Meeting-House. — Pewholders. — Clock. — First Stoves. — Erection of the Fourth Meeting-House in 1854. — Dedication. — Description of the Same. — Sale of Pews.

THE first meeting-house in the North Parish was built in 1737, on or near the spot where the present edifice now stands. The dedication sermon was preached by Rev. Mr. Dunbar, of Stoughton, from Solomon's Songs, viii. 8: "We have a little sister, and she hath no breasts: what shall we do for our sister in the day when she shall be spoken for?"

From the best information gained, it was a small, plain structure, in keeping with the times, facing south, without steeple, bell, or chimney; the windows had diamond-shaped glass, walls plastered, but not warmed by stove or furnace.

> "Our meeting-house — our meeting-house —
>   It stood upon a hill,
> Where autumn gales and wintry blasts
>   Piped round it loud and shrill.
> No maple-tree with leafy shade,
>   Nor tall, protecting oak
> Stood near to guard the ancient house
>   When tempest round it broke.
>
> No steeple graced its homely roof
>   With upward-pointing spire ;
> Our villagers were much too meek
>   A steeple to desire.
> And never did the welcome tones
>   Of Sabbath-morning bell
> Our humble village worshippers
>   The hour of worship tell."

To this place the people of the parish gathered from Sabbath to Sabbath with commendable regularity, on horseback or on foot. They "kept the Sabbath and reverenced the Sanctuary."

At the time of the incorporation of the parish the house was "Erected and Inclosed," but not finished. At a meeting held March 12th, 1739, " Timothy Keith, Benjamin Edson, David Packard, Daniel Howard, Edward Curtis, were chosen a committee for the finishing the meeting-house in s^d Precinct," also " voted to raise two Hundred and fifty pounds for the finishing of the same, to be paid by the last of August," chose Abiel Packard, " Receiver of stuf and meterels," March 26th, 1739. " The committee appointed to finish the meeting-house made demand of the several inhabitants how they would pay their Reats, or what they could percure tords the prosecution of the work of finishing the meeting-house. In order to pay their Raits Whare upon a number subscribed what they would percure, as first: " —

James Packard to do the Glazing of the House, and what it amounts to more than his Reats Come to, to take his pay at the forge, In Iron ore or Cole next fall Insewing. John Johnson and John Kingman, to do the masing work, and nails, and to take his pay over and Abuv, his Raits at the fornes or forge, In Labour, or Cole, or Iron ore the next fall Insewing. David Packard, Solomon Packard, and Jacob Allen, to find Lime.

Robert Haward, to find one thousand of pine Bords,
Zacheus Packard, to find one thousand of oak Bords,
Solomon Packard, to find one thousand of pine Bords,
Benjamin Edson, to find one thousand of pine Bords,
Abiel Packard, to find one thousand of pine Bords,
Timothy Keith, to find one thousand of oak Bords,
Daniel Haward, to find one thousand of pine Bords,
Theofilus Curtis, to find five hundred of pine Bords,
Edward Curtis, to find five hundred of pine Bords,
James Barret, to find one thousand of pine Bords,

Joshua Warren, to find Henges, Timothy Keith, David Packard, Solomon Packard, Jacob Allen, Benjamin Edson, Daniel Haward, to find all the sheet work.

The above offers were accepted, by vote of the meeting in " Lue of money so far as shall pay their Raits." Oct. 8th, 1739, " voted to sell roome for pews in the meeting-house."

Dec. 10th, 1739, " voted to sell room for pews in order to Raise money to buy a Cushing." *   Jan. 15th, 1740, " voted to chuse three men to set a prise upon the pews to be Gin to Bid at, so that no man should Beed below the prise thay should set, maid choise of James Packard, Abiel Packard, and Isaac Kingman, for the same."   Jan. 21st, 1740, " meeting was held to-day," and " voted to sell the pews to the highest bidder."   " John Kingman, vendue master, who seet up the first pew on the west side of the pulpit to be sold to the highest Beder, and so all the Rest Sucksesevely Round the meetin house, to the Number of 13 pews."

	£	s.	d.
Voted that John Kingman shuld have the first pew, It being five feet Two inches front, and five feet Three inches deep for he being the highest Beder,	17	05	0
Voted that Daniel Haward should have the *Seckond* pew, It being 5 ft 2 inches front and 5 feet 2 inches deep for	13	00	0
Voted that Charles Snell should have the *Thurd* pew, It being 7 ft 8 inches front and 4 ft 6 inches deep for	14	10	0
Voted that John Johnson should have the *Forth* pew, It being 6 ft 10 inches front and 4 ft and 6 inches deep for	13	00	0
Voted that Jabez Field should have the *Fifth* pew, It being 7 ft 9 inches front and 4 ft and 6 inches deep for	12	10	0
Voted that Walter Downe should have the sixth pew, It being 6 ft and 10 inches front and 4 ft 7 inches deep for	5	00	0
Voted that James Packard should have the Seventh pew, It being 7 ft 3 inches front and 4 ft 7 inches deep for	23	00	0
Voted that Nathan Keith should have the Eighth pew, It being 7 ft 3 inches front and 4 ft 7 inches deep for	26	15	0
Voted that Weddow Ledah Packard should have the ninth pew, It being 6 ft 10 inches front and 4 ft 7 inches deep for (No amount given.)			
Voted that Zachriah Snell should have the tenth pew, It being 7 ft 9 inches front and 4 ft 6 inches deep for	16	15	0
Voted that Abiel Packard should have the Eleventh pew, It being 7 ft 9 inches front and 4 ft 6 inches deep for	15	00	0
Voted that David Packard should have the twelfth pew, It being 7 ft 10 inches front and 4 ft 6 inches deep for	23	05	0
Voted that Robert Haward should have the thirteenth pew, It being 6 ft 9 inches front and 5 ft 6 inches deep for	27	00	0

Robert Haward was chosen, " recever of the Bonds," given for the pews.

---

* Probably this was for the pulpit.

A LIST OF CHARGES GIVEN IN TO THE PRECINCT FOR BUILDING THE NEW
MEETING HOUSE.

	£ s. d.		£ s. d.
James Packard,	55 19 0	Theofllus Curtis,	05 13 8
Abiel Packard,	24 15 0	Solomon Packard,	12 00 0
Weddow Ledah Packard,	15 09 6	Benjamin Edson,	04 11 0
Zacheus Packard,	11 09 0	Timothy Keith,	07 00 0
Jacob Allen,	10 01 0	David Packard,	53 12 0
Joshua Warren,	07 16 0	John Kingman,	05 06 5
James Barret,	08 02 6	Josiah Snell,	16 00 0
John Johnson.	39 15 9	Mr. Barnabas Pratt,	08 02 0
Daniel Howard,	11 00 6	Zachariah Snell,	00 15 0
Robert Howard,	8 00 0	John Colly,	06 06 0
Elezer Washburn,	74 17 0		——————
		Total	386 11 4

January 12, 1741. "Voted that John Colly should have Thirty-five shillings for sweeping the meeting house the year Insuing." March 23, 1742. Abiel Packard to sweep the meeting house the present year for 35 shillings.

March 28, 1743. John Coly to have 40 shillings for sweeping the meeting house this year coming.

June 6, 1743. A meeting was held "to see whether the precinct would vote to Buld Seats In the Galiryes, and it was voted in the negative." It was then put to vote to see whether the precinct would "sell Roome over the stairs and behind the front Galiry next to the wall for pews and it was voted in the Affirmative."

From the above it appears that the house had galleries put up, but not finished. The usual practice in building churches in early times was to finish the inside and sell "pew room," or sections, which each purchaser would finish to suit himself. Hence we frequently find votes in the records as follows : —

June 20, 1743. "It was put to vote by the moderator of the meeting to see whether the precinct would vote to sell fore pews Behind the front Galary, and over the Stayers at a publick vandue to the highest Beder. The Demenshions of s^d Pews are as followeth : 'over the womens Stairs 6 feet front and five feet and half deep. Behind womens front Galary, 8 feet front and five feet deep. Behind men's front Galary six feet and a half front, and five feet deep, over the mens stairs six feet front, and five and a half deep, alowing Convenant Roome to pase up and down the stairs.' Voted in the afirmative."

"The pew over the mens stairs was seet up by the moderator to sail and Timothy Keith Beding two pounds and ten shillings upon s^d pew, It was struck of to him, he being the highest Beder."

" The pew over the womens stairs was bid off by Daniel Howard he Beding two pounds and ten shillings on s^d pew."

" The pew Behind the mens front galary was seet up, and Simeon Brett Beding twenty seven pounds upon s^d pew, It was struck off to him."

" The pew behind the womens front galary was set up by the moderator to sail and Constant Southworth Beding twenty pounds and five shillings upon s^d pew, It was struck off to him, he being the highest Beder."

Abiel Packard, Robert Haward, and Zachariah Snell were a committee to give confirmation to the above " sail of pews."

September 3, 1744.   " Voted to buld two seats in each side Gallery."

The first thing to be done after building a church in early times was to " seet the peopel " and provide a pew for the minister.

September 3, 1744.   We find " Jabez Field & charge voted for Bulding Mr. Porter's pew, £3 10 shillings."

June 28, 1746.   It was put to vote "to see If the Precinct would vote to finish the meeting-house this year, and it was voted in the affirmative."

" Voted that James Packard, Henry Kingman, and Jabez Field be a committee to see the meeting house be finished."

What the effect of the above vote was we find no record, and are left to judge that it was never carried into effect, as appears by the following record, aiming at the same thing; namely, to have the " meeting House " completed.

Aug. 15, 1748.   " Voted that Abiel Packard, Constant Southworth, and Samuel Brett be a committee to finish the meeting house the present year."

The following persons were supposed to have worked upon

the house in the completion of the same as it appears March 27, 1749. The following sums were voted to be paid: to Samuel Brett for work "Don In the meeting House " £6 7 shillings. To Luke Perkins £1 10 shillings. March 29, 1750, " money voted to Simeon Cary for Labour Don abought the Meeting House, to be Drawed out of the Treasury, £8 1 4." " Voted to Archabiel Robson for Bannisters for the Meeting House £4 10 shillings Lawfull Money."

At a meeting held September 27, 1756, it was " voted that the Petition between the men and womens frount Gallery Shuld be bult up a gain where it first stood. Also voted that the Rume on the wemens side of the Petition should be for the wemen."

By the above votes we see the custom prevailed of keeping the men and women in separate pews, and have no doubt the work was completed, and that they were kept in their proper places ; for we find Barnabas Pratt was allowed £3 8 shillings for putting up a " petition " between the " Gallereyes and the Hind Seets."

At a meeting of the Precinct held December 4, 1758, " voted that the committee provide an Iron Latch and Bolt for the South Dore of the meeting house."

The subject of building a new church, or of enlarging the old one, was talked of in 1760, and a meeting called to see what the Precinct would do, which was held December 1st, 1760,

" To see if the Precinct will vote to enlarge the Meeting House by spliting of It In tow, or making an addition to it or both and also to See if any person, or persons, will under-take the Doing of it for the Rume In the addition that shall be maid to the meeting house, and in case the Precinct should not vote to Inlarge the meeting house, then to see if the Precinct will vote to Buld a new Meeting House and when and where it shall be set, and of what Bigness it shall be bult." The vote was first put " to see if the Precinct would build a new House which was voted in the negative." " Then to see if the Precinct would vote to Inlarge the Meeting House by spliting of it. Voted in the negative."

Thus things remained for over a year, when the subject
was again brought up at a meeting held December 29, 1761,
at ten o'clock A. M. "To see what sum of money can be
raised to wards the Bulding a new Meeting House. In the
North Precinct of Bridgewater, by selling the pew Rome
to the Highest Beders. In a Meeting House of the same
Demenshons of the South Meeting House, in Bridgewater, the
number of them and the Setuation and Begness may be seen
by a plan that will be Provided in said meeting on said day."
"voted that Capt. Simeon Cary shuld be marster of the vandue to sell the pews to the Hiest Beders," and also "voted
that the pew on the Right Hand of the pulpet stairs shuld be
for the use of the menestry In said Precinct," and it was further "voted that Every person that had a pew struck of to
him by the vandue master, shuld pay Down a Dolor, as Enerst
for his pew."

"The master of the vandue, chose by the precinct then
proseded to the sail of the Pews, to the Number of 47, on
the flore of the Meeting House." The number, names, and
price of each being as follows : —

			£	s.	d.
Pew No.	1	Ebenezer Snell,	18	16	0
"	" 2	Ebenezer Packard,	16	18	8
"	" 3	Nehemiah Lincoln,	15	9	4
"	" 4	Zachariah Gurney Jr.,	10	10	8
"	" 5	Issachar Snell,	14	2	8
"	" 6	Daniel Manly and Ephraim Cole,	17	17	4
"	" 7	Elisha Gurney,	17	12	0
"	" 8	Josiah Packard,	18	0	0
"	" 9	Matthew Kingman,	18	10	8
"	" 10	Simeon Brett,	13	12	0
"	" 11	Abiezer Packard,	17	6	8
"	" 12	Thomas Thompson,	16	0	0
"	" 13	Isaac Packard,	21	12	0
"	" 14	Barnabas Howard,	18	13	4
"	" 15	Alexander Kingman,	17	6	8
"	" 16	Adam Howard and Zebedee Snell,	22	0	0
"	" 17	Nathaniel Southworth,	14	8	0
"	" 18	Josiah Hayden,	18	13	4

			£	s.	d.
Pew No. 19	Abia Keith,		22	5	4
" " 20	Daniel Ames		16	16	0
" " 21	William Packard,		14	13	4
" " 22	Abia Packard,		14	2	8
" " 23	Simeon Cary,		15	9	4
" " 24	Jonathan Cary,		15	1	4
" " 25	Thomas Packard,		14	18	8
" " 26	John Howard,		14	16	0
" " 27	Jacob Packard,		no account		
" " 28	Barnabas Pratt,		13	6	8
" " 29	Robert Howard,		18	16	0
" " 30	Charles Snell,		18	16	0
" " 31	Thomas Reynolds,		20	13	4
" " 32	Zachariah Cary,		16	0	0
" " 33	Samuel Brett,		14	16	0
" " 34	Benjamin Ames and Nathaniel Linfield,		14	18	8
" " 35	Reuben Packard,		14	13	4
" " 36	Issachar Snell,		22	2	8
" " 37	Joseph Richards,		18	13	4
" " 38	Daniel Richards,		24	16	0
" " 39	Robert Thompson,		15	14	8
" " 40	Barnabas Packard,		16	2	8
" " 41	Abel Packard,		23	12	0
" " 42	David Packard,		18	16	0
" " 43	Ensign Henry Kingman,		14	18	8
" " 44	Capt. Lemuel Dunbar,		14	16	0
" " 45	Jabez Field,		13	6	8
" " 46	Seth Harris,		14	16	0
" " 47	Eliphalet Philips,		16	0	0

After the sale of the above pews " the Precinct aGorned the meeting to Monday the forth Day of Jenuary at twelve o'ck, M." "agreeably to agornment the precinct gathered together and the vandue master, chosen by the precinct, for the sail of the pews proseded and made sail of sixteen pews In the front Gallery," the number, names, and prices of which were as follows: namely, —

	NAMES.		£	s.	d.
Pew No. 1	Isaac Fuller,		20	13	4
" " 2	Issachar Snell,		20	8	0
" " 3	Luke Perkins,		26	13	4
" " 4	Issachar Snell,		21	2	6
" " 5	Issachar Snell,		24	5	4

NAMES.	£	s.	d.
Pew. No. 6 Jonathan Hayden,	14	8	0
" " 7 William Edson,	14	5	4
" " 8 Barnabas Howard and Jabez Field,	18	8	0
" " 9 Joshua Packard,	13	17	4
" " 10 Jacob Packard,	29	17	4
" " 11 Nathan Packard and Simeon Packard,	10	0	0
" " 12 William Shaw,	10	16	0
" " 13 Josiah Perkins,	9	9	4
" " 14 Dependence French & Theopolis Curtis Jr.,	12	13	4
" " 15 Levi French & Isaac Brett,	12	8	0
" " 16 Dr. Phillip Bryant & Seth Bryant,	12	2	8

January 5, 1762. " Voted to Buld a meeting house of the same demenshons of the South meeting house In Bridgewater, excepting two side Gallary to be bult in seets," also " voted to Buld the meeting House the next summer, within twelve month from the aforsaid Date hereof," and " voted that all the posts of the Body of the meeting House shuld be sawed and the house faced South." Robert Haward, Captain Simeon Cary, and Mr. Abia Keith were chosen a committee for " prosicuting the Bulding the meeting House in the North Precinct." " Voted that the house shuld be Shilingled with sedar shingles."

Monday, November 8, 1762. " A meeting was called to see if the precinct will vote to Buld a Belfree to the meeting house," and it was voted to " Build one over the East Dore," also " voted to Buld a porch over the west Dore, and to sell the stairways for pews to the highest Beder." It seems nothing had been done towards forwarding the building of the " Belfree " in January, as another meeting was called to meet January 17, " to see if the precinct will vote to buld the Belfree, and spire, already voted to be built, provided it can be don by subscription, and without taxing the precinct," which was voted in the affirmative, also " voted that the Belfry should be twelve feet square, and eighty-five feet high from the grown." Capt. Simeon Cary, Isaac Packard, and Barnabas Howard were chosen a committee to

FIRST CONGREGATIONAL CHURCH (Centre Village).
Second Edifice—Erected in 1762; taken down in 1827.

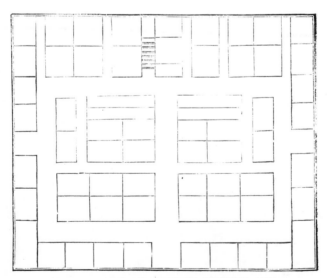

PLAN OF PEWS IN SECOND EDIFICE, 1762.

"Buld" the same. In the spring of 1762 the building was commenced. The frame was raised in June, 1763, and in December of the same year the house was completed, and dedicated to the worship of God the last week of that month. Rev. Mr. Dunbar preached the sermon in the forenoon of the day of dedication, from text, Isaiah lx. 7 : " I will glorify the house of my glory." Rev. John Angier, of the East Parish * preached a sermon in the afternoon from the text, Psalms cxxii. 1 : " I was glad when they said unto me let us go into the house of the Lord." The first sermon preached in the new meeting-house, by Rev. Mr. Porter, was from text, Haggai ii. 9 : " The glory of this latter house shall be greater than the former." The carpenters that performed the carpenter work upon this house were Dea. Jonathan Cary, Benjamin Packard, Micah Packard, Seth Packard, Barnabas Pratt, Thomas Pratt, Job Bryant, Gamaliel Bryant, Samuel Hayden, Phinehas Paine, Jeremiah Beals. Col. Josiah Hayden was the master workman of the inside of the house. Col. Simeon Cary, who was one of the building committee, was master of the outside of the house. Col. Hayden also built the pulpit and sounding-board. All of the above mechanics belonged in the town.

We have already seen that the precinct voted to have a steeple built by subscription; but for some reason which does not appear on record, it was not all paid in. For this purpose the pew back of the " Deckon seet " was put up for " sail " to help pay the committee that built it what expense had been incurred. May 17, 1764. " Voted to sell the old meeting house for the use of the precinct in jenerail."

> " Alas ! there came a luckless day,
>   Our meeting house grew old, —
> The paint was worn, the shingles loose ;
>   In winter it was too cold.

---

* Now East Bridgewater.

> They called it an old-fashioned thing,
> And said it must be sold."

Also voted the same day to " Geet a Bell for the New Meeting House, not exceeding six hundred Wate." Daniel Howard Esq., Capt. Abiel Packard, and Lieut. Henry Kingman were chosen a committee to purchase the same. October 24, 1765, "Voted to Build stairs to the Belfree." It seems the bell of the new meeting-house became broken from some cause, and at a meeting held October 10, 1768, to see if the precinct would vote to mend the bell, voted in the affirmative, also " voted that Lt. Henry Kingman should geet it mended." We presume that the bell was past mending, as we afterwards find, December 11, 1769, a vote " to geet a new Bell of Seven hundred wate. Lt. Henry Kingman, Col. Simeon Cary, and Capt. Isaac Packard were appointed a committee to go and agree with Mr. Hubbard, for the making and taking down of the old Bell and hanging the new one." January 11, 1770. " Voted to Imploy Mr. Aaron Huburd and Mr. Gellomer to new Run the Bell, and that it shall be of Seven hundred wate." In the early part of 1772, a number of persons became " larned " in the rules of " musick " under Mr. Billings, and asked that seats might be assigned to them in the south part of the women's gallery. This request was complied with, as follows : November 30, 1772, " Voted to the singers the South part of the women's Gallary During pleasure." We find this produced some dissatisfaction, and efforts were made to restore the seats back to the women. Various meetings were called until, April 8, 1773, a special meeting being called, the " Question was put by the moderator to see if the precinct will vote to restore the Southerly part of the womens gallary to the womens use again." It was " voted in the negative." April 3, 1775. The above vote was reconsidered, and a vote passed " allowing the north part of the womens seets During the pleasure of the Parish," also "voted to build a pair of stairs in the Belfree." December 11, 1788. "Voted to sell the Deef Seet." Also "voted to sell the two hind seets each side of the Broad alley." Now the parish begin to think that some repairs are needed, and a committee of three were chosen to report what repairs were necessary. Job Bryant, Moses Cary, and Jeremiah Beals were that committee, who reported the following to be done: "new sett the Glass in putty, paint the Door, windows, and walls, and the platform of the Belfree be covered with Led." Voted "that the window frames and sashes be painted white."

March 19, 1789. "Voted to build a porch provided it can be Don without expense to the parish, and also to put seats in the porch and Belfree for the negroes, and sell the room where the stairs and negro pew now are." Thus we see that in this year the negroes were to sit in the loft provided on purpose, which created no little feeling on the part of the colored population.

March 4, 1795. "Voted to shingel the Meeting House the front side, to be completed by the 15 of Sept."

In the year 1800, we again find a disagreement between the colored people attending worship and sitting in the same seat with the white people, which very much annoyed some of them, and to remedy this trouble a meeting was held August 4, "To see what measures the Parish will take to prevent the *blacks* from occupying the seats appropriated to the use of the white people, so as to prevent any disturbances in time of Public worshipe," at which time it was "Voted that the side galleries and the seats in the Body of the meeting house be appropriated to the use of the white people, and the seats in the porch above to the use of the blacks."

January 19, 1801. "Voted to erect seats in the front gallery for the singers, in front of the front pews," and "voted that they be erected in a surkerler forme." April 30, 1801.

"Voted to paint the inside work that has heretofore been
painted, to be under the direction of the Parish Committee."
Early in the year 1805, the people of the parish, wishing to
improve the looks of their house of worship, called a meeting,
which was held March 11, 1805, "To see if the Parish will
repair the meeting Hous, and what repairs they will make
the year insuing." At this meeting a committee of nine was
chosen to view the house and report at the adjournment of
the meeting. This committee consisted of the following persons : Capt. Abel Kingman, Capt. Howard Cary, Major Caleb
Howard, Jeremiah Beal, Jesse Perkins, Gideon Howard Esq.,
Perez Southworth, Silas Packard, Daniel Packard. This
committee report "that it was necessary to make new the
wast bords and water table from the north east corner of the
meeting hous, and on the South side, to the South side of the
Porch door, that as many of the sashes as are defective should
be made new, and such repairs on the doors as shall be found
neccessary ; that the bell fraim, banisters, &c., be made new,
and all the trimmings together with the spire be painted,
that the body of the house together with the rouff be painted." A committee of five were appointed to select a color
for painting, who reported "white, one shade on the yallow."
Moses Cary, Jonathan Beals, and John Wales were chosen a
committee to carry the above repairs into execution. August 30, 1805. "Voted to Polish the Vain."

December 5, 1816. We again find a vote respecting the
seating of the colored people, as follows : Voted "that the
Peopel of color may occupy the two Back seats in the west
gallery of our meeting house & no other seats, or that they
may have ground for one pew in the north west corner of the
Gallery and ground for another pew in the North East corner
of the Gallery as they Choose, and that the Parish clerk serve
the people of color with a copy of this vote."

In 1818 the subject of warming the meeting-house came

up in the following manner: some of the churches in the neighboring towns, having found it a luxury to have the house of God warmed and made comfortable, thought it would not be too much of a sin to enjoy the same comfort. The idea at first met with serious opposition; for the first article in a warrant, concerning the purchasing of a cast-iron stove, was negatived, which move was made December 10, 1818, as follows: "Voted to have the article of getting a stove inserted in a warrant for the next spring meeting;" and in the following spring, March 25, 1819, "voted the stove or stoves to a committee of five," consisting of Col. Caleb Howard, Daniel Howard, Esq., Abel Kingman, Esq., Capt. Zachariah Gurney, Eliphalet Kingman. December 13, 1819. This committee reported it "inexpedient to get a Stove." March 7, 1822. "Voted the South part of the East Gallery for the use of the young women." Previous to February, 1823, this Parish had been known by the name of the "North Parish in Bridgewater." December 2, 1822. The parish "voted to take measures to alter the name of the North Parish of Bridgewater, and that it be called the 'First Parish in North Bridgewater,' also voted that the Parish take measures to petition the Legislature to carry the above into effect." Caleb Howard, Esq., Perez Crocker, and Perez Southworth were appointed to petition the Legislature in behalf of said parish;* so that from that time forward it was known as the "First Parish in North Bridgewater." In the early part of 1824, the bell of this parish was found broken, and Abel Kingman, Esq., Caleb Howard, Esq., and Rev. Daniel Huntington were chosen a committee to purchase a new one, March 2, 1824, with discretionary power to "gitt a Bell of the wate of from 10 to 12 cwt." A bell was purchased of George H. Holbrook of West Medway, Mass., April 17, 1824, which was

* The town of North Bridgewater, having been incorporated June 15, 1821, is the reason for having the name of the parish changed.

13

warranted for one year with fair common usage, and weighing 1,242 lbs., at an expense of $465.75. An article was inserted in a warrant for parish meeting, March 2, 1824. "To see if the Parish will agree to make any alteration in the form or shape of the Meeting House either inside or out, or to make any repairs to either." This was the first movement toward rebuilding or repairing the old house. At this meeting it was voted to make some alteration, providing that they can agree with the pew-holders on reasonable terms. For this purpose a committee was chosen to see upon what terms the pew-holders would consent to "give up thare pews." This committee consisted of Howard Cary, Silas Packard, Capt. David Ames, Nathaniel Littlefield, Bela Keith, Eliphalet Kingman, Capt. John Packard, Capt. Asa Jones, Col. E. Southworth, Israel Packard, Capt. Jeremiah Beals, who were to report at the next meeting, which report was as follows: "25 were willing to have their pews apprised, 24 willing to sell, 13 willing to exchange their old for new ones." "Voted not to accept of the committee's report," and also "Voted they wouldn't make any alteration in the Meeting House." February 25, 1825. "Voted to dismiss the article concerning alteration of the Meeting House." September 4, 1826, the subject was again brought before the Parish, "To see if the Parish will agree to alter, repair, or rebuild thair Meeting House." A committee of fifteen were chosen to take the subject into consideration, who reported in favor of building a new house. October 23, 1826. Voted to choose a committee of five out of town to apprise the pews in said meeting-house. Col. Royal Turner, of Randolph, Ezra Fobes, of Bridgewater, Wade Daley, of Easton, John Belcher, Micah Nash, of Abington, were appointed said committee, who proceeded to their duty November 7, 1826, and apprised the whole, amounting to $2,750. February 16, 1827. Chose a committee of eleven to nominate three as building committee,

FIRST CONGREGATIONAL CHURCH (Centre Village).
Third Edifice—Erected 1828.

Destroyed by fire, Nov. 7, 1860.

and six as advising. Abel Kingman, Lieut. Isaac Packard, and Benjamin Kingman were appointed as the building committee, and the two first named resigning, B. Kingman was chosen as agent to build the house, and Bela Keith, Esq., Asa Jones, Daniel H. Cary, Col. Isaac Littlefield, Lieut. Ephraim Cole, and John Tilden, Jr., were chosen as advising committee. A committee of five were appointed to locate the house, consisting of the following persons: Silas Packard, Jesse Perkins, Esq., Col. Edward Southworth, Col. Cyrus Porter, Abel Kingman, Esq., who reported in favor of setting the house its width south, and half its length west. Report accepted March 16, 1827.

The old house was taken down in April of this year. On the first day of the week in which this was to be done, and the ground cleared for another house, a sermon was delivered by Rev. D. Huntington, the pastor of the church, from Zachariah xii. 6: "And Jerusalem shall be inhabited again in her own place, even in Jerusalem." And as many of the society could not go abroad to worship while the new house was in process of building, it was thought best to provide temporary accommodations. For this purpose an addition was made to the sheds at the southwest corner of the green, in which seats were provided for the congregation, and to which the pulpit of the old house was removed. And the author has often been told that, in that humble place, there were many precious hours spent, and some of the most interesting seasons of religious exercise enjoyed there that ever they experienced. The new house of worship was completed in November; so that the sheds were occupied by them during the interval of time between those dates. The house was dedicated November 27, 1827, with highly appropriate and interesting exercises.

November 15, 1827. At a meeting of the parish the following persons were chosen a committee of arrangements for the dedication of the new house; namely, Benjamin Kingman, Capt. David Ames, Col. Nathan Jones, Col. Isaac Littlefield, Lieut. Ephraim Cole, also Silas Packard and Benjamin Kingman were appointed and authorized to convey the pews to those that purchased. Voted that the sale of pews take place Wednesday, November 28, 1827, to commence at nine o'clock A. M.

The following shows a list of the pews sold, the number, names of owners, and price for which they sold. Zenas French of Randolph, Vandue Master.

5	Azel Gurney,	101.50	37	Micah Shaw,	125.00
6	Robert Howard,	104.00	38	Arza Keith,	128.00
7	James Cary,	110.50	39	Col. Edward Southworth,	140.00
8	David Edson, Jr.,	106.00	40	Thomas Wales,	173.00
9	Simeon Packard,	103.00	41	Lieut. Ephraim Cole,	195.00
10	Hezekiah Packard,	98.50	42	James Littlefield,	206.00
11	Eliphalet Kingman,	98.00	43	Jacob Fuller,	204.00
12	Joel Ames,	100.50	44	Isaac Packard,	205.00
13	Ornan Cole,	85.50	45	Jeremiah Beals,	200.00
14	Francis Cary,	94.00	46	Arza Packard,	190.00
15	Moses Packard,	93.50	47	Theron Ames,	180.00
16	Ezekiel Merritt,	86.00	48	Abel Kingman, Esq.,	175.50
17	Zibeon French,	75.00	49	Josiah W. Kingman,	155.00
18	Col. Edward Southworth,	72.00	50	John W. Kingman,	140.50
19	Asa Ford,	56.00	51	Charles Keith,	132.50
20	Apollas Packard,	38.00	52	Alpheus French & Son,	124.00
21	Ambrose Packard,	21.00	53	Lysander Howard,	95.50
22	Bela Keith,	40.00	54	Joel Packard,	56.00
23	Josiah Fuller,	49.50	55	David Ames,	32.25
24	Josiah Packard,	69.50	56	Abel Kingman, Esq.,	30.00
25	Ziba Keith,	94.00	57	Samuel Tribou,	54.00
26	Robert Packard, Jr.,	94.50	58	Martin Cary,	80.00
27	Simeon Leach,	102.00	59	Noah Ford,	120.50
28	Abel Kingman, Esq.,	103.00	60	Col. Cyrus Porter,	133.50
29	David Ames,	108.50	61	Eliphalet Kingman,	140.00
30	Luke Packard,	117.00	62	Bela Keith,	155.00
31	Benjamin Kingman,	115.00	63	John Thompson,	169.50
32	Josiah Brett,	123.00	64	Col. Nathan Jones.	178.50
33	Micah Faxon,	127.00	65	Isaac Littlefield,	182.00
34	Isaac & Jonas Keith,	128.50	66	Turner Torrey,	202.00
35	Silvanus French,	127.50	67	Josiah Ames,	203.00
36	Isaac Curtis,	134.10	68	Rositer Jones,	196.00

69	Asa Jones,	197.50	
70	Silas Packard, Esq.	195.50	
71	Micah Faxon,	173.50	
73	Nathaniel Ames,	123.50	
74	Howard Packard,	127.00	
75	Nahum Perkins,	135.50	
76	Darius Littlefield,	136.00	
77	Silas Packard,	133.50	
78	Jabez Kingman,	128.50	
79	Benjamin Ames &		
	Galen Pratt,	125.00	
80	Isaac Littlefield,	122.50	
81	Alva Noyes,	117.50	
82	Galen Warren,	112.50	
83	Martin Cary,	107.00	
84	Lysander Howard,	102.50	
85	Daniel Ford,	94.00	
86	Samuel Alden,	71.00	
87	Eliphalet Kingman,	58.50	
88	Benjamin Packard,	48.50	
89	Seth Copeland,	31.50	
90	Zenas Thayer,	30.50	
91	William Lewis,	37.25	
92	Zenas Brett,	42.50	
93	Marcus Copeland,	47.00	
94	Eliphalet Kingman,	57.00	
95	Alva Noyes,	60.00	
96	Daniel H. Cary,	73.50	
98	Jesse Perkins,	66.50	
99	Jesse Perkins,	70.00	
100	Heman Packard,	103.00	
101	Lieut. Ephraim Cole,	105.25	

102	Mark Perkins,	107.00
103	Isaac Packard,	89.00
104	Barzilla Cary,	90.00
105	Oliver Leach,	77.00
106	Jonas Reynolds,	85.00
107	Barzilla Field,	114.00
108	Josiah Dunbar (half),	54.25
	Mark Perkins (half),	54.25
109	Albert Smith,	97.00
110	Oliver Dike (half),	38.75
	Hosea Alden (half),	38.75
111	Nehemiah Lincoln,	42.50
114	Benjamin Ames &	
	Galen Pratt,	47.00
115	Isaac Curtis (half),	43.00
	Luke Packard (half),	43.00
119	Bela Keith,	26.00
121	John Wales,	20.00
124	Simeon & Hezekiah	
	Packard,	24.50
126	Josiah Brett (half),	18.75
126	Moses & David Packard	
	(half),	18.75
127	Bela Keith,	30.00
129	John Shankland,	26.00
132	Silas Packard,	18.75
134	Isaac Keith,	23.00
135	John Wales,	33.50
137	Eliphalet Kingman,	43.50
140	Lemuel French,	44.00
141	Abel Kingman,	40.50

November 28, 1827. Voted that the three easterly pews in the north side of the gallery be reserved for young women. And again the subject of seating the colored people comes up, and. it was "Voted that the South west and North west pews be reserved for the people of Colour." January 14, 1828. At a meeting held this day, "To see if the parish will vote to procure a timepiece," it was "voted to defer the subject of getting a timepiece to a future meeting." January 28, the same subject was brought before the parish for action, when it was "voted not to do anything respecting getting a timepiece."

The report of the agent in building the new house reported as follows, January 14, 1828 : —

"The total cost of the new house, including the furniture, as furnished at the expense of the parish, was seven thousand five hundred and nine dollars and seventeen cents. The old house sold for four hundred and three dollars and thirty-seven cents, which, deducted from the cost of the new building, leaves the nett cost seven thousand and ninety-five dollars and eighty cents."

Also at the same time " voted that the Parish committee be instructed to build Horse sheds for those that want them at cost. Benjamin Kingman chosen as agent to build them." March 24, 1828. Jesse Perkins, Col. Edward Southworth, and Benjamin Kingman were appointed to view the ground in front of the meeting-house with reference to erecting a fence, who reported in favor of erecting one, " to extend 40 feet front of the house of a circular form, of 20 Stone Posts, and Iron rods or chains." January 24, 1832. A new bell was procured. Thomas Gurney and Abel Kingman, Esq., were the purchasing committee. The bell was manu-factured by George Holbrook, of Medway, Mass. Also, in April of the same year, a clock was procured by subscription, which was made by George Holbrook above named, costing three hundred dollars, placed upon the church April 11, 1832. The proprietors of the clock offered it to the parish upon their paying what outstanding accounts were unpaid, which offer was accepted, and $62.88 paid for the same. Monday, January 21, 1833. The subject of warming the house was brought before the society again, "To see if the Parish will pro-cure a stove or any other apparatus for warming their meet-ing house." A committee of five were chosen "to get infor-mation respecting the best mode of warming their Meeting House, and to what course is pursued in other Societies, and report at the next March meeting." Turner Torrey, Lysander Howard, Darius Littlefield, Eliphalet Kingman, and Ephraim Cole, committee for the above. After report of committee, December 30, 1833, "Voted that they would not consent to have a stove in our meeting house providing it was done free of expense to the Parish." Monday, August 10, 1835. Chose a building committee of five persons to build a parsonage house, — Edward Southworth, Abel Kingman, Benjamin Kingman, Bela Keith, and Rositer Jones, committee. At last the parish concluded to warm the house, which appears by a vote passed November 28, 1835. Heman Packard, Col. E. Southworth, and Ephraim Cole were chosen a committee to provide stoves for the meeting-house. Truly a most remarkable innovation when compared with the former custom of sitting during long sermons, shivering and shaking as though it were wicked to be made comfortable. Judging by the records, this people, like most other societies, were occasionally troubled with naughty boys, as April 13, 1844, "Voted to choose a number of persons to take care of the boys in the gallery." March 8, 1852. An article was inserted in the warrant, calling a meeting of the parish, "To see if the Parish will make a general repair and revision of their meeting house, and take measures that may be proper to settle with the pew holders." "Voted unanimously to make a general repair and revision of their meeting house." "Also made choice of Benjamin Kingman, Oakes S. Soule, and Marcus Packard a committee to procure plans for reseating and repairing the meeting house, and report at a future meeting." March 22, 1852. The committee appointed to get a plan for reseating and repairing "reported in favor of building a new house, and recommend that the Parish thoroughly review the whole subject deliberately." This report was accepted, and the same committee were appointed to "investigate and get such information in relation to the whole matter of building and repairing their house as they may think best calculated to enable the parish to judge correctly as to what is best to be done, to examine modern built houses at their discretion."

The same day " voted to reconsider the vote to repair and reseat the Meeting House."

The above-named persons were chosen as building committee. April 26, 1852. Benjamin Kingman, Ozen Gurney, and Marcus Packard were appointed to settle with pew-holders, sell the old house, and provide another place of worship. December 27, 1852. " Voted to instruct the building committee to proceed in building a house when the sum of Eight Thousand Dollars is subscribed." March 17, 1853. Made choice of three persons to apprise the old pews; namely, John W. Loud, of Weymouth, Joseph Lewis, of Duxbury, Nathan Randall, of Duxbury were chosen.

The ladies of the First Congregational Church and society held a levee for social intercourse and fellowship at the Satucket Hall, February 15, 1853. The object of the meeting was to increase the fund for furnishing the new meeting-house which was then talked of building. The meeting was largely attended, the weather mild, the travelling good, with a bright moon. The meeting made choice of William P. Howard as president. The " North Bridgewater Brass Band" was present, and made the first impression; then prayer was offered by Rev. Paul Couch; then a musical treat by Isaac T. Packard; remarks appropriate to the occasion by Rev. Paul Couch; amusements; refreshments for five hundred persons; and a little later in the evening the following song was sung by the organist of the church.

THE OLD VILLAGE CHURCH.

1 A song for the church, — the old village church,
  Which has stood full many a year;
  We'll sing to its praise in the loftiest lays;
  For we love its portals dear.

2 The storms they have beat on that sacred retreat,
    While its inmates have bowed in prayer ;
The lightnings have flashed and the deep thunder crashed
    With the notes of the chanting choir.

3 Memory now can look back through time's beaten track
    And remember the joyful day
When its frame was reared, while the workmen cheered, —
    To them it was sport and play.

4 They saw the tower rise, pointing up to the skies,
    While within the deep-toned bell
Gave forth the glad sound to the people around
    That the building was finished well

5 Then a song for the church, — the old village church,
    Which has stood full many a year ;
We'll sing to its praise in the loftiest lays ;
    For we love its portals dear.

6 But old Father Time, he thinks it no crime
    To crumble the stateliest towers ;
In silence he's spaced, and the beauty defaced
    That was once in this temple of ours.

7 And progression appears in these later years
    To make it our duty clear
That we must in our might, while contending for right,
    A fine new structure rear.

8 Then a song for the church, — for the new village church,
    Which we hope we then shall see ;
In which we may raise glad notes of praise
    To thee, Great One in Three.

9 The work has begun, and the ladies have done
    And are doing, from day to day,
An honorable part to encourage each heart
    To labor without delay.

10 They have invited us here, and with right good cheer
    We respond to their festive call ;
And we'll do nothing worse than to fill their purse,
    To discount in the fall,

11 In decking the church, — the new village church,
    Which we hope we then shall see,
In which we may raise glad notes of praise
    To thee, Great One in Three.

14

The frame of the new house was raised August 25, 1853, in the afternoon, when the following ceremony took place : 1. Hymn, sung by the children ; 2. Prayer, by Rev. Charles L. Mills, of the Porter Church ; 3. Prayer, by Rev. A. B. Wheeler, of the Second Methodist Episcopal Church ; 4. Hymn, written by Isaac T. Packard, the organist of the church : —

1 Praise to thy name, eternal King,
 In grateful numbers here we bring ;
 Oh, now behold us from above,
 And smile upon us in thy love.

2 Here on this hallowed ground we meet,
 And now thy blessing we entreat ;
 Oh, may these walls in order rise
 Through help that cometh from the skies.

3 Oh, build this house, — this house of **prayer** !
 Make it the object of thy care ;
 Here with thy people ever dwell :
 Here may thy saints thy glories tell.

4 And from this earthly house below
 May multitudes redeemèd go
 To that prepared by thee above,
 There join to sing redeeming love.

The old meeting-house was sold to Messrs. Winthrop S. Baker and Rufus P. Kingman for $1,226.60, who took a lease of the land upon which the building stood, a few feet south of where the present building now stands, for the term of fifty years from March 21, 1854, at the rate of one hundred dollars per year. The building was remodelled and used as a hall for public meetings until destroyed by fire, November 7, 1860.

The present new and splendid edifice was opened to the public at two o'clock on Thursday, July 27, 1854. There were present from fifteen hundred to two thousand persons, and the exercises were in the following order : 1. Voluntary on the organ ; 2. Chant : —

FIRST CONGREGATIONAL CHURCH (Centre Village).
Fourth Edifice—Erected 1854.

" Holy, holy, holy Lord God of hosts ; "

3. Invocation and Reading of the Scriptures; 4. Anthem:—

" Let all the nations fear ; "

5. Prayer; 6. Hymn:—

1 To thee this temple we devote,
   Our Father and our God ;
Accept it thine, and seal it now,
   Thy Spirit's blest abode.

2 Here may the prayer of faith ascend,
   The voice of praise arise ;
Oh, may each lowly service prove
   Accepted sacrifice.

3 Here may the sinner learn his guilt,
   And weep before his Lord ;
Here, pardoned, sing a Saviour's love,
   And here his vows record.

4 Here may affliction dry the tear,
   And learn to trust in God,
Convinced it is a Father smites,
   And love that guides the rod.

5 Peace be within these sacred walls ;
   Prosperity be here ;
Long smile upon thy people, Lord,
   And evermore be near.

7. Sermon, by Rev. Paul Couch, text, Isaiah ii. 2–5, showing that the house of God is to be a central and controlling power in the world's reformation; 8. Hymn, Anthem:—

" Peace be to this habitation ; "

9. Dedicatory Prayer ; 10. Anthem:—

" Hark ! the song of jubilee ; "

11. Closing Prayer; 12. Hymn and Doxology, by the congregation:—

" From all that dwell below the skies ; "

Doxology :—

" Praise God, from whom all blessings flow ; "

13. Benediction.

The sermon is spoken of as having been of a high order.
Many a golden thought was presented to the people, and
will be treasured up by them.   The singing also was of the
most excellent kind, and entitled to great praise.   The last
hymn was sung to the tune of " Old Hundred," in which the
congregation joined; and seldom has that tune been sung
with such great power and in such correct time as on that
occasion.   The organ poured forth a flood of harmony from
which no deviation could be made, and every one present
seemed pleased with the arrangements and detail of the exercises.   This occasion afforded many an opportunity to
view the house for the first time.   The day was pleasant and
the attendance very large.   Few houses are to be found in
the country that will compare favorably with this.   Its exterior is rendered attractive and pleasing to the eye by its
beautiful proportions, which, while they present and possess
unusual strength, are so arranged that the whole appearance
is not only satisfactory, but very graceful and imposing.
The length of the building is 96 feet, width 64 feet, with a
spire 185 feet in height, and contains 116 pews on the
floor and 28 in the gallery.   It is built in the Romanesque
style of architecture, designed by Messrs. Towle & Foster,
of Boston, was built by Samuel Vaughn, of Boston.   The
pews are all neatly carpeted, cushioned, and upholstered
both in the gallery and below.   The gallery contains a large
and beautiful organ, built by W. B. D. Simmons, of Cambridge Street, Boston, which was finished May 17, 1854.   On
entering the building, we find, on the first floor, a vestry of
good size and a large room, carpeted and well furnished, for
the use of the "Ladies' Association," connected with the society.   In the rear of these rooms are two convenient and
well-arranged tenements, which are rented.   Ascending from
the main entrance on either side stairs of very easy grade,
we find ourselves in the vestibule, from which we enter the

auditory, or ascend to the galleries. The interior effect is exceedingly fine. The spacious floor, well-arranged pews, all uniform and somewhat richly upholstered, the ample galleries, not projecting from the sides with huge, overshadowing effect, but rather relieving the height and presenting a corresponding finish, the chaste and elegant pulpit, finely frescoed walls and ceiling, are in perfect harmony with each other and their design and uses, and beautifully wrought without glaring effect. Upon the west end of the building, on the ceiling to the left of the pulpit, is the following inscription: " Ye shall keep my Sabbaths and reverence my sanctuary. I am the Lord." To the right of the pulpit is the following: "The Lord hath chosen Zion. He hath desired it for his habitation." The outlay in erecting this house, including the organ, was about $24,000. The first sale of pews took place on Monday following the dedication, at which 73 pews were sold for the sum of $22,282.50. The choice money paid was $1,746.50. After the sale there were 43 pews remaining unsold on the floor of the auditory, many of which were very desirable, and several in the galleries, all of which were carpeted and furnished as below.

The bell that belonged on the old church, when sold, was transferred to the new house above described in June, 1854. The following legend was upon the same : —

> " I to the church the living call,
> And to the graveyard summon all."

This bell, after having done many years of faithful service, gave out but a short time after it was removed; for we find, September 5, 1855, a new bell was purchased of Messrs. Henry N. Hooper & Co., of Boston, weighing 2,035 lbs.

CHAPTER VI.

EDUCATIONAL HISTORY.

Free Schools. — Their Origin. — School Committee of the North Parish. — Division of the Parish into Districts. — School Committee. — Annual Appropriations. — School Districts. — Adelphian Academy. — North Bridgewater Academy. — High School. — Private Schools.

FOR the past two centuries our country has enjoyed a system of education that has had no parallel. The progress of our country with all its varied interests may be attributed to the education of her people. There is no one thing in which the happiness and prosperity of society is so much involved as in the proper education, the moral training, and discipline of youth, and the many advantages arising from the same cannot be too highly estimated or overstated. The boldness of the measure aiming at universal education through the medium of *free schools* has no precedent in the history of the world. Every nation abroad, as well as States at home, are imitating our example. The credit of originating these free institutions is due to our *Pilgrim Fathers*. It was in the cabin of the "Mayflower" that they agreed among themselves to a written constitution of government which was the nucleus of all the free governments of the earth. At the time they landed on our shores, two grand ideas pervaded their minds; namely, religion, or the spiritual interest of their people, and knowledge, or the education of the young. The fisheries of Cape Cod were early laid under contributions for the support of free schools in 1671. At a public festival a few years since, the following sentiments were offered:

110

"Mackerel Schools and Free Schools, the one the support of the other;" another, "The Fishermen of Cape Cod, they get their learning on their own Hook." These institutions have long been under the control of the government, by them supported and controlled, sanctioned and protected by law as much as the right of a person to their own mode of worship; and the distinguishing feature of the system is in the advantage of common-school instruction, which is free to all, without distinction of race, color, or position, and is secured to every child in the State, that the property of the commonwealth shall be subservient to equal and adequate instruction. The mass of the people have been educated, and we have enjoyed what no other nation has been permitted to enjoy, — we have learned for ourselves how to conduct a free government, and the success of the same may be seen in the progress that has been and is now being made in all that contributes to make a nation prosperous and happy.

From earliest time the policy of Massachusetts has been to develop the minds of her people and to imbue them with the principles of duty. In doing this she has had the aid of the many towns within her limits, and has a system which is destined to greater and more elevated usefulness than has ever before been seen.

The town of North Bridgewater has ever been ready to contribute of her public funds for educational purposes. Previous to the incorporation of the old North Parish, the parish paid their proportional part of school expenses of the town of Bridgewater, and received a share of the benefits of the same. At a meeting of the town of Bridgewater, held November 24, 1746, a committee of twelve were chosen, "To consult what method may be most beneficial to the Town in improving of ye school for the futer." Robert Howard, Abiel Packard were chosen on the part of the North Parish.

The committee made the following report: December 1, 1746. " Voted that the sum of £250 old Tenor, to support schooling in the town one year next following, and that the grammar school has been kept longer in a precinct than has been useful when it comes to their turn, and that the west precinct shall have the improvement of ye grammar school the first year and then the other precincts in order shall have the grammar school according to their proportion of ye Tax." We next find a record in the parish books as follows: March 21, 1747. " At a meeting held this day To chuse a committee to take care of the money, and gat a scole masture, or a scoole dame, and to see if the precinct can agree whare the scoole shall be keept this year," it was voted " That Timothy Keith, Robert Howard and Abiel Packard should be a committee to take care of the scoole the year Insewing." Also, " Voted by the precinct, that the precinct should be devided into three scoole Ricks, to begin at Elisha Dunbars, and from thence to Abia Keiths and from thence to Henery Kingmans all to the South of that line to be the South Rick, And the meedal Rick to extend North as far as the north side of Abiel Packards field that Joynes Zachariah Gurneys, by an east and west Line from said place.

" Each peart having Equal parte In the town treasury for draft of money belonging to the precinct for the use of the scoole to be drawed by the committee for the scoole or their order." For a long time after the establishment of the North Parish, or precinct, there were but three school districts, which were divided as above. " The subject of new school Houses was brot to the attention of the parish, August 15, 1748, To chuse a man or men to receive the money due from the town to maintain a scoole and to dispose of the same in the best method, Alsow To see if the precinct will build one or more scool houses for the use of the Parish scool, and to act anything proper for accomplishing the same. The meeting was setteled by the choise of Daniel Howard, moderator.

"Voted that Timothy Keith, Abiel Packard, and Robert Howard shuld bee a committee to draw the money out of the town treasury this present year, their perporsionabel part for the use of the Parash Scools and to dispose of the same in the way and manner voted by the precinct last year past." December 9, 1751. A meeting was held "To agree How, and whare the scoole shall be keept the Insueing year. Voted that the scool shuld be keept in three places in the precinct, also Voted that the meddal part shuld have the scool the first fore months and the south part shuld have it the next two months, and the north part which extends from the north line of the middle rick as far north as the town extends, should have it the next three months." Again, March 28, 1753, the laying out of the money, and "settelling of the scool" was left to the precinct committee. The people of the precinct, feeling dissatisfied with the division, called a meeting which was held March 11, 1784, "To take the minds of the precinct respecting the grammar school for the future, and act what may be thought proper concerning the same," at which it was "Voted to divide the precinct into four Ricks for the Grammar School, also Voted that Barnabas Howard, Dea. Jonathan Cary, Mr. Matthew Kingman, and Ensign Issachar Snell, be a committee for the purpose aforesaid and make report at the fall meeting." September 6, 1784. The committee for dividing the district into four ricks for the grammar school gave in the following report : —

We the subscribers, being chosen a committee by the North Precinct in Bridgewater, in order to divide said precinct into four parts for the better accommodation of the Inhabitants of said precinct to improve the Grammar School, and having considered the same, do report as followeth ; namely, That a line be drawn from Mr. Zachariah Cary's westerly to Ephraim Churchill's, and from thence to Easton Line, and those families on the south side of said line to be the South Rick, and those on the north side of said

15

line to be the North Rick, and from said Cary's easterly to William Shaw's and from thence to Abington line, to divide the easterly part of said precinct, those families on the south side of said Road to be the South Rick, the before mentioned Ricks to be divided North and South by the Country Road.

ISSACHAR SNELL.
BARNABAS HOWARD.
MATTHEW KINGMAN.
JONATHAN CARY.

The above report being read, it was accepted, and the meeting voted "that the Grammar School be keept six weeks in each Rick." "Voted that the two Ricks on the west side of the Country Road have the Grammar School this year."

After the above division of the parish into districts, or ricks, the precinct committee had charge of the division of the school fund as it was drawn from the town treasury, and upon them devolved the duties that afterward were assigned to the committee chosen for each district.

March 4, 1794. The parish "voted to raise £15 to be assessed on the inhabitants of the parish for the purpose of English schooling." March 17, 1794. At a meeting of the parish it was "voted to chose a Committy in Each English School District to take care of the school money, and see that it is well laid out for the benefit of each Destrict." The duties of this committee were to procure rooms, teachers, fuel, etc., for the schools in their several districts.

The plan adopted in the following table is to place the first person in office at the head of the list with the year in full, and any subsequent years in an abbreviated form, as follows: 1794, 95, 97. When a person is re-elected to office during several consecutive years, the first and last years are placed in full, with a dash between, to show that the intermediate years are included: as 1801–1826. This plan has been adopted to save repetition of names, and is one which will be easily understood by the reader.

THE FOLLOWING IS A LIST OF THE SCHOOL COMMITTEE CHOSEN BY THE TOWN
FOR THE SEVERAL DISTRICTS FROM 1794 to 1826, INCLUSIVE.

Lieut. Nathaniel Orcutt, 1794.

Ensign Howard Cary, 1794, 95, 1802, 4, 6, 11, 16, 17.

Daniel Cary, 1794, 95, 1801.

Perez Southworth, 1794, 95, 1805.

Issachar Snell, Esq., 1794–1798.

Ichabod Howard, 1794, 95, 98, 99, 1800, 1, 2, 7, 19.

Levi Keith, 1794, 95.

Benjamin Howard, 1794.

Parmenas Packard, 1794, 95, 99, 1802.

Captain Lemuel Packard, 1794, 96, 1802, 8.

Barnabas Curtis, 1794, 95.

Lieut. Robert Packard, 1795–1801, 14, 21.

Daniel Manley, 1795, 1800.

Ephraim Cole, 1795, 1801, 10, 14, 18.

Capt. Jesse Perkins, 1796, 99, 1800.

Lieut. Eleazer Snow, 1796.

Job Ames, 1796.

Oliver Howard, 1796, 1803, 5.

Waldo Hayward, 1796.

John Wales, 1796, 1804.

Samuel Dike, 1796, 1803, 7.

Joseph Hayward, 1796, 1805.

Eliphalet Packard, 1797.

Moses Cary, 1797, 1814, 16.

William Brett, 1797.

Jonathan Perkins, Jr., 1797, 1806, 7, 11, 13, 16, 19.

Jeremiah Beals, 1797.

Rufus Brett, 1797.

Capt. Zebedee Snell, 1797, 98.

William Shaw, Jr., 1797.

Nathaniel Manley, 1797.

Dea. James Perkins, 1798.

Ensign Mark Perkins, 1798, 1804, 6, 8, 11, 17, 19.

Samuel Cheesman, 1798.

Timothy Ames, 1798, 1805.

Ebenezer Warren, 1798.

Seth Kingman, 1798, 1815.

Jonathan Keith, 1798, 1801, 2, 3.

Thomas Thompson, 1799, 1813, 19, 22.

Nathaniel Leach, 1799.

Zachariah Gurney, Jr., 1799, 1804, 9, 14, 18.

Benjamin Keith, 1799, 1805–1809.

Asaph Hayward, 1799.

Japhet Beals, 1799.

Noah Ames, 1799.

Josiah Perkins, 1800, 5.

Amzi Brett, 1800.

Abiah Packard, 1800.

Jonathan Cary, 1800.

Dea. David Edson, 1800, 8.

Doctor Phillip Bryant, 1800, 8, 9.

Ensign Jonathan Snow, 1800, 26.

Micah Shaw, 1801, 6, 13, 22.

Hayward Marshall, 1801, 10, 14, 24.

Barzilla Field, 1801, 5, 9, 23.

Ephraim Jackson, 1801, 4.

Samuel Brett, Jr., 1801.

Caleb Howard, 1802.

John Tilden, 1802, 7, 9, 12, 22.

Lieut. Ephraim Noyes, 1802, 4, 11, 14, 17.

Isaiah Packard, 1802, 8.

Ensign Asa Jones, 1803, 9, 18.

Job Bryant, 1803.

Asa Ford, 1803.

Cyrus Packard, 1803, 6, 15, 21.

Thomas Packard, Jr., 1803, 10.

Joseph Alden, 1803.

Capt. Abel Kingman, 1804, 22, 26.

John Howard, 1804.

Daniel Packard, 1804.

Shepard Perkins, 1804, 9, 17.

Seth Snow, 1805.

Zachariah Snell, 1805.

Abijah Knapp, 1805.

Perez Crocker, 1806, 17.

Gideon Howard, Esq., 1806, 12, 13, 15, 16.

Oliver Snell, 1806, 10.

William Edson, 1806.

Ensign Nehemiah Lincoln, 1807, 9, 12.

Seth Edson, 1807, 11.

Noah Cheesman, 1807.

Samuel Alden, Jr., 1807.

Joseph Brett, 1807, 14.

Joseph Sylvester, Jr., 1808, 14.

Daniel Howard, Esq., 1808, 9, 11.

John Ames, 1808.

Levi Packard, 1808, 13.

John Burrill, 1809.

Benjamin Ames, 1809, 14, 19, 23.

Adin Packard, Jr., 1810.

Eliphalet Kingman, 1810, 17, 20.

Barnabas Curtis, 1810.

Ebenezer Dunbar, 1810.

Jonathan Beal, 1811.

Zebedee Snell, Jr., 1811.

Caleb Jackson, 1811, 15.

Joseph Reynolds, Jr., 1811.

Silas Snow, 1812.

Turner Torrey, 1812, 14, 17, 24.

Silvanus French, 1812, 19, 23.

Jacob Fuller, 1812, 20.

Isaac Eames, 1812.

Shepard Snell, 1812.

Galen Packard, 1812, 21.

Alpha Brett, 1813.

Luke Packard, 1813, 21.

Josiah Dunbar, 1813, 18.

Micah Packard, 1813, 17, 23.

Manley Hayward, 1813, 16, 21.

Asa Howard, 1815, 22.

Capt. John Packard, 1815, 16, 19, 20.

Jeremiah Beals, Jr., 1815, 19.

Lewis Dailey, 1815.

Capt. Oliver Jackson, 1815, 21, 26.

James Cary, 1815.

Howard Packard, 1815, 17.

Isaac Keith, 1816, 26.

Enos Thayer, 1816.

Apollas Packard, 1816.

Darius Howard, 1817, 26.

Ziba Keith, 1817, 21.

Thomas Wales, 1818.

Howard Manley, 1818, 23.

Jacob Dunbar, 1818.

Ezekiel Merritt, 1818.

Samuel Packard, 1818.

Josiah Ames, 1818.

John Smith, 1818, 24.

John Crafts, 1819.

Parmenas Brett, 1819.

Jabez Kingman, 1819, 26.

David Ford, 1820.

Azor Packard, 1820, 24.

Oliver Leach, 1820.

Theron Ames, 1820.

Zenas Brett, 1820.

Isaac Packard, 1820.

Nathan Packard, 1820.

Isaac Hartwell, Jr., 1820, 22.

Nathaniel Wales, 1821.

David Battles, 1821.

Azel Gurney, 1821.

Barnabas Edson, 1821.

David Ames, 1822.

Josiah Brett, 1822.

William Tribou, 1822.

Jonas Reynolds, 1822.

Zibeon Brett, 1822, 23.

Simeon Dunbar, 1823.

Jesse Perkins, Jr., 1823, 26.

Williams Alden, 1823.

Hezekiah Packard, 1823.

Martin Southworth, 1823.

Martin Dunbar, 1823.

Isaac Curtis, 1823.

Sullivan Packard, 1824.

Charles Packard, 1824.

Samuel Dike, Jr., 1824.

Caleb Copeland, Jr., 1824.

Zophar Field, 1824.

Nahum Perkins, 1826.

Joel Ames, 1826.

This was the commencement of the practice of choosing a

committee man in the several districts to manage the affairs independently of the town.

March 16, 1795. The parish came together " to hear the Report of a committee chosen to see if they can fix upon any plan that shall operate more equally in the division of the Grammar School District."

" The committee appointed by the North Parish of Bridgewater at their meeting in November last to consider whether any alterations can be made in the Grammar School wricks in said Parish wich will be of more general advantage to the inhabitants thereof Beg leave to make the following reporte ; namely, —

" *First*, your committee are of opinion that the South west and South east wricks, as to their extent and bounds, remain as they now are. *Secondly*, your committee are of opinion that it will be for the general advantage of the inhabitants of the North west and North East wricks to be divided into three wricks in the following manner, and form, to wit, The first or north west wrick to be bounded Northerly and Westerly, on Stoughton and Easton, Southerly on the South west wrick and easterly on the river whareon Reynolds sawmill stands, including also Lieut. Parmenas Packard, and Benjamin Silvesters familys. The *Second* or north wrick to be bounded northerly on Stoughton, westerly on Reynolds mill River aforesaid, Southerly on the Southern wrick, and easterly on trout Brook excluding the before mentioned families of Lieut. Parmenas Packard and Benjamin Silvester, including Daniel Howard, Esq., Gideon Howard and Thomas White and their families before mentioned. The *Third* or North East wrick to be bounded easterly and northerly on Abington and Randolph ; westerly, on Trout Book, and southerly on the South east wrick, excluding Daniel Howard, Esq., Gideon Howard and Thomas White's families, before mentioned. *Thirdly*, your committee are also of opinion that the Grammar School ought to be kept in the two southern wricks every other year, — one half in the South west wrick, and the other half in the South east wrick. We are also of opinion that said Grammar School ought to be kept in the three northern wricks every other year in the following proportion ; namely, one Third part of the time in the north west wrick, one third part in the middle or north wrick, and one third part of the time in the North East wrick. *Fourthly*, your committee are furthermore of the opinion that the school in the north or middle wrick ought to be kept alternately at the school House near Nathaniel Snells and the school House near the Meeting House, and that the school in the South east wrick ought to be kept at or between Seth Kingmans, Abel Kingmans and Eliab Packards, and that the School in the North east wricks

ought to be kept alternately at the school house near Deacon Jonathan
Carys, and the School house near William Shaws, unless the inhabitants of
said wrick can agree on a more central place, which we judge to be at or between Ames Packards, Josiah Packards, Josiah Eames, and Perez South-
worths.

" All wich is submitted to Said parish for consedoration and acceptance.

ISSACHAR SNELL, ⎫
ELEAZER SNOW, ⎪
DANIEL HOWARD, ⎬Committee."
JESSE PERKINS, ⎪
LEMUEL PACKARD, ⎭

A true record.

DANIEL CARY, Precinct Clerk.

Again, the grammar school did not suit all the people in
the parish; for, November 14, 1796, we find a meeting called
" To see if some more advantageous method cannot be de-
vised for the improvement of the Grammar School," at which
it was " voted to postpone the subject to the next March
meeting."

March 9, 1797. " Voted to choose a committee of one
from each school District, to make some alteration in the
Grammar School Districts, and report at next fall meeting."
Daniel Howard, Esq., Issachar Snell, Esq., Waldo Hayward,
Capt. Lemuel Packard, Moses Cary, Capt. Zebedee Snell,
Capt. Jesse Perkins, Jeremiah Thayer, Jr., Barnabas Curtis,
Daniel Manley Jr., were the committee who made the follow-
ing report November 13, 1797 : " The committee appointed
to report a plan for keeping the Grammar School have agreed
upon the following mode ; namely, —

" *First*, That Said School shall not be kept in a dwelling House.   *Second*,
That Said School be kept in each English district through the parish, provided they Shall build School Houses and fit them with seats in the same
manner the School house near the meeting house is and otherwise convenient
in the judgment of the Selectmen for the time being, and find sufficiency of
Fire wood.   *Third*, In case any district shall not comply with the forgoing
conditions the school is to be keept in the next Distrect according to their
turn.   The school shall be keept first in Issachar Snells, 2d in Jesse Perkins,
3d Jonathan Carys, 4th Amzi Bretts, 5th William Shaws, 6th Ichabod Ed-
sons, 7th Charles Snells, 8th Ephraim Coles, 9th Daniel Manlys, 10th Capt.

Zebedee Snells — all of which is Submitted to the parish for consideration and acceptance.

" The above report was accepted and agreed to by the Parish.

" A trew record.

" DANIEL CARY, Parish Clerk."

Previous to the organization of the town in 1821, the North Parish had the charge of the school funds which were set apart by the town to them, and the precinct committee were the committee when no others were chosen especially for that purpose. The amount was assessed upon the inhabitants according to their valuation. We find no systematic account of the amount appropriated yearly, or the manner in which it was spent, but presume it was well expended. The schools were usually from six to eight weeks in a year, and we should judge the people would make the most of their time. We have found occasionally separate amounts additional to that voted by the town to be assessed by the parish, as March 16, 1795. " Voted £15 for English Schooling." Also February 27, 1798. " Voted to raise two hundred dollars for the use of schooling." This above vote was reconsidered August 19, 1798. The precinct voted sums only when an extra outlay had been made, or a schoolhouse built. The first appropriations are from 1821 to 1825, inclusive, when the sum of six hundred and twenty-five dollars was voted. Early the next year, 1826, the State passed a general law, placing the entire care and superintendence of the public schools in a town in the hands of a committee which consisted of three, five, or seven persons, whose duty it was to examine into the qualifications of teachers, and to visit the several schools at the commencement and closing of them. Their duty was to provide books for those that fail to provide for themselves, under certain rules, and also to determine what books should be used in the schools.

The following is a list of the school committee from **1827**
to 1864, inclusive, together with the years of their election : —

Eliab Whitman, 1827, 40, 41, 42, 43, 44, 46, 47.
Linus Howard, 1827, 29, 30, 31.
Dr. Nathan Perry, 1827.
Rev. D. Huntington, 1828, 40, 41, 42, 43, 44, 45, 46, 47,
Dr. John S. Crafts, 1828, 29, 30.
Rev. John Goldsbury, 1828.
Heman Packard, 1829, 30, 31, 32, 33, 34.
Albert Smith, 1829, 35, 38, 39.
Jesse Perkins, 1829, 30, 31, 32, 33, 36 37 39
Jabez Kingman, 1830.
Erastus Wales, 1832, 33.
Lucius Kingman, 1834, 35.
Zibeon Shaw, 1834, 35, 36, 37.
Joseph A. Rainsford, 1836, 37.
Isaac Eames, 1838.
Josiah W. Kingman 1838.
Rev. John Dwight, 1838.
Rev. Paul Couch, 1838, 39, 40, 41, 42, 43, 44, 45, 46, 47, 48, 49, 50, 51,
52, 53, 54, 56, 57, 58.
Rev. A. S. Dudley, 1845.
Adoniram Bisbee, 1848, 49, 50, 51, 52.
Rev. William Whiting, 1848, 49, 50.
Henry A. Ford, 1851, 52, 56, 57, 58, 59, 60, 61.
Rev. Henry Baylies, 1853, 54.
Rev. A. B. Wheeler, 1854, 55.
Rev. Warren Goddard, 1853,
George T. Ryder, 1855.
Charles C. Bixby, 1855.
Rev. Charles L. Mills, 1856, 57, 58, 59, 60.
Elbridge G. Ames, 1859, 60, 61, 62, 63.
Galen E. Pratt, 1860, 61, 62, 63.
Rev. Charles W. Wood, 1862, 63, 64.
Augustus F. Jones, 1864.
Rev. F. A. Crafts, 1864.

This committee were also required to make an annual report of the number of schools, scholars, amount appropriated,
and such other details as was deemed of interest to the secretary of the commonwealth. From these reports, now on
file in his office, from North Bridgewater, we find the follow-

ing reports, which we publish to exhibit at a glance the condition of the schools at different dates: —

Year.	No. scholars attending school.	Amount appropriated.	No. schools in town.
1827	425	$800	11
1828	425	800	11
1829	550	800	11
1830	580	800	11
1831	593	800	11
1832	569	800	11
1833	669	800	11
1834	650	1000	11
1835	657	1000	11
1836	676	1000	11

We see by the above returns that, prior to the year 1837, the amount annually appropriated for the support of the public schools in the town has not increased in proportion to the increase in the number of scholars. During this year a change was made in the laws regulating the schools throughout the commonwealth, by the organization of the " *Board of Education* " in June, 1837, and by which all the school committees in the several towns were required to make a detailed report to them, annually, of the condition of the schools in their respective towns, which report was either to be read in open town meeting, or printed for circulation among the inhabitants. The effect of these reports has been of universal advantage to the commonwealth, as by this system the experience of each town is laid open to the others, so that they may be benefited by another's experience. By it the several portions of the State are brought nearer each other, causing a spirit of emulation to pervade the entire community. It is this that has given the Old Bay State a name worthy of being handed down to future generations, and has made her so celebrated for her educational advantages

The returns above named were usually made in March or April, and presented to the town for their approval. Below we present the reader with a copy of the returns from

1838, the year following the organization of the Board, to the year 1864, inclusive.

Year.	No. schools.	Amount appropriated by taxation.	No. scholars between 4 and 16.
1838	11	$1000	704
1839	13	1188.83	717
1840	11	1200	701
1841	11	1500	678
1842	11	1500	713
1843	11	1500	739
1844	11	1761.56	799
1845	13	1926.20	800
1846	13	1926.20	800
1847	13	1630	790
1848	13	1630	817
1849	15	2000	891

Year.	No. schools.	Amount appropriated by taxation.	No. scholars between 5 and 15.
1850	16	2000	802
1851	16	2000	867
1852	16	2600	905
1853	16	2600	979
1854	16	3000	1043
1855	18	3000	1124
1856	19	3500	1135
1857	18	3500	1135
1858	19	3500	1191
1859	19	3500	1174
1860	19	3500	1177
1861	20	3500	1263
1862	21	3500	1271
1863	21	3500	1343
1864	21	3500	1302

NOTE. The reports in the several towns being made in the early part of the year, the figures opposite the dates above are, in fact, the record of the preceding year, as, in 1838, the return being for the year ending in March, it would be the record for 1837, and so on to the end of the list.

For eight years previous to 1864 the town of North Bridgewater has not expended as much money per scholar as most of the towns in the State. In that year the people with a commendable spirit added one thousand dollars to their appropriation, making it $4,500, which sum is divided among the several districts through the town: also another appropriation of $1,200 for high school purposes, making a total of $5,700 for schools. To show how the town has been in past times, we will present to the reader a few figures for 1863 with an appropriation of $3,500. There are in the commonwealth three hundred and thirty-three towns. Of this number three hundred and six towns pay more for each scholar between the ages of five and fifteen than this town, while there are but twenty-six towns that do not pay as much. There are

Four that pay one dollar and over.
Fifty-one that pay two dollars and over.
Ninety-nine that pay three dollars and a fraction.
Ninety-two   "   " four   "   "   "
Thirty-six   "   " five   "   "   "
Nineteen   "   " six   "   "   "
Ten   "   " seven   "   "   "
Eleven   "   " eight   "   "   "
Four   "   " nine   "   "   "
One   "   " ten   "   "   "
One   "   " twelve   "   "   "
Two   "   " fourteen   "   "   "
One   "   " nineteen   "   " and is the highest town in the State.
North Bridgewater pays $2.606 per scholar.
East Bridgewater   "   3.369   "   "
West Bridgewater   "   3.518   "   "
Bridgewater   "   3.597   "   "

In comparison with the other towns in Plymouth County, while this town stands second in point of population, fifth in valuation, fourth in the number of her schools, yet she pays the smallest sum per scholar of any town in the county. We think, however, that the public sentiment has begun to change in regard to the great importance of keeping up the schools, and the additional sum appropriated in 1864 will give a new impulse to the cause of popular education. September 5, 1864, a new high school was opened in the building formerly occupied by Mr. S. D. Hunt for school purposes; and judging by the appearance of the school at the end of the first term, it will be a valuable addition to the educational department of the town.

During the first settlement of the North Parish, there was but one school district, and that included the entire parish. Only one teacher was required and that was usually the minister of the parish, or some person sufficiently " larned " to teach the young to " Read, Wright, and Sifer," which at that time was all that was deemed necessary for common business pursuits, except those intending to enter some professional calling.

As the different portions of the precinct became settled, movable schools were held in private dwellings, mechanic shops, and cornhouses, or such places as could be best and most easily procured. The minds of the people were occupied in agricultural pursuits, clearing land, and providing for the support of their families, and such other matters as were necessary for subsistence. They were like all people in new places : they had not an abundance of money or means to do with as at the present day, and he was lucky who could be spared from labor long enough to get even six weeks' schooling in a year.

In 1751, the people saw the necessity of a division of the school funds, and for the purpose of dividing the time equally and accommodating all portions of the precinct, voted to divide the parish into three school districts, or " Ricks." Again, in 1784, the parish was divided into four districts, or " Ricks," and the school was kept in the two westerly districts, which were west of the present Main Street, the first year, and the two easterly districts to have it the next year. Again, in 1795, the two northerly districts were divided into three districts, making five in the parish. In 1794, a system of choosing a district " committee man " to look after the

CENTRE SCHOOL-HOUSE (District No. 1).

NORTH CENTRE SCHOOL-HOUSE (District No. 12.)

schools in the several districts was adopted, which served to give new interest in school matters. In 1797, a committee of one from each district were appointed to rearrange the "keeping of the School." This committee reported against keeping schools in private houses, and in favor of having schools kept in order around the town, provided each district would furnish a schoolhouse and find fuel. Various changes were made in the division of the territory till, at the present time, there are fourteen school districts in the town.

No. 1, or "CENTRE."

The first house erected in this district was near the old church; the next was situated just south of the present hotel and on the spot where Kingman's brick block now stands. The third was located on School Street, east of the hotel and near the present new house. The present building was erected in 1847, and is a neat, roomy building, two stories in height, with a cupola and bell, and is painted white, with green blinds, and enclosed with a substantial fence.

NO 2, OR HOWARD.

This district comprises the northerly portion of the town, near Stoughton line. The first house erected in this part of the town was built previous to 1795, and was removed in 1860 to give place for a new and larger edifice. The present building was erected during the years 1860 and 1861, under the direction of Lucien B. Keith, Charles S. Johnson, Nahum Battles, Willard Howard, and Henry Howard as building committee, and who were the trustees in behalf of the district. The building is fifty by thirty-three feet, with twenty-three feet posts. The contractor and master-builder was John F. Beal, of Stoughton, who performed his part in a faithful and workmanlike manner. The school-room is thirty-five by forty-two feet, with seats for eighty scholars, which are of the modern style, furnished by Mr. W. G. Shattuck, of Boston. Around the outside of the room are seats for sixty scholars more. The rooms are well furnished with blackboards. There is a large room in the second story, well adapted for public gatherings of any kind, furnished with settees. There is also a retiring room in the house, fifteen feet square, with seats for those wishing to remain during intermission. In the entry is a large amount of wardrobe hooks and iron sinks for the use of the pupils. The arrangement of the house is excellent, and the interior as well as exterior appearance reflects great credit upon the building committee. The house was dedicated March 20, 1861, with the following exercises: Voluntary; Invocacation, by Rev. N. B. Blanchard; Singing, by the children; Remarks, by Galen E. Pratt, of the school committee; Address, by Mr. Farwell, the teacher at that time; Finale, Singing, under the direction of Robert Sumner, of Stoughton.

NO. 3 IS "WEST SHARES, OR NORTHWEST BRIDGEWATER."

This district is provided with a small, neat schoolhouse, situated upon the road leading from the centre village to Stoughton. It consists of a one-story building, painted white, with green blinds.

NO. 4 IS "TILDEN."

This building is situated on the Boston and Taunton Turnpike, and near the road leading from Easton to North Bridgewater Village, and near to the shoe manufactory of H. T. Marshall; it is a small building, similar to that at the West Shares.

NO. 5 IS THE "AMES" DISTRICT.

Situated on the road leading to Easton from the Centre Village, and near the residence of the late Dr. Fiske Ames.

NO. 6, OR CAMPELLO DISTRICT.

The first schoolhouse in this village was one of the first

in the town; was erected previous to 1784. This was sold at auction, and removed by Major Nathan Hayward to the north part of the town, in 1842, and a new one erected by Bela Keith, twenty-eight by eighteen feet, at an expense of about five hundred dollars, one story in height, painted white. In 1854 this house was raised, and one story added, and in 1862 a new house was built by Otis Cobb, costing four hundred and fifty dollars, situated south of the old building. The time is not far distant when these two buildings must give place to one large and more commodious building.

NO. 7, OR "COPELAND."

There have been three houses in this district. The first was built about 1800. The present neat and tidy house was erected in 1852; is a one-story building, painted and blinded, and is an ornament to that portion of the town, when compared to the old red schoolhouse of ancient days. This district is situated about one mile east from the village of Campello, on the east side of Salisbury River, and the bounds of which extend to West Bridgewater line.

NO. 8, OR "SHAW'S."

This district was one of the early formed, the old house being built previous to 1794. The present house was erected in 1843, costing about five hundred dollars, one story high and painted; is located on or near the same spot that the old house stood, which is near to what is called "Shaw's Corner."

NO. 9, OR "CARY HILL."

This is one of the oldest districts in town, a house having been built previous to 1794. It is situated in the north-east part of the town, upon a high spot of land called "Cary Hill." First house burned in March, 1840, rebuilt by Marcus Packard, in July, same year, costing four hundred and twenty-five dollars.

NO. 10 IS THE "FIELD DISTRICT."

The school in this district is situated on a prominent height of land, on the south side of Prospect Street, between the houses of John Field, and the late Joseph Brett. They have a new house erected within a short time.

NO. 11, OR "SPRAGUE'S."

This portion of the town has had two schoolhouses. The first was built about 1800; the second was built in 1852, under the care of Chandler Sprague, Esq., and is a neat, two-story building, with a cupola containing a bell, the whole painted white, with green blinds, and is located in a very sightly position.

NO. 12, OR "NORTH WING."

This is a comparatively new district. It was formed of a portion of the Centre District, being set apart from them in 1846. At first a large, two-story house was erected, but of late it has increased in numbers to such an extent that in a few years a second house was erected for the primary department, and both are well filled with pupils.

NO. 13, OR "SOUTH WING."

This, like the North Wing District, is also a new district, they having been set off by themselves at the same time the Centre was divided, and the North Wing taken from them, in 1846. A new schoolhouse was erected near the residence of Mr. Sumner A. Hayward, on the east side of Main Street, and has quite a large school.

NO. 14, OR "SNOW'S."

This district comprises the territory between West Shares and Tilden Districts. The house is situated near the First Methodist Church, on the turnpike, and has been erected but a few years.

ADELPHIAN ACADEMY.

About the middle of August, 1844, two young men, brothers, who had just finished their collegiate studies, came into town, entire strangers, without letters of introduction, or money, and opened a school in a building owned by Major Nathan Hayward, south of the hotel and quite near the "Old Unitarian Church." They commenced with thirty students, September 4, 1844, and steadily increased in numbers as follows: the first term they had forty-six students; second term, fifty; third term, ninety-six; fourth term, sixty-nine; fifth term, one hundred and twenty-one. The second year the building proved inadequate to their wants, and the church above named was procured for the same purpose. The school continued in favor and was doing well, when a meeting was held to consider the propriety of erecting a suitable building for the permanent establishing of the academy. Three thousand dollars were agreed upon as the amount needed to accomplish the object: Failing to get enough subscribed, the project was abandoned for a time. Struggling against adverse circumstances, and after much thought and many solicitations to go elsewhere, they concluded to remain at North Bridgewater, and to make that town a permanent home. A small hillock of about four acres, a short distance north of the railroad depot, was purchased, which they called Montello, upon which they erected buildings suitable for their purpose, involving an expenditure of nearly ten thousand dollars. The friends of the enterprise made them a dedicatory visit soon after the completion of the buildings, and presented them with a valuable bell for the academy building. In the spring of 1847, an Act of Incorporation was granted to the proprietors with corporate powers. The following is a copy of the Act: —

" Be it enacted by the Senate and House of Representatives in General Court assembled, and by Authority of the Same as follows : —

17

" Silas L. Loomis, L. F. C. Loomis, Nathan Jones, and their associates and successors are hereby made a corporation by the name of the Adelphian Academy, to be established in the town of North Bridgewater in the county of Plymouth, with all the powers and privileges, and subject to all the duties, restrictions, and liabilities, set forth in the forty-fourth chapter of the Revised Statutes."

This corporation had permission to hold real estate to the amount of fifteen thousand dollars, and personal estate to the amount of ten thousand dollars, to be exclusively devoted to the purposes of education.

Approved March 11, 1847.

The following were elected officers of the institution: Joseph Sylvester, *President;* L. C. Loomis, *Secretary;* S. L Loomis, *Treasurer.* Hon. Jesse Perkins, L. C. Loomis, Josiah W. Kingman, Edwin H. Kingman, David Cobb, Newton Shaw, Silas L. Loomis, George Clark, Caleb Copeland, Franklin Ames, Isaac Eames, *Trustees.*

This institution continued to increase in numbers, until a high school was thought of being established in the town, which the Messrs. Loomis supposed might injure their school, when they concluded to close it as soon as it might be done without too great a sacrifice. Thus the academy was brought to a close, in 1854, after a term of ten years from its commencement. During this time they had gathered a library of over one thousand volumes and a cabinet of over ten thousand specimens. The following are among those that had taught in that institution: —

Prof. Silas L. Loomis, A. M., M. D., now surgeon in the U. S. Army, Prof. L. C. Loomis, A. M., M. D., now president of the Wesleyan Female College, Wilmington, Delaware, J. E. Marsh, A. M., M. D., now surgeon in the U. S. Army, Rev. Horace C. Atwater, A. M., Hon. Isaac Atwater, A. M., Chief Justice of Iowa, Rev. J. H. Burr, A. M., Rev. Daniel Steele, A. M., J. Mason Everett, E. A. Kingsbury, Maximilian Hall, B. A. Tidd, Miss Emma L. Loomis, Miss Susan T. Howard,

Otis S. Moulton, Annie E. Belcher, S. M. Saunders, Emery Seaman, O. W. Winchester, A. B., Mrs. Mary A. Winchester.

The building formerly used as an academy has since been removed to the corner of Centre and Montello Streets, near the railroad depot, and is used as a manufactory. It was a three-story building, painted white, with green blinds, and crowned with a cupola for a bell.

NORTH BRIDGEWATER ACADEMY.

This institution was founded by Mr. Sereno D. Hunt, who came from Concord, Mass., where he had been keeping a high school for eight years. It commenced in the middle of May, 1855. He first purchased the building previously used as a house of worship by the " New Jerusalem Society " at an expense of two thousand dollars, and remodelled it into a well-arranged and comfortable schoolroom, and fitted it with modern desks and chairs, of the most approved kind, sufficient for ninety-six scholars, at an additional expense of upwards of three thousand dollars. The first term commenced with seventy-five scholars; the second term had over one hundred scholars; and the average of attendance for the first five years was seventy-five scholars per term. After the breaking out of the rebellion, for the last four years of its existence, it had an average of over sixty pupils, and the last two terms were larger than for several terms previous. Owing to a large proportion of the students belonging in the town, it was thought the establishment of a high school there would tend to diminish or interfere with the success of the institution. It was therefore brought to a close at the end of its thirty-seventh term.

There were connected with the school philosophical and chemical apparatus, a cabinet of minerals, shells, etc., and a small but choice library. The principal, Mr. S. D. Hunt,

was assisted at different times by the following teachers:
Mrs. Hunt, wife of the principal, Miss Mary H. Clough,
Miss Clara Kingman, Miss Sarah B. Fiske, Miss E. Marion
Hurlbut, Miss Helen Eveleth, Edwin Hunt, A. B., Miss
Hattie F. Stacy, and Miss Julia M. Howard.

PRIVATE SCHOOLS.

Among the most prominent of these institutions in the
town is Mrs. Nathan Jones's school. We take pleasure in
recording the fact that for more than thirty years Mrs.
Jones has kept a private boarding-school for children of
both sexes at her residence ; and few there are to be found
of the young persons, natives of the town, who have not
attended "Mrs. Jones's School," at least for one term.

Deacon Heman Packard kept a select school at the north
end of the town on Prospect Hill for several years, previous
to his leaving town for New Orleans, which had a good reputation.

Rev. E. Porter Dyer kept a select school in the town in
1835 and 1836. How long he continued, we have no partic-
lars from which to write.

CHAPTER VII.

BIOGRAPHICAL HISTORY.

List of Graduates of Colleges. — Students of Normal School. — Rev. John Porter. — Rev. Asa Meech. — Rev. Daniel Huntington. — Rev. James Thompson. — Rev. John Porter, Jr. — Rev. Huntington Porter. — Rev. Eliphalet Porter, D. D. — Rev. Thomas Crafts. — Rev. Asa Packard. — Rev. Hezekiah Packard. — Rev. Joshua Cushman. — Rev. Napthali Shaw. — Rev. Theophilus Packard. — Rev. Jonas Perkins. — Rev. Eliphalet P. Crafts. — Rev. Levi Packard. — Rev. Austin Cary. — Rev. Zechariah Howard.

LIST OF GRADUATES FROM DIFFERENT COLLEGES OF PERSONS FROM NORTH BRIDGEWATER, SO FAR AS CAN BE ASCERTAINED.

Names.	Date.	Institution.	Professional Calling
James Thompson,	1761,	Princeton, N. J.,	Clergyman and preceptor.
John Porter, Jr.	1770,	Harvard,	Clergyman.
Huntington Porter,	1777,	Harvard,	Clergyman.
Jonathan Porter,	1777,	Harvard,	Physician.
Eliphalet Porter,	1777,	Harvard,	Clergyman.
Thomas Crafts,	1783,	Harvard,	Clergyman.
Asa Packard,	1783,	Harvard,	Clergyman.
Zechariah Howard,	1784,	Harvard,	Clergyman.
Hezekiah Packard,	1787,	Harvard,	Clergyman.
Joshua Cushman,	1787,	Harvard,	Clergyman and statesman.
Naphtali Shaw,	1790,	Dartmouth,	Clergyman.
Theophilus Packard,	1796,	Dartmouth,	Clergyman.
Daniel Howard,	1797,	Harvard,	Attorney-at-Law.
Issachar Snell,	1797,	Harvard,	Physician.
Lucius Cary,	1798,	Brown University,	Attorney-at-Law.
Daniel Noyes,	1813,	Yale,	Merchant.
Jonas Perkins,	1813,	Brown University,	Clergyman.
Frederick Crafts,	1816,	Brown University,	Preceptor.
Jonathan P. Crafts,	1817,	Brown University,	
Austin Packard,	1821,	Brown University,	Attorney-at-Law.
Levi Packard,	1821,	Brown University,	Clergyman.
Eliphalet P. Crafts,	1821,	Brown University,	Clergyman.
Thomas Jefferson Snow,	1823,	Brown University,	Preceptor.
Lucius Kingman,	1830,	Brown University,	Attorney-at-Law.
Abel W. Kingman,	1830,	Amherst,	Physician.
Austin Cary,	1837,	Amherst,	Clergyman.
Samuel Dike,	1838,	Brown University,	Clergyman.

Names.	Date.	Institution.	Professional Calling.
Abel Kingman Packard,	1845,	Amherst,	Clergyman.
David Temple Packard,	1850,	Amherst,	Clergyman.
Lysander Dickerman,	1851,	Brown University,	Clergyman.
Augustus T. Jones,	1856,	Yale,	Editor and Publisher.
John P. Apthorp,	1861,	Amherst.	
Heman Packard DeForest,	1862,	Yale.	
Ebenezer Couch,	1864,	Harvard.	

Miss Elizabeth A. Packard, M. D., graduated at N. E. F. Medical College.
John Goddard entered at Amherst, 1858, but owing to ill-health did not graduate.

Henry T. Eddy is now in Yale College.

LIST OF PERSONS HAVING ATTENDED THE STATE NORMAL SCHOOL AT BRIDGE-
WATER, WITH THE YEARS OF THEIR ATTENDANCE, MOST OF WHOM ARE
GRADUATES.

Mr. Lucius Gurney, ... 1841	Miss Almaria Kingman, . . 1858
Miss Melinda A. Carey, . . 1841	Miss Arabella Ames, ... 1859
Miss Vesta Holbrook, . . . 1841	Mr. Henry Manley, . . . 1859
Mr. Chauncy Conant, . . . 1842	Miss Lizzie A. Kingman, . . 1860
Mr. Nathaniel Wales, . . . 1842	Mr. Isaac Kingman Harris, . 1860
Mr. Elbridge G. Ames, . . 1843	Mr. Thomas S. Kingman, . . 1861
Mr. Lysander Dickerman, . . 1843	Miss Mary E. Hughes, . . 1863
Mr. Frederick Perkins, . . 1843	Miss Julia A. Packard, . . . 1863
Mr. Josiah V. Bisbee, . . . 1853	Miss Mary A. Hollis, . . . 1863
Mr. Augustus Remick, . . 1857	Miss Martha J. Packard, . . 1863
Miss Harriet N. Kingman, . . 1857	Miss Esther M. Simmons, . 1863
Mr. Ellis V. Lyon, ... 1858	Mr. Charles H. W. Wood, . . 1863
Mr. Jonas Reynolds, ... 1858	Miss Lucia A. Kingman, . . 1864

REV. JOHN PORTER was the son of Samuel and Mary
Porter, of Abington, Mass.; born in 1716; graduated at
Harvard College in 1736; commenced preaching as a candidate for the "Fourth Church in Bridgewater" (now the
First Church of North Bridgewater") in December, 1739.
Soon after the incorporation of the North Parish, he received
a call to settle with them as pastor, August 25, 1740, which
call he accepted, and was ordained October 15, 1740. Mr.
Porter entered upon the duties of his office with all the advantages which a faithful church and affectionate society could
afford. Their hearts were deservedly united in him, and
seldom has any minister of the gospel been enabled to exert

a more general and salutary influence over the people of his charge. His qualifications, both natural and acquired, were peculiarly respectable. He was taught, not only of men, but of God. Much of what was estimable in his Christian and ministerial character he gratefully ascribed to the labors of that justly celebrated and eminently useful servant of Christ, the Rev. Mr. Whitefield, under whose ministry of the word he received the most deep and salutary impressions a little before his entrance upon the duties of the sacred office. With that great and good man he formed an intimate acquaintance, invited him to his pulpit, and, with his beloved flock, enjoyed the benefit of his evangelical instructions. This circumstance undoubtedly contributed to increase that zealous spirit of reformation by which the Rev. Mr. Porter's long and faithful ministry was so happily characterized. He clearly exhibited and ably defended the great doctrines of the gospel, and, though not fond of controversy, wielded the sword of the Spirit with uncommon skill, vigor, and success against all the assailants of evangelical truth. His labors among his people in the sanctuary and from house to house were greatly blessed. Mr. Porter continued to labor with this people until September 1, 1800, when, finding the infirmities of age creeping upon him, and a frame worn out in the service of his Master, he asked for assistance in his labors. His son-in-law, Rev. Thomas Crafts, and Rev. Asa Meech, then a candidate for the ministry, from Connecticut, came to his help, and Mr. Meech received a call to become a colleague pastor with him, which call he accepted, and was ordained October 15, 1800. Rev. Mr. Porter continued to perform pastoral labor, preaching occasionally, till his decease. The last sermon he preached was from John ix. 4: " I must work the works of him that sent me while it is day : the night cometh when no man can work." This sermon is often spoken of as having been peculiarly and prophetically appropriate, and most tenderly affecting to those who were listening to the last message of truth and love from the lips of one whom very many regarded as a *spiritual father*, and *all*, as an affectionate and *faithful friend*. He departed this life March 12, 1802, in the eighty-seventh year of his age, and in the sixty-second year of his ministry. His sickness was of three weeks' duration, which commenced about one week after the delivery of the above-named discourse. His wife, with whom he had so long and so happily lived for more than one half a century, died about four months previous to his death. This circumstance seemed to render his death more welcome to him than otherwise. She was a woman of very exemplary habits, and a devoted mother in Israel. His funeral was attended by Rev. Zedekiah Sanger, D. D., of Bridgewater, Mass. His remains lie buried in the graveyard near the residence of the late William Tribou, at Campello. On the gravestone may be found the following inscription: "They that be wise shall shine as the brightness of the firmament; and they that turn many to righteousness, as the stars forever and ever." To the virtues of Rev. Mr. Porter's private life, and the usefulness of his ministerial qualifications and labors, the affection and respect with which he was viewed by his family and acquaintances, the love and veneration of the large and respectable religious society with which he so long lived in harmony, and labored with success, the manner in which his services were accepted in other societies where he occasionally preached, and the lasting reputation he maintained in the church, are the most unequivocal and honorable testimonies. To the influence of this good man, more than any other thing, is the community indebted for the love of order, industry, economy, enterprise, and religious character of many of the descendants of that society. His influence had very much to do with formation of the character of the early inhabitants of the town of North Bridgewater.

D. Huntington

Rev. Asa Meech. (See page 27.)

Rev. Daniel Huntington was the son of Gen. Jedediah,
and grandson of Gen. Jabez Huntington, of Norwich, Conn.,
both of whom were generals in the army of the Revolution,
1775, also brother of the late Rev. Joshua Huntington, of the
Old South Church, Boston. He was born at Norwich,
Conn., October 17, 1788; graduated at Yale College, New
Haven, Conn., in 1807; studied theology; and was first
ordained at North Bridgewater, October 28, 1812, where
he remained as pastor of the First Congregational Church
until prostrating disease compelled him to retire from
that field of labor, greatly to his own grief and that of
a devoted church and society, in March, 1833, being dismissed by council March 27, 1833. In May following, he
removed his family to New London. After a brief respite
from pastoral labors, he gained sufficient strength to gratify
his fine literary taste in the instruction of successive classes
of young ladies in the higher branches of an educational
course while a resident of New London, the city of his birth
and death. In this employment, combined with occasional
preaching as returning health permitted, seven years passed
away usefully and pleasantly. At the end of this period his
heart yearned for a return to the labors of his love ; and receiving an earnest call from a portion of his original church *
and congregation to take charge of them in the Lord, he
cheerfully consented to the arrangement, and was received
not only by them, but by the original church and all the
churches and pastors who had known his going out and coming in, in former years, with open arms. His installation took
place January 1, 1840, where he continued to labor for thirteen years as a gospel preacher, winning souls to Christ, and
making glad the hearts of all by his tender love and faithful-

* South Congregational Church at Campello

18

ness.   At the end of that period he tendered his resignation, May 2, 1853, which was accepted, and he was permitted to retire to the home of his youth, and pass the evening of his days amid the scenes of his earliest aspirations.   From that day, for about six years, till near the time of his departure, he continued to preach the gospel " in season and out of season " as " the open door was set before him," all the while setting his house in order.   At the moment when his Master called him, he was diligent in business, fervent in spirit, serving the Lord, preaching his last sermon to the mission church at Mohegan just four weeks before the messenger of Death met him.*   The physical sufferings of his last days were very great, owing to the complicated diseases which, with fierce strength, assailed his delicate frame ; but his patience and faith failed not ; no complaining or murmuring word fell from his lips ; his mind was clear and unclouded to the last.   To the affectionate daughter, who was trying to arrange the pillows for his aching head, he said, " Let me go, for the day breaketh," and to another who asked if he would not lie down, he answered, " Lay me down in Jesus' arms ; " " Other refuge have I none."   To a brother according to the flesh, who said to him, " I hope you can say with the apostle, ' I know in whom I have believed,' " he replied, after a moment's pause, " I am persuaded that he is able to keep that which I have committed to him against that day."   Thus closed a life eminently devoted in its progress to the happiness of his family and friends, to the honor of his Redeemer, and the salvation of men, in peace, and the joyful hope of a glorious immortality.   Mr. Huntington was a man of refined sensibilities, generous sympathies, unfeigned humility, and extreme modesty, that imposed a restraint on the putting forth of his native genius : of pleasant aspect, voice, and manner, of genial humor, and gifted with good judgment.   He sought

* His death took place May 21, 1858, at New London, Conn.

to make home agreeable to children and guests; as a man and companion, affable, courteous, and true; a zealous defender of the faith, a clear, logical, earnest minister of the New Testament. As a pastor, he had few equals, being eminently kind, sympathizing, prudent, and studious. As a husband, father, brother, son, he was affectionate and faithful, and greatly beloved in his domestic and social relations; distinguished above most others in consolation to the afflicted and bereaved. His preaching was such as might convince any one of his sincerity and belief in those truths which he professed to believe. He sought not for abstruse matters, hard to be understood, neither did he aim at beauty of style, or pomp of display, either in language or person, but was simple, earnest, scriptural, practical. Many must have felt upon learning of his death that they had lost a friend. All who knew him will acknowledge that a good man has gone. Thus has ended the life of one who, when he first entered the ministry, declared his intention to continue in that profession, God permitting, to his death.

> "Rest here, blest saint, till from his throne,
> The morning break and pierce the shade."

REV. JAMES THOMPSON was son of Archibald Thompson, who came from Ireland to America in 1724; graduated at the New Jersey College, Princeton, N. J., in 1761; became a clergyman; preached only a short time; was a preceptor of an academy at Charleston, S. C.

REV. JOHN PORTER, JR., was son of Rev. John and Mary (Huntington) Porter; was born in North Bridgewater, February 27, 1752; graduated at Yale College, New Haven, Conn., in 1770; studied divinity, and became a minister. Soon after the war broke out between England and America in 1775, he received a captain's commission, and went into the army, where he is said to have been a superior officer. From captain he was promoted to major; left the army but a short time before peace was declared. He afterward went to the West Indies, and there died.

Rev. Huntington Porter was son of Rev. John and Mary (Huntington) Porter; was born March 27, 1755; graduated at Harvard College, Cambridge, Mass., in 1777; married Susannah Sargent, of Haverhill, Mass.; commenced preaching at Rye, N. H., in August, 1784, supplying the pulpit till, December 29, 1784, he was ordained as colleague pastor with Rev. Samuel Parsons. He continued to preach in that place for upwards of fifty years. The people of his society were for a long series of years remarkable for their unanimity in their religious as well as civil concerns, and for more than thirty years there was no division. All attended his church; union and peace was the prevailing sentiment among the people. After that time other denominations sprung up; still he continued to labor until 1828, when the civil contract between him and his society was dissolved. He continued to preach occasionally for several years after that time, till near the close of his life.

Rev. Eliphalet Porter, D. D., was born in North Bridgewater June 11, 1758; was son of Rev. John and Mary (Huntington) Porter; graduated at Harvard College 1777; was settled as pastor of the " First Church " in Roxbury, Mass., October 2, 1782. He was called to supply a vacancy caused by the death of Rev. Amos Adams, who died in 1775. Of his pastoral labors, we may say they were well suited to the times in which he lived. Frequent visits for social intercourse were not expected, and for these he had neither taste nor fitness; his manners were grave, and did not encourage familiarity, nor had he that easy flow of language so essential to sustain a conversation on the familiar topics of the day. But in the chamber of the sick, or wherever there was affliction which the sympathies of a pastor could alleviate, he was a constant and welcome visitor. Says one who knew him well, " Few men ever spoke with more meaning, or to so good a purpose. He did not dazzle, but he enlightened ; and the weight of his influence and character and the remarkable purity and uprightness of his life gave an influence and interest to whatever he said, and impressed his sententious remarks deeply on the mind." As a citizen, his influence was widely and beneficially felt ; he had frequent calls for assistance and counsel in the secular affairs of the town. In the various offices of trust to which he was often called, whether for objects of charity, or for the promotion of education or religion, they were fulfilled with a characteristic caution, prudence, and fidelity, which obtained and justified unlimited confidence. In 1818 he was elected fellow of Harvard College. The period of his connection with this institution was one of great difficulty ; yet he took his full share of the labors and responsibilities incident to his official position. He was a warm, constant friend of the college, and the notices of his death on the records of the corporation manifest the strong sense of " the great loss our literary and religious community have sustained by the death of this learned divine and exemplary Christian, whose intelligence, fidelity, and zeal in support of the interests of literature, and especially of those connected with the prosperity of Harvard University, they have had uniform occasion to witness during the many years he has been one of the members of this board." As a preacher, Dr. Porter exhibited few, if any, of the characteristics of a popular preacher of the present day, although few modern preachers of to-day are listened to more attentively, or regarded with more reverence than he was. He was not excitable ; therefore he was not likely to produce excitement in others. There was a calmness and solemnity in his manner which gave to his discourses a peculiar impressiveness. He never was dogmatical or bigoted ; he had clear and settled opinions on the controverted points of theology, and was always ready to sustain them; but he had no taste for controversy, and therefore rarely preached on subjects which occasioned it. He regarded the religious opinions of others without prejudice, and never allowed a difference of opinion to interrupt Christian fellowship. Dr. Porter died at Roxbury, December 7, 1833, aged seventy-six years. The funeral was held in his church December 11, 1833, Rev. Dr. Lowell offering the funeral prayer. Rev. George Putnam, D. D.,* preached the funeral sermon from Genesis xxv. 8 : "He died in a good old age, an old man, and full of years, and was gathered to his people." Rev. John Pierce, D. D., of Brookline, made the concluding prayer. †

REV. THOMAS CRAFTS was son of Dr. Thomas Staples Crafts (from Newton); was born in North Bridgewater; graduated at Harvard College 1783; married Polly, daughter of Rev. John Porter, December 28, 1786; settled at Princeton, Mass., 1786, and dismissed in 1791 and settled at Middleboro'. After remaining at Princeton several years, his physicians decided that his life depended on his leaving the ministry, and engaging in more active or some out-of-door pursuit. He consequently removed to Weymouth, Mass., where he entered into commercial business, and was quite successful. After his health had become somewhat improved, he received a call to preach from the " Middleboro' and Taunton Precinct," and was installed in 1802, where he enjoyed a happy ministry for many years, and there died, February 27, 1819, aged sixty years. His family then removed to North Bridgewater.

REV. ASA PACKARD was son of Jacob and Dorothy (Perkins) Packard; was born in North Bridgewater May 3, 1758. His life was a very eventful one. At the age of sixteen, he

---

* Dr. Putnam was settled with Dr. Porter July 7, 1830, after he had preached for fifty-one years.

† For an account of his publications that have been published, see list.

entered the Revolutionary service as a fifer. In an engagement near Harlaem Heights, in 1776, a companion who had made great boasts of his bravery seized Mr. Packard's fife, and, handing him his musket in return, fled to a place of safety, preferring, it would seem, the music he could make with a stolen fife to that made by the balls of the enemy. Mr. Packard, thus armed, engaged in the conflict, but soon received a wound which nearly proved fatal. The ball entered his back just above the hip, and though an attempt was made to extract it, yet so severe was the operation that the surgeon feared he would die in his hands, and so was induced to desist. A severe illness followed in consequence, and when sufficiently recovered, he left the army and returned home, and commenced a course of studies preparatory to entering college. The ball he received was never extracted; but remained in his back during his life. Mr. Packard was a man of great facetiousness, and often alluded in pleasantry to the circumstance of his having fought and bled for his country. Once in a merry circle he said, —

" I bear about in my body a weighty testimonial of my bravery ; " * to which a jovial companion replied, —

" I think from the position of the wound our hero must have been playing a retreat."

" Playing a retreat ! " said Mr. Packard ; " I had a musket in my hand, and was found skilful as a grenadier."

" I think," rejoined the other, " our friend must have been skilled in the motion ' to the right about face ! ' and must have performed it well when he received his wound."

The joke was appreciated by Mr. Packard and the rest of the company. Mr. Packard graduated at Harvard University in 1783 ; received a call, and settled in Marlboro', March 23, 1785, — a day long to be remembered from the fact that the

* The ball he received was never extracted, but remained in his back during his life. Rev. George Trask, of Fitchburg, has the ball now in his possession.

snow was so deep as to cover the tops of the fences, notwithstanding there had been a thaw which settled the snow, so
that, in freezing, it became sufficiently solid to bear up a
team.   The people went to the ordination in their sleighs
upon the crust across lots, over the tops of fences and walls
without difficulty.   The depth of snow was so remarkable
that it became and continued for a long time a standard of
comparison. He was settled on a salary of £100, "and twenty
cords of good marketable oak wood, cut and brought to
the door annually, so long as he remains our minister."
They also voted him a settlement of £300, — one half to be
paid in one year, the other half in two years from his ordination.   Mr. Packard was a man of sprightly talent, and was
noted for his readiness rather than for his profundity.   He
had great conversational powers, and was remarkable for his
eccentricity.   His sermons were practical rather than doctrinal, and more distinguished for happy descriptions of life
and manners than for connected views of gospel truths.   He
was liberal in his theological opinions, belonging to what is
denominated the Arminian School.   As Unitarianism devel-
oped itself in Massachusetts, he was considered as coincid-
ing with that class of his brethren, though later in life his
sentiments are supposed to have undergone some change.
"Perhaps it will be more correct to say that he never
formed for himself any definite system of doctrinal belief;
his mind was more distinguished for its readiness than for its
method, and seemed to have held opinions in regard to different doctrines which were not consistent with each other,
and which could not have been blended into a logical system.   Different persons who knew him well have, for this
reason, claimed him with different denominations, since on
some points his views seemed to coincide with Unitarians,
and on others, with the Orthodox standard of doctrine."
These are the views entertained by one of the most distin-

guished preachers of New England on his theological opinions. Mr. Packard remained pastor of the first and the only parish in Marlboro' for about twenty years, and the people were happy under his ministry. In the year 1805, an unpleasant controversy arose in regard to the subject of locating a meeting-house, which ended in the erection of two houses, and ultimately in two parishes. During this controversy he remained neutral, both parties anxious to retain him ; but he continued to remain in the old church, and being unwilling to take part in the dedication of the new house, and realizing that a majority had a right to command his services while he remained their pastor, he wisely asked a dismission from the church and society as the best way of avoiding a public approval of the removal of the meeting-house, which was the sole cause of the unhappy feeling. On March 6, 1806, the matter was brought before the Marlboro' Association, and after due consideration it was decided by them that the town had a claim to Mr. P. in the new house. "The association, while they lament the occasion for it, both on their own and the people's account, cannot but acquiesce in his determination to be dismissed." After much opposition, the west parish in Marlboro' received an act of incorporation, February 23, 1808, by the name of the Second Parish in Marlboro'; on the 23d of March, the same year, Rev. Asa Packard, who had labored with the society since his dismission from the town, was installed over the west parish, and retained his pastoral relation until May 12, 1819, when he took a dismission and removed to Lancaster where he resided till his death, which took place March 20, 1843, in the eighty-fifth year of his age. He was in his usual health in the morning, and on coming into the house, he sat down to listen to a letter from a distant brother; while it was being read, he sunk back, and immediately expired.

19

Rev. HEZEKIAH PACKARD, D. D., was born in North Bridgewater, Mass., December 6, 1761, son of Jacob and Dorothy
(Perkins) Packard, and was the youngest of ten children.
And of his parents and their influence he used to speak
with pleasure, affection, and respect.   Being the youngest
of the family, he no doubt experienced the indulgence common to the youngest of a large family.   The humble circumstances of his father's family accustomed him to habits of
active industry, rigid economy, and self-reliance.   Their
narrow means, together with their discretion, restrained him
from associating with other lads.   One amusement his parents indulged him in had an influence they little thought of.
He says, " At what precise period I procured a fife I do not
distinctly remember; but the acquisition was to me very gratifying and delightful.   Martial music was very animating to
me, and I soon learned several martial airs.   The tunes sung
and played during the incipient state of the Revolution had
a wonderful influence.   The exciting remarks made in favor
of the Revolution had a thrilling effect upon my mind.   I became anxious to attend musters and meetings for enlisting
soldiers.   The battle of Bunker Hill had an exciting influence.   It seemed to electrify the whole community.   On
that memorable day I was in a neighbor's field hoeing corn,
and heard the roaring of the cannon.   I was then in my
fourteenth year.   The captain of the militia lived near my
father's, and as he knew the family were high Whigs, and
that I had some skill with the fife, he appointed me a fifer in
the company under his command.   Soon after this, he was
drafted for five months, and solicited me to go with him as
fifer, promising to use me as a son, which promise he always
kept.   Although young and fond of home, I never had any
scruples or hesitation about enlisting, nor do I recollect that
my parents opened their lips in the way of discouragement.
Distinctly do I remember when my mother took my hand

and said, 'Hezekiah, remember praying will make thee leave
sinning, and sinning will make thee leave praying.' These
words were to me full of meaning and of practical truth.   Indeed, the devout desires and earnest prayers of my affectionate and pious parents were, as it appeared to me, preserved
as memorials before God on my behalf.   For though I neglected prayer when a soldier, my moral habits were in other
respects correct.   I was averse to vices in the army to which
youth are exposed; no profane word escaped my lips from
the time I left my father's house till I returned to it again.
I was more and more disgusted at the profaneness common
among the soldiers, and even the officers of the Revolution.
My brother (the late Rev. Asa Packard, of Marlboro', Mass.)
had already become a soldier in the eight months' service,
and was stationed at Roxbury.   The regiment to which I
belonged was ordered to Cambridge, and we dwelt in tents
near Cambridgeport.   Soon after we pitched our tents and
drew our provisions from College Hall, where beef, pork,
etc., were kept for our army, and other arrangements were
made for a campaign, and I felt myself a soldier in camp, I
had a furlough for a day or two to visit my brother at Roxbury.   From the time we marched into Boston, late in autumn, until the following June, Col. Sargent's regiment in
which my name was enrolled was destined to occupy several
stations.   After being in Boston a few weeks, we were ordered to Bunker Hill.   In the spring of 1776, we were stationed at Castle William, now Fort Independence.   Here we
remained till June, when orders were given for us to march
to New York.   We went to New London by land, and from
thence by water to New York.   The regiment was stationed
near Hurlgate.   Six miles below the city, upon the banks of
East River, opposite to our fort on the other side of the
river, the enemy built a fort to annoy us, the distance between the two forts being a little over a mile.   A soldier,

soon after the balls and bombs began to fly into our camp, walking proudly upon the parapet, boastfully exclaimed that the ball had not been made that was to kill him. Not many minutes after, a ball came and almost cut him asunder, thus warning others not to expose themselves needlessly. This cannonading and bombarding continued for several weeks, killing some and wounding some. I remember an old man belonging to our camp who, seeing a bomb fall and bury itself in the ground a few rods from him, started hastily toward the spot, hoping to save the powder, for which he would get a dollar; but just before he reached the place there was a tremendous explosion, and he was covered with dirt and nearly suffocated. He received, however, no serious injury, and was for a time the subject of facetious remark. About the same time, two young men belonging to the same mess found a bomb, the fuse of which had been somehow extinguished, and thoughtlessly attempted to open the vent with a pickaxe. This rash and inconsiderate attempt was fatal to both. A spark from the axe reached the powder, and these young men were awfully mangled by the explosion. One expired immediately; the other survived a few days. Soon after this there was a general excitement. Intelligence reached us that troops were leaving Long Island, and that the British were pressing upon them, orders being given for retreat, and New York was evacuated. It was the Sabbath, in the last of August or the first of September. The heat was extreme, the roads were crowded with troops, with men, women, and children, together with cattle, goods, and chattels, overspread with thick clouds of dust. The night following was dark and rainy. I slept under a blanket with my captain, who had always treated me like a son, according to the promise he made when I enlisted. The next morning while the cooks were preparing breakfast, and the soldiers were adjusting their packs and cleaning their guns, etc., after the rain, alarm guns were heard; our army was aroused; the enemy were at hand. A detachment of one hundred and thirty-six in number, among them my brother, was sent out to check the enemy, and in a few hours he was on his way to the hospital at West Chester. On the same day was the battle of Harlaem Heights. Our regiment was near the centre of the line extending from Hudson to East River. The line of battle was not far from King's Bridge. The number killed and wounded I do not remember. The sick and wounded were taken to the hospital. I visited my brother several times. His wound became alarming, and his surgeons gave no encouragement. We both nearly despaired of his restoration. At the second or third visit I took charge of a letter to our parents, in which he took leave of them and of the family; and we took leave of each other. I afterward went to the hospital, not knowing whether he was among the living, and found him somewhat relieved. His body was less swollen; his hopes of recovery revived. After this, as far as my memory serves, we did not see each other till we met at home in our father's house. In the autumn of that year, I was sick, and destined to breathe the polluting, infectious air of the hospital, and suffered much for want of things comfortable. Having the itch shockingly, without the means of getting rid of that loathsome disease, and being reduced by other complaints without the medical aid I required, I thought much of home and a mother's cares; but I was a stranger in a strange land. The hospital was extremely filthy, its atmosphere pestilential. My case was so much neglected, and my whole frame so diseased and shattered, that I had serious apprehensions I should not long survive. My term of service expired at the end of the year; I was no longer a soldier. Finding myself some better, although still feeble, I set my face and directed my tottering steps toward home. The first day I travelled about

three or four miles toward the object of my affection. About
the third day on my homeward march, I reached the great
road from White Plains to my native home, and was providen-
tially overtaken by my captain's elder brother and his waiter.
He had purchased a cheap horse before he left camp, and was
homeward bound ; but finding me feeble, unprotected, and
solitary, he readily dismounted, and allowed me the privilege of riding. I rode nearly the whole distance of two hundred miles.   I have no remembrance of my friend's riding five
miles till we reached Easton, Mass., his native town, and where
my oldest brother then lived. We often received many a
good bit on our way, in consequence of the piteous and oft-
repeated story my friend told of the poor destitute and suffering fifer upon the horse, so that people were kind to us,
cheered and comforted us on our way homeward. My parents had not heard a word from me after the battle at Harlaem Heights, except that I was there, but in doubt what to
expect. My brother's letter not reaching home, the same
doubt existed in regard to him. After my return from the
army, I was so reduced in strength, my whole frame so diseased and wrecked, that for a long time I was unfit for business. I was long exposed to suffering, and unable to labor.
I was, however, afterward induced to enlist for six months.
That I should have again entered the army was a mystery.
I was stationed at Providence, and afterward at Newport.
Gen. Sullivan, who had command, intended to gain possession of Newport, then in the hands of the British. After
quitting the service, I made up my mind to live at home and
become a farmer. But changes and events occurred in our
domestic circle which greatly affected my condition and prospects.   (My father died February 2, 1777, aged fifty-six.)
My brother, as before mentioned, being wounded, was
probably led by that circumstance to change his purpose of
life. He accordingly fitted for college, and entered Harvard

in the summer of 1779. In the course of the revival of 1780, did I first receive my religious impressions; at a meeting called by my brother my own mind was deeply and solemnly impressed. I did feel I had some encouraging evidence that God in Christ did appeal for me in mercy. The burden of sin which had borne with oppressive weight upon my soul was removed, and I think I found peace in believing. Calmness, peace, and serenity prevailed in my own mind. Availing myself as I had opportunity of the advice and experience of neighbors, I had the reputation of taking good care of the farm and rendering it productive. I labored to the extent of my strength, and made some improvements by subduing rough parts of the land, and building walls. Meeting the approbation of my neighbors and family, and seeing the good effect of my labors, I acquired a fondness for husbandry, and readily devoted myself to it. I was well satisfied with my condition and sphere of life, and had no idea of relinquishing the pursuits of agriculture until the spring of 1782. At that time I was afflicted and discouraged by an injury done my arm in making wall. Being young and ambitious, I strained my arm at the elbow. The injury was such that it disqualified me from pursuing my favorite occupation. I showed my arm to several physicians, but received no encouragement. I then made arrangements for acquiring an education, and soon left home and placed myself under the instruction of Rev. Dr. John Reed, minister of the west parish. I pursued my studies with great diligence, deducting the time I was obliged to suspend my studies on account of weak eyes. I was not more than a year fitting for college. When fitting, I often visited the home of my childhood and early youth, and reluctantly denied myself its endearments. The distance, not being more than five or six miles, I could easily walk home Saturday night and return on Monday morning. In July, 1783, that being Cambridge commencement, I entered college with rather gloomy prospects: my small patrimony, in consequence of bad debts and fraudulent men, was reduced from five or six hundred dollars to a mere trifle. I had no patron to whom I could go for advice, encouragement, and help; I had no place I could properly call home; I had no place to call my home through my college studies; I had to make my way through many difficulties. I spent most of my vacations at college, where I had good opportunity for study, and I defrayed the expenses of board by keeping a morning school for misses, by the care of college buildings, etc. I kept school nine or ten weeks winters. I waited in Common Hall more than three years during college life. In justice to myself and for the benefit of others, I can state with all the confidence of truth that I passed through college without fine or censure, and with a respectable literary character. The first year after leaving college, I kept a grammar school in Cambridge. The year passed pleasantly, and I found myself in the way of improvement. The next year I took charge of the library as assistant; was one of the three who in the course of the year prepared the first printed catalogue of the college library. The other two were Rev. Isaac Smith, the librarian, and Professor Sewall. At the commencement of 1789, I entered the tutorship in the mathematical department as successor of Mr., afterward Professor, and subsequently President Webber. I continued as tutor four years, enjoying enlightened society in college, and in the town and vicinity of Cambridge."

In October, 1793, Mr. Packard was ordained over the church in Chelmsford, with the prospect of a comfortable and useful ministry, where he labored with conscientious diligence in the work of the ministry eight years, when, receiving an invitation to settle at Wiscasset, Me., he asked his dismission, and it was granted by a mutual council called July 29, 1802. He was installed at Wiscasset, Me., September 8,

1802, Professor Tappan, of Cambridge College, preaching the sermon. He entered upon his new field of labor with a fair prospect of comfort and usefulness. When he had been in Wiscasset three or four years, he was invited to take charge of a private school. The school was full, and succeeded so well that in the course of the year a plan for an academy was in train. A brick building was erected costing four thousand dollars. He kept this academy several years, and his labors in it and his pastoral and ministerial duties were too much for his constitution, and brought on infirmities which have been at times troublesome companions. His labors at this place were terminated by a mutual council in the spring of 1830. Again Providence opened for him a smaller field of labor and usefulness at Middlesex Village, a remote part of his former parish in Chelmsford, where were living many of those who, as parents or children, had been under his preaching thirty years before. It was while residing at this place his son William, then a student of Bowdoin College, died, January, 1834. He exercised his ministry at Middlesex six years, and in the fall of 1836 dissolved his connection with that church. He moved to Saco, Me., November 11, 1836. During the remaining years of Mr. P.'s life, he resided at Saco, Me., Salem, Mass., and Brunswick, Me., making occasional visits to each and all of his children. He took a lively interest in passing events and social life, and to the last had a cheerful temperament and strong social affections. He never secluded himself, nor seemed to feel too old to meet and fulfil the claims of society upon him. In his eighty-fifth year he took the principal charge of a garden, and in winter he used the axe and saw. He participated in all schemes for good; mourned with those that mourned; rejoiced with those that rejoiced. The passer-by ever met him with a kind word or a bow. He possessed great dignity of bearing and character, combined with ease and elegance

of manners which adorn the most cultivated society, and an
ever-playful, genial humor.   For nearly fifty years he was connected with various literary institutions, much of the time
being engaged in training the youth.   For seventeen years
he was a trustee of Bowdoin College, and ten years vice-
president of the same ; and from the day of his admission to
the university he was a college man to the close of his days,
always glowing in college scenes, reminiscences, and attach-
ments.   He was the originator of the Bible society in Lincoln County, Me.   He died April 25, 1849.   Agreeable to
his own request, his remains were conveyed to Wiscasset for
interment, the place where he had labored twenty years before.   The funeral took the place of the afternoon service,
Rev. Dr. Adams, of Brunswick, preaching the sermon.

> " The last long journey of his life now o'er,
>   His gentle voice and cheerful smile no more
>   Shall tell the tale of life's uncertain dream ; —
>   For his is now in heaven, a higher theme."

Rev. Joshua Cushman was born 1758 or 9, and resided in
North Bridgewater, Mass. ; graduated at Harvard College in
1787.   In the early part of the Revolutionary War, at the age
of seventeen or eighteen, he entered the military service of
the United States.   A paper found among his papers and
books contains the following account of his services in that
war in his own handwriting : —

" I enlisted on the 1st day of April, 1777, under Caleb
King, then in Bridgewater, Mass., and served in the ninth
regiment of the Massachusetts line.   The field officers were
Col. Wesson, Lieut. Col. Mellen, and Major Badlam.   I was
in Capt. Bartlett's company.   My first rendezvous was
at Cambridge, near Boston ; then proceeded to Albany,
thence up the Mohawk to the German Flats ; joined Arnold's
attachment from Gates's Army for the relief of Fort Stanvix.
After the dispersion of the enemy, we joined the northern

army, near Stillwater, on the Hudson; thence took ground
and encamped on Bemis Heights; was in the decisive battle
which led to the capture of the British forces in that quarter.   After the surrender of Burgoyne, we moved down the
Hudson to Albany, and thence across the country to White
Marsh in Pennsylvania.   After facing the enemy for a day or
two, we went into winter quarters at Valley Forge.   After
the enemy evacuated Philadelphia, we moved with the main
army under Gates, first to Danbury, then to Hartford, Conn.,
thence to Fishkill.   There, and in the vicinity of West Point,
N. Y., I was stationed with the regiment during the rest of
my term of service.   I was discharged the latter part of
March, 1780, having completed the term of my engagement
lacking a few days, an indulgence obtained through the cour-
tesy of the colonel."

After leaving the military service, he fitted for college;
graduated in the same class with Hon. John Quincy Adams;
studied theology with Rev. Ephraim Briggs, and was ordained as pastor of the Congregational church in Winslow,
Me., on June 10, 1795, at the age of thirty-six, where he remained nearly twenty years.   At a little later period after
his settlement, he adopted the views of that branch of Con-
gregationalists called Unitarians.   His ordination sermon
was preached by Rev. Mr. Whitman, of Pembroke, and the
other services of the occasion were performed by Rev. Mr.
Porter, of Roxbury, Rev. Mr. Porter, of Rye, N. H., Rev. Mr.
Winthrop, of Woolwich, Me., Rev. Mr. Ellis, of Topsham, Me.,
and Rev. Mr. Calef, of Canaan, Me.   The church where his
ordination took place not being large enough to contain the
audience, a bower was made covered with green boughs and
supported by twenty pillars interwoven at the sides, and
when filled with people, presented quite a unique and picturesque appearance.   After his dismissal from the ministry,
which was not from any disagreement between him and the

parish, but from inability to support a minister, he continued
to preach in that vicinity for awhile, but never was installed
over any society. He soon became an eminent political man,
commencing by representing the county of Kennebec in the
Senate of Massachusetts (of which Maine was then a part) in
the political year 1810; represented the town of Winslow in
the House of Representatives in 1811 and 1812; was elected
on the Executive Council of Massachusetts, but declined the
office; in 1819 was elected as Representative to Congress
from the Kennebec district, and after Maine was separated
from Massachusetts in 1820, he continued in Congress for six
consecutive years. In 1828 he was again elected from his
district to the Senate, and in 1834 again represented his
adopted town of Winslow in the House, and this was the last
of his public services. " His course was run, his days were
numbered." Being the senior member at the opening of the
Legislature in January, 1834, it became his duty to call the
House to order at its organization; but his health being feeble, he never took his seat again in that body. He died at
his boarding-house Monday morning, January 27, 1834, aged
seventy-five years. Immediately upon the opening of the
two branches of the Legislature, the House voted to adjourn,
and the members to wear black crape during the remainder
of the session as a mark of respect to the memory of Hon.
Joshua Cushman. And the Senate also adjourned from a regard to his services and worth. His funeral was attended by
the members of both branches of the Legislature; and, although the snow was extremely deep at the time, there was
a large gathering, and the duty of following his remains was
consequently fatiguing. He was interred at Augusta, Me.,
and a plain marble slab erected to his memory, bearing this
simple inscription: " Our fathers, where are they ? " The
Legislature of Maine afterward, however, removed his remains
to the tomb erected for the burial of those who died in the

service of the government, and his name was engraved on the top of the tomb among those who had gone before him. He was a good scholar, was imbued with Christian and statesmanlike principles, and was a respectable speaker. Progress and reform were among the leading traits of his mind. The test of time and the judgment of men which truly tries the character and acts of all has pronounced its verdict, — " A good and faithful servant."

> " Tranquil amidst alarms,
>   It found him on the field,
> A veteran slumbering on his arms,
>   Beneath his red cross shield."

REV. NAPHTALI SHAW was the son of William and Hannah (West) Shaw; born in North Bridgewater June 20, 1764. His ancestors, as far back as he had any knowledge of them, were pious people. When a lad, he had but little time for reading, excepting on the Sabbath; then he read the Bible and religious books. He was religiously educated, and from such works as he had, he early received religious impressions, which proved of the greatest value to him. Of the divine authority of the Scriptures he never had a doubt, and at an early period of his life he had determined to make them the rule of his faith and practice. At the age of fifteen, he enlisted in the service as a soldier of the Revolutionary War for a special service at Rhode Island; and again the next year, with his two older brothers, marched to the call of his country to aid in suppressing Shay's Rebellion and a threatened assault on one of our maritime places. In all this he did not have to engage in battle. He was, however, always through life patriotic. When he came back from military service the last time, being then seventeen years of age, he prevailed upon others in his native town to unite with him in purchasing a social library, and the first book he selected was " Mason on Self-Knowledge," which he always thought was of

great value to him, and one that no person could study without profit.   After preparation for college under the care of
Dr. Crane, a physician of Titicut Parish, and Rev. Dr. John
Reed, of West Bridgewater, in 1786, at the age of twenty-
two, he entered Dartmouth College, Hanover, N. H., where,
after applying himself closely to his studies, and after a hard
struggle with difficulties arising from limited means and a
new state of things in the vicinity of the college, he graduated with honor in 1790, receiving the Bachelor's degree.
After this he taught school in Easton, Mass., and Boston, as
an assistant of Mr. Caleb Brigham, an instructor of great celebrity.   After studying theology seven months, he was ap-
probated (as it was then called) by the Plymouth association
of ministers August 1, 1792.   He pursued the study of theology under the care of Rev. Zedekiah Sanger, D. D., of Bridgewater, who was in the habit of instructing young men for the
ministry.   Immediately after he was licensed to preach, he
received a call to preach at Kensington, N. H., where they
had already heard more than twenty candidates.   He was ordained at that place January 30, 1793, as pastor of the Congregational church, then at the age of twenty-nine years.
He remained in that place till January 13, 1813, when, his
health failing him, he had to ask his resignation.   His ministry was pacific and useful; peace and harmony were restored, and the cause of education, morals, and religion was
promoted.   Upon his resigning his pastoral labors, his health
continued such that he devoted himself to agricultural pursuits.   He purchased a farm in Bradford, Vt., where he continued during the remaining forty years of his life, giving up
preaching entirely.   In due time he united with the Congregational church in Bradford, Vt., and, to the day of his death
continued a most worthy and exemplary member, highly respected by all who knew him.   Although an educated man,
he was far from being dictatorial or overbearing or fault-find-

ing, but habitually exhibited that meek, humble, and quiet spirit that manifested itself in all his actions, and which, in, the sight of God, is of great price.

Rev. Theophilus Packard., D. D., was the son of Abel and Esther (Porter) Packard, and was born in North Bridgewater, Mass., March 4, 1769. When he was five years old, he re moved with his father's family to Cummington, Mass., the western part of the State, where he lived until he entered Dartmouth College. His early years were spent in working upon his father's farm. At the age of twenty-one he began to fit up a farm for himself; but, by overtasking his bodily powers, he disabled himself in a great degree for that kind of labor. Shortly after this, his mind became deeply exercised on the subject of religion; and at length so far settled that he became a member of the church. He began now to meditate the purpose of devoting himself to the Christian ministry; and, with a view to this, commenced his preparation for college under the instruction of his pastor, the Rev. James Briggs. He entered college in 1792, and graduated in 1796. Immediately after his graduation, he commenced the study of theology under the Rev. Dr. Burton, of Thetford, Vt., and at the end of six months was licensed to preach by the Orange Association, to which his theological teacher belonged. His first labors, as a minister, were among the churches in the region in which he was licensed. He went to Shelburne, Mass., to preach as a candidate, early in the autumn of 1798. He was ordained on the 20th of February, 1799, the sermon being preached by the Rev. John Emerson, of Conway, Mass. The honorary degree of Doctor of Divinity was conferred upon him by Dartmouth College in 1824. Dr. Packard continued in sole charge of the church at Shelburne until March 12, 1828, when his son Theophilus was ordained as his colleague. The charge was given to the young pastor by the Rev. Jonathan Grout, of Hawley, who had performed the same service in connection with his father's ordination twenty-nine years before. From this time the father and son continued to supply the pulpit alternately till February 20, 1842, when Dr. Packard gave notice to his people that he should relinquish all pastoral service, and from that time he never received from them any compensation. He was, however, not dismissed, but retained the pastoral relation till his death. During the fourteen years in which the two were associated in supplying the Shelburne pulpit, they both labored extensively in destitute parishes in the neighborhood, and were instrumental, in several instances, in preparing the way for a stated ministry. Dr. Packard having reached the age of seventy-three, and finding the infirmities of age were rapidly increasing upon him, went, in the spring of 1846, to live with a widowed daughter in South Deerfield. Here he remained four years, but returned to Shelburne in the summer of 1854. His last sermon was preached in Deerfield in November, 1847. He suffered severe injury from a fall upon the ice in the early part of January, 1855, and from that time was confined to his house, and mostly to his bed. He was afflicted by a complication of maladies, from which, during the last few weeks of his life particularly, he experienced intense suffering. He died on the 17th of September, 1855. The Franklin County Church Conference and Benevolent Anniversaries having been appointed to be held on the 18th and 19th, his funeral took the place of the Conference exercises on the afternoon of the 19th, a very large number of ministers being in attendance. His funeral sermon was preached by the Rev. Dr. Hitchcock, late president of Amherst College. He was married to Mary, daughter of Isaac Tirrill, of Abington, Mass., February 9, 1800. He had eight children, one of whom, Theophilus, was graduated at Amherst College in 1823, and, as has been already noticed, was associated with his father in the ministry. Mrs. Packard was living in 1856. Dr. Packard, in the course of his ministry, instructed thirty-one students * in theology, all of whom became preachers of the gospel.

REV. JONAS PERKINS was the oldest son of Josiah and Anna (Reynolds) Perkins; was born in the North Parish of Bridge-water, October 15, 1790. At the age of seventeen he com-menced fitting for college at Phillips' Academy, Andover, Mass., having, from the time of his conversion, at the age of ten, a strong desire to devote himself to the ministry of the gospel. He enjoyed the instruction of Rev. Mark Newman and John Adams at the academy, and when examined for ad-mission to Brown University, offered himself as a candidate for advanced standing, and was received as a member of the Sophomore Class. He graduated at this institution with dis-tinguished honor in 1813. He immediately commenced a course of theological studies under the instruction of Rev. Otis Thompson, of Rehoboth, Mass.; was licensed by the Mendon Association October 11, 1814, and was invited to preach as a candidate for the Union Society of Weymouth and Braintree, at the age of twenty-four. After preaching a short time, he received a unanimous call to become their pastor, which call he accepted, and was ordained June 14, 1815. With this society he has labored for forty-six years, prosperous, united, and happy; and the church under his care has been constantly increasing in numbers. At the annual meeting of the society in 1861, he gave them notice that he should resign his pastoral charge at his seventieth birthday, the 15th of the following October. Accordingly, he preached his fare-well sermon on the Sabbath following that day, and by the mutual consent of pastor and people and approval of a coun-cil, his official connection with them was dissolved. At a

* See Packard's " History of Churches and Ministers of Franklin County, Mass."

21

meeting of the church and parish, held soon after, the following resolutions were passed, showing the estimation in which his labors were held by them : —

" *Resolved,* that we recognize with devout gratitude the goodness of God to this society in preserving the life and continuing the labors of our pastor, Rev. Jonas Perkins, so many years.

" *Resolved,* that the union and prosperity of this church and people during his pastorate testify to his fidelity and success as a minister of Jesus Christ.

" *Resolved,* that we tender our heartfelt thanks to him, as the shepherd of this flock, for his constancy and his unwearied efforts to promote our spiritual and temporal good.

"*Resolved,* that while the dissolution of this relation awakens many tender and painful emotions, we are comforted and cheered by the thought that he and his beloved companion are to spend the evening of their life with us, and that we shall still enjoy their counsels, the light of their example, and their prayers.

" *Resolved,* that we assure him and his family of our continued respect and love, and that we fully reciprocate the wish expressed in his farewell discourse, — for a mutual and truly Christian remembrance until death."

REV. ELIPHALET P. CRAFTS is son of Rev. Thomas and Polly (Porter) Crafts ; was born in North Bridgewater, November 23, 1800. At an early age he, with the rest of the family, removed to Middleboro', where he received his early education ; fitted for college with his father ; graduated at Brown University, Providence, R. I., in 1821 ; studied theology at the theological school of Cambridge, where he graduated for the ministry. He was first settled at East Bridgewater, in 1828, where he enjoyed a happy ministry for seven years, and was dismissed at his own request. After regaining his

health, he was installed over the "First Congregational
Church and Society" at Sandwich, Mass., in 1839, minister-
ing to a harmonious and affectionate people for about fifteen
years. Receiving a dismission, at his request, he removed to
Lexington, Mass., where he has been engaged in educating
young Spanish gentlemen, also supplying vacant pulpits in
Lexington and vicinity.

REV. LEVI PACKARD was the son of Levi and Ruth
(Snow) Packard, born in North Bridgewater, Mass., February
4, 1793. His early days were spent under the parental
roof in the discharge of filial and fraternal duty. At the
age of fourteen he became the hopeful subject of renew-
ing grace, and was received into the communion of the
church in his native town. Here he gave himself up to
God, it is believed, with a "purpose of heart to cleave
unto him" which was never relinquished. His thoughts
were early turned toward the Christian ministry, and he
longed to devote himself to the work of preaching that
gospel which he had found so precious; but his circumstances were unfavorable, and for several years he endured
a painful mental conflict on the subject. Still he urged the
anxious inquiry, "Lord, what wilt thou have me to do?"
cherishing the hope from year to year that the Saviour
whom he loved would yet permit him, as an under shepherd, to feed his lambs. Having at length attained his majority, he felt at liberty to devote the avails of his personal
labor to the object which lay nearest his heart, and which
years of doubt and difficulty had but rendered more and
more dear to him. His preparation for college was retarded
by the expedients which he was constrained to adopt for de-
fraying its expenses; but at length, at the age of twenty-
eight, his efforts and sacrifices were rewarded, and he graduated with the highest honors at Brown University. He

then continued his theological studies under private instructors, and after having preached temporarily in several places,
he was ordained at Spencer, Mass., the 14th day of June, 1826.
A ministry of twenty-seven years in that place leaves but
little need of any testimony to his personal or official character. He had learned the truths of the gospel experiment-
ally, and he preached them in a corresponding manner. He
preached plainly, directly, affectionately, unreservedly, prac-
tically. Though he sought not literary distinction, or the
gratification of intellectual pride, he was not wanting in orig-
inality of thought; he was not a retailer of other men's ideas;
his sermons were his own, — the fruits of his own inquiry,
solemn meditation, and earnest prayer. He shunned no subject on account of its difficulty or its unpopularity, but aimed
to declare the whole counsel of God. The cross was ever
prominent in the religious instruction which he gave; yet,
while determined not to know anything among his people
save Jesus Christ and him crucified, he ever remembered
that the object of the Lord's coming was to destroy the
works of the Devil, and that the gospel develops and enforces
principles and rules of action applicable to all the relations,
obligations, and interests of social life. While desirous that
every sermon should have a Saviour in it, he endeavored to
give each doctrine and precept of revealed religion its place
and proportion in the Christian system. Not constitutionally
inclined to controversy, he opposed error, not so much by direct attack, as by giving his hearers an opportunity to detect
it for themselves in the light of the truth which shone upon
it. Against every violation of the divine law, whether in the
private walks of life, or in the high places of public authority, by individuals or communities, he bore his honest and
fearless testimony, esteeming it comparatively a light thing
to be judged of man's judgment, and mainly anxious to be
free from " the blood of all men," even should his faithfulness

as a reprover provoke the displeasure of those whose friendship he most highly valued, and whom he was most reluctant to offend. At length, he, having received the impression that he could no longer be useful as a pastor, resolved that for their good, he would seek employment in some other vineyard. His pastoral attachment, however, still survived, making a request "that his last sermon to them should be from his silent lips, and that his dust might lie among those with whom he had taken sweet counsel, and with whom he hoped to meet in the sanctuary above." Mr. Packard was not long allowed to remain idle; he was dismissed from his people in Spencer in September, 1853, and was settled over the Congregational church in Woonsocket, R. I., in December of the same year. Here he labored about one year; from that time he gradually failed, through the withering power of pulmonary disease, until his death, which took place at Stafford Springs, Conn., January 11, 1857. The most remarkable characteristic of Mr. Packard may be designated as honesty. In whatever he said or did, he was sincere, frank, and guileless. No one could hear him preach without coming to the conclusion that he felt what he said. There was no room for suspicion; and for simplicity of character he may be considered as a model; and during all his long last sickness says one who was seldom absent from his bed of languishing, " he has given us a bright pattern of patience and quiet submission to his heavenly Father's will."

> " Servant of Christ, well done .
> Praise be thy new employ ;
> And while eternal ages run,
> Rest in thy Saviour's joy."

Rev. Austin Cary was the son of James and Hannah (Wales) Cary; born in North Bridgewater October 1, 1809. His early life was marked with amiableness and morality, and as is usual with children of pious parents, he was from his early years the subject of serious impressions. The first he distinctly remembered was when he was about seven years old; but, as he advanced in youth, he left the Sabbath-school, as is the dangerous custom of many lads when they begin to approach manhood.   From that time, though extremely fond of reading, he neglected the Bible and lost all relish for it.   He also, for the pleasure of showing what he could say, and of provoking discussion, allowed himself to advance objections against its divine origin.   As the result he became sceptical, and ultimately an atheist, entirely callous to religious impressions.   His recovery from this state was peculiar and striking.   Returning home late at night, he had fallen asleep in the wagon, as he was wont to do when thus kept abroad by business.   His thoughts had not been turned to the subject of God's existence, or any kindred subject, either then, or for some time before.   The night was cloudy.   As he awoke and looked on the dim objects about him, a strong and instantaneous impression was on his mind, — "There is a God.   He keeps myself and everything in being; he is here, he is everywhere."   This sudden and abiding conviction he ascribed to the Spirit of God.   From that time he became the subject of frequent religious impressions.   He re-entered the Sabbath-school now as a teacher; but the employment only made him wretched by conscious unfitness.   These occasional impressions and periods even of wretchedness he concealed.   In this state he continued about two years; at the end of this time, and near the close of a protracted meeting, he finally and forever gave his heart to Christ, and openly avowed himself his disciple.   Soon after this, in the spring of 1832 and in the twenty-third year of his age, he began fitting for college with the hope of entering the ministry. In 1833 he entered Waterville College, Me., from which, in the Sophomore year, he removed to Amherst, where he graduated with honor in 1837.   The same year he entered the

Theological Seminary at East Windsor, Conn., where he completed his theological course in 1840. He soon after received
calls from three churches. He accepted that from Sunderland,
where he was ordained November 11, 1840. Here he labored
with great fidelity and success. He enjoyed two special re-
vivals in 1843 and 1849, and one hundred and thirty-six were
added to the church during his ministry. In the autumn of
1849 it pleased God to send distressing sickness on all the
members of his family, which interrupted his public labors.
The last time he preached, he went from the bedside of his
wife, then scarcely expected to recover, and preached extem-
poraneously from these words: "We all do fade as a leaf."
His last public act was on a Sabbath subsequent to his last
sermon, when he left his sick family long enough to baptize
six children. As his family became slightly better, worn out
himself with fatigue and anxiety, he was attacked by hemor-
rhage from the lungs, followed by three similar attacks. He
became, however, more comfortable, and his physician entertained the hope that, after a few months, he might be restored to a measure of comfortable health; but a typhoid
fever set in, and he died soon after, on Tuesday, November
27, 1849, at ten o'clock, P. M., aged forty years, after a ministry of nine years.* He was remarkably winning in his
manners, speedily securing the interest of a stranger, which
was usually increased and consolidated into friendship by
further acquaintance. He was always modest and unassuming; he was ardent in his feelings, firm and trustworthy in
his friendships; he was social, frank, and generous, above all
shadow of meanness; he was eminently manly; and remarkably unselfish. Before experiencing religion, he was
becoming more and more absorbed in the love of money; he
was bent upon being rich; but grace had effected a complete
triumph over this; his heart was not set on property; money

* Rev. Samuel Harris, of Conway, preached his funeral sermon.

flowed from him freely for every good object. He was firm in his decisions, and in the least, as well as the greatest, matter, where principle was at stake, absolutely inflexible; and yet he maintained his convictions and carried through his purposes with such suavity that they who yielded to his decision seemed almost to suppose that he had yielded to them. He possessed sound judgment and strong common sense. With all his warmth of feeling, he had great self-control; and few, if any, have seen him thrown off his guard by even a momentary passion. He had immense energy; and what he undertook he would at all hazards accomplish; and this, with his scrupulous fidelity, caused any matters pertaining to the interests of the church which were intrusted to him to be done seasonably and thoroughly; and in whatever he undertook, he was almost recklessly unsparing of himself. His own convenience, interests, time, and health seemed literally the last thing he ever thought of. Hence he was led unquestionably to an unjustifiable excess of labor, which the remonstrances of friends were inadequate to restrain, and which brought him to an untimely end. As a preacher and writer he had ability, as his prize tract on dancing, and his report on the desecration of the Sabbath show. His peculiar characteristic was unction; he was a son of consolation rather than a Boanerges; a John rather than a Peter. He spoke to the heart; and the peculiar warmth of his soul glowed in his sermons and melted the hearts of his hearers. As a Christian, he was unusually spiritual. He spoke * of " free and confiding intimacy with God in Christ, and comparing the Christian to a little child flinging his arms around his parent's neck, and affectionately whispering his wants in his ear."

As a pastor, he felt an absorbing interest in his people. In his last hours any reference to the interests of the

* At a meeting of conference held at Shelburne a few days before his death.

church seemed to arouse him when nothing else would. He was one of the most active in forming and executing plans to promote the general interests of the churches in the county; and few men of nine years' standing in the ministry had been called on so many councils, or had so great an influence in them. The following epitaph is on his gravestone: "His uniform Christian deportment, his zeal, fidelity, and success in the cause of Christ, have engraven his memorial imperishably upon the hearts of those who knew him." " Blessed is that servant whom his Lord, when he cometh, shall find so doing."

Rev. Zachariah Howard was son of Robert and Abigail (Snell) Howard; born in North Bridgewater, May 21, 1758. For a short time he was a soldier in the Revolutionary army; graduated at Harvard College in 1784; settled in the ministry as successor of Rev. Samuel Dunbar, over the First Church in Stoughton,* 1787, where he died, in 1806, leaving no children. His widow died at Canton, March 11, 1856, aged ninety-five years.

* That portion of Stoughton where this Church is located was incorporated into a town by the name of Canton, February 23, 1797.

CHAPTER VIII.

BIOGRAPHICAL HISTORY — CONTINUED.

Rev. William Thompson. — Rev. John Goldsbury. — Rev. Paul Couch. — Rev. Nathaniel B. Blanchard. — Rev. Edward L. Clark. — Rev. Warren Goddard. — Rev. Nathaniel Wales. — Rev. John F. Norton. — Rev. Charles L. Mills. — Rev. Samuel H. Lee. — Rev. Matthew Kingman. — Rev. Abel K. Packard. — Rev. John Dwight. — Rev. D. Temple Packard. — Rev. Charles W. Wood. — Rev. Lysander Dickerman. — Rev. Zenas P. Wild. — Rev. Azariah B. Wheeler. — Rev. T. B. McNulty. — Dr. Philip Bryant. — Dr. Peter Bryant. — Dr. Luther Cary. — Dr. Issachar Snell. — Dr. Elisha Tillson. — Dr. Ziba Bass. — Dr. Nathan Perry. — Dr. Jonathan P. Crafts. — Dr. Adolphus K. Borden. — Dr. Abel W. Kingman. — Dr. James F. Richards. — Dr. Edgar E. Dean. — Dr. Horatio Bryant. — Dr. Thomas Stockbridge. — Dr. James Easton. — Dr. Nahum Smith. — Dr. E. R. Wade. — Dr. Henry Eddy. — Dr. James L. Hunt. — Dr. Silas L. Loomis. — Dr. L. C. Loomis. — Lucius Cary, Esq. — Eliab Whitman, Esq. — Jonathan White, Esq. — Jonas R. Perkins, Esq. — Austin Packard, Esq. — Daniel Howard, Esq. — Lucius Kingman, Esq. — Caleb Howard, Esq. — Melville Hayward, Esq. — Ellis W. Morton, Esq. — Bradford Kingman, Esq. — Thomas J. Snow. — Frederick Crafts, A. M. — Dea. Heman Packard. — Angustus T. Jones, A. M. — Heman P. De Forrest. — S. D. Hunt.

REV. WILLIAM THOMPSON came from Connecticut to North Bridgewater, and was ordained September 18, 1833, as pastor of the First Congregational Church, with whom he remained but a short time, owing to pressing calls from the Theological Institute at East Windsor, Conn., where he now resides as Professor of Biblical Literature. He was dismissed by council September 4, 1834.

REV. JOHN GOLDSBURY. (See page 48.)

REV. PAUL COUCH was born in Newburyport, June 21, 1803; attended the public schools of his native town till the age of sixteen years, attending one year in a private academy; entered the Freshman Class in Dartmouth College, N. H., 1820; graduated in 1823; studied three years in the Theological Seminary at Andover, Mass.; commenced preaching in the fall of 1826; first ordained at West Newbury, Mass., in March, 1827; married Miss Harriette Tyler, of Griswold, Conn., May 28, 1827; settled at Bethlehem, Conn., in 1829; left there in 1834, and was installed in North Bridgewater in October, 1835, and dismissed at his own request, after a service of twenty-four years, in 1859. Since that time he has been preaching in North Cambridge one year, and in various places, and now, in 1865, has been preaching at Stonington, Conn., for upwards of a year. They have had seven children, five of whom are now living, — the oldest son living in Brooklyn, N. Y.; second son is in Victoria, Vancouver's Island: third is in the 18th Regiment of Conn. Volunteers; fourth was a graduate of Harvard College in 1864; his daughter is married, and resides in Jewett City, Conn.

REV. NATHANIEL BAILEY BLANCHARD was born in Abington, Mass., July 16, 1827. In 1848 he became a member of the Congregational Church in East Abington; in 1853, graduated at Amherst College; in 1855, he completed his theological course at Bangor, Me.; July 15, 1856, he was ordained to the Christian ministry of Edgartown, Mass; while at this place he was married. He became a pastor of the Pilgrim Church in Plymouth, Mass., where he remained three years. On September 18, 1861, he was installed as pastor of the First Congregational Church in North Bridgewater. While preaching at that place, his health failed him and he became unable to perform the services incumbent upon a pastor. He started on a journey for his health, and, on his way to Plymouth, N. H., stopping at Concord, grew worse, and died August 7, 1862, aged thirty-five years. He was a man universally loved and respected wherever he went; and from his youth was a thoughtful boy, with high aims and noble purposes, faithful in all the minor duties, and true in all the social and fraternal relations. He made the most of his opportunities, entering with a heart full of zeal and love upon his work, — his joy of preaching Christ. Sincerity, kindness, and the constraining love of Christ shone forth in all his walk. *

REV. EDWARD L. CLARK. (See page 45.

REV. WARREN GODDARD was the son of the late Dr. John Goddard, of Portsmouth, N. H., where he was born, September 12, 1800. He married Mary Crowell Tobey, of Sandwich, Mass., August 6, 1829. He fitted for college at the "Portsmouth Academy," and entered Harvard University September, 1815, one year in advance; graduated at that institution August, 1818. In the spring of 1819, he became fully satisfied of the truths of the doctrines contained in the writings of Emmanuel Swedenborg, and entered as a student of theology in the family of Rev. Thaddeus M. Harris, D. D., of Dorchester, Mass. At the completion of his studies, there being only one society of the New Church in all New England, — namely, that in Boston, consisting of less than a score of members, and already provided with a pastor elect, — and the few societies in the United States being also provided with ministers, he was obliged to postpone his former purpose of entering the ministry until there should be some society needing ministerial services. At this time an opening presented itself in the academy at Sandwich, Mass. He therefore accepted the office of principal, and was very successful, commencing with twelve pupils, all belonging in that town. Soon after this, applications for admission continued to increase, first from the adjoining towns, then from more distant places, even as far as South Carolina. At the end of two years, he commenced and pursued the study of law in the office of the late Lieut. Governor John Reed, of Yar-

* See resolutions passed by the church on page 45.

mouth, Mass., and was admitted to the bar of Barnstable County; practised law two years in Barnstable, and nearly a year in Boston in connection with Professor Parsons, when, becoming dissatisfied with the practice, so far as it related to the management before juries, he relinquished the practice of law, and accepted an appointment as principal of the English and Classical School at Princeton, Mass., where he labored two or three years with signal success. Several societies having during this time been formed, and needing ministerial services, Mr. Goddard returned to the profession of his first choice, and after preaching and receiving several calls to settle in Abington, Portland, and North Bridgewater, he at length settled at the latter place, where he was installed September 19, 1839, and where he has continued to labor in the ministry until the present time, as one of the most acceptable and useful New Church ministers to be found in the country.

Rev. Nathaniel Wales was son of Thomas and Polly (Hobart) Wales; born in North Bridgewater April 2, 1793; studied theology at Bangor Theological Seminary; settled in the ministry at Belfast, Me., September 26, 1827. At the time of his entering the ministry, the church over which he was settled was supported partly by missionary aid, and was in a neighborhood where he met with an unusual opposition from those who differed from him in their belief. They were unusually hostile to the faith his church professed. The wealth, fashion, and influence of the place were arrayed against its young men, who were early taught not to frequent their house of worship. Seldom has a church sprung up with such a strong opposition as the one over which he was placed. To breast this influence and make progress against it, they needed a man of strength of mind and moral courage. In Mr. Wales the church found such a man. He, having entered the

ministry late in life, had the advantage of mature years.   He
had no fear of man; for, having been called of God to preach
the everlasting gospel, he shunned not to declare the counsel
of God, however received by men.   He warmly embraced
the "faith once delivered to the saints,"—the faith of the Pilgrim Fathers,—not doubting that its faithful exposition and
enforcement were God's appointed means of spiritual profit.
His was no time-serving policy; he had not learned that, to
win souls, the offensive features of divine truth must be ig-
nored or kept out of sight.   As a speaker, Mr. Wales was
bold, emphatic, and impressive; he grasped the truth with a
strong hand, and sent it forth on its mission all glowing with
the ardor of his own intense feeling.   His honest purpose,
his ardent desire to do good savingly, to bless those to whom
he ministered, could not be doubted.   He sought to make his
influence tell upon the eternal well-being of his people.   He
was abundant in labor, preaching much in the surrounding
towns, striving to win and save wherever he went.   He was
an earnest student, an able preacher, a faithful pastor, cheerfully spending and being spent, that he might enlarge the
boundaries of the Redeemer's kingdom, and bring glory to
Him on whom all his own hopes reposed; nor did he labor in
vain.   While his ministry was too brief to reap large results,
he still made an impression on the community in favor of the
true gospel and a faithful ministry, whose influence is felt to
this day; so that the once feeble church has, under his
and his successors' instrumentality, gathered courage and
strength till it has grown to be one of the able churches
of that vicinity.   In stature Mr. Wales was above the medium; he had a manly countenance and dignified bearing; the sight of him inspired respect.   In the warm season of 1828, while returning home from a public meeting,
he took a severe cold, which fastened upon his lungs and
brought on consumption.   His disease baffled medical skill

and the most assiduous care. He gradually declined till, on the 20th day of January, 1829, he sunk peacefully to rest, and a rising light was thus early quenched. His early death was one of those mysterious providences that try the faith, and one which was sincerely mourned by the people of his charge and by numerous friends. " Blessed are the dead who die in the Lord." " The memory of the just is blessed." Says one who was an intimate friend, —

" My recollections of Mr. Wales are very pleasant, and I cherish great respect for his memory, and as being a man of more than ordinary power."

Rev. John F. Norton. (See page 71.)

Rev. Charles L. Mills. (See page 72.)

Rev. Samuel H. Lee. (See page 73.)

Rev. Matthew Kingman is son of Eliphalet and Zilpha (Edson) Kingman; born February 24, 1807. He was engaged in early life in teaching school; studied theology at Gilmanton, N. H.; was afterward agent of that institution for one year; was ordained in the ministry June 26, 1845, at Bethel, Vt.; dismissed from there April 19, 1854; was installed pastor of the First Congregational Church in Charlemont, Mass., June 6, 1854. While preaching at Bethel, the degree of Master of Arts was conferred upon him.

Rev. Abel Kingman Packard is son of Dea. Simeon and Harmony (Kingman) Packard; was born in North Bridgewater, March 19, 1823; became a member of the First Congregational Church in North Bridgewater, November 6, 1836; graduated at Phillips Academy, Andover, August, 1841; entered Amherst College the same year, and graduated August

14, 1845; became principal of an academy at Millbury, Mass., where he remained two years; graduated at Andover Theological Seminary, Andover, Mass., September 4, 1850; was a resident licentiate and student one year; was ordained pastor of the Congregational Church at Yarmouth, Mass., December 16, 1851; was dismissed at his own request October 17, 1859, and removed immediately to Minnesota; supplied the Congregational Church at St. Anthony six months, during the absence of their pastor, and was installed pastor of the church at Anoka, Minn., June 14, 1860, where he now resides.

REV. JOHN DWIGHT.   (See page 58.)

REV. DAVID TEMPLE PACKARD is son of David and Elizabeth (Drake) Packard; was born in North Bridgewater August 24, 1824. After the usual course of common district schools, Mr. Packard fitted for college under the private instruction of Rev. Paul Couch, and at the Adelphian Academy, and the Phillips Academy, Andover, Mass. He graduated at Amherst College, August, 1850; taught high school at East Braintree, Mass., one year, and entered Bangor Theological Seminary October, 1851, and graduated August 30, 1854. Previous to leaving the seminary, he had received two calls to labor in the ministry, — one from the Congregational Church in Bucksport, Me., the other from the South Congregational Church in Campello, the latter of which he accepted, and was ordained as their pastor September 21, 1854. Here he labored with acknowledged success, having become deservedly popular, and, as the glorious results of his efforts, considerable accessions were made to the church for about two years, when he, with his family, wishing to enjoy the benefits of a Western climate, he asked a dismission, which was granted, and he was dismissed October 1, 1856. He then removed to Rock Island, Ill., and preached for the Second

Presbyterian Church in that city. The next year he took charge of the Second Presbyterian Church in Davenport, Iowa. Here he received a unanimous call to settle with them; but preferring New England for a permanent field of labor, after an absence of two years, he returned to Massachusetts in 1858, and in June of that year commenced preaching for the First Congregational Society in Somerville, Mass., and soon after received a call to settle with them as their pastor. In 1860 the call was renewed, and accepted by Mr. P., and he was installed September 21 of that same year, where he now resides.

REV. CHARLES W. WOOD. (See page 64.)

REV. LYSANDER DICKERMAN is the son of Lyman and Vienna (Sproat) Dickerman; born in North Bridgewater June 8, 1825; began a preparatory course of study with the Rev. Paul Couch of that town; entered Phillips Academy, Andover, Mass., under the care of Samuel H. Taylor, L.L. D. In the autumn of 1847, he entered the Freshman Class of Brown University, Providence, R. I., and graduated in 1851; was principal of Rockingham Academy, Hampton Falls, N. H., two years; entered the Theological Seminary, Andover, Mass. in 1853, and graduated in 1856. And on leaving the seminary, his health being poor, he was not settled till April 29, 1858, when he was ordained and installed pastor of the Congregational Church in Gloucester, Mass.; was dismissed by an ecclesiastical council from the pastorate of that church January 19, 1860, and was installed as pastor over the Congregational Church and Society in Weymouth, where Rev. Jonas Perkins had preached for forty-six years, January 17, 1861.

REV. ZENAS P. WILD was born in North Bridgewater October 16, 1818; united with the church under the care of Rev.

John Dwight at Campello, Mass., 1837; fitted for college at Pierce Academy, Middleboro'; became a member of the Baptist Church at North Randolph, Mass., and was there licensed to preach; afterward studied theology at Thomaston and Waterville, Me., also with Rev. E. B. Smith, D. D., of New Hampton, N. H., and Rev. John Newton Brown, D. D., graduating in 1844. He then received an invitation to preach at Unionville (now Ashland), Mass., where he was ordained in March, 1845. With this people he remained two years, laboring with great success, large numbers being added to the list of church members. He next became pastor of the Baptist Church in Marblehead, Mass., remaining there two years. Receiving a call to settle with the Baptist Church in Rowley, Mass., he remained with them three years with satisfactory results; was pastor of the Baptist Church in Billerica, Mass., two years; since then settled at West Boylston, Mass.; from thence he removed to New York, where he labored as pastor for four years, when, his health failing, he resigned the office of pastor and received an appointment from the City Tract Society as city missionary April, 1860, where he now resides.

REV. AZARIAH B. WHEELER is the son of Beriah and Lucy Wheeler, of East Haddam, Conn.; born March 23, 1817. He pursued his academic studies at the East Haddam Academy; was ordained in the ministry in 1840. After preaching in various places, he was stationed at North Bridgewater, as pastor of the Second Methodist Episcopal Church, in April, 1851. He has held several public offices; at one time was president of the North Bridgewater Loan Fund Association. In 1855 he was a representative to the General Court from North Bridgewater. In 1856 was senator from Plymouth County, also a member of the Fremont Electoral College.

REV. T. B. McNULTY. (See page 76.)

PHYSICIANS.

DR. PHILIP BRYANT was born in Middleboro', Mass., in December, 1732. He lived some time with his father in Titicut (Teightaquid), a parish formed of part of Middleboro' and part of South Bridgewater. With his father, he removed to North Bridgewater, concerning which he was wont to say that he remembered the time when a greater part of it was thought quite unfit for the purposes of settlement. He studied medicine with Dr. Abiel Howard, of West Bridgewater, whose daughter he married. He was a man of great bodily activity, a calm and even temper, healthful habits, and kindly manners. He continued to practise medicine with much success to a very old age, which was terminated by his death, which took place February, 1817, in the eighty-fifth year of his age.

DR. PETER BRYANT (son of Dr. Philip Bryant) was born in North Bridgewater August 12, 1767. This man early distinguished himself by his love of study. In his frequent visits to the house of his grandfather, Dr. Abiel Howard, of West Bridgewater, he found, in a library well stocked for that time, the means of gratifying his thirst for knowledge. He studied medicine and surgery, completing his course with Dr. Lewis Leprilete, a French physician of eminent skill and a celebrated surgeon of Norton, Mass. He then removed to Cummington, in the western part of Massachusetts, which was just beginning to fill up rapidly with settlers from the eastern counties of the State. Here he established himself as a physician, and married a daughter of Ebenezer Snell, Esq., also a North Bridgewater family. For several years he represented the town of Cummington in the Legislature of the State, and in the latter part of his life held a seat in the Senate. While in the Legislature he took a prominent part in bringing forward and passing laws still in force to raise the standard of medi-

cal education in the State. In politics he belonged to the
Federal party, whose doctrines and measures he supported
with zeal. He wrote for the county paper, "Hampshire Gazette," certain humorous poems of a satirical cast, the design
of which was political. With these he took great pains,
pruning and retouching them, and polishing and invigorating
the lines. His scholarship, though not extensive, was remarkably exact. He had, subsequently to his settlement in
Cummington, made a voyage to the Indian Ocean and passed
six months in the Isle of France, where he acquired the
French language and preserved his familiarity with it for
the rest of his life. He was a surgeon of great dexterity,
firmness of hand, and precision in his operations; in private
life amiable and much beloved. His life was closed in consumption the 19th of March, 1820.

LUTHER CARY was son of Zachariah and Susannah (Bass)
Cary, and was born in North Bridgewater May 30, 1761;
married Nabby, daughter of Benjamin King, of Raynham,
Mass.; studied medicine with Dr. James Freeland, of Sutton,
Worcester County, Mass., 1782; appointed Justice of the
Peace June 8, 1800; Justice of Peace and of Quorum August
23, 1804, and Justice of the Court of Common Pleas for Oxford County March 30, 1805. He first resided at Sterling,
Mass; removed from there to Williamsburgh, Mass., from
which place he removed to Turner, Oxford County, Me., April
2, 1798. He was an excellent physician, had a very extensive practice, and was very successful; raised up a large
and respectable family, the most of whom are now living,
one a clergyman residing in Iowa.

ISSACHAR SNELL was son of Issachar, Esq., and Mary (Keith)
Snell; was born in North Bridgewater, Mass., June, 1775;
graduated at Harvard College in 1797; studied medicine, and

became an eminent physician. He had given especial attention to surgery, and had practised as a physician previous to
his removal to Winthrop, Me. He had performed the operation of lithotomy with great success, and soon gained large
practice in town, especially among those that emigrated from
Bridgewater, Mass., of whom there were not a few. His success as a surgeon gave him such celebrity that he was often
called to the neighboring towns, many miles away from his
home, to perform operations. To the great regret of the
people of Winthrop, he removed to Augusta, Me., in 1828,
where he continued to practise till his death, which took place
very suddenly in 1847, aged seventy-two years and five
months. He was a member of the Massachusetts Medical
Society.

DR. ELISHA TILLSON resided in the town a short time;
married Molly, daughter of Capt. Zebedee Snell, September
2, 1792, and had one son, Elisha Snell, born in 1794; married Betsy Chandler, of Easton, 1819.

ZIBA BASS, M. D., was son of Edward Bass. He was born
in Braintree May 28, 1774; studied medicine with Dr. Ebenezer Alden, of Randolph, Mass., and commenced practice in
North Bridgewater about 1800 under the most favorable au-
spices, with the fairest prospects of usefulness to his fellow-
men. He was a man of very pleasing address, of an affectionate and amiable disposition, and gave unwearied attention
to the welfare of his patients. His assiduity in search of
knowledge and his constant and undeviating fidelity in all
the duties of his profession won the affection and established
the confidence of a numerous class of the community in the
circle of his acquaintance; but he was suddenly called, soon
after commencing in life, from his earthly labors, leaving a
weeping multitude to deplore his loss. The following is on
his tombstone : —

" Erected to the memory of Dr. Ziba Bass, who died September 23, A. D., 1804, in the thirty-first year of his age, giving full proof that usefulness was his grand object in life. He was a pattern of modesty, temperance, fidelity, prudence, economy, and uprightness, and died in hope of eternal rest and glory.   Hence the following appropriation : ' Blessed are the dead who die in the Lord from henceforth : Yea, saith the Spirit, that they may rest from their labors; and their works do follow them.' "

DR. NATHAN PERRY.   This good man was born in Norton May 27, 1776; was educated in the common schools of his native town, never having received a college education ; pursued the study of medicine under the direction of Dr. Isaac Fowler, of Rehoboth, Mass., and Dr. Ebenezer Alden, Senior, of Randolph, both of whom were physicians of eminence in their day and accustomed to the instruction of young men. Having completed his pupilage, Dr. Perry commenced practice in Reading, Mass., 1802 or 3, where he acquired a good reputation and a competent share of employment.   On the death of Dr. Ziba Bass, which took place, September 3, 1804, at North Bridgewater, on the recommendation of his instructor, and by the solicitations of many respectable citizens of that town, he was induced to change his residence and take the place of his deceased friend.   He was immediately introduced into a wide circle of practice, and during a period of nearly thirty years was the principal physician in the town.   At length, in connection with reverses in his worldly circumstances, and the loss of most of the members of his family by death, his spirits became greatly depressed and his mind impaired.   Subsequently he suffered from paralysis, and never fully recovered the perfect exercise of either his bodily or mental powers; consequently, during the last twenty-five years of his life, he relinquished to a great extent the active duties of his profession. In 1823 he became a fellow of the Massachusetts Medical Society by election, and a retired member in 1830. He was a good physician, a man of sound judgment and sterling integrity, always pursuing the course he judged to be right, whatever might be the consequences to himself. In early life he made a public profession of his faith in Christ, and his character was in perfect harmony with his profession. He died peacefully in a ripe old age more from the debility incident to decay of his vital powers than from any manifest disease. Such was Dr. Perry, — a good man and a worthy citizen. He closed his earthly career Sabbath morning, August 16, 1857, at the advanced age of eighty-one years, leaving behind a memory cherished with affectionate regard by those who have shared his friendships and benefited by his counsels.

The following incident in relation to Dr. Perry is found in Clark's " History of Norton : " —

"About the year 1792, Nathan Perry, afterward Dr. Perry, of North Bridgewater, then a youth of some sixteen years of age, was one day passing by Judge Leonard's deer-park in Norton ; he playfully reached his hands through the fence and took hold of one of the old buck's horns, and for some time annoyed him in that way. At length the deer got out of patience, broke away from his hold, and quite unexpectedly leaped over the fence, seven or eight feet high, and made a furious attack upon young Perry, throwing him upon the ground ; but very fortunately the horns of the enraged deer, instead of striking his body, passed down on each side of it. While in this position, Nathan grasped the horns of the buck, and succeeded in preventing him from doing any injury till his brothers, Gardiner and Alvin, with one of Judge Leonard's men, came and rescued him from his perilous situation."

ADOLPHUS K. BORDEN, M. D., was born in Horton, Nova Scotia January 26, 1802 ; was educated at Windsor College ; received his medical degree from Harvard College, in 1824: first entered upon the practice of his profession in Wareham, Mass., where he remained seven years: from thence he removed to North Bridgewater, where he now resides in the enjoyment of a successful practice.

ABEL W. KINGMAN, M. D., is son of Abel and Lucy (Washburn) Kingman; born in North Bridgewater April 22, 1806;
graduated at Amherst College in 1830; commenced the practice of physician and surgeon at North Bridgewater, where
he now resides; he was appointed postmaster of that village
during Buchanan's administration.

JAMES F. RICHARDS, M. D., is son of Col. Jason and Sophia
(Forsaith) Richards, of Plainfield, Mass.; was born July 16,
1832; taught school in Virginia; studied medicine with Dr.
Forsaith, M. D., of South Abington, Mass.; graduated at the
College of Physicians and Surgeons of New York in 1859:
and is now a resident of Campello, enjoying a highly lucrative practice.

EDGAR EVERETT DEAN, M. D., is the son of Charles Dean, of
Easton, Mass.; born December 17, 1837; came to North
Bridgewater in June, 1861, and succeeded Dr. Alexander
Hichborn in the practice of medicine.   He received his early
education in the district schools of his native town till he
was fourteen years of age; student at Bristol Academy from
1853 to 1856; studied medicine with Dr. Luther Clark, of
Pinckney Street, Boston; graduated at Medical School, Harvard, March 6, 1861; practised in Boston for a short time,
and from thence to this town, where he enjoys a lucrative
and successful practice.

HORATIO BRYANT, M. D., is son of Micah and Drusilla
(Harlow) Bryant; born in Plympton, Mass.; fitted for college
with Rev. Elijah Dexter, and at Amherst Academy; entered
Amherst College; taught school at Castleton, Vt.; graduated
at Union College, Schenectady, N. Y.; taught academy at
Plainfield, N. J.; studied medicine at Yale College, where
he graduated in 1839; he commenced practice as a physician

and surgeon at Blandford, Mass., where he remained several years. He married Lucretia, daughter of Ebenezer Clark, of Conway, Mass., and has one daughter. He removed from Blandford to Campello, Mass., about 1848. He now resides at Independence, Iowa.

DR. THOMAS STOCKBRIDGE was born in Scituate, Mass.; came to North Bridgewater about 1837, and practised as a physician several years, until he removed to New York; he continued his practice in that city till about 1855, when he returned to North Bridgewater, and continued to practise as before till his death, which took place January 14, 1863.

DR. JAMES EASTON was in practice for some time.

DR. NAHUM SMITH was a botanic physician in the town for many years till he removed to Haverhill, Mass.

DR. E. R. WADE came to North Bridgewater about fifteen years since, and is a botanic physician.

HENRY EDDY, M. D., came to North Bridgewater, as a physician, from Guilford, Conn. He was formerly an Orthodox clergyman; settled in East Stoughton, Mass.

DR. JAMES LEWIS HUNT was born in Jay, Essex County, N. Y., November 27, 1817; educated at Kimball Union Academy, Meriden, N. H., and graduated at Dartmouth College, Hanover, N. H., in 1842; attended medical lectures at Cleveland and Cincinnati, Ohio; graduated at the Ohio Medical College, Cincinnati, in 1851; married Miss Maria Baldwin, of Medina, Ohio, September 11, 1850; practised medicine at Bellevue, Ohio, Plymouth, Mass., and North Bridgewater; removed from the last-named place but a few years since, and now resides at Painesville, Ohio.

SILAS L. LOOMIS, A. M., M. D., was born in North Coventry, Conn., May 22, 1832; son of Silas and Esther (Case)
Loomis; educated at the public schools of his native town
till fourteen years of age; studied six months at Wesleyan
Academy, Wilbraham, Mass.; three years at Holliston, Mass.;
graduated at Wesleyan University, Middletown, Conn., at the
age of sixteen; taught school; elected teacher of mathematics
and natural sciences at Holliston Academy, in 1839; held
that position during preparatory and part of his collegiate
studies; in connection with his brother, established the Adelphian Academy in North Bridgewater in 1844, of which he
was associate principal for ten years; was elected member of
the American Association for the Advancement of Science in
1853 at the Cleveland meeting; principal of Western Academy, Washington, D. C., 1855; graduated Doctor of Medicine,
Georgetown College, 1856; accepted the appointment of chief
astronomer of the United States Lake Survey Expedition in
1856; published the "Normal Arithmetic" and "Analytical
Arithmetic" in 1859; elected professor of chemistry, physiol-
ogy, and hygiene of Georgetown College in 1861, and the
same year was elected president of the Washington Scientific Association; in 1862 was appointed assistant surgeon,
U. S. A., and accompanied the Union Army of Gen. McClel-
lan from Fortress Monroe to Harrison's Landing, and afterward stationed at the United States General Hospitals; in
1863, elected to the chair of Chemistry and Texicology, medical department, Georgetown College, and has written various
articles upon medical and scientific subjects, many of which
are highly recommended by the press and distinguished men
of all classes.

LAFAYETTE CHARLES LOOMIS, A. M., M. D.; born in North
Coventry, Conn., July 7, 1824; son of Silas and Esther
(Case) Loomis; he was educated at the public school till the

age of thirteen; studied at Wesleyan Academy, Wilbraham, Mass., and at Holliston, Mass.; graduated at Wesleyan University, Middletown, Conn., in 1844; he commenced teaching in the public schools at the age of fifteen, which he continued to do winters through his academic and collegiate studies; In connection with his brother established the Adelphian Academy in North Bridgewater in 1844, of which he was associate principal till 1851, afterward principal of Irving Institute, Tarrytown, N. Y., in 1852-3; elected Professor of Rhetoric and Natural Science in Wesleyan Female College, Wilmington, Del., in 1853; Professor of Moral and Mental Philosophy in 1854, which chair he held till his election as president of the college in 1857. Several articles appeared in the "National Magazine" during that time. He was elected a member of the American Association for the Advancement of Science in 1856. In 1857 elected president of the Delaware State Teachers' Association. In 1858 he published " Mizpah, Prayer and Friendship," a devotional work of great merit: removed to Washington, D. C., and established the "Lafayette Institute," a seminary for young ladies; edited "Mrs. Thomas's Travels in Europe, Egypt, and Palestine" in 1860 and in 1861; wrote upon various subjects; graduated Doctor of Medicine and Surgery, medical department, Georgetown College, in 1863.

LAWYERS.

LUCIUS CARY was son of Moses Cary; born 1776; graduated at Brown University 1791; was an attorney-at-law, and died at Charleston, S. C., 1806, aged thirty years.

ELIAB WHITMAN, the subject of this notice, was the son of Seth Allen Whitman; born in that part of Bridgewater now known as East Bridgewater May 30, 1788. He prepared for

college at the Bridgewater Academy under the tuition of
John Shaw, then the preceptor of the academy (and who is
still living in Bridgewater); graduated at Brown University,
at Providence, 1817; returned to his native town, and there
studied law in the office of Hon. Nahum Mitchell, afterward
Judge of the Probate Court, and later Judge of the Court of
Commonpleas for Plymouth County. After his admission to
the bar, he settled in Lisbon, Me., where he practised his profession for about two years. In 1813 he returned to Bridgewater and settled in that portion of the town which was afterward incorporated as North Bridgewater; married Susannah, daughter of John Wales, May 18, 1817; here he passed
his life without ambition in the quiet discharge of the duties
that rested upon him. He was twice representative of the
town in the Massachusetts Legislature, in the years 1840 and
1841, but generally shrunk from public office. He is described by one who knew him well, as a man of severe integrity, whom neither money nor emolument of any kind
could induce to practise any misrepresentation, trick, artifice,
or injustice. He was not an advocate, rarely engaged in
trials before a jury, or even before the bench; but his integrity, punctuality, diligence, and carefulness brought him a
considerable office business, and he was present to attend to
it at all proper hours until age and infirmity prevented. In a
word he minded his own business and that of his clients, and
was utterly devoid of the ambition of making a figure in the
world. He was the only attorney in the town for many
years; was on the school committee several years. He had
three children.

JONATHAN WHITE, ESQ., is son of Jonathan and Abigail
(Holbrook) White; born in East Randolph, Mass., August
22, 1819; fitted for college at Phillips Academy, Andover;
entered Yale College in 1840; graduated in 1844; studied

law at Cambridge Law School; opened a law office in North
Bridgewater in 1849; appointed Justice of the Peace March
19, 1851, and Justice of Peace and Quorum throughout the
commonwealth March 15, 1859; represented the town of
North Bridgewater in the Legislature in 1864; is a successful attorney and counsellor at law.

Jonas R. Perkins, son of Rev. Jonas and Rhoda (Keith)
Perkins; born in Braintree, Mass., February 18, 1822; fitted
for college with his father; entered Brown University in
1837, and graduated in 1841; kept school two years in Rochester Academy, Mass.; studied law in the office of Timothy
G. Coffin, of New Bedford, Mass.; was associated with Mr.
Coffin in the practice of law three years; from thence sailed
for California July 10, 1849; returned to Massachusetts in
July, 1852, and in September of the same year opened a law
office in North Bridgewater, where he continues to practise
with success. He was appointed Justice of the Peace in
1852; Captain of North Bridgewater Dragoon Company,
1857; elected selectman of the town in 1864.

Austin Packard, Esq., was son of Thomas Packard; was
born in North Bridgewater January 15, 1801; graduated at
Brown University in 1821; studied law in the office of Hon.
William Baylies, of West Bridgewater, and was admitted to the
bar in 1824, and is now an attorney and counsellor at law in
West Bridgewater; is a successful practitioner. He has been
a prominent man in town affairs, having held many public offices of trust; represented the town of West Bridgewater in
the Massachusetts Legislature in 1848; is a Justice of Peace
and Trial Justice for Plymouth County, which office he has
held since that office was created; he has also been selectman, assessor, and overseer of the poor for eighteen years
in succession; married Charlotte, daughter of Abiel Ames,
of West Bridgewater.

DANIEL HOWARD was the son of Daniel and Vesta Howard; born in North Bridgewater February 6, 1775; graduated at Harvard College, Cambridge, in 1797; studied law with Hon. Judge Nahum Mitchell, of East Bridgewater, Mass.: commenced practice at Turner, Me.; from thence he removed to Buckfield, Me., afterward to New Gloucester, Me., then to Jay, Me., from which place he removed to East Vassalboro', about 1832 or 1833. He was a man of very respectable talent, although not distinguished; of modest, unassuming demeanor, and having never taken an active part in political matters, has never occupied any public offices; he was not a political office-seeker, choosing private life to that of public contention and strife; he was a man of very temperate habits and strict integrity; has had a family of seven children, most of whom are married and have families of respectability; fitted for college with Rev. Jonathan Strong, of Randolph, and Rev. John Reed, of West Bridgewater; taught school one year at Weymouth Landing.

LUCIUS KINGMAN is son of Eliphalet and Zilpha (Edson) Kingman; born January 23, 1803; graduated at Brown University, Providence, 1830; represented the town of North Bridgewater in the Legislature of Massachusetts several times; is now engaged in the Land Office of the United States at Quincy, Ill., and an attorney and counsellor at law.

CALEB HOWARD is son of Thomas Jefferson and Lavinia (Tilden) Howard; born in North Bridgewater August 2, 1834; studied law at Philadelphia and the Cambridge Law School; removed to the Sandwich Islands.

MELVILLE HAYWARD is son of Ambrose and Hannah Hayward; born in North Bridgewater April 21, 1836; was a student at the Adelphian Academy, graduating in January,

1850; removed to Williamsburgh, L. I., in May, 1851; studied law with P. J. Fish, Esq.; admitted to the bar in New York in 1857. In the call for troops in April, 1861, he enlisted with the famous New York Seventh Regiment for service, and again in May, 1862.

ELLIS WESLEY MORTON was born in North Bridgewater October 8, 1840; is son of Ellis J. and Abby S. (Anthony) Morton. He received his early education at the Adelphian Academy and North Bridgewater Academy under the care of S. D. Hunt, Esq.; graduated at the Classical High School, Providence, R. I.; studied law at Cambridge Law School; graduated with degree of Bachelor of Laws in 1861; admitted to the Suffolk Bar, Boston, October 8, 1861; appointed Assistant United States Attorney for Massachusetts November 1, 1861; received the appointment of Justice of the Peace January 13, 1862; admitted to the bar of the United States Circuit Court for Massachusetts February 17, 1862; admitted to the bar of the United States Supreme Court at Washington, D. C., March, 1864; is now a resident of Boston.

BRADFORD KINGMAN was born January 5, 1831; is son of Josiah W. and Mary (Packard) Kingman. After the usual attendance in the district schools of his native town, he attended the Adelphian Academy, North Bridgewater, Williston Seminary, East Hampton, Mass.; studied law with Lyman Mason, Esq., of Boston; admitted to the Suffolk Bar April 21, 1863; elected member of the New England Historic-Genealogical Society of Boston February 6, 1861; appointed Justice of the Peace for Norfolk County, January 22, 1864; is now an attorney and counsellor at law, resident of Brookline, Mass. and Trial Justice for the County of Norfolk.

MISCELLANEOUS.

THOMAS JEFFERSON SNOW was the son of Jonathan and Huldah Snow; born February 21, 1802, in that part of North Bridgewater called North-West Bridgewater, or West Shares. He had early in life acquired a fondness for books, and his parents, discovering that he had more than ordinary thinking powers and a desire for learning, decided to give him a collegiate education; he fitted for college under the tuition of Dr. Caleb Swan, of Easton, Mass., and Thomas Tolman, Esq., of Canton, Mass.; he entered Brown University, Providence, R. I., a year in advance, and graduated in 1825 with the usual honors. His natural inclinations were of a literary cast. He never published works of any kind, but was frequently employed to deliver lectures. The most of his life was spent in teaching, with the exception of three years. He was a very successful teacher. He was first principal of Hingham Academy, afterward principal of Franklin High School, in Nantucket, Mass.; he then accepted the principalship of the Milton Academy, Milton, Mass., where he taught six years, and was elected honorary member of Harvard College. This position he resigned for the purpose of removing West, which was in 1835, when he moved to Michigan City, in the northern part of Indiana: from thence he removed to Kentucky, where he resided twelve years, teaching and educating his sons; but fearing to have his sons brought up and coming under the influence of slavery, he removed to Illinois in 1851. He opened a school the same year in Peoria, where he taught till his death, October 6, 1851, aged forty-nine years. He was buried in the Masonic Cemetery with the honors of that order. He held the office of " Royal Arch Mason." He left a wife and seven children to mourn his loss as a kind friend, a good teacher, and good counsellor; he was a warm receiver and firm advocate of the doctrines of the " New Jerusalem

Church." His eldest son, Hector O. Snow, was formerly professor in Shelbyville College, also professor in the commercial colleges, Chicago, and is now principal of the Tazewell High School, Tazewell County, Ill.; his second son, Orin T. Snow, is principal of Batavia High School, Kane County, Ill.; Croyden P. Snow is principal of the Second District Grammar School, Peoria, Ill.; Herman W. Snow was a teacher in the last-named school for seven years, when he resigned to enter upon the profession of law, and is now settled in Peoria, Ill., attorney-at-law, member of Peoria bar.

FREDERICK CRAFTS, A. M., is son of Rev. Thomas and Polly (Porter) Crafts; born June 5, 1797. In early life he resided in the West Parish of Middleboro', Mass., of which his father was pastor; he fitted for college at Pierce Academy, Middleboro'; graduated at Brown University, Providence, R. I., in 1816; studied law and was admitted to the bar of Plymouth County. He soon left the practice of law, and, after teaching at Boston, Taunton, and other places, was appointed principal of the Bridgewater Academy, where he remained till 1861, when he resigned. He is now a resident of Bridgewater.

HEMAN PACKARD, born in North Bridgewater, was the son of Levi and Ruth (Snow) Packard; resided in that town teaching school for many years; at length, his health being such that he could not reside in the northern climate, he engaged in travelling as colporteur; for four years he distributed tracts up and down the Mississippi among the flatboat and rafts men coming down the river. In the year 1842 he was appointed colporteur for the American Bible Society in the city of New Orleans, afterward receiving the agency of the South-West Bible Society and American Sunday-school Union, also of the Presbyterian Board of Publication. He was a warm-hearted, devoted Christian man, whose whole aim and
25

purpose seemed to be devoted to doing good, cheerfully giving of his time and substance to that object. He left his native town about the year 1838 or 1840, having spent about twenty years in his labor of love. He died January 12, 1858, at New Orleans.

At a meeting of the Bible Society, held at New Orleans on the day of his death, resolutions were passed expressive of the sorrow for the friends of the departed, also, " That in his death the society has lost one of its best and truest friends and servants. So long as he lived we always felt that it had the earnest, faithful, effectual, and fervent prayers of a right-eous man ascending to the throne of God's grace in its be-half."

AUGUSTUS T. JONES, A. M., was born in North Bridgewater May 21, 1832; fitted for college at Adelphian Academy and at Phillips Academy, Andover, Mass; entered Amherst College September, 1854, where he remained two years; entered junior class at Yale College, New Haven, Conn., September, 1856, and graduated in July, 1858; had the degree of Master of Arts conferred upon him in 1862; was principal of high school at Williamsburgh, Mass., from 1860 to 1862; began to publish the "North Bridgewater Gazette" in September, 1863, of which he is now publisher and editor.

HEMAN PACKARD DE FOREST* is son of Isaac and Jane Baker (Packard) Packard; born August 20, 1839. After receiving the usual common school education in his native school district, at the age of fifteen, he entered the North Bridgewater Academy, which had then been in existence but a short time; commenced fitting for college in the fall of 1856; graduated

* The name of De Forest is an adopted name in honor of David C. De Forest, who had left a sum of money to Yale College to be appropriated to the education of those who should adopt his name.

at Yale College in July, 1862; entered Yale Theological Seminary in September, 1863.

S. D. Hunt was born in Sudbury, Mass., June 8, 1823; son of Sewall Hunt; received his education at the academies in Derry, N. H., and Framingham, Mass.; taught high school at Concord, Mass., eight years, ending 1854; removed to North Bridgewater, and established the North Bridgewater Academy in 1855.

Dr. Jonathan Porter Crafts was son of John and Olive (Porter) Crafts; born in North Bridgewater September 9, 1792; graduated at Brown University, Providence, R. I., in 1817; studied medicine, but never practised his profession; died in 1822, aged thirty years.

Dr. George B. Cogswell had an office in Wheeler's Block in 1859, where he remained but a short time.

Dr. Alexander Hichborn had an office in the village, and practised as a physician till 1861, when he enlisted as a captain in Co. F, 12th Regiment, Colonel Fletcher Webster; afterward became surgeon in the army.

Rev. Samuel Fuller Dike is son of Samuel and Betsy (Burrill) Dike; was born in North Bridgewater March 17, 1815; fitted for college under the instruction of Rev. Daniel Huntington, and at the Weymouth and Braintree Academy, Samuel T. Worcester, instructor, and the Bridgewater Academy, Hon. John Shaw, instructor; entered Brown University Providence, R. I., in 1834; graduated in 1838; was a preceptor of Yarmouth Academy, Yarmouth Port, Mass., one and a half years; studied theology with Rev. Thomas Worcester, of Boston; completed his studies for the ministry in

1840; was ordained as minister of the New Jerusalem Church at the session of the General Convention of New Jerusalem Churches at Philadelphia, June 7, 1840, by Rev. Thomas Worcester, of Boston; commenced preaching as a candidate in Bath, Me., June 14, 1840. At the end of the same year, he received a call to settle with the society where he now labors; this call he accepted, and was duly installed Sunday, October 10, 1841. He has continued his labors of love to that church and society to the present time. On the Sabbath, June 13, 1847, he was made an ordaining minister of the New Jerusalem churches by the general convention holden in the city of New York. He has been president of the Maine and New Hampshire Association of the New Jerusalem Churches for nearly twenty years; also, superintendent of the public schools of Bath from 1847 to 1863.

CHAPTER IX.

OFFICIAL HISTORY.

WE present to our readers in this chapter the names of those who have held public office, and although it may not be of interest to every one, yet there are those that like to know who have had the management of public affairs both in town and state. To see a list of those having held positions of trust and confidence can hardly fail to be of interest to us as showing the estimate in which they were held by their fellow-citizens. To be a Selectman or " Townsman," as they were sometimes called, was considered as being one of the " fathers of the town." The Selectmen have nearly the control of the affairs of a town, and it is very common, even to this day, in town meetings " to refer the matter to the Selectmen, with full powers," or to leave business at the discretion of the Selectmen with suggestions from the town. Hence the value that should be placed upon such officers, and the reason why none but men of good judgment and integrity should be selected. Anything and everything, not otherwise provided by law, in regard to town affairs, falls by custom to the care of the Selectmen; and generally such men have been chosen.

LIST OF SELECTMEN FROM THE INCORPORATION OF THE TOWN OF NORTH BRIDGE-
WATER TO THE PRESENT YEAR.*

Howard Cary, 1821–24.

Zachariah Gurney, 1821–23.

Abel Kingman, 1821–23.

Eliphalet Kingman, 1824–28.

Ephraim Cole, Jr., 1824–28.

John Packard, 1824, 25.

Robert Packard, 1824.

Caleb Howard, 1824.

* The Selectmen have performed the duties of assessors and overseers of the poor ever since the incorporation of the town.

Jesse Perkins, 1826–28.
Benjamin Kingman, 1829–33.
Darius Howard, 1829–35.
Nahum Perkins, 1829–33, 39, 40, 45.
Linus Howard, 1834, 35.
Lucius Kingman, 1834, 35.
Albert Smith, 1836–38.
Lorenzo Wade, 1836.
Nathaniel H. Cross, 1836, 37.
Isaac Eames, 1837, 39, 40, 50.
Newton Shaw, 1840–44.
Caleb Copeland, 1836, 40–42, 45.
Josiah W. Kingman, 1838–41, 58, 60–63.
Perez Marshall, 1842–44.
Col. Nathan Jones, 1843, 44.

George Clark, 1846–54.
Bela Keith, 1845–48, 51–54.
Frederick Howard, 1849.
John Field, 1849.
Marcus Packard, 1851–53.
Ellis Packard, 1855, 59–61.
William H. Cooper, 1855.
Vinal Lyon, 1855.
Franklin Ames, 1856–63.
Edwin H. Kingman, 1846–48, 56, 57.
Franklin Keith, 1856–58.
Nelson J. Foss, 1859, 64, 65.
Isaac Kingman, 1850, 65.
Ruel Richmond, 1854.
Nathan Packard, 2d, 1862, 63.
Jonas R. Perkins, 1864.

Rufus L. Thatcher, 1864, 65.

TOWN CLERKS.

Next in importance among the officers of a town is the Town Clerk. Upon him devolves the care of all the records and doings of the Selectmen and town meetings; and this office requires a man of accuracy and good judgment, as well as firm integrity; experience, also, is an important requisition for good clerks. Hence we find most of the clerks of this town have served long terms.

LIST OF TOWN CLERKS OF NORTH BRIDGEWATER FROM ITS INCORPORATION TO THE PRESENT TIME, WITH THE YEARS EACH HAS SERVED.

Edward Southworth, 1821–29.
Jesse Perkins, 1830–38.

Franklin Ames, 1839–54.
Horatio Paine, 1855–61.

Welcome H. Wales, 1862–65.

LIST OF TREASURERS OF THE TOWN OF NORTH BRIDGEWATER TO THE PRESENT TIME.

Edward Southworth, 1821–29.
Jesse Perkins, 1830–37.
Franklin Ames, 1838–54.

Francis M. French, 1855.
Rufus P. Kingman, 1856–64.
Oakes S. Soule, 1865.

LIST OF MODERATORS OF TOWN MEETINGS FROM THE INCORPORATION OF THE TOWN TO THE PRESENT TIME.

Joseph Sylvester, 1821, 23–26, 28, 29, 32–35, 38.
Eliphalet Kingman, 1822.
Abel Kingman, 1827, 30, 31.

Col. Nathan Jones, 1836, 37, 39–42.
Jesse Perkins, 1843–54.
William H. Cooper, 1855, 60.
George Clark, 1856–58, 59.

R. H. Williams, 1861–65.

LIST OF REPRESENTATIVES TO THE GENERAL COURT FROM THE TOWN OF NORTH BRIDGEWATER FROM ITS INCORPORATION TO THE PRESENT TIME.

Caleb Howard, 1822.
Howard Cary, 1823, 24.
Capt. John Packard, 1825.
Abel Kingman, 1828–30, 36, 37.
Ephraim Cole, 1829, 30.
Rev. John Goldsbury, 1831.
Eliphalet Kingman, 1831.
Lucius Kingman, 1834, 35.
Albert Smith, 1838, 39.
Eliab Whitman, 1840, 41.
Benjamin Kingman, 1842, 43.
Daniel Huntington, 1844.
Henry French, 1845, 46.

Josiah W. Kingman, 1847, 48.
Jesse Perkins, 1831, 33–37, 39, 40, 49, 51, 52.
No choice 1850.
Nahum Perkins, 1853.
No choice 1854.
Lewis Fisher, 1855.
Rev. A. B. Wheeler, 1856.
Rev. Paul Couch, 1857, 58.
Edward Southworth, Jr., 1859, 60.
Lorenzo D. Hervey, 1861, 62.
George B. Dunbar, 1863.
Jonathan White, 1864.

Nelson J. Foss, 1865.

LIST OF REPRESENTATIVES OF THE TOWN OF BRIDGEWATER FROM THE NORTH PARISH.

Gideon Howard, 1813.

Daniel Howard, 1815–20.

STATE SENATORS FROM NORTH BRIDGEWATER.

Hon. Abel Kingman, 1836, 37.
Hon. Jesse Perkins, 1841, 43.

Rev. A. B. Wheeler, 1857.
Hon. Edward Southworth, Jr., 1861.

EXECUTIVE COUNCILLOR FROM DISTRICT NO. 8.

Franklin Ames, 1859.

LIST OF ENGINEERS OF THE FIRE DEPARTMENT SINCE ITS ORGANIZATION IN 1846.

Benjamin Kingman, 1846–48.
Edward Southworth, 1846–58.
Josiah W. Kingman, 1846–52, 54.
Charles Lincoln, 1846–52, 55–59.
Ruel Richmond, 1846–52, 54.
Chandler Sprague, 1846–51, 53.
William S. Gay, 1846–48.
Bela Keith, 1849–52.
Benjamin G. Stoddard, 1849–52.
Charles Howard, 1852, 55–59.
Lorenzo D. Hervey, 1853, 54.
Francis M. French, 1853, 55–57.

Aaron B. Drake, 1853–57.
Edwin H. Kingman, 1854.
Darius Howard, 1854–57, 60, 61.
Lewis Fisher, 1855–59.
Nelson J. Foss, 1857, 58, 60, 61.
Barnabas H. Gray, 1858, 59.
Charles L. Hathaway, 1858, 59.
Daniel Dunbar, 1859.
Alpheus K. Harmon, 1860.
Benjamin P. Lucas, 1861–65.
George Sawyer, 1864, 65.
Samuel McLaughlin, 1864, 65.

Isaac H. Hartwell, 1864, 65.

LIST OF JUSTICES OF THE PEACE, WITH THE DATE OF THEIR COMMISSION.

Nathaniel Reynolds, June 14, 1776.
Barnabas Howard, March 14, 1782.

Daniel Howard, * May 17, 1787.
Daniel Howard, 2d, June 19, 1790.

Issachar Snell, March 11, 1791.
Gideon Howard, July 4, 1803.
Issachar Snell, Jr., March 5, 1804.
Caleb Howard, January 25, 1806.
Howard Cary, July 10, 1807.
Simeon Dunbar, February 17, 1810.
Abel Kingman, February 22, 1811.
Lemuel Packard, February 25, 1812.
Joseph Sylvester, February 25, 1812.
Eliab Whitman, * † July 3, 1816.
Silas Packard, July 3, 1818.
Edward Southworth, Feb. 1, 1819.
Micah Packard, August 20, 1823.
Jonathan Snow, January 7, 1824.
Eliphalet Kingman, March 1, 1827.
Linus Howard, August 27, 1829.
George Clark, June 25, 1830.
Jesse Perkins, * † June 16, 1831.
Austin Packard, † ‡ Sept. 29, 1835.
Bela Keith, July 7, 1837.
Franklin Ames, * † § March 31, 1842.
Isaac Eames, June 20, 1843.
Perez Crocker, June 20, 1843.
George W. Bryant, † ‡ March 31, 1846.
Isaac Kingman, October 13, 1847.
Jonathan White, * § March 19, 1851.
Edwin H. Kingman, March 26, 1851.
Perez Marshall, April 25, 1851.
Jonas R. Perkins, † Nov. 20, 1852.

Charles Lincoln, February 9, 1855.
Francis M. French, Feb. 9, 1855.
Hiram Jernegan, October 1, 1855.
Dennis Snow, February 11, 1856.
Rufus L. Thatcher, Feb. 9, 1857.
Manley Packard, March 24, 1857.
Nathan Jones, March 24, 1857.
Ellis Packard, March 24, 1857.
Cornelius H. Dunham, March 24, 1857.
Willard Keith, October 29, 1857.
Franklin Keith, February 15, 1858.
William H. Cooper, March 10, 1858.
Horatio E. Paine, January 26, 1858.
Loring W. Puffer, February 8, 1859.
Algernon S. Sylvester, Feb. 15, 1859.
Edward Southworth, Jr., March 29, 1859.
Chandler Sprague, Nov. 23, 1859.
Galen E. Pratt, January 2, 1860.
Daniel Crocker, April 30, 1860.
Sumner A. Hayward, Nov. 27, 1860.
Isaac E. Snell, February 6, 1861.
Arza B. Keith, February 19, 1861.
Charles Gurney, February 26, 1861.
Nelson J. Foss, May 17, 1861.
Ellis W. Morton, January 13, 1862.
David L. Cowell, Dec. 31, 1862.
William Perry, January 30, 1863.
Josiah W. Kingman, Jan. 14, 1864.

Bradford Kingman, Jan. 22, 1864.

NOTE. Those marked with * are of the Quorum; those marked with † are to qualify civil officers; those marked with ‡ are Trial Justices; those marked with § are Justices throughout the commonwealth. All others are county appointments.

CORONERS IN THE TOWN OF NORTH BRIDGEWATER.

Thomas Packard, December 17, 1811.   Thomas Wales, Jr., July 3, 1821.
Benjamin A. Packard, February 11, 1856.

NOTARY PUBLIC.

George W. Bryant, May 10, 1854.   Jonas R. Perkins, December 6, 1853.

DEPUTY SHERIFFS RESIDENT IN THE TOWN.

Darius Howard, 1806–12.
Benjamin Kingman, 1819–51, 54, 55.
Fiske Ames, 1815–22.

Sumner A. Hayward, 1852, 53, 57, 59.
Charles J. F. Packard, 1856–59.

Otis Hayward, 1862–65.

LIST OF MILITARY OFFICERS, WITH THE DATES OF THEIR COMMISSION.

COLONELS.

Simeon Cary, 1758.   Josiah Hayden.

Nahum Reynolds.

LIEUTENANT-COLONELS.

Caleb Howard, May 21, 1810.   Nathan Jones, October 3, 1829.
Edward Southworth, April 29, 1817. Martin Cary, October 1, 1832.

MAJORS.

John Porter, May 30, 1777.   Nathan Hayward, March 23, 1824.
Josiah Hayden.   Moses Noyes, July 22, 1824.
Daniel Cary, September 6, 1792.   Nathan Jones, September 15, 1828.
Caleb Howard, June 15, 1802.   Martin Cary, September 22, 1831.
Edward Southworth, Aug. 22, 1815.   Nahum Reynolds, August 28. 1837.

Uriah Macoy, July 30, 1864.

CAPTAINS.

Daniel Howard.   Abiel Packard, November 27, 1819.
Robert Howard.   Luke Packard, July 4, 1820.
Abiel Packard.   Moses Noyes, March 19, 1822.
Barnabas Howard.   David Ames, May 7, 1822.
Isaac Packard.   Ziba Keith, September 5, 1822.
Jeremiah Beals.   Nathan Hayward, Sept. 20, 1823.
John Porter, December 9, 1774.   Jabez Kingman, May 4, 1824.
Simeon Cary, December 9, 1774.   John Battles, July 15, 1825.
Nathan Packard, July 25, 1778.   Nathan Jones, May 30, 1827.
Lemuel Dunbar, July 25, 1778.   John W. Kingman, July 4, 1828.
Joseph Cole, July 25, 1778.   Ornan Cole, October 7, 1828.
David Packard, July 23, 1780.   Alvah Noyes, August 10, 1829.
Lemuel Packard, March 10, 1785.   Augustus Jones, August 10, 1831.
Anthony Dike, July 16, 1792.   Martin Cary, August 10, 1831.
Parmenas Packard, March 28, 1795.   Charles Gurney, December 3, 1831.
Leavitt Thayer, May 2, 1796.   Thomas Hathaway, October 27, 1832.
Robert Packard, May 29, 1796.   Cary Howard, November 1, 1834.
Abel Kingman, May 5, 1799.   Nahum Reynolds, May 3, 1836.
Howard Cary, May 14, 1799.   Nahum Reynolds, June 27, 1853.
Zachariah Gurney, 3d, May 25, 1802. Robert A. Stoddard, Sept. 28, 1853.
Gideon Howard, May 25, 1803.   J. Freeman Ellis, April 25, 1854.
Oliver Jackson, June 17, 1804.   Henry A. Raymond, May 8, 1856.
Jonathan Snow, May 6, 1806.   Jonas R. Perkins, July 11, 1857.
Thomas Thompson, May 6, 1806.   Lucius Richmond, August 27, 1860.
Asa Jones, September 16, 1809.   Alexander Hichborn, June 26, 1861.
Noah Chessman, September 23, 1811.   Charles T. Packard. Aug. 20, 1862.
Nehemiah Lincoln, 2d, May 25, 1814. John S. Stoddard, July 23, 1862.
Adin Packard, May 31, 1815.   Alpheus K. Harmon, May 10, 1862.
Silas Dunbar, May 26, 1816.   Uriah Macoy, July 11, 1864.
Adin Packard, Jr., April 12, 1817.   Charles L. Sproul, July 30, 1864.

26

Elisha Tillson, Surgeon's Mate, September 30, 1794.
Daniel Hartwell, Adjutant, September 6, 1792.
Caleb Howard, Adjutant, August 27, 1795.
Issachar Snell, Surgeon's Mate, December 13, 1800.
Rev. Daniel Huntington, Chaplain, May 6, 1816.
John Tilden, Jr., Adjutant, January 1, 1827.
Rev. Edward L. Clark, June 26, 1861.
Rev. Israel Washburn, Chaplain, September 1, 1862.
Rev. W. A. Start, Chaplain, April 18, 1864.

When our government was first organized, there were no party organizations. In 1785, political parties sprung up upon questions of light importance, and soon were done away. From 1798 to 1800, two great parties came into being; namely, Federal and Republican, or, as sometimes called, Anti-Federal. The Federal were those in favor of a strong national government, while the advocates of Thomas Jefferson were opposed to our present constitution on the ground that it was opposed to the States' rights. From that day to the present, these parties have assumed new positions as new questions came up, and new issues were made, till at last the Republican party became the advocate of a strong national government, and the Federal party became strict constructionists. After the War of 1812, the Federal party gradually faded away, and a new party arose, taking the name of National Republicans, and afterward that of Whigs, to show that they were opposed to the executive prerogative; these were also opposed to the Democratic party through the States. In 1848, the Free-Soil party arose in the Northern States, and supported Martin Van Buren. About 1850, the Coalition party sprung up, being a compound of "Free-Soil" with a portion of the Democratic party. In 1854, there was a sudden, secret, and effectual breaking up of the Whig, Free-Soil, and Democratic parties, giving a new character to political affairs, and known as "American Know-Nothings." In 1857, the present Republican party was formed in Massachusetts and some of the Northern States, and most of the Whig party have become merged in this party.

The following list shows how the people of North Bridgewater have voted since it became a town : —

VOTES FOR GOVERNOR SINCE THE INCORPORATION OF THE TOWN OF NORTH BRIDGEWATER, IN JUNE, 1821.

Year	Candidate	Votes	Year	Candidate	Votes
1822.	William Eustis	165	1835.	Edward Everett	214
	John Brooks	38		Marcus Morton	77
1823.	William Eustis	211	1836.	Marcus Morton	157
	Harrison G. Otis	28		Edward Everett	144
1824.	William Eustis	220	1837.	Edward Everett	280
	Samuel Lothrop	34		Marcus Morton	151
1825.	Levi Lincoln	184	1838.	Edward Everett	228
	Marcus Morton	3		Marcus Morton	149
1826.	Levi Lincoln	213	1839.	Edward Everett	293
	Samuel Hubbard	2		Marcus Morton	179
1827.	Levi Lincoln	124	1840.	John Davis	400
	William C. Jarvis	3		Marcus Morton	180
1828.	Levi Lincoln	140	1841.	John Davis	383
	Marcus Morton	3		Marcus Morton	178
1829.	Levi Lincoln	190	1842.	John Davis	358
	Marcus Morton	4		Marcus Morton	184
1830.	Levi Lincoln	169		Samuel E. Sewall	31
	Marcus Morton	6	1843.	George N. Briggs	323
1831.	Levi Lincoln	245		Marcus Morton	187
	Marcus Morton	7		Samuel E. Sewall	37
1831.*	Levi Lincoln	125	1844.	George N. Briggs	385
	Samuel Lothrop	66		George Bancroft	140
	Marcus Morton	6		Samuel E. Sewall	80
1832.	Levi Lincoln	121	1845.	George N. Briggs	325
	Samuel Lothrop	100		Isaac Davis	138
	Marcus Morton	15		Samuel E. Sewall	68
1833.	John Q. Adams	209	1846.	George N. Briggs	293
	John Davis	61		Isaac Davis	121
	Marcus Morton	29		Samuel E. Sewall	66
1834.	John Bailey	128	1847.	George N. Briggs	290
	John Davis	108		Caleb Cushing	136
	Marcus Morton	29		John M. Brewster	64

* Owing to an amendment in the Constitution, there were two elections in 1831, which required the governor to be chosen in November instead of April, and to take his seat on the first Wednesday of January instead of the last of May. The reader will therefore understand that, from 1832, those who are elected in November are chosen for the following year.

1848.	George N. Briggs	315		Erastus D. Beach	207
	Stephen C. Phillips	298	1856.	Henry J. Gardner	668
	Caleb Cushing	67		George W. Gordon	36
1849.	George N. Briggs	328		Erastus D. Beach	217
	Stephen C. Phillips	226		Luther V. Bell	43
	George S. Boutwell	98	1857.	N. P. Banks	368
1850.	George N. Briggs	324		Henry J. Gardner	197
	Stephen C. Phillips	309		Erastus D. Beach	182
	George S. Boutwell	84	1858.	N. P. Banks	434
1851.	Robert C. Winthrop	381		E. D. Beach	184
	John G. Palfrey	315		Amos A. Lawrence	27
	George S. Boutwell	123	1859.	N. P. Banks	325
1852.	Horace Mann	374		B. F. Butler	156
	John H. Clifford	355		George N. Briggs	40
	Henry W. Bishop	98	1860.	John A. Andrew	677
1853.	Emery Washburn	347		Erastus D. Beach	193
	Henry Wilson	305		Amos A. Lawrence	103
	Henry W. Bishop	90	1861.	John A. Andrew	258
	Bradford L. Wales	50		Isaac Davis	162
1854.	Henry J. Gardner	537	1862.	John A. Andrew	596
	Emery Washburn	97		Charles Devens, Jr.	230
	Henry Wilson	52	1863.	John A. Andrew	579
	Henry W. Bishop	51		Henry W. Paine	56
1855.	Julius Rockwell	270	1864.	John A. Andrew	733
	Henry J. Gardner	265		Henry W. Paine	190

THE FOLLOWING LIST OF GOVERNORS OF THE STATE WILL SHOW WHEN NORTH BRIDGEWATER ACTED WITH A MAJORITY OF THE PEOPLE OF THE COMMONWEALTH.

John Brooks, 1816–22.
William Eustis, 1823, 24.
Levi Lincoln, 1825–33.
John Davis, 1834, 35.
Edward Everett, 1836–39.
Marcus Morton, 1840.
John Davis, 1841, 42.

Marcus Morton, 1843.
George N. Briggs, 1844–50.
George S. Boutwell, 1851, 52.
John H. Clifford, 1853.
Emery Washburn, 1854.
Henry J. Gardner, 1855–57.
Nathaniel P. Banks, 1858–60.

John A. Andrew, 1861–65.

MODERATORS OF THE YEARLY PRECINCT MEETINGS FOR THE CHOICE OF OFFICERS FROM 1738 TO THE INCORPORATION OF THE TOWN IN 1821.

Timothy Keith, February 5, 1739.
Timothy Keith, March 12, 1739.
James Packard, March 26, 1739.
John Kingman, March 24, 1740.
Daniel Howard, March 23, 1741.

Daniel Howard, March 23, 1742.
Abiel Packard. March 28, 1743.
Daniel Howard, March 28, 1744.
Shepard Fiske, March 25, 1745.
Daniel Howard, March 26, 1746.

Daniel Howard, March 25, 1747.
Daniel Howard, March 28, 1748.
Abiel Packard, March 27, 1749.
Abiel Packard, March 29, 1750.
Abiel Packard, March 25, 1751.
Shepard Fiske, March 25, 1752.
Constant Southworth, March 28, 1753.
Shepard Fiske, March 28, 1754.
Daniel Howard, March 26, 1755.
Shepard Fiske, March 29, 1756.
Shepard Fiske, March 28, 1757.
Daniel Howard, March 28, 1758.
Zachariah Snell, March 20, 1759.
Simeon Cary, March 19, 1760.
Constant Southworth, March 16, 1761.
Daniel Howard, March 22, 1762.
Daniel Howard, March 25, 1763.
Shepard Fiske, March 19, 1764.
Simeon Brett, March 27, 1765.
Daniel Howard, March 19, 1766.
Daniel Howard, March 18, 1767.
Constant Southworth, March 22, 1768.
Simeon Cary, March 20, 1769
Simeon Cary, March 20, 1770.
Nathaniel Reynolds, March 20, 1771.
Nathaniel Reynolds, March 12, 1772.
Simeon Cary, March 22, 1773.
Simeon Brett, March 28, 1774.
Nathaniel Reynolds, March 20, 1775.
Simeon Cary, March 14, 1776.
Simeon Cary, March 17, 1777.
Simeon Cary, March 25, 1778.
Simeon Cary, March 17, 1779.
Thomas Thompson, March 27, 1780.
Simeon Brett, March 19, 1781.
Capt. Jesse Perkins, March 19, 1782.

Col. Josiah Hayden, March 13, 1783.
Issachar Snell, Esq., March 11, 1784.
Matthew Kingman, March 17, 1785.
Barnabas Howard, March 29, 1786.
Dr. Philip Bryant, March 21, 1787.
Capt, Zebedee Snell, March 18, 1788.
Issachar Snell, Esq., March 19, 1789.
Daniel Howard, March 18, 1790.
Issachar Snell, March 22, 1791.
Issachar Snell, March 19, 1292.
Issachar Snell, March 19, 1793.
Matthew Kingman, March 17, 1794.
Dr. Elisha Tillson, March 16, 1795.
Dr. Philip Bryant, March 21, 1796.
Lemuel Packard, March 9, 1797.
Daniel Howard, March 8, 1798.
Caleb Howard, March 7, 1799.
Matthew Kingman, March 6, 1800.
Joseph Sylvester, Jr., March 2, 1801.
Daniel Howard, Jr., March 4, 1802.
Daniel Howard, Jr., March 28, 1803.
Moses Cary, March 27, 1804.
Abel Kingman, March 11, 1805.
Caleb Howard, March 27, 1806.
Jonathan Perkins, March 30, 1807.
Howard Cary, March 24, 1808.
Dr. Nathan Perry, March 20, 1809.
Jonathan Perkins, March 19, 1810.
Gideon Howard, March 18, 1811.
Caleb Howard, March 23, 1812.
Jonathan Perkins, March 15, 1813.
Joseph Sylvester, March 14, 1814.
Joseph Sylvester, March 13, 1815.
Caleb Howard, March 4, 1816.
Joseph Sylvester, Jr., March 24, 1817.
Joseph Sylvester, Jr., April 3, 1818.
Howard Cary, Esq., March 25, 1819.
Caleb Howard, March 10, 1820.
Dr. John S. Crafts, March 10, 1821.

Previous to 1700, the number of Selectmen in the old town of Bridgewater was three, and they were chosen by nomination, which custom was continued till 1757, when the number chosen yearly was five, — one from each parish, — till the incorporation of the town of North Bridgewater.

THE FOLLOWING ARE THOSE CHOSEN FOR THE NORTH PARISH.

Shepard Fiske, 1757–74.
Col. Simeon Cary, 1770–75.
Nathaniel Reynolds, 1776, 77.
Col. Josiah Hayden, 1770–80.
Lieut. John Howard, 1781.
Col. Josiah Hayden, 1782.

Capt. Jesse Perkins, 1783–85.
Issachar Snell, Esq., 1786–88.
Capt. Jesse Perkins, 1789–95.
Major Daniel Cary, 1796–1801.
Capt. Abel Kingman, 1802–17, 19–
    21.

Eliphalet Kingman, Esq., 1818.

LIST OF CLERKS IN THE NORTH PARISH OF BRIDGEWATER, AND THE YEARS
EACH HAS SERVED.

Robert Howard, 1739–71.
John Howard, 1772–81.
Daniel Howard, 1782–85.
Capt. Jesse Perkins, 1786–91.

Daniel Cary, 1792–1802.
Capt. Jesse Perkins, 1802–15.
Jesse Perkins, Jr., 1816–18.
Adin Packard, 1819.

Lemuel French, 1820, 21.

TREASURERS OF THE NORTH PARISH FROM 1738 TO 1821.

Abiel Packard, 1738–43.
Deacon Samuel West, 1744, 45.
Samuel Brett, 1746–48.
Constant Southworth, 1747.
Daniel Howard, 1749–51.
Isaac Packard, 1752–54.
Abia Keith, 1755, 59–61.
Thomas Torrey, 1756, 58.
Jabez Field, 1757.
Abel Packard, 1762.
Dr. John Staples Crafts, 1763, 64.
Zachariah Cary, 1765.
Barnabas Packard, 1766–71.
Nathaniel Southworth, 1772, 76, 77.

Capt. Jesse Perkins, 1773, 81, 82.
Issachar Snell, 1774.
Reuben Packard, 1775.
Simeon Packard, 1778, 79.
Simeon Cary, 1780.
Capt. David Packard, 1783.
Lieut. Daniel Cary, 1784–92.
Jonathan Perkins, 1793, 94.
Abel Kingman, 1795–1800.
Caleb Howard, 1801.
Capt. Howard Cary, 1802–9.
Perez Crocker, 1810.
Jonathan Beals, 1811, 12.
Ichabod Howard, 1813.

Edward Southworth, 1814–21.

COMMITTEE OF THE NORTH PARISH OF BRIDGEWATER FROM 1738 TO 1821,
SHOWING THE YEARS EACH HAS SERVED.

Timothy Keith, 1738–40, 49.
David Packard, 1738–45.
Daniel Howard, 1738, 39, 41–48, 52
    –55.
Samuel Kingman, 1739, 40.
James Packard, 1741, 42, 51, 52.
Zachariah Snell, 1743, 46, 47, 54.
Samuel West, 1744, 45.

Abiel Packard, 1746–48, 50, 52, 54,
    56–58, 60, 61, 63–69.
Moses Curtis, 1748, 49.
Solomon Packard, 1749.
Robert Howard, 1750, 51, 56, 70, 81.
Henry Kingman, 1750, 51, 55, 67, 68.
Shepard Fiske, 1753, 55–58.
Simeon Cary, 1759, 61, 77, 79, 91.

Nathaniel Reynolds, 1759, 66, 70, 72, 74, 75.

Constant Southworth, 1760, 62, 64.

Ebenezer Packard, 1762, 63, 68, 69, 73, 74.

Isaac Packard, 1765, 72.

Abia Keith, 1770.

Barnabas Howard, 1771, 72, 74, 76, 78.

Dr. Philip Bryant, 1771, 75, 76, 79, 95, 97.

Jacob Packard, 1772.

Simeon Brett, 1777.

Dea. David Edson, 1776.

Josiah Hayden, 1778.

Jesse Perkins, 1780, 83, 91, 93, 96, 98-1800.

Jonathan Cary, 1780, 84, 85, 87-90.

Capt. Zebedee Snell, 1780, 86, 94, 95.

Zechariah Gurney, 1781, 1812, 21.

Ichabod Edson, 1781.

Issachar Snell, 1782, 84-93.

Matthew Kingman, 1782-93, 98.

Reuben Packard, 1782.

William Shaw, 1783.

Ichabod Howard, 1794, 1802, 4-6.

Dr. Elisha Tillson, 1794, 95, 97.

Capt. Lemuel Packard, 1796, 99, 1803, 7, 8.

Timothy Ames, 1796.

Dr. John S. Crafts, 1797.

Col. Caleb Howard, 1798, 1801, 3, 11-13, 15-21.

Joseph Silvester, Esq., 1799, 1800.

Jonathan Perkins, Jr., 1800, 10, 15, 19, 20.

Issachar Snell, Jr., 1801.

Daniel Cary, 1801.

Perez Southworth, 1802, 4-10, 12-14, 21.

Howard Cary, 1803.

Capt. Gideon Howard, 1804-10.

Moses Cary. 1807-9.

Asa Jones, 1809.

Col. Edward Southworth, 1816.

Abel Kingman, Esq., 1811, 13, 14.

Thomas Packard, 1811.

Capt. Robert Packard, 1817, 18.

CHAPTER X.

STATISTICAL HISTORY.

Population of the North Parish in 1764, 1790, 1810, 1820, 1830, 1840, 1850, 1855, 1860, 1835. — Parish Rates in 1744. — List of Polls in the Parish in 1770. — Owners of, and Valuation of Dwelling-Houses in 1798. — Industrial Table for 1837. — Valuation in 1840, 1850, 1860. — Industrial Tables for 1845 and 1855. — Number cf persons engaged in various trades.

IN order that we may more fully realize the rapid strides that have been and are now being made in this country, let us imagine ourselves in a wilderness, surrounded with wild beasts and wilder men, where the deer, panther, the wild-cat, bear, and other beasts roamed over the forests subject to no law but might, when the red man prowled over its surface, regardless of life only to take it. When we think of the hardships our ancestors endured, the sufferings they passed through, we can but feel astonished at the onward progress that has been and is now being made in all that contributes to make us happy, prosperous, and useful to our country and to ourselves. To witness the progress of civilization, the rapidity with which this country has grown, the development of her resources, its advance in agriculture, religion, and literature ; to note the refinement and the elevated position of our present inhabitants, is interesting to the student, the man of business, the farmer, and all who are curious to watch the changes as they occur.

We have observed in another part of this work that the early inhabitants of this town were farmers or agriculturists, and the soil not being adapted for extensive tillage, many parts of the town being stony and rough, it was not as inviting as some other places for that purpose. Hence, in early times, emigration to other parts of the country was great ; a large number removed to Plainfield, Cummington, Pelham, and other towns in the westerly portion of the State, and many to Winthrop, Turner, and Minot in the State of Maine, then a part of Massachusetts. This will in a great measure account for the slow peopling of the town in early days.

An order was passed by the Assembly, February 2, 1764, directing the selectmen of each town and district to "take an exact account of the number of dwelling-houses, families, and people in their respective towns and districts, including Indians civilized, negroes and mulattoes, as well as white people, and females as well as males."

At this period there were one hundred and twenty houses in the North Parish, — one hundred and thirty-one families, with a population of eight hundred and thirty-three.

The above was the first attempt to take the census in Massachusetts.

In 1790, the first United States census was taken, since which time there has been a statement of the population every ten years, each one varying from the other in the system of classification.

In the years 1790 and 1800, the account is not separately given in a manner to show what the population of the North Parish was.

The population of the Parish in 1810 was 1,354.

THE FOLLOWING IS THE CENSUS OF THE NORTH PARISH IN 1820 :

Free white	males	under 10,.......................	190
"	"	" of 10 and under 16,...............	107
"	"	" of 16 and under 26,...............	153
"	"	" of 26 and under 45,...............	145
"	"	" of 45 and upwards,...............	123
Colored Persons,....................................			23

Free white females under 10,........................ 181
"   "   "   of 10 and under 16,............... 113
"   "   "   of 16 and under 26,............... 151
"   "   "   of 26 and under 45,............... 156
"   "   "   of 45 and upwards,............... 134
Foreigners not naturalized,.......................... 4
Number of dwelling-houses,.......................... 220
Total number of inhabitants,........................1,480

POPULATION IN 1830, 1,953, WITH THE FOLLOWING DETAILS :

MALES. Under 5, 129 ; 5 to 10, 112 ; 10 to 15, 129 ; 15 to 20, 122 ;
20 to 30, 177 ; 30 to 40, 105 ; 40 to 50, 73 ; 50 to 60, 36 ; 60 to 70, 41 ;
70 to 80, 19 ; 80 to 90, 8 ; 90 to 100, 1.

FEMALES.   Under 5, 122: 5 to 10, 110 ; 10 to 15, 102 ; 15 to 20, 92 ;
20 to 30, 211 ; 30 to 40, 106 ; 40 to 50, 85 ; 50 to 60, 58 ; 60 to 70, 42 ;
70 to 80, 24 ; 80 to 90, 9 ; 90 to 100, 0.

COLORED PERSONS.

MALES. Under 10, 6 ; 10 to 24, 9 ; 24 to 36, 3 ; 36 to 55, 3 ; 55 to 100, 2.
FEMALES.   Under 10, 3 ; 10 to 24, 5 ; 24 to 36, 1 ; 36 to 55, 4 ; 55 to
100, 4.

POPULATION IN 1840, 2,094, WITH THE FOLLOWING DETAILS :

MALES. Under 5, 0 ; 5 to 10, 170 ; 10 to 15, 147 ; 15 to 20, 156 ; 20 to
30, 167 ; 30 to 40, 187 ; 40 to 50, 93 ; 50 to 60, 72 ; 60 to 70, 30 ; 70 to 80,
23 ; 80 to 90, 11 ; 90 to 100, 2.   Total 1,058.

FEMALES.   Under 5, 0 ; 5 to 10, 170 ; 10 to 15, 135 ; 15 to 20, 114 ; 20
to 30, 132 ; 30 to 40, 202 ; 40 to 50, 100 ; 50 to 60, 72 ; 60 to 70, 48 ;
70 to 80, 26 ; 80 to 90, 15 ; 90 to 100, 0.   Total 1,014.   Colored, 22.

POPULATION IN 1850, 3,939, WITH THE FOLLOWING DETAILS :

Under 1, 101 ; 1 to 5, 379 ; 5 to 10, 418 ; 10 to 15, 364 ; 15 to 20, 452 ;
20 to 25, 449 ; 25 to 30, 402 ; 30 to 35, 320 ; 35 to 40, 248 ; 40 to 45,
198 ; 45 to 50, 156 ; 50 to 55, 115 ; 55 to 60, 91 ; 60 to 65, 79 ; 65 to 70,
56 ; 70 to 75, 35 ; 75 to 80, 21 ; 80 to 85, 13 ; 85 to 90, 5 ; 90 to 95, 4 ;
95 to 100, 3 ; colored, 30.   Total 3,939.

POPULATION IN 1855, 5,205, BY THE STATE CENSUS, WITH THE FOLLOWING
DETAILS :

Under 5, 707 ; 5 to 10, 533 ; 10 to 15, 523 ; 15 to 20, 507 ; 20 to 30,
1,125 ; 30 to 40, 790 ; 40 to 50, 451 ; 50 to 60, 298 ; 60 to 70, 170 ; 70 to
80, 71 ; 80 to 90, 15 ; 90 to 100, 2.

POPULATION IN 1860, 6,584, WITH THE FOLLOWING DETAILS:

MALES. Under 1, 92; 1 to 5, 397; 5 to 10, 361; 10 to 15, 298; 15 to 20, 360; 20 to 30, 705; 30 to 40, 490; 40 to 50, 338; 50 to 60, 171; 60 to 70, 99; 70 to 80, 47; 80 to 90, 8: 90 to 100, 1. Total 3,367.

FEMALES. Under 1, 118; 1 to 5, 347; 5 to 10, 343; 10 to 15, 248; 15 to 20, 292; 20 to 30, 694; 30 to 40, 462; 40 to 50, 288; 50 to 60, 200; 60 to 70, 115: 70 to 80, 61; 80 to 90, 12: 90 to 100, 0. Total 3,185.

COLORED PEOPLE.

MALES. Under 1, 0; 1 to 5, 4; 5 to 10, 3; 10 to 15, 1; 15 to 20, 1; 20 to 30, 2; 30 to 40, 3; 40 to 50, 1; 50 to 60, 1; 60 to 70, 1. Total 18.

FEMALES. Under 1, 0; 1 to 5, 2; 5 to 10, 3; 10 to 15, 0; 15 to 20, 1; 20 to 30, 3; 30 to 40, 3; 40 to 50, 1; 50 to 60, 0; 60 to 70, 1. Total 14. Number of dwelling-houses, 1,023; number of families, 1,377.

Population in 1865, 6,335. Number of dwellings, 1,249. Number of families, 1,391. Number of churches, 8. Number of schoolhouses, 15. Number of ratable polls, 1,708. Number of legal voters, 1,362. Number of naturalized voters, 141.

The following is a list of rates as made out by the assessors in the North Parish of Bridgewater, for the payment of Rev. John Porter's salary, for the year 1744, as made out by Daniel Howard and Robert Howard, *Assessors* of the Precinct, September ye 14th, 1744, and committed to Joshua Warren, *Constable*, for collection, and is inserted to show the inhabitants of the parish at that date: —

Names.	Polls.	Tax. £ s. d.	Names.	Polls.	Tax. £ s. d.
Timothy Keith,	2	2 7 6	Isaac Fuller,	1	1 3 9
David Packard,	3	3 11 3	Jacob Packard,	1	1 3 9
Solomon Packard,	2	2 7 6	Alexander Wilson,	1	1 3 9
Jacob Allen,	1	1 3 9	David Brown,	1	1 3 9
John Kingman, 2d,	1	1 3 9	Daniel Ames,	1	1 3 9
Benjamin Edson,	3	3 11 3	Daniel Howard,	1	1 3 9
John Kingman, 3d,	1	1 3 9	Robert Howard,	2	2 7 6
Henry Kingman,	1	1 3 9	Samuel West,	1	1 3 9
Deacon Packard,	2	2 7 6	Pelatiah Phinney,	1	1 3 9
Zechariah Packard,	2	2 7 6	Seth Packard,	1	1 3 9
James Torrey,	0	0 3 0	David Packard, Jr.,	1	1 3 9
Joshua Warren,	2	2 7 6	William Packard,	2	2 7 6
James Hewett,	1	1 3 9	Mark Perkins,	3	3 11 3
Micah Langford,	1	1 3 9	Samuel Brett,	1	1 3 9

Names.	Polls.	Tax.		
		£	s.	d.
Daniel Rickard,	1	1	3	9
Abiel Packard,	2	2	7	6
Constant Southworth,	2	2	7	6
Widow Lydia Packard,	0	0	0	0
Caleb Phillips,	1	1	3	9
John Johnson,	0	0	0	0
Zachariah Cary,	2	2	7	6
John Pratt,	1	1	3	9
Zechariah Snell,	2	2	7	6
William French,	0	0	0	0
Elisha Dunbar,	1	1	3	9
Abiah Keith,	1	1	3	9
Daniel Field, Jr.,	1	1	3	9
Ebenezer Hill,	1	1	3	9
John Battles,	1	1	3	9
Joseph Phinney,	1	1	3	9
Nathaniel Reynolds,	1	1	3	9
Thomas Reynolds,	1	1	3	9
Samuel Pettingill,	1	1	3	9
Akerman Pettingill,	2	2	7	6
Isaac Allen,	1	1	3	9
Benjamin Hayward,	1	1	3	9
Zechariah Cary,	1	1	3	9
Edward White,	1	1	3	9
John Randall,	2	2	7	6
William French,	1	1	3	9
David French,	1	1	3	9

Names.	Polls.	Tax.		
		£	s.	d.
Archibald Thompson,	2	2	7	6
Jabez Field,	2	2	7	6
Walter Downie,	2	2	7	6
Benjamin Pettingill,	1	1	3	9
Joseph Pettingill,	1	1	3	9
Peter Edson,	1	1	3	9
Benjamin Worrick,	1	1	3	9
John Buck,	1	1	3	9
Simeon Cary,	1	1	3	9
Jonathan Cary,	1	1	3	9
Thomas Terrill,	1	1	3	9
John Coley,	1	1	3	9
Zepio (Col'd),	1	1	3	9
Thomas Henry,	1	1	3	9
Matthew Buck,	1	1	3	9
Abiah Keith,	1	1	3	9
Widow Keith,	0	0	0	0
Ames,	0	1	3	9
Japhet Rickard,	0	1	3	9
Ephraim Willis,	0	0	0	0
John Brett,	1	1	3	9
Thomas Buck,	1	1	3	9
Benjamin Edson, Jr.,	1	1	3	0
John Dailey,	0	0	0	9
Charles Snell,	1	1	3	9
Edward Southworth,	2	2	7	6
Shepard Fisk,	0	0	0	0

The following list is inserted to show the residents of the North Parish in 1770, with the number of polls against each householder : —

Names.	Polls.	Names.	Polls.
Joseph Allen,	1	Ephraim Cole,	1
Samuel Brett,	1	Joseph Cole, Jr.,	1
Simeon Brett,	3	Ephraim Churchill,	2
Matthew Buck,	3	Ashley Curtis, Jr.,	1
Dr. Philip Bryant,	1	Elisha Dunbar,	0
Seth Bryant,	1	Elisha Dunbar, Jr.,	1
Job Bryant,	1	Seth Dunbar,	1
Jeremiah Beal,	2	Silas Dunbar,	1
Japhet Beal,	1	Jesse Dunbar,	1
Zechariah Cary,	1	Ensign John Dailey,	1
Joseph Cole,	1	Jabez Field,	3
Samuel Cole,	2	Levi French,	1

Names.	Polls.	Names.	Polls.
Zachariah Gurney,	1	Ebenezer Snell,	2
Lt Elisha Gurney,	1	Cornet Charles Snell,	2
Micah Gurney,	1	Eleazer Snow, Jr.,	2
Daniel Howard, Esq.,	1	Samuel Sturtevant,	1
Capt. Barnabas Howard,	1	Ezekiel Southworth,	1
Capt. Robert Howard,	2	Edmund Soper,	1
Robert Howard, Jr.,	1	Jacob Thayer,	1
Elisha Hayward,	1	Enoch Thayer,	1
Joseph Hayward,	1	Zechariah Watkins, Jr.,	1
Jonathan Hayden,	1	Eleazer Cole,	1
Josiah Hayden,	2	Ephraim Willis,	1
Abiah Keith,	2	Demetrius Rickard,	1
Nathan Keith,	2	Fobes Field,	1
Jacob Keith,	1	Samuel Brett, Jr.,	1
Daniel Manly,	1	Ezra Cary,	1
John Brett,	1	Abram Packard,	1
Capt. Abiel Packard,	2	Enos Thayer,	1
Thomas Packard,	1	Barnabas Curtis,	1
Timothy Packard,	1	Eleazer Cole,	1
David Packard,	2	Daniel Ames,	3
David Packard, Jr.,	1	Timothy Ames,	1
Abiezer Packard,	1	Noah Ames,	1
William Packard,	2	Benjamin Ames,	1
William Packard, Jr.,	1	Simeon Alden,	1
Lemuel Packard,	1	Isaac Brett,	1
Capt. Isaac Packard,	2	Simeon Cary,	1
Abia Packard,	1	Jonathan Cary,	1
Ensign Abel Packard,	2	Dr. John Staples Crafts,	1
John Packard,	1	Deacon David Edson,	1
Nathan Packard, Jr.,	1	James Edson,	1
Barnabas Pratt,	1	Benjamin Edson,	1
Thomas Pratt,	1	Jacob Edson,	1
Jonathan Perkins,	1	William Edson,	1
Daniel Pettingill,	1	Ichabod Edson,	1
Stephen Pettingill,	1	Ebenezer Edson,	2
Caleb Phillips,	1	Isaac Fuller,	1
Capt. Eliphalet Phillips,	1	Mark Ford,	1
Nathaniel Reynolds,	1	Thomas Hendry, *Estate*,	
Philip Reynolds,	1	Lt. John Howard,	2
Jonas Reynolds,	1	Adam Howard,	0
Timothy Reynolds,	1	Lt. Henry Kingman,	2
Thomas Reynolds,	3	Matthew Kingman,	1
Jacob Rickard,	1	Henry Kingman, Jr.,	1
Charles Richardson,	1	John and Adam Kingman,	1
Ensign Issachar Snell,	1	John Kingman, Jr.,	1
Zebedee Snell,	2	Levi Keith,	2

Names.	Polls.	Names.	Polls
Nehemiah Lincoln,	1	Lemuel Southworth,	1
Ebenezer Packard,	2	Benjamin Southworth,	1
Jacob Packard,	1	William Shaw,	3
Nathan Packard,	2	Joseph Sylvester,	1
Simeon Packard,	1	Thomas Thompson,	2
James Packard,	1	Seth Thayer,	2
Reuben Packard,	2	Joshua Warren,	1
Seth Packard,	1	Ebenezer Warren,	1
Lt. Josiah Packard,	1	Ezra Warren,	1
Joshua Packard,	1	Thomas West,	1
Daniel Packard,	1	William French,	1
Eliab Packard,	1	Isaiah Fuller,	1
Barnabas Packard,	1	Lt. Daniel Noyes,	0
George Packard,	1	Jacob Noyes,	0
Josiah Perkins,	1	Samuel Noyes,	0
Samuel Pettingill,	3	David Porter,	0
Edmund Pettingill,	1	Joseph Porter,	1
Joseph Pettingill,	2	Samuel Dike,	1
Daniel Richards,	2	Jesse Perkins,	1
John Richards,	0	Jacob Packard, Jr.,	1
Constant and Nath. Southworth,	1	Moses Cary,	1
Edward Southworth,	2		

" General list of all Dwelling Houses which, with the Out Houses appurtenant thereto and the Lots on which the Same are erected, not exceeding two Acres in any Case, were owned, possessed, or occupied, on the 1st day of October, 1798, within the Assessment District, No. 10, in the Sixth Division of the State of Massachusetts, *exceeding* in value the Sum of One Hundred Dollars."

Names of reputed owners.	Valuation in dolls.	Names of reputed owners.	Valuation in dolls.
Daniel Alden,	200	Jeremiah Beal,	175
Timothy Ames,	230	Isaac and Joseph Brett,	620
Noah Ames,	225	Samuel Brett,	150
Job Ames,	225	Rufus Brett,	110
Joseph Alden,	110	Daniel Cary,	350
Daniel Alden,	230	Thomas Craft,	550
Philip Bryant,	500	Ephraim Churchill,	105
Amzi Brett,	110	Barnabas Curtis.	120
Job Bryant,	200	Joseph and B. Crosswell,	105
Samuel and William Brett,	275	Moses Cary,	110
Japhet Beal,	250	Samuel Chesman,	175

Names of reputed owners.	Valuation in dolls.
Ephraim Cole,	500
Jonathan and James Cary,	325
Jonathan Cary, Jr.,	200
Simeon and Howard Cary,	325
Jacob and Ebenezer Dunbar,	220
Jacob Dunbar, Jr.,	150
Samuel Dike, Jr.,	120
Mannasseh and Sam. Dickerman,	325
Ichabod Edson,	250
Seth Edson,	105
William and William Edson,	120
David Edson,	230
James and Josiah Edson,	120
Josiah and Elisha Eames,	200
James Eaton,	105
Fobes, Jabez, and Daniel Field,	500
William Field,	175
Asa Ford,	175
Mark and Samuel Ford,	150
Bezaleel and Bethuel Field,	200
Zechariah Gurney, Zechariah Gurney, Jr.,	105
Silas Sturtevant, Ephraim Groves,	200
Caleb Hayward,	125
Ichabod Howard,	625
John Howard,	500
Alfred Howard,	230
Robert and Robert Howard, Jr.,	400
Mary Howard, Solomon Hill,	200
Waldo Howard,	110
Asaph Howard,	200
Asaph Hayward,	275
Joseph Hayward,	175
Barnabas and Jonas Hayward,	500
Daniel Howard, 2d,	300
John Hunt,	180
Oliver Howard,	350
Gideon Howard,	400
William Jameson,	
Asa Jones,	175
Ephraim Jackson,	230
Jonathan Keith,	230
Levi Keith,	350

Names of reputed owners.	Valuation in dolls.
Benjamin Keith,	275
Shepard Keith,	150
Seth Kingman,	500
Matthew Kingman,	275
Matthew Kingman,	325
Guardian of Isaac Packard,	
Abel Kingman,	150
Nathan Keith,	120
Henry Kingman,	150
Solomon Keith,	
Daniel Keith and Son,	
Seth Keith,	
Jeremiah Keith,	
Edward Keith,	
Samuel Keith,	
Nehemiah Lincoln,	175
Nathan Leach,	130
Nathaniel Manley,	230
Daniel Manley,	230
Daniel Manley, Jr.	110
Thomas Macomber,	200
Hayward Marshall,	175
Ephraim Noyes,	500
Josiah Packard,	500
Eliphalet Packard,	150
Nathaniel and Leonard Orcutt,	135
Silas Packard,	625
Jonathan Perkins, Jr.	150
Ames Packard,	110
Eben'r., Lot and Robt. Packard,	360
Jonas Packard,	150
James Porter,	120
Josiah Packard,	200
Lemuel Packard,	650
Jonathan Perkins,	110
Nathan Packard,	325
Jesse and Zadoc Perkins,	625
Rebecca Perkins, Noah Packard,	120
James Perkins,	600
Thomas Packard,	130
John Porter,	
Luke Perkins,	200
Shepard Perkins, Widow Abigail Perkins,	275

Names of reputed owners.	Valuation in dolls.	Names of reputed owners.	Valuation in dolls.
Luke Perkins and Isaac Porter,..		Zebedee Snell,................	175
Josiah Perkins,................	120	Issachar Snell,................	400
Benjamin Packard,............	450	Joseph Snell,.................	110
Joseph Packard,..............	105	Joseph Sylvester,.............	120
Widow Content Packard,......	150	Joseph Sylvester, Jr.,.........	350
Mark Perkins,................	175	Benjamin Southworth,.........	105
Levi Packard,................	325	Shepard Snell,................	150
Widow Dorothy Packard,......	275	William and Micah Shaw,.....	300
Cyrus Packard,...............	175	Nathaniel Snell,..............	275
Thomas and Elijah Packard,...	175	Perez Southworth,............	210
Abiah and Howard Packard,...	250	John Tilden,.................	275
Josiah Pratt,.		Thos. and Thos. Thompson, Jr.,.	460
Jonas Reynolds,..............	150	James Thompson,.............	
Widow Elizabeth Reynolds,...	150	Seth Thayer,.................	110
Seth Snow,...................	105	Jeremiah Thayer,.............	110
Ephraim Sturtevant,.........	275	Enos Thayer,.................	220
Jonathan Snow,..............	200	John Wales,.................	130
Silas and Widow Snow,.......	550	Thomas Willis,...............	500
Zechariah and Oliver Snow,...	275	Ephraim Willis,..............	250

NAHUM MITCHELL, *Assessor.*

JOHN WHITMAN,
SOLOMON HAYWARD,
DANIEL CARY,   } *Assistant Assessors.*
JONATHAN COPELAND,
DANIEL FOBES,

BRIDGEWATER, March 5, 1799.

The Legislature of Massachusetts, by an act passed April 19, 1837, required the Assessors of the several towns in Massachusetts to return to the Secretary of the Commonwealth, an accurate account of the various branches of industry. The following is the product of North Bridgewater, for 1837 : —

Cotton mill, 1 ; number of spindles, 350 ; cotton consumed, 16,000 lbs. ; number of yards of cotton cloth manufactured, 60,000; value of the same, $4,800 ; males employed, 3 ; females, 12 ; capital invested, $8,666. Common sheep, 60 ; common wool produced, 210 lbs. ; average weight of fleece, $3\frac{1}{2}$ lbs. ; value of same, 84 ; capital invested, $120. Boots manufactured, 79,000 pairs. Shoes manufactured, 22,300 pairs ; value of boots and shoes, $184,200 ; males employed, 750; females, 375.   Hat manufactories, 1 ; hats manufactured, 2,000 ; value of same, $6,000 ; males employed, 3 ; females, 3.   Manufactories of forks and hoes, 1; value of same, $1,000 ; hands employed, 2 ; capital invested, $400. Manufactories of chairs and cabinet ware, 3 ; value of the same, $38,500 ; hands employed, 39.   Value of wooden ware manufactured, $300 ; hands employed, 1.   Shoe tool manufactories, 2 ; value of the same, 1,900 ; hands employed, 22 ; capital invested, $5,000.

VALUATION FOR 1840.

Number of polls over 16, 679 ; number of polls supported by the town, 5 ; number of polls not taxed, 20.   Number of houses, 388 ; number of shops adjoining, 153 ; number of warehouses, stores, etc., 6 ; number of barns, 264 ; all other buildings, 69.   Tillage land, 663 acres ; English and upland mowing, 1,043 acres ; tons of hay, 744 ; fresh meadow, 692 ; tons of hay on the same, 399 ; pasture, 2,789 ; woodland, 2,243 ; unimproved land, 2,283 ; unimprovable, 613 ; town land, 120 acres ; roads, 245 acres ; water, 20 acres.   Horses, one year old and over ; oxen, four years old and over, 467 ; steers and heifers, 83 ; sheep, 22 ; swine, 314.   Number of chaises, 47.   Grist-mills, 3 ; sawmills, 3 ; other mills, 1.   Oats, 1,063 bushels ; rye, 405 bushels ; barley, 331 bushels ; corn, 3,833 bushels.

VALUATION FOR 1850.

Polls 1,067, 20 years and upwards.   Dwelling-houses, 616 ; shops adjoining houses, 96 ; other shops, 134 ; warehouses and stores, 13 ; grist-mills, 4 ; saw-mills, 2 ; Barns, 29 ; all other buildings of the value of $20 and upwards, 155.   Stock in trade, $75,655 ; interest money, $68.96 ; stocks, $28,170 ; shares in incorporated companies, 475 ; tillage land,

574 acres; unimproved land, 97 acres; unimprovable land,
65; land owned by town, 100 acres; land taken for roads,
300 acres; land covered by water, 100 acres. Number of
horses, 278; number of oxen, four and over, 82; number
of cows, three and over, 487; steers and heifers, 151.
Rye, bushels, 244; oats, bushels, 543; corn, bushels, 4,344;
barley, bushels, 139. Acres mowing, 1,527; tons of hay,
1,128; fresh meadow, 642; tons of hay, 409; pasturing,
3,310; woodland, 3,499; swine, 264; all other property
not enumerated, value, $12,541.

VALUATION FOR 1860.

Ratable polls, 1,574, 20 years and upward. Male polls,
3, not taxed nor supported by the town. Male polls, 2,
supported by the town. Dwelling-houses, 952; each $900,
$856,800. Shops within or adjoining to dwelling-houses,
94: each $75, $7,050. Other shops, 206; each $200, $41,-
200. Warehouses and stores, 38; at $1,500 each, $5,700.
Barns, 388; at $250 each, $97,000. Grist-mills, 4; at $2,000
each, $8,000. Saw-mills, 2; at $2,550 each, $5,100. Steam
mills, and other mills not above enumerated, 5; at $3,180
each, $15,900. Boot factories, 5; $13,000. Shoe factories,
37: at $1,000 each, $37,000. Piano-forte factories, 1;
$1,000. Tool factories, 2; at $850 each, $1,700. Nail
and tack machines, 1; $400. Other manufactories of iron,
copper, brass, and metals, 2; at $850 each, $1,700. All
other buildings between $20 and $100 in value, 6; at $75
each, $450. All other buildings of more than $100 value,
5; at $1,000, $5,000. Amount of every person's stock in
trade, $209,786. Amount of money at interest more than
any creditor pays interest for, including United States and
State securities, $86,500. Amount of stock held by stock-
holders in any bank or insurance company, $140,114.
Shares in toll-bridges, canals, railroads, 323; value, $34,500.

Acres of land annually tilled, exclusive of orchards tilled, 1,106; at $130 each, $143,780. Amount of orcharding, all kinds of fruit, 77 acres; at $200, $15,400. Acres of upland mowed, excluding orcharding mowed, 1,505; at $130, $195,650; tons of hay produced, yearly produce of same, 1,281. Acres of orcharding mowed, 8; $200, $1,600; tons of hay, the yearly produce of the same, 5. Acres of fresh meadow, 591; tons of hay, the yearly produce of the same, 364. Acres of land, excluding orcharding pastured, 2,872; at $20, $57,440. Acres of woodland, 4,384, excluding pasture land enclosed; at $15 each, $65,760. Cords of wood, 4,827. Acres of land owned by any town or other proprietors, 92; at $40 each, $3,680. Acres of land used for roads, 329. Acres of land covered by water, 1,000. Acres of land in town from actual survey, 12,619. Horses one year old and upwards, 279; at $75, $20,925. Oxen four years old and upwards, 60; at $40, $2,400. Cows three years old and upwards, 403; at $25, $10,075. Steers and heifers one year old and upwards, 115; at $10, $1,150. Swine six months old and upwards, 190; at $6, $1,140. Value and description of all other ratable estate, not before enumerated, $20,990. Total value, $2,173,965.

A census of the productions of the State, published in 1845, shows the product of North Bridgewater, Mass., as follows :—

Manufactories of shovels, spades, forks, and hoes, 1; value of articles manufactured, $2,000; capital, $500; men employed 2.

Musical instrument manufactories, 1; value of instruments manufactured, $900; capital, $350; men employed, 2.

Brush manufactories, 1; value of brushes manufactured, $21,500; capital, $6,000; men employed, 21.

Saddle, harness, and trunk makers, 1; value of articles manufactured, $1,500; capital, $300; employ 3 men.

Hat and cap manufactories, 1; value of hats and caps manufactured, $1,040; valued, $2,500; capital, $500; employ 3 men.

Establishments for manufacturing railroad cars, coaches, chaises, and other vehicles, 1; value manufactured, $1,590; capital, $300; employ 3 men.

Chair and cabinet ware manufactories, 2; value of goods manufactured, $38,000; capital, $18,571; men employed, 48.

Tin ware and stove manufactories, 2; value of goods manufactured, $6,074; capital, $2,200; employ 11 hands.

Boots manufactured, 44,711 pairs; 155,476 pairs shoes; value, $179,716; men employed, 301; females, 203.

Value of snuff, cigars, and tobacco, $5,200; employ 9 persons.

Value of pumps, blocks, $361; employ 2 men.

Value of mechanics' tools manufactured, $8,250; employ 19 hands.

Shoe-last and boot-tree manufactories, 1; value of goods manufactured, $7,995; capital, $1,500; employ 7 men.

Value of machines for rolling leather, $1,599; capital, $300; employ 1 man.

Value of packing boxes manufactured, $2,132; capital, $400; employ 6 men.

Lumber prepared, 300,000 feet; value, $3,531.

Firewood prepared, 1,155 cords; value' $4,620.

Horses, 292; value, $17,520; neat cattle, 632; value, $15,800; swine, 338; value, 5,070.

Indian corn or maize raised, 5,000 bushels; value, $3,333. Rye, 366 bushels; value $293. Barley, 239 bushels; value, $143. Oats, 585 bushels; value, $234. Potatoes, 23,111 bushels; value, $5,777. Other esculent vegetables, 2,000 bushels; value, $600. Millet, 4 tons; value, $50. Hay, 1,445 tons; value, $20,230. Fruit raised, 7,249; value, $1,812. Butter, 20,496 lbs.; value, $3,279. Cheese, 23,280 lbs.; value, $1,862. Honey, 235 lbs.; value, $28. Beeswax, 16 lbs.; value, $4.

The Industrial Tables for 1855 show the following as the production of North Bridgewater: —

Musical instrument manufactories 2; value of instruments manufactured, $8,780; capital, $2,000; employ 9 hands.

Daguerrotype artists, 1; daguerrotypes taken, 800; capital, $450; employ 1 man.

Brush manufactories, 2; value of brushes, $8,000; capital, $3,000; employ 11 men.

Saddle, harness, and trunk manufactories, 1; value of saddles, etc., $6,000; capital, $2,000; employ 4 men.

Establishments for the manufacture of chaises, wagons, sleighs, and other vehicles, 3; value of carriages manufactured, $5,200; capital, $1,600; employ 8 men.

Establishments for making soap and tallow candles, 2; soap manufactured, 280 barrels; value of soap, $1,120.

Chair and cabinet ware manufactories, 1; value of chairs and cabinet ware manufactured, $20,000; capital, $10,000; employ 32 men.

Tin-ware manufactories, 2; value of tin-ware, $13,000; capital, 4,600; employ 7 men.

Boots of all kinds manufactured, pairs, 66,956; shoes of all kinds manufactured, 694,760 pairs; value of boots and shoes, $724,847; employ 692 males; females employed, 484.

Value of building stone quarried and prepared for building $500; employ 4 men.

Value of blacking, $8,000; employ 4 men.

Value of blocks and pumps manufactured, $50; employ 1 man.

Value of mechanics' tools manufactured, $2,540; employ 44 men.

Number of lasts manufactured, 40,000; value, $10,000.

Lumber prepared for market, 213,000 feet; value of timber, $32,025.

Firewood prepared for market, 3,348 cords; value of firewood, $13,796; employ 60 men.

Number of sheep, 5; value, $10; wool produced, 20 lbs. Horses, 343; value of horses, $29,880. Oxen over three years old, 74; steers under three years old, 26; value of oxen and steers, $5,760; milch cows, 420; heifers, 36; value of cows and heifers, $17,068. Butter, 20,075 lbs.; value of butter, $5,018.75; cheese, 6,505 lbs.; value of cheese, $650.50. Honey, 620 lbs.; value of honey, $155. Indian corn, 216 acres; Indian corn per acre, 28 bushels; value, $6,075. Rye, 25 acres; rye per acre, 15 bushels; value, $567. Barley, 7 acres; barley per acre, 23 bushels; value, $240. Oats, 20 acres; oats per acre, 19 bushels; value, $225.60. Potatoes, 310 acres; potatoes per acre, 90 bushels; value, $27,667. Turnips, 5 acres; turnips per acre, 200 bushels; value, $250. Carrots, ½ acre; carrots per acre, 400 bushels; value, $50. Beets and other esculent vegetables, 20 acres; value, $5,000. English mowing, 1,550 acres; English hay, 1,266; value, $25,320; wet meadow, or swale hay, 375 tons; value, $3,750. Apple-trees, 7,700; value of apples ,$3,000. Pear-trees, 818; value of pears, $100. Cranberries, 16 acres; value, $3,200. Beeswax, 100 lbs.; value, $73.

Bakeries, 1; flour consumed, 200 barrels; value of bread manufactured, $5,000; capital, $4,000; employ 6 men.

Establishments for manufacturing shoe boxes, 1; value of boxes manufactured, $1,500; capital, $1,000; value of boot trees and forms manufactured, $2,000.

Peat, 500 cords; value, $2,000. Swine raised, 526; value, $4,208.

The following list gives the number of persons employed in the various trades and professions, as collected in 1855 : —

Shoemakers,	420	Shoe tool makers,	9	Harness makers,	3
Farmers,	153	Shoe tool manf'rs,	2	Box manufacturer,	1
Boot-makers,	134	Students,	7	Watch makers,	5
Laborers,	139	Soap maker,	1	Cabinet manuf'rs,	2
Carpenters,	72	Printers,	6	Horse trader,	1
Shoe-cutters,	37	Last manufacturer,	1	Railroad men,	3
Cabinet makers,	31	Newspaper,	1	Jeweller,	1
Clerks,	28	Editor,	1	Awl manufacturers,	3
Merchants,	19	Musician,	1	Expresses,	2
Shoe manufacturers,	21	Lumber dealer,	1	Brush manufacturer,	1
Painters,	14	Physicians,	6	Brush makers,	6
Boot manufacturers,	10	Cigar manufacturers,	2	Pat. leather makers,	3
Masons,	13	Cigar makers,	8	Postmaster,	1
Awl makers,	13	Tailors,	10	Singing-school	
Blacksmiths,	18	Pump maker,	1	teacher,	1
Machinists,	7	Pump pedler,	1	Musical instrument	
Carriage makers,	7	Hotel,	1	manufacturers,	2
Last makers,	7	Barber,	1	Musical instrument	
Bakers,	5	Academy,	1	makers,	9
Stone masons,	3	Refreshment rooms,	3	Clergymen,	8
Boot formers,	6	Marble worker,	1	Warden almshouse,	1
Butchers,	6	Lawyer,	1	Pedlers,	7
Provision dealers,	2	Rolling machine		Boot treer,	6
Stage drivers,	2	manufacturer,	1	Livery stables,	2
Boot tree makers,	2	Moulder,	1	Currier,	1
Hatters,	2	Hames manuf'r,	1	Trimmer,	5
Writing master,	1	Lighthouse keeper,	1	Sailor,	1
Teamsters,	5	Assistant "	1	Hat manufacturer,	1
		Railroad engineers, 2.			

MANUFACTURING STATISTICS FOR 1865.

Gross value of mechanics' tools, $28,525; capital, 4,500; hands employed, 33. Number of tack and brad manufactories, 1; value of stock, $2,000; capital invested, $2,500; hands employed, 2. Melodeon and organ manufactories, 2; number of instruments manufactured, 70; value of the same, $6,860. Number of marble manufactories, 1; value of productions, $6,422; hands employed, 10. Number of cabinet manufactories, 1; value of goods manufactured,

$30,000; capital invested; hands employed, 30. Number of pairs of boots manufactured, 103,066; number of pairs of shoes manufactured, 1,009,700; hands employed, — males, 1,059; females, 208; value of goods manufactured, $1,466,900. Number of blacking establishments, 3; hands employed, 8; value of stock, $25,808.97; value of blacking manufactured, $43,806.95; capital invested, $12,300. Number of shoe-last manufactories, 1; number of lasts manufactured, 48,000; value of the same, $12,000; capital invested, $10,000; hands employed, 12. Number of shoe-box manufactories, 1; value of boxes made, $9,000; hands employed, 7; capital invested, $1,000.

AGRICULTURAL STATISTICS FOR 1865.

Cords of firewood cut, 3,065; value of the same, $10,890. Acres of farming land, 3,972; value of the same, including buildings, $255,188. Acres of improved land, 3,761. Acres of woodland, 3,034; value of the same, $74,415. Bushels of Indian corn raised, 5,625. Acres of rye, 41. Acres of barley, 25. Acres of oats, $12\frac{1}{4}$. Bushels of potatoes, 17,650. Tons of English hay, 2,233. Apple-trees cultivated for fruit, 6,848. Pear-trees cultivated for fruit, 1,150. Number of horses, 385; value of same, $38,140. Number of oxen and steers, 68; value of same, $3,965. Number of cows and heifers, 427; value of same, $18,719. Gallons of milk sold, 24,421; value of same. Pounds of butter sold, 5,448. Pounds of cheese sold, 1,225. Pounds of beef dressed, 378,000. Pounds of pork dressed, 77,700. Pounds of veal dressed, 32,115. Number of swine, 232; value of same, $4,618.

CHAPTER XI.

THE OLD FRENCH, AND FRENCH AND INDIAN WARS.

Capture of Louisburg. — Treaty at Aix-La-Chapelle. — War renewed in 1754. — Attack on Nova Scotia by the Colonies. — Crown Point. — Niagara. — List of Men in the Crown Point Expedition. — Capt. Simeon Cary's Company. — Capt. Josiah Dunbar's Company. — Expedition against Canada. — Capt. Lemuel Dunbar's Company. — At Crown Point.

THE OLD FRENCH WAR.

BY a treaty made between the English and French at Utrecht in 1713, the French had ceded the Provinces of Nova Scotia and Newfoundland to Great Britain. The French, finding need of a fortress in that region, had built Louisburg on the Island of Cape Breton, at a cost of 30,000 livres, and twenty-five years of labor.

When the war of 1744 broke out between France, Spain, and Great Britain, the New England Colonies soon found the French made use of this fortress as a hiding-place for the privateers that annoyed their vessels. A naval force was got ready for sea. Four thousand three hundred and sixty-six men were raised from the various Colonies, properly equipped, and placed under the command of Gov. Shirley, assisted by Commodore Warren, a British officer from the West Indies, who succeeded in the capture of the fortress after a siege of forty-nine days. The town and island surrendered June 17, 1745. Nothing now occurred of importance till the treaty made between England and France in October, 1748, at Aix-La-Chapelle. This war has been called, by way of distinction from a later one, the "OLD FRENCH WAR," or otherwise known as "KING GEORGE'S WAR."

Owing to the irregularity and torn condition of the rolls, and no record of the names of those who took part in this expedition being on the old town records, we are unable to present their names.

FRENCH AND INDIAN WAR.

By the treaty at Aix-La-Chapelle between the French and English, hostilities had ceased for a few years, although occasional depredations and incursions were made into the border towns, rendering it necessary to keep up some of the garrisons; and in many places people were obliged to go armed to their fields to work, for fear of Indian massacre and assault. The war was renewed in 1754, although it was not formally declared till 1756.

Early in the year 1755, the Colonies proceeded to attack the French at four different points, — Nova Scotia, Crown Point, Niagara, and Ohio River.

In these expeditions Massachusetts bore a prominent part, and contributed both men and means to carry on the war. We find among the names of those that went from the North Parish of Bridgewater the following list. In a return of sick in Colonel Pomeroy's regiment at Lake George, November 25, 1755, is the name of

Nathan Packard.

In the muster-roll of Captain Joseph Washburn's company on the Crown Point expedition, from September 11 to December 22, 1755, —

Lemuel Dunbar, *Sergeant.*
Joseph Cole, *Corporal.*   Isaac Perkins, *Corporal.*

Also, in Captain Samuel Clark's company, on the Crown Point expedition, from September 15 to December 16, 1775,—

Zechariah Gurney.

In the muster-roll of Captain John Clapp, in Colonel Dwight's regiment, we find, —

Lemuel Dunbar, *Ensign.*
Joseph Cole, *Sergeant.*   Benjamin Southworth, Elisha Gurney, *Corporals.*

In camp at Fort Edward, July 26, 1756, in service from February 18 to November 15, 1756.

In the muster-roll of Captain Simeon Cary's company, in Colonel Thomas Doty's regiment, in service from March 13 to December 11, 1758,—

Simeon Cary, *Captain.*
Lemuel Dunbar, *First Lieutenant.*   James Packard, Jr. *Sergeant.*

PRIVATES.

Edmund Pettingill, Isaac Packard, Jr., Isaac Fuller, Jr., Archibald Thompson, Jr., Abijah Hill, John McBride, Henry Kingman, Jr., Adam Kingman, James Loring, Jonathan Snow, John Packard, Ephraim Jackson, Lemuel Kingman.

In the roll of Captain Josiah Dunbar's company, in service from February 14, 1759, to December 28, 1760,—

Elisha Gurney, *First Lieutenant.*

PRIVATES.
Ephraim Cole, Abijah Hill.

The following is a list of men in Captain Simeon Cary's company, in an expedition against Canada, in service from May 14, 1759, to January 2, 1760 : —

Simeon Cary, *Captain.*   Jonathan Snow, *Sergeant.*

PRIVATES.

Samuel Cole, Jesse Perkins, Joseph Pettingill, Joshua Packard.

In the muster-roll of Captain Lemuel Dunbar's company, stationed at Halifax, N. S., in service from March 31, 1759, to November 1, 1760, are

Lemuel Dunbar, *Captain.*   Eleazer Packard, *Drummer.*

PRIVATES.
Isaac Fuller, James Loring, Lemuel Kingman, Seth Packard, Jonathan Perkins.

In Captain Lemuel Dunbar's company, in service from April 18, 1761, to January 14, 1762, we find the names of

Lemuel Dunbar, *Captain.*   Peter Dunbar, *Corporal.*

PRIVATES.

Lemuel Fuller, Adam Kingman, Lemuel Kingman, Stephen Pettingill.

Also in the muster-rolls of Captain Lemuel Dunbar's company, enlisted for an expedition to Crown Point, in service from March 4, 1762, to December 5, 1762, —

Lemuel Dunbar, *Captain.*

PRIVATES.

Hugh Carr, Thomas Carr, Lemuel Fuller, Ephraim Groves, Abijah Hill, John Pratt, Philip Reynolds.

We have thus far endeavored to present the names of all those who did service during the French wars. Doubtless, many have served in these expeditions that are not on the rolls, or have entered other companies, not belonging in the Bridgewater rolls.

We can see, however, by the foregoing lists, that the North Parish of Bridgewater did her part in the service in which Massachusetts took the lead.

CHAPTER XII.

THE REVOLUTIONARY WAR.

Controversy between England and America. — Acts of Trade. — Sugar Act. — Stamp Act. — Tea Destroyed in Boston Harbor. — Boston Port Bill. — Preparations for War. — Minute-Men. — Company marched on Lexington Alarm. — List of Persons in the various Companies in the Service during the War. — Shay's Rebellion. — List of Soldiers called into the Service to quell the same at Taunton.

NO period in the history of the world is more interesting, or more full of moral and political instruction than that of the American Revolution. The controversy between Great Britain and the American Colonies arose in regard to the right of Parliament to tax the Colonies while they were not allowed the privilege of representation in that body. Parliament determined to make the experiment, which it did, and the result of which is familiar to all readers of history. The first of a series of oppressive acts was that known as the " Acts of Trade," that tended to destroy all trade with the Colonies. The second act required a duty to be paid into the English treasury on all sugar, molasses, indigo, coffee, wines, etc., that came into the Colonies. This act passed April 5, 1764, and was called the " Sugar Act." *

At the time of the passage of this act, it was resolved to quarter 10,000 soldiers somewhere in America. Both of these acts were strongly opposed by the Colonies, and laid the foundation for a still greater breach in the trade between the two countries. Trade in the Colonies was principally confined to home productions, and the people determined not to import anything that it was possible to do without. Parliament find-

* The tax on rum was ninepence, molasses, sixpence per gallon, and sugar, five shillings per hundred.

ing the source of income very small, sought for another way to raise funds.

On the 22d of March, 1765, the famous " Stamp Act " was passed, to go into effect on the 1st of November following. This act required all colonial documents, as bonds, notes, and deeds, to be written on stamped paper, and to bear the royal seal, or to be of no value.

A general burst of indignation followed the passage of this act. Legislative bodies passed resolves, and protested against the measure. Societies in great numbers were formed, called " Sons of Liberty," who determined to resist parliamentary oppression. People began to wear cloth of their own manufacture, and denied themselves of foreign luxuries. Economy became the order of the day, the excess of which was soon felt in England, as many manufacturers were idle for want of a market for their goods, and laborers began to feel the consequences of her folly.

The King and Parliament soon saw their error, and repealed this act March 18, 1766, at the same time declaring they had a right to tax the Colonies whenever they " deemed it expedient," thereby intending not to give up their right to taxation, but only to change the form ; for the next year they passed an act levying a duty on glass, paper, paint, tea, etc. This only created continued opposition, which was such that Parliament thought proper to repeal all former resolves in regard to taxation, reserving a small tax of threepence a pound on tea. The strong resolutions passed by the Colonies not to import or consume tea finally deprived the English Government of a revenue from that source, and an attempt was made to import it through the agency of the East India Company, who had a right to export teas to all ports free of duty. Several ships were sent to the large cities in America. Those sent to Boston were consigned to some of Gov. Hutchinson's relatives. The inhabitants were determined it should not be landed, and it was not. It was thrown into the sea by a body of men disguised as Indians. As soon as the news of the destruction of the tea arrived in England, Parliament resolved to punish the devoted town of Boston. Next came the "Boston Port Bill," forbidding the landing or loading of goods in the harbor, passed March 25, 1774.

All these measures that were passed by Parliament did not intimidate the Americans, but served to strengthen their firm purpose not to submit to their oppression in any form.

When the Legislature of Massachusetts met at Salem in June, 1774, a meeting of delegates from all the Colonies was proposed, which soon after met at Philadelphia September 4, 1774, when a declaration of rights was agreed upon.

At this time everything assumed the appearance of opposition by force. Fortifications were thrown up in Boston by Gen. Gage, who had been appointed governor by Parliament. The Provincial Congress met at Concord October 11, 1774, where measures were taken for arming the whole province. Twelve thousand men were ordered to be raised, and to hold themselves in readiness at a moment's warning, and were called " Minute Men." Companies were formed through all parts of the country. Provisions and military stores were collected at various places, particularly at Concord. Gen. Gage, wishing to destroy the means of carrying on the war by the provincials, detached Lieut.-Colonel Smith and Major Pitcairn, April 18, 1775, to proceed to Concord for the purpose of destroying the military stores which he had learned had been stored there. Information having been sent in advance to Concord of their movements, the people flew to arms, and marched in small squads to where they were needed.

When the British troops arrived at Lexington, about five o'clock on the morning of the 19th, they were met by a small band of militia, paraded in front of the village church. Major

Pitcairn rode up to them and bade them disperse, which command was followed by a scattering fire, and a general skirmish ensued, in which eight men were killed and several wounded. The main body of the troops passed on to Concord, where they arrived soon after sunrise, and a fight known as the "Concord Fight" took place. At Lexington was the first blood shed in defence of the liberty of the people, and immediately on the departure of the troops from that place, by an arrangement previously made, the committees of safety throughout the whole country despatched messengers on horse in every direction, so that by evening every town within one hundred miles was informed that the war had commenced. The news was scattered throughout the towns by guns being fired, and other signals being given, so that people in the remote sections of a town were soon aware that they were needed. The news of this battle arrived in Bridgewater early in the day, and before sunset the company had collected and were ready for a march.

After a long and laborious search among the Revolutionary rolls, we have found the following names, of those who have taken part in the Revolutionary War, from North Bridgewater. The first we find is the company of Minute Men that marched on the 19th of April, 1775, on the occasion of the Lexington alarm.

List of Captain Josiah Hayden's company in Colonel Bailey's regiment of Minute Men, April 19, 1775: —

Josiah Hayden, *Captain.*

Nathan Packard, *First Lieut.*	William Packard, *Corporal.*
Zechariah Gurney, *Second Lieut.*	Timothy Ames, *Corporal.*
Reuben Packard, *Sergeant.*	Jeremiah Beals, *Corporal.*
Joseph Cole, *Sergeant.*	Eleazer Cole, *Drummer.*
Henry Kingman, *Sergeant.*	Silvanus Packard, *Drummer,*

PRIVATES.

Simeon Alden,	Fobes Field,	Jonathan Packard,
Noah Ames,	Mark Ford,	Jonathan Perkins, Jr.
Daniel Ames,	Richard Field,	Jonas Reynolds,

Japhet Beal,
Simeon Brett,
Samuel Brett,
Seth Bryant,
William Cole,
Ephraim Cole,
Jonathan Cary,
Daniel Dickerman,
Nathan Edson,
Barnabas Edson,

Ephraim Groves,
John Gurney,
Micah Gurney,
Anthony Dike,
Robert Howard,
Daniel Howard,
Oliver Howard,
Bela Howard,
Simeon Keith,
Lemuel Packard,

Joseph Reynolds,
Joseph Sylvester,
Charles Snell,
Uriah Southworth,
John Thompson,
Enos Thayer,
Ezekiel Washburn,
Ebenezer Warren,
Job Bryant,
Mannasseh Dickerman,

Jacob Edson,   Thomas Pratt.

Also Captain Robert Orr's company, Col. John Bailey's regiment, who marched from Bridgewater in consequence of the Lexington alarm: —

> Daniel Cary, one month and one day in service.
> Luke Packard, one month and one day in service.

Captain Robert Webster's company, Gen. Pomeroy's regiment: —

> Asa Packard, *Fifer*, in service three months and twelve days from April 27, 1775.

We find in the roll of Captain Nathan Mitchell's company, that marched from Bridgewater in consequence of the Lexington alarm, the 19th of April, 1775, the name of

> Jonathan Cary, in service eleven days.

Again on the 23d of April, 1775, the Provincial Congress resolved to raise thirteen thousand five hundred men from Massachusetts immediately, the term of service to be eight months. Among these we find the following companies: —

A muster-roll of Captain John Porter's company in Col. Paul D. Sargent's regiment.

		Time of service.	
John Porter, *Captain*	June 29	to August, 1775.	
Isaiah Fuller, *Sergeant*	July 7	"	"
Uriah Southworth, *Corporal*	June 29	"	"
Ezekiel Washburn, *Corporal*	June 29	"	"
Samuel Cole, *Drummer*	July 7	"	"

Luther Cary, *Fifer*....................June 29 to August, **1775.**
Daniel Ames, *Private*................July 7   "   "
Ebenezer Edson, "   ....June 30   "   "
Benjamin Fuller, "   ....June 30   "   "
William Shaw,   "   ....June 27   "   "

No man of this company received any guns, bayonets, car-
tridge-boxes, or clothing, excepting what he provided himself with.

A complete list of men in Captain Josiah Hayden's company, in Col. John Thomas's regiment, to August 1, 1775 : —

	M.	W.	D.
Josiah Hayden, *Captain*,	3	1	1
Zechariah Gurney, *First Lieutenant*,	3	1	1
Joseph Cole, *Ensign*,	3	1	1
Eleazer Cole, *Sergeant*,	3	1	1
Ephraim Groves, *Sergeant*,	3	1	1
Job Bryant, *Corporal*,	3	1	1
Richard Field, *Corporal*,	3	1	1
Silvanus Packard, *Drummer*,	3	1	1
Simeon Brett, *Private*,	3	1	1
Luther Cary, "	3	0	5
Southworth Cole, "	2	0	5
Thomas Crafts, "	3	1	1
Daniel Dickerman, "	3	1	1
Anthony Dike, "		Armorer.	
William French, "	0	3	3
Micah Gurney, "	3	1	1
Jonathan Packard, "	3	1	1
Oliver Packard, "	3	1	1
Thaddeus Pratt, "	3	1	1
Joseph Snell, "	2	1	1

In Captain Daniel Lothrop's company, in Col. John Bailey's
regiment, for eight months' service, from May 3, 1775, were
the following : —

		Time of service.
Ephraim Jackson,	Three months.	
Ebenezer Dunbar,	One "	
Adam Howard	Three " and six days.	
Nathan Leach,	One " " two "	
Daniel Packard,	One " " two "	
Matthew Pettingill,	One " " two "	

A muster-roll of Captain Frederick Pope's company, to August 1, 1775 : —

Eight months' Service.	Time of Enlistment.
Eleazer Snow,	June 25, 1775.
Mannassah Dickerman,	June 24, 1775.
Eleazer Snow,	June 27, 1775.

Names of men enlisted in Captain Thomas Pierce's company of artillery, in Colonel Knox's regiment, for service at Roxbury, December 16, 1775 : —

Elijah Packard,　　Jonathan Packard.

An exact roll of Captain Elisha Mitchell's company, in Colonel Simeon Cary's regiment, that marched April 2, 1775 : —

Joseph Cole, *Lieutenant.*
Joseph Snell, *Corporal.*　　Samuel Cole, *Drummer.*

PRIVATES.

Daniel Ames,	Thomas Craft,	Daniel Cary,
Jonathan Cary,	Jonathan Keith,	Simeon Keith,
Josiah Packard,	Ichabod Packard,	Luke Packard.

Captain Eliakim Howard's company, in Colonel Edward Mitchell's regiment, that was ordered to march to the service of the United States, March 4, 1776 : —

Daniel Howard,　　Simeon Keith,　　Jeremiah Thayer, Jr.

Captain Henry Prentiss's company, in Colonel Marshall's regiment, raised for the defence of Boston, July 5, 1776 : —

Zechariah Gurney, *Lieutenant.*　　Joseph Cole, *Lieutenant.*

List of Abiel Pierce's company, in Colonel Nicholas Dike's regiment, from August 3, 1776, to November 29, 1776 : —

Barzillai Field,　　Stephen Pettingill,　　Ichabod Packard.

The following persons were in the service under Captain Henry Prentiss, in Colonel Thomas Marshall's regiment, to August 1, 1776 : —

Zechariah Gurney,	May 4
John Thompson,	June 8
Ezekiel Washburn,	June 8
Zechariah Gurney,	June 8
Gideon Lincoln,	June 8
Mark Ford,	June 8
Enos Thayer,	July 8
Joseph Reynolds,	July 12
David Reynolds,	July 12

This company was also in service from August to November 1, 1776, at the expiration of which time they enlisted for one month additional service.

A muster-roll of Captain Snell's company, in Colonel Mitchell's regiment of militia, who marched on the alarm to Rhode Island, December 8, 1776, and were in service two weeks and two days : —

David Packard, *First Lieutenant.*   Jeremiah Beal, *Sergeant.*
John Packard, *Second Lieutenant.*   Ezra Cary, *Sergeant.*
William Packard, *Sergeant.*   Samuel Brett, *Corporal.*

PRIVATES.

Timothy Ames,	Jonathan Hayden,	Charles Snell,
Daniel Ames,	Fobes Field,	Eleazer Snow,
Jonas Packard,	Joshua Ames,	Ephraim Packard,
	Simeon Alden,	Henry Thayer.

The following are those having served in the artillery companies.

A roll of officers and men in Captain Daniel Lothrop's company, in Colonel Thomas Crafts's regiment of artillery, in the service of Massachusetts Bay, up to the first day of August, 1776 : —

Joseph Cole, *First Lieutenant,*	May 9, 1776
Richard Field, *Sergeant,*	May 13, 1776
Samuel Cole, *Drummer,*	May 16, 1776
Jeremiah Thayer, *Mattross,*	May 20, 1776

This company was also in service from August 1 to November 1, 1776, also from November 1, 1776, to February 1, 1777.

Eleazer Snow enlisted in this company November 1, and was in service with the above-named men from February 1, 1776, to the 7th of May of the same year.

January 26, 1777, a resolve was passed by the Assembly, making a requisition on Massachusetts for every seventh man of sixteen years old and upward, without any exception (save the people called Quakers), to fill up the fifteen battalions called for by the Continental Congress, to serve three years or during the war. The following are those enlisted from Bridgewater: —

	Regiment.	Time of Service.	Time of Enlistment.	Names of Companies or Captains.
Ebenezer Edson,	Crane's,	36	3 years	Frothingham.
Micah Gurney,	Thirteenth,	35 24	3 years	Light Infantry.
Joshua Cushman,	Ninth,	33 0	3 years	Miller.
Ephraim Groves,	Crane's,	36 0	3 years	Frothingham.
Nehemiah Packard,	Thirteenth,	45 16	During war.	Light Infantry.
Benjamin Packard,	Thirteenth,	45 3	During war.	Allen.
Daniel Packard,	Fourteenth,	32 39	3 years	8th Company.

The following persons marched on a secret expedition to Tiverton, Rhode Island, and were in service from September 25 to October 30, 1777: —

Nathan Packard, *First Lieutenant.* Jonathan Packard, *Second Lieutenant.* Nathaniel Manley, *Sergeant.*

PRIVATES.

Seth Edson,   Simeon Packard,   Elijah Packard,
Caleb Howard,   Shepard Packard,   John Pratt,
        John Pratt, 2d,   John Packard.

Each of this company received a bounty of twenty dollars per month.

Captain Edward Cobb's company that marched from Bridgewater to Bristol, Rhode Island, April 21, 1777, for two months' service: —

	M.	W.	D.
Daniel Howard, *First Lieutenant,*	2	4	0
Hezekiah Packard, *Fifer,*	2	0	4½

Barzillai Field,.............................2......0.....4½
Zechariah Gurney,..........................2......0.....4½
Oliver Packard,............................2......0.....4½
Jonathan Snow,............................2......0.....4
Hugh Carr,................................2......0.....4

We also find in Captain Stetson's company, Colonel Marshall's regiment, the name of

Daniel Packard, enlisted April 9th, 1777.

Joshua Warren was in Captain Bartlett's company, in Colonel Wesson's regiment, May 7, 1777.

Solomon Packard was in service in Captain Benjamin Edgell's company, Colonel John Jacobs's regiment, five months and sixteen days, 1777.

A draft was made for men to reinforce the northern army, January 1, 1778. For this service, in Captain Jacob Allen's company, Colonel John Bailey's regiment, from Massachusetts, in the camp at Valley Forge, January 24, 1778, is the name of

Caleb Howard, *Corporal.*

A pay-roll of Captain Nathan Packard's company, in Colonel Thomas Carpenter's regiment of militia, in the State of Massachusetts, from July 25 to September 9, 1778, in service in Rhode Island : —

Nathan Packard, *Captain.*

Jesse Perkins, *First Lieutenant.*   Nathaniel Orcutt, *Third Lieutenant.*
Joseph Reynolds, *Corporal.*   Ebenezer Dunbar, *Corporal.*

PRIVATES.

Mannasseh Dickerman,	Amzi Brett,	John Pratt,
Simeon Keith,	Samuel Craft,	Daniel Pettingill,
David Packard,	Mark Ford,	Simeon Packard,
	David Reynolds,	John Thompson.

Captain John Ames's company of militia, who marched to Rhode Island and joined Colonel Nathaniel Wade's regiment on the 27th of June, 1778, for a term of twenty days, agreeably to a resolve of the General Court : —

Daniel Howard, *First Lieutenant.*
Lemuel Gurney, *Fifer.*

PRIVATES.

Daniel Cary,	Joshua Warren,	Thomas Pratt,
Seth Edson,	Thomas Packard,	Barzillai Field,
Asa Keith,	Oliver Packard,	Micah Pratt.

"A return of men mustered for Colonel Robinson's regiment by James Hatch, muster-master for the county of Plymouth, to serve in ye New England States until January, 1778 : " —

Uriah Southworth,	Simeon Dunbar,	Southworth Cole,
Alpheus Cary,	Eleazer Snow,	Oliver Packard,
Peter Edson,	Daniel Howard,	Luther Cary,

Abiah Southworth, July 26, 1778.

In Captain Joseph Cole's company, Colonel John Jacobs's regiment, in the Continental service one year from January 1, 1778, we find the following names : —

Joseph Cole, *Captain.*
Isaiah Fuller, *First Lieutenant.*   Hezekiah Packard, *Fifer.*

PRIVATES.

| Alpheus Cary, | Peter Edson, | Ephraim Churchill, |
| | Joshua Warren, | Luther Cary. |

In September, 1778, the following persons were mustered into the service of the States, to serve till January 1, 1779 : —

| Hezekiah Packard, | Jeremiah Thayer, | Zechariah Gurney, |
| | Oliver Packard. | |

Isaiah Fuller was a lieutenant in Captain Joseph Cole's company, in Colonel John Jacobs's regiment, from April 1, 1778, to January, 1779, for nine months' service.

In Captain Calvin Partridge's company of militia, in Colonel Samuel Pierce's regiment, stationed at Little Compton, Rhode Island, April 30, 1779 : —

Zechariah Gurney, *First Lieutenant.*   James Packard, *Sergeant.*
Lemuel Gurney, *Private.*

Zechariah Watkins, *Lieutenant.*

PRIVATES.

Solomon Hill,	Daniel Brett,	Shepard Packard,

were in Colonel Ezra Wood's regiment for one month; enlisted for service at Ticonderoga in May and part of June, 1778.

Shepard Packard also enlisted in Captain Edward Sparrow's company, Colonel Nathan Tyler's regiment, in June, 1779.

Joseph Sylvester enlisted in Colonel Bailey's regiment, for three years or during the war, October 24, 1779.

The pay-roll for six-months men raised in the town of Bridgewater in July, 1780, for Continental service, contains the following names from the North Parish: —

Akerman Pettingill,	Zechariah Gurney,	Hugh Carr,
	Solomon Packard.	

Also

Simeon Keith, *Sergeant.*   Jeremiah Thayer, *Corporal.*
Jacob Packard, *Private.*

That marched on the alarm to Rhode Island, by order of Council, July 22, 1780, in service from July 30 to August 9.

Captain David Packard's company, in Colonel Eliphalet Cary's regiment, who marched on the alarm to Rhode Island, July 22, 1780, in service from July 23 to August 9, 1780: —

David Packard, *Captain.*   Eleazer Snow, *Second Lieutenant.*

SERGEANTS.

Daniel Howard,	William Packard,	Ephraim Packard,
	Samuel Brett.	

CORPORALS.

Fobes Field,	Ephraim Cole,	Jonathan Cary,
Luther Cary, *Fife Major.*		Micah Gurney, *Drummer.*

PRIVATES.

Philip Packard,	Richard Field,	Barnabas Pratt,
Daniel Howard,	Ephraim Field,	Nathaniel Snell,
Bela Howard,	Zechariah Howard,	Joseph Reynolds,
William Brett,	Jonathan Reynolds,	Enos Thayer,
Joshua Ames,	James Perkins,	Eleazer Cole,
Alpheus Cary,	Daniel Dickerman,	Timothy Reynolds,
Timothy Ames,	Daniel Ames,	Jeremiah Beal,

Howard Cary,
Lemuel Packard,
Barnabas Pratt, Jr.,
Thomas Packard,
Charles Hayden,
David Gurney,

Solomon Hill,
Adin Packard,
Levi Packard,
Abiah Packard,
Joshua Cushman,
Ichabod Howard,

Samuel Chesman,
Eleazer Snow, Jr.,
Mannasseh Dickerman,
Job Ames,
Noah Ames,
John Gurney.

An order was passed by the Assembly, to raise two thousand men to reinforce northern armies, in 1780.

In this service, we find from the North Parish, in Bridgewater, —

Hugh Carr,   Akerman Pettingill,

in Captain Hancock's company, who marched from Springfield July 4, 1780, for six months.

Zechariah Gurney was in the Eleventh Division, and marched from Springfield under command of Ensign Bancroft, for six months, July 11, 1780.

Solomon Packard was in the seventh division of six-months men, who marched from Springfield under the command of Captain Dix, July 7th, 1780.

The following is a list of Captain Nathan Packard's company, in Major Eliphalet Cary's regiment, that marched on account of the alarm in Rhode Island, July 22, 1780. By order of council from North Bridgewater: —

Nathan Packard, *Captain.*

Jesse Perkins, *First Lieutenant.*   John Thompson, *Sergeant.*

PRIVATES.

Mark Packard,
Josiah Packard,
Anthony Dike,
Mark Perkins,
Barnabas Edson,
Seth Edson,
Ebenezer Edson,
Benjamin Keith,

Seth Kingman,
Daniel Manley,
Shepard Packard,
Jonathan Perkins,
Caleb Packard,
Simeon Packard, Jr.,
Jacob Packard,
William Shaw, Jr.,

Daniel Shaw,
Naphtali Shaw,
Gilbert Snell,
John Tilden,
Rufus Brett,
Asa Packard,
Josiah Edson,
Josiah Perkins, Jr.

Again, we find in the company of Captain Luke Bicknell, in Colonel Putnam's regiment at West Point, New York, 1781, several persons from North Bridgewater : —

Joshua Cushman,	Thomas Packard,	Isaiah Packard,
Simeon Packard,	Marlboro' Packard,	Daniel Alden.

The following persons enlisted in Colonel John Bailey's regiment, January 25, 1782, to reinforce the Continental army : —

Joseph Sylvester,	Benjamin Kingman,	Daniel Packard,
	Noah Pratt, John Thompson.	

We have now given the readers an account of those who took part in the war that resulted in our national independence. Imperfect as this list may be, owing to the unconnected tattered rolls at the State House, we have endeavored to get the names of all who did military duty during the eight years' strife between England and America, and place them in readable form. We have brought the account down to the close of the war, or to the time of the signing of the treaty at Paris, in November, 1782. The war had grown exceedingly unpopular after the surrender of Cornwallis at Yorktown, in October, 1781, although nothing definite was done till March, 1782, when the House of Commons voted not to prosecute the war any further. At the close of that year, commissioners were chosen on both sides, who met at Paris, and after a long consultation, they agreed upon the articles of peace. These were signed November 30th of that year, and on the 20th of January, 1783, hostilities ceased between the two countries.

On the 19th of April, just eight years after the battle of Lexington, Washington issued his proclamation of peace. Thus ended a war of nearly eight years' duration, in which a hundred thousand lives were lost, and millions of property destroyed. It was the decision of this war that established the United States among the powers of the earth. In looking over the list of persons that took part in the battles of our country, we should not forget those who were left at home to provide for the families of absent ones. In many instances the women of the town had to till the soil to obtain what food was actually needed for subsistence; in short, every nerve was brought into requisition to provide home-made cloth, stockings, shirts, and blankets, that were called for by the government in large quantities; and although the women, wives and mothers of those who fought the battles, could not fight in the face of the foe with muskets, they did their part in aiding and abetting; and their deeds were as heroic in many instances as those we record; may their memory ever be cherished with gratitude, and stimulate us all to act well our part, and thus be mutual helpers to each other through life, that at its close we may have the satisfaction of feeling that we have done our whole duty, and done it well.

SHAY'S REBELLION.

At the conclusion of the Revolutionary War, peace and independence having been established, the attention of the people was directed to the finances of the country. The English merchants flooded the country with foreign goods, and thereby drained us of specie, and ruined the manufacturers. This involved merchants and others in debt.

The masses of the people, finding themselves burdened under the weight of taxes and loss of employment, became quite disheartened and uneasy, and hence could easily be led into almost any kind of a scheme to relieve their burdens. Debts could not be collected, and the heavy taxes were the ruin of a great many. During this state of feeling, a few persons, taking advantage of that condition of affairs, called a public meeting, which was held at Hatfield, Massachusetts, in August, 1786, to see what they could do to better themselves.

This meeting so inflamed the people that a mob of fifteen hundred persons assembled at Northampton, to prevent the sitting of the courts. From thence the insurrection fire continued to burn and spread throughout the State. One Daniel Shay, of Pelham, Massachusetts, was one of the principal movers in the scheme. A similar company was collected at Springfield, in September following. Here they found a military force sufficient to stop their proceedings. Similar gatherings were had in the towns where the county courts were held, in other parts of the State, the object being to stop all means of collecting debts by the usual process of law. Such a gathering was had at the court-house in Taunton, Bristol County, in September, 1786.

At this place, as before, the insurgents found that preparations had been made for a grand reception; and after a delay of a day or two, in frightening the people in that vicinity, the mob dispersed.

Among those called to suppress this rebellion at Taunton, were the following companies from Bridgewater. The list below gives the names of those from the North Parish of Bridgewater: —

" A muster and pay role of ye 7th company of militea in the 3d regiment, in the county of Plymouth, and commanded by Lieutenant-Colonel Orr, —

Lemuel Packard, *Captain.*
Daniel Cary, *First Lieutenant.*
Samuel Brett, *Second Lieutenant.*
Parmenas Packard, *Sergeant.*

Howard Cary, *Sergeant.*
Ephraim Field, *Corporal.*
Josiah Reynolds, *Drummer.*
Ephraim Sturtevant, *Fifer.*

PRIVATES.

Oliver Howard,
Robert Howard,
John Howard,
Jonas Howard,

William Reynolds,
Barzillai Field,
Gideon Howard,
Seth Edson,

James Cary,
Daniel Ames,
Thomas Packard,
John Crafts.

"The above-named persons were in service from September 9th to the 13th, 1786.

Sworn to before   JUSTICE HOWARD.
                                               LEMUEL PACKARD, Captain."

"A muster and pay role of Captain John Thompson's company of militia, in service from September 9 to September 13, 1786 : —

John Thompson, *Captain.*

PRIVATES.

Levi Washburn,
Jeremiah Thayer,
Mark Perkins,
Josiah Perkins,
Amasa Brett,
Leonard Orcutt,
Oliver Packard.
Obadiah West,
Nathan Packard,
Nathan Packard, Jr.,
David Edson, Jr.,

Thomas Thompson, Jr.,
Jonathan Keith,
Josiah Packard,
Jonathan Perkins, Jr.,
Elijah Packard.
Peter Bruyint,
Ichabod Bruyint,
Calvin Bruyint,
Job Bruyint,
Job Bruyint, Jr.,
Daniel Perkins,

Nathan Keith,
Daniel Bruyint,
Seth Kingman,
Calvin Brett,
William Shaw,
Henry Kingman,
Ichabod Edson,
Ephraim Groves,
Japhet Beals,
Jonas Howard,
Beza Bruyint.

Sworn to before   JUSTICE HOWARD.
                                               JOHN THOMPSON, Captain."

"Bridgewater, September ye 9th, 1786.

CHAPTER XIII.

WAR OF 1812.

Impressment of Seamen. — Embargo. — War declared by the President. — Calls for Troops from Militia. — Pay-Role of Company from North Bridgewater, stationed at Plymouth.

THE war of 1812 was memorable as the opening of a second war with England. The difficulty existing between the two nations consisted in the English Government impressing our seamen on board their ships, and by a series of depredations upon our commerce, even upon our own coasts, together with insults to the American flag in various ways.

On the 4th of April, an embargo was placed upon all vessels within the jurisdiction of the United States for ninety days, and on the 18th of June, war was formally declared by the President between England and the United States. Various incidents and many interesting events occurred both on land and sea during the years 1812, 1813, and 1814, which we have not space to publish. The skirmishing on the sea was spirited, and resulted in many victories to our forces, and on land was as favorable as could be expected, and in the end secured to us our rights as Americans.

The plan of operations at first, was to guard our sea-coasts, sending troops to man them, by calls on the militia at various times, the whole under the direction of the regular army. The spring of 1814 opened with the loss of the ship " Essex " of the navy, at Valparaiso, which served to stimulate the people of the United States to renewed activity, although the war was considered by many as uncalled for. Fortunately there were those who thought it best to maintain their dignity, and not allow any injustice to be done to our seamen. During the year 1814, the militia along the seaboard towns were called upon to guard the forts. Among those who responded to the call from North Bridgewater was the following company : —

" Pay-roll of a company of infantry, under command of Captain Nehemiah Lincoln, detached from the Third Regiment, First Brigade, in the Fifth Division, stationed at Plymouth, under the command of Lieutenant-Colonel Caleb Howard, commandant."

Nehemiah Lincoln, *Captain*.

Ephraim Cole, Jr., *Lieutenant*.   Silas Dunbar, *Ensign*.

SERGEANTS.

Gustavus Sylvester,   Josiah Dunbar,   Martin Kingman.

CORPORALS.

Jabez Kingman,   Galen Manley,   Daniel Packard,   Nathan Jones.

MUSICIANS.

Robert S. Holbrook.   George W. Burt.

PRIVATES.

John Ames,	Ira Hayward,	Loring White,
Benjamin Ames,	Manley Hayward,	Nathaniel Ames,
Oliver Bryant,	James Hatch,	Theron Ames,
John Burrill, Jr.,	Bernard Jackson,	Joseph Packard,
Samuel Brett,	Isaac Whiting,	Cyrus B. Phillips,
Zibeon Brett,	Benjamin Kingman,	Waldo Hayward,
Zenas Brett,	James Loring,	Martin Drake,
John Battles,	John May,	Isaac Packard,
William Battles,	Ambrose Packard,	Lemuel Sumner,
Chester Cooley,	Luke Packard,	David Packard,
Zenas Cary,	Jesse Packard,	Silvanus French,
Luther Cary,	Sullivan Packard,	Simeon Cary,
Martin Cary,	Arza Packard,	Enos Thayer,
Simeon Dunbar,	Zibeon Packard.	Galen Packard,
Samuel Dike, Jr.,	Thomas Reynolds,	Charles Clapp,
Bela C. Dike,	Matthew Snell,	Hezekiah Packard,
Samuel Dickerman,	Oliver Snell,	Charles Lincoln,
John Delano,	Jeremiah Snell,	Sidney Howard,
Isaac Eames,	John Smith,	Sprague Snow,
John Field,	Newton Shaw,	Galen Warren,

Asa Howard,
Cyrus Howard,
Lewis Howard,
Oliver Howard, Jr.,
Otis Howard,
Gideon Howard,
Austin Howard,

Simeon Warren,
Cyrus Warren,
Ephraim Willis, Jr.,
James Willis,
Ebenezer Crocker,
Jason Packard,
David Packard, 2d,
Oliver Howard.

Jonathan Edson,
Nathaniel Ames,
Howard Manley,
John Thompson,
Waldo Field,
Salmon Manley,
Ozen Gurney,

Plymouth, October 12, 1814.

"This may certify that the above is a true and correct roll of the company under my command, from the 20th of September to the 12th of October, 1814.

NEHEMIAH LINCOLN, Captain."

The following persons were also in service three days, — from the 12th to the 15th of October, 1814, — under the command of Captain Nehemiah Lincoln, and not included in the above list : —

Nahum Leonard, *Lieutenant.*

Seth Keith, *Sergeant.*
Simeon Taylor, *Corporal.*

Ansel Alger, *Sergeant.*
Jonathan Copeland, 3d *Corporal.*

PRIVATES.

David Ames,
Charles Copeland,
Ebenezer Caldwell, Jr.,
Perez Robinson,
Daniel Hartwell, Jr.,
Asa Briggs.

Perez Williams, Jr.,
Seba Howard,
Eleazer Churchill, Jr.,
John Colwell,
Charles Ames,
Bezer Lathrop,

Gershom Orcutt,
Howard Alger,
Kingman Cook,
Benjamin Randall,
Asa Packard,
Edward C. Howard,

Samuel Packard,   Charles Dunbar.

CHAPTER XIV.

THE REBELLION OF 1861.

Election of 1860. — State of the Country at the Commencement of the Rebellion. — Steamer " Star of the West." — Secession of South Carolina. — Firing upon Fort Sumter. — Call for 75,000 Volunteers for Three Months. — Company F, Twelfth Massachusetts Regiment. — Casualties and Changes in the Twelfth Regiment. — North Bridgewater Brass Band. — Call for more Troops. — Company I, First Massachusetts Cavalry. — List of Changes and Casualties in the same. — Companies and Regiments in which Soldiers have been in the Service. — List of Changes, Prisoners, Promotions, Deaths, etc., during the Rebellion. — Narrative of the Twelfth Regiment.

IT is well known that there had existed for a long time a bitter antagonism between the Northern and Southern portions of the United States upon the great subject of Slavery. Fierce party contentions had long existed, and ever will continue under a free elective government.

Till the election of November, 1860, however, there never was a Southern presidential candidate that did not receive electoral votes at the North, nor a Northern candidate who did not receive electoral votes at the South. The country at this time was in a state of unexampled prosperity. Agriculture, commerce, and manufactures, East, West, North, and South, had just recovered from the great financial crisis of 1857, and our country was spoken of, and regarded by the rest of the civilized world, as among the most prosperous nations of the world. We had been classed with England, France, and Russia, as one of the four leading powers of the age. No sooner had the results of the election of November 6th been made known than it appeared on the part of one of the Southern States, and whose example was soon after followed by others, that it had been the firm intention of those States not to abide the result of the election, unless it resulted in giving them their candidate. They were not satisfied with having had their own choice for sixty years, and now they had agreed not to abide by the decision of the majority, in the event of the election of Abraham Lincoln, and in consequence of this, the greatest conspiracy of the nineteenth century came to light, and the nation at once became involved in a civil war.

The first overt act of war committed in pursuance of this treasonable conspiracy, after the formal act of South Carolina passing its secession ordinance, was the firing upon a national transport, laden with men and supplies for the garrison in Charleston harbor. The date of the ordinance was December 20, 1860. The firing upon the steamer "Star of the West," was January 9, 1861. The commencement of the rebellion is dated from April 12, 1861, when the rebels, who numbered by hundreds, commenced firing upon Fort Sumter from every direction.

It was then the intention of the rebels to follow up this first blow by seizing the capital at Washington. In this they were frustrated; for, on the 15th of April, the War Department called for 75,000 troops from the militia of the several States, for three months' service, who hastened to Washington, and thus saved the capital of the nation. In no portion of the world was ever an army gathered so quickly; in less than two months, over 200,000 men were in the army, ready for action. The response to the President's calls was truly wonderful, both in men and money.

On the 16th, the Sixth Massachusetts Regiment was on its way to the seat of government, by railroad, and the Third and Fourth Regiments moved by steamers; on the 18th, the Eighth Regiment marched under General Butler; on the 20th, the Third Battalion of Rifles, under Major Devens; and the Fifth Infantry, with Cook's Battery of Light Artillery, on the morning of the 21st. The number of troops furnished by

Massachusetts under these calls for three months' service were 3,736.

The call for volunteers in the month of April, 1861, was met in the spirit of '76. Frequent meetings were held; patriotic speeches were made, and volunteers came up nobly to fill the ranks.

On Saturday evening, April 20, 1861, a large and enthusiastic meeting was held in the vestry of the "New Jerusalem Church," for the purpose of forming a new military company. Dr. Alexander Hichborn was chairman of the meeting, Jonas R. Perkins, Esq., secretary. There were about one thousand persons present. Spirited and patriotic addresses were made, and over one hundred came forward and enlisted in the service of their country.

The following company enlisted as volunteers for three years, or during the war : —

Roll of Company F, Twelfth Regiment, Captain Alexander Hichborn, as corrected at Fort Warren, July 13, 1861, under command of Col. Fletcher Webster : —

Name.	Age.	Rank.	Place.	Occupation.	Married or Single.
Alexander Hichborn,	39	Capt.	N. Bridgewater.	Physician.	Married.
Alpheus K. Harmon,	34	1st Ln't.	"	Painter.	"
Hiram W. Copeland,	26	2d "	"	Clerk.	Single.
John S. Stoddard,	31	1st Sgt.	"	Brush Mf'r.	Married.
Nathan H. Crosby,	29	2d "	Bridgewater.	Awl Forger.	"
Charles L. Sproul,	25	3d "	N. Bridgewater.	Stitcher.	"
Francis P. Holmes,	31	4th "	"	Awl Forger.	"
James B. Sampson,	24	5th "	"	Merchant.	Single.
James S. Tennet,	30	Corporal.	"	Wood T'n'r.	Married.
Uriah Macoy,	35	"	"	Trader.	
Roswell C. Amsden,	33	"	"	Boot-Cutter.	Married.
Galen Edson,	33	"	"	Cabinet M'r.	"
Charles H. Reinhart,	39	"	"	Carpenter.	"
Frederick C. Packard.	18	"	"	Melod'n M'r.	Single.
Walter D. Packard,	20	"	"	Clerk.	"
Edwin T. Cowell,	19	"	"	Bag. Master.	"
James Sullivan,	12	Music'n.	Boston.		"
Joseph Lynch,	22	Wagn'r.	E. Stoughton.	Teamster.	"
James A. Allen,	23	Private.	N. Bridgewater.	Machinist.	"

Name.	Age.	Rank.	Place.	Occupation.	Married or Single.
Luther E. Alden,	30	Private.	N. Bridgewater.	Boot-Cutter.	Married.
James F. Andrews,	35	"	"	Cabinet M'r.	"
Leander B. Andrews,	30	"	"	Painter.	"
Lawrence Burke,	19	"	"	Cooper.	Single.
John Barry,	19	"	North Andover.	Machinist.	"
Isaac W. Blanchard,	25	"	N. Bridgewater.	Butcher.	Married.
Henry Burns,	28	"	"	Shoemaker.	Single.
Eli Bunker,	20	"	"	"	"
Henry L. Bunker,	18	"	"	"	"
William H. Benney,	22	"	"	Boot-maker.	"
John L. Colter,	21	"	"	Shoemaker.	"
Henry R. Coots,	40	"	Chelsea.	"	Married.
George W. Childs,	21	"	N. Bridgewater.	"	Single.
John Creighton,	21	"	Boston.	Laborer.	"
Malcolm D. Halberg,	30	"	N. Bridgewater.	Shoemaker.	"
Thomas Doyle,	30	"	"	"	"
Albert S. Dean,	27	"	"	Machinist.	Married.
Aaron B. Dodge,	22	"	"	Boot-Maker.	Single.
Joseph P. Davis,	23	"	East Randolph.	Shoemaker.	Married.
Sargent Daniels,	37	"	N. Bridgewater.	Butcher.	
Seth Edson,	33	"	"	Carpenter.	Married.
Aaron B. Frost,	23	"	Lowell.	Shoemaker.	Single.
Joseph W. Freeman,	22	"	N. Bridgewater.	Needle Mk'r.	"
Henry W. Freeman,	33	"	"	Shoemaker.	Married.
Robert F. Fuller,	29	"	"	Shoe-Cutter.	"
John E. Ford,	25	"	Boston.	Barber.	Single.
Andrew J. Frost,	31	"	N. Bridgewater.	Boot-Maker.	"
John C. Greeley,	33	"	"	Shoemaker.	Married.
Warren A. Holmes,	20	"	"	"	Single.
Linus P. Howard,	24	"	"	Shoe-Cutter.	"
Rufus F. Hull,	23	"	Georgetown.	Manf'r.	Married.
Albert P. Hovey,	32	"	Boxford.	Wheel'r't.	"
Nathaniel H. Hall,	30	"	N. Bridgewater.	Stitcher.	"
Christopher T. Harris.	21	"	Plymouth.	Tin Worker.	Single.
Volney Howard,	21	"	Randolph.	Boot-Maker.	"
Clarence E. Hartwell,	25	"	N. Bridgewater.	"	Married.
John S. Hamilton,	25	"	"	"	Single.
John Hallihan,	24	"	Lowell.	Shoemaker.	Married.
Charles Howard,	20	"	N. Bridgewater.	Farmer.	Single.
William W. Hayden,	17	"	South "	Clerk.	"
Andrew Jackson,	22	"	West "	Shoe-Cutter.	"
Laban Jackson,	20	"	N. Bridgewater.	Farmer.	"
Thaddeus Keith,	28	"	"	"	"
Dexter D. Keith	29	"	"	Shoemaker.	Married.
Benjamin J. Keith,	19	"	South "	Blacksmith.	Single.
Martin M Keith,	22	"	" "	Shoemaker.	"

Name.	Age.	Rank.	Place.	Occupation.	Married or Single.
Carl A. Linstead,	27	Private.	N. Bridgewater.	Shoemaker.	Married.
Timothy Leary,	18	"	West "	"	Single.
F. A. Manchester,	33	"	N. "	Shoe-Cutter.	Married.
Francis N. Maroni,	20	"	"	Shoemaker.	Single.
Henry E. Morley,	22	"	"	"	"
William W. Newson,	28	"	Boston.	Mechanic.	"
Arthur J. F. O'Keefe,	18	"	"	Printer.	"
Isaac S. Porter,	19	"	Stoughton.	Farmer,	"
James A. Packard,	25	"	N. Bridgewater.	Shoe-Cutter.	Married.
Samuel N. Packard,	37	"	"	Shoemaker.	"
Anthony P. Phillips,	19	"	"	"	Single.
Herbert A. Phillips,	24	"	"	Boot-Maker.	"
George A. Perkins,	23	"	"	"	"
Gilman B. Parker,	21	"	West Boxford.	Shoemaker.	"
Henry C. Richardson,	18	"	"	Mechanic.	"
William H. Rugg,	21	"	Boxford.	Shoemaker.	"
William F. Robinson,	27	"	N. Bridgewater.	Farmer.	Married.
Osgood Ring,	40	"	"	Boot-Trees.	Single.
Charles Reed,	20	"	"	Shoemaker.	"
Henry Rogers,	27	"	South "	"	"
Frederick S. Symonds,	33	"	North "	Awl Forger.	"
Frank M. Stoddard,	19	"	East Stoughton.	Shoe-Cutter.	"
Francis A. Sanford,	21	"	N. Bridgewater.	Shoemaker.	"
George G. Smith,	22	"	Easton.	"	"
Luther T. Snell,	18	"	N. Bridgewater.	Machinist.	"
Harrison Stevens,	18	"	Boston.	Clerk.	"
George F. Tinkham,	24	"	N. Bridgewater.	Shoemaker.	"
Ephraim Tinkham,	28	"	"	"	"
Nathan M. Tripp,	25	"	"	Carpenter.	Married.
Ira Temple,	23	"	Boston.	Teamster.	Single.
Joseph J. Vincent,	21	'	N. Bridgewater.	Shoe-Cutter.	"
George B. Walker,	22	"	Weymouth.	Boot-Maker.	"
George F. Whitcomb,	19	"	Randolph.	Last-Maker.	"
Thomas W. Wall,	21	"	East Stoughton.	Shoemaker.	"
Lewis B. Wade,	19	"	N. W. Bridg't'r.	Boot-Maker.	"
Herbert O. Morse,	21	"	Boxford.	Shoemaker.	"
Webster Howard,	24	"	N. Bridgewater.	"	Married.
Jerome R. Hodge,	27	"	Canton, Me.	"	"
Franklin M. Godfrey,	23	"	Easton.	Carpenter.	Single.
Richard Packard,	20	"	N. Bridgewater.	Shoe Striper.	"
Samuel E. Chandler,	24	"	Charlestown.	Clerk.	"
Freeman Ranney,	44	"	Boston.	Merchant.	Married.
John Howard,		"	E. Bridgewater.	School T'h'r.	Single.
William Woods,	21	"	Boston,	M. Student.	"

The Twelfth Regiment of which Company F, of North Bridgewater, formed a part, was organized at Fort Warren by Col. Fletcher Webster (son of the late lamented and illustrious Hon. Daniel Webster, of Marshfield, Massachusetts), "a brave and generous gentleman," who fell in the battle of Bull Run August 30, 1862. The regiment, when mustered into service on the 26th day of June, 1861, numbered 1,040 men. Company F was recruited at North Bridgewater, and left that town April 29, 1861, at 9 o'clock A. M. The event of leaving the town was the occasion of a grand demonstration by the people of the town, thousands of whom had turned out to bid them farewell. The company assembled in their armory, which they left under the escort of the North Bridgewater Light Dragoons, Captain Lucius Richmond, with the Engine Companies Nos. 2, 3, 5, and 6, and a large body of citizens, marching, to the music of the North Bridgewater Brass Band, through the village to the railroad depot. The gathering was very numerous, probably never exceeded upon any occasion in that town. A sober feeling pervaded the concourse, in view of the peril to be encountered by our townsmen, and sympathy for those who were parting with husbands, brothers, and sons, and perhaps forever. A large company of citizens with the band, accompanied the soldiers in the train to Boston, and when arriving in Boston, marched in procession to Faneuil Hall, and from thence to their temporary quarters at 71 Clinton Street. The company numbered eighty, rank and file, when they left the town for Boston, to which there were large additions made soon after. *

Roll of North Bridgewater Brass Band, attached to the Twelfth Massachusetts Regiment of Volunteers : —

William J. Martland, *Band Master.*

MUSICIANS.

Amasa S. Glover,	Robert S. White,	Richard B. Atkinson,
Thaddeus M. Packard,	Lucius H. Packard,	William Dubois,
George E. Sturtevant,	Henry C. Packard,	George A. Bates,

* See account of Twelfth Regiment at the end of "History of the Rebellion

Samuel C. Perkins,	Joseph Kennedy,	James S. Bean,
Isaac C. Dunham,	Fernando De Argome,	Louis A. Beaumont,
John B. Emmes,	Minot Thayer,	Charles M. Capin,
	Nathaniel Carver, John Calnan.	

This band was mustered out of the service May 8, 1862.

An account of casualties, deaths, desertions, promotions, and changes, in Company F, Twelfth Massachusetts Regiment : —

Alexander Hichborn, *Captain*, commissioned June 26, 1861; discharged May 13, 1862.

Alpheus K. Harmon, *First Lieutenant*, June 26, 1861, Captain, May 10, 1862; wounded at the battle of Bull Run ; discharged July 8, 1864, at the expiration of three years' service ; promoted acting provost marshal of the Ninth Massachusetts District June, 1864.

Hiram W. Copeland, *Second Lieutenant*, commissioned June 26, 1861; discharged January 8, 1862.

John S. Stoddard enlisted in Company F, of the Twelfth Regiment of Massachusetts Volunteers, as a private, and immediately upon the organization of the company was appointed Orderly Sergeant ; afterward commissioned as Second Lieutenant May 13, 1862 ; promoted First Lieutenant December 14, 1862. He was in the battle of Gettysburg, and narrowly escaped being taken prisoner ; but by his native shrewdness and strategy, he succeeded in getting back to his regiment ; immediately after this he received a Captain's commission, dated July 23, 1862; he fell while leading his men on in the very face of the enemy, pierced by a bullet, killing him instantly, May 10, 1864, in the battle of Spottsylvania, Virginia.

In all the positions that he was called to fill, he proved himself faithful, and an officer of unusual capacity, while his kind and considerate regard for his men, and his ever genial disposition, made him a favorite with all, whereever he was known, and the community in which he lived have reason to deplore the loss of one whose soldierly qualities commanded the respect of his associates. He was buried on the battle-field by his men.

Nathan H. Crosby, *First Sergeant*, discharged for disability October, 1862.

Charles L. Sproul, *Sergeant*, discharged by order from War Department August 1, 1863 ; afterward attached to the Navy on the Mississippi River ; commissioned as First Lieutenant in Company C, Sixtieth Massachusetts Regiment, for one hundred days' service, July 11, 1864 ; Captain, July 30.

Francis P. Holmes, *Sergeant*, discharged September 1, 1861 ; afterward re-enlisted, and was killed.

James B. Sampson, *Sergeant*, promoted Second Lieutenant September 18, 1862, and assigned to Company A January 13, 1863 ; taken prisoner at the battle of Gettysburg, Virginia, and was an inmate of Libby Prison, Richmond, Virginia ; was a prisoner at Columbia, South Carolina, where he ran past the guard with two other fellow-captives, and reached the Union lines in safety, after a perilous journey of three hundred miles.

James S. Tannett, *Corporal*, afterwards Sergeant, died July 13, 1862, of typhoid fever, at Manassas.

Uriah Macoy, *Corporal*, afterwards First Sergeant ; taken prisoner at the battle of Gettysburg, and was a resident of Belle Isle Prison, Richmond, Virginia, till March, 1864; commissioned as Captain of Company C, Sixtieth Massachusetts Regiment, in one hundred days' service, July 11 ; promoted Major July 30, 1864 ; mustered out of service November 30, 1864.

Roswell C. Amsden, *Corporal*, discharged for disability August 18, 1862.

Galen Edson, *Corporal*, promoted Sergeant ; died February 20, 1864, at Culpepper Court House, Virginia. He was engaged in the battle at Cedar Mountain, Thoroughfare Gap, Second Bull Run, Fredericksburg, Antietam, and Gettysburg. He was spoken of by his superior officers, as a brave and faithful soldier, always at his post, never shrinking from duty or danger.

Charles H. Reinhardt, *Corporal*, discharged for disability May 30, 1862.

Frederic C. Packard, *Corporal*, transferred to Company D November 18, 1861, and discharged for disability October 17, 1862.

Walter D. Packard, *Corporal*, detached as Hospital Clerk, at Frederick, Maryland, and honorably discharged July 8, 1864.

Edwin T. Cowell, *Corporal*, transferred to the United States Signal Corps January 13, 1864.

James Sullivan, *Musician*, discharged for disability January 26, 1864.

Joseph H. Lynch, *Wagoner*, mustered out of service July 8, 1864.

James A. Allen, *Sergeant*, promoted to First Lieutenant July 23, 1863, Sergeant Major, January 25, 1863.

Luther E. Alden, *Corporal*, transferred to Invalid Corps March 15, 1862, and afterward to Veteran Reserve Corps ; wounded at the battle of Bull Run.

James F. Andrews, *Private*, mustered out at the expiration of service, July 8, 1864 ; wounded at battle of Bull Run ; released from Libby Prison January, 1864.

Leander B. Andrews, *Private*, mustered out at expiration of service, July 8, 1864.

John Barry, *Private*, slightly wounded at the battle of Antietam, September, 1862 ; mustered out at the expiration of service, July 8, 1864.

Henry Burns, *Private*, slightly wounded at the battle of Antietam, September, 1862 ; mustered out at expiration of service, July 8, 1864.

Eli Bunker, *Private*, slightly wounded at the battle of Antietam, September, 1862 ; transferred to the Invalid Corps January 16, 1864.

Henry L. Bunker, *Private*, slightly wounded at the battle of Antietam, September, 1862 ; mustered out of service July 8, 1864.

William H. Bennie, *Private*, discharged, on account of wounds received at Bull Run, February 12, 1863.

George W. Childs, *Corporal*, killed in action, at the battle of Fredericksburg, Virginia, December 18, 1862.

John D. Creighton, *Private*, discharged, on account of wounds received at Bull Run, June 11, 1863.

Malcolm F. Dhalberg, *Private*, severely wounded at the battle of Antietam ; died December 17, 1862.

Thomas Doyle, *Private*, severely wounded at the battle of Bull Run ; discharged, on account of wounds, December 15, 1862.

Albert S. Dean, *Private*, discharged for disability June 4, 1862.

Aaron B. Dodge, *Private*, discharged for disability January 9, 1863.

Joseph P. Davis, *Private*, mustered out of service July 8, 1864.

Sargent Daniels, *Private*, transferred to the United States Cavalry October 13, 1861.

Seth Edson, *Private*, discharged for disability December 19, 1862.

Aaron B. Frost, *Private*, died in battle of Bull Run, August 30, 1862.

Joseph W. Freeman, *Private*, discharged for disability December 12, 1862.

Henry W. Freeman, *Private*, mustered out of service July 8, 1864.

Robert F. Fuller, *Private*, transferred to the Veteran Reserve Corps January 16, 1864.

Andrew J. Frost, *Private*, died at Fairfax Court House August 28, 1862.

John C. Greeley, *Private*, transferred to brigade head-quarters ; wounded at the battle of Bull Run, mustered out of service July 8, 1864.

Warren A. Holmes, *Private*, discharged for disability March 14, 1863.

Linus P. Howard, *Private*, killed at the second battle of Bull Run August 30, 1862.

Rufus F. Hull, *Private*, discharged for disability October, 1862.

Albert P. Hovey, *Private*, mustered out of service July 8, 1864.

Nathaniel H. Hall, *Private*, transferred to division head-quarters ; mustered out of service July 8, 1864.

Christopher T. Harris, *Private*, discharged for disability September 26, 1862.

Volney Howard, *Sergeant*, promoted to Brigade Commissary Sergeant July 12, 1863.

Clarence E. Hartwell, *Private*, transferred to the United States Cavalry October 13, 1861.

John S. Hamilton, *Private*, died of small-pox, near Washington, December, 1862.

John Hallihan, *Private*, discharged for disability June 11, 1863

Charles Howard 2d, *Private*, wounded at the battle of Bull Run ; discharged for disability, on account of wounds, October 10, 1862.

William W. Hayden, minor, *Private*, discharged June 28, 1862.

Andrew Jackson, *Sergeant*, slightly wounded in the eye at the battle of the Wilderness ; mustered out of service, July 8, 1864.

Laban Jackson, *Private*, wounded in the side, at the battle of the Wilderness ; mustered out of service July 8, 1864.

Thaddeus Keith, *First Sergeant*, killed at the battle of the Wilderness May 6, 1864. At the time of his death, he was at the fore front of the battle, where he gallantly and bravely resisted several onsets of the enemy. His frank and generous nature made him a favorite in the company.

Benjamin J. Keith, *Private*, discharged for disability December 28, 1861.

Dexter D. Keith, *Private*, discharged for disability January 29, 1863 ;

afterward re-enlisted ; lost his right hand in the battle at Plymouth, North Carolina, April, 1864, and taken prisoner.

Martin M. Keith, *Private*, severely wounded at the battle of Bull Run.

Carl A. Lindstedt, *Private*, slightly wounded at the battle of Fredericksburg ; mustered out of service July 8, 1864.

Timothy O'Leary, *Private*, transferred to New York Battery ; mustered out of service July 8, 1864.

Francis A. Manchester, *Private*, slightly wounded at Antietam.

Francis N. Maroni, *Corporal*, killed in action, at second battle of Bull Run, August 30, 1862.

Henry E. Morley, *Private*, slightly wounded at the battle of Antietam ; mustered out of service July 8, 1864.

Isaac S. Porter, *Private*, transferred to the Veteran Reserve Corps July 1, 1863.

James A. Packard, *Corporal*, detached for hospital duty ; mustered out of service July 8, 1864.

Samuel N. Packard, *Private*, discharged for disability July 3, 1863.

Anthony P. Phillips, *Private*, discharged March 4, 1863 ; transferred to the Seventy-third Ohio Regiment.

George A. Perkins, *Private*, killed in the battle of Antietam, September 17, 1862.

Gilman B. Parker, *Private*, slightly wounded at the battle of Bull Run.

Henry C. Richardson, *Private*, transferred to the Thirty-ninth Massachusetts Regiment June 25, 1864.

William H. Rugg, *Corporal*, mustered out of service July 8, 1864.

Herbert Phillips, *Private*, mustered out of service July 8, 1864.

William F. Robinson, *Private*, mustered out of service July 8, 1864.

Osgood King, *Private*, transferred to the Veteran Reserve Corps September 18, 1863.

Henry Rogers, *Private*, discharged for disability March 4, 1863.

Frederick S. Simonds, *Private*, severely wounded at the battle of Bull Run ; discharged for disability March 13, 1863.

Frank M. Stoddard, *Sergeant*, wounded at the battle of Fredericksburg ; killed at the battle of Spottsylvania, Virginia, May 10, 1864.

Francis A. Sanford, *Private*, killed at the second battle of Bull Run, August 30, 1862.

George S. Smith, *Private*, transferred to the Veteran Reserve Corps February 20, 1864.

Luther T. Snell, *Private*, severely wounded at the battle of Antietam ; discharged for disability March 3, 1863.

Harrison Stevens, *Private*, severely wounded at the battle of Antietam ; discharged for disability December 25, 1862.

George F. Tinkham, *Private*, severely wounded at the battle of Antietam ; discharged on account of wounds March 4, 1863.

Ephraim Tinkham, *Private*, wounded at Fredericksburg ; transferred to the Veteran Reserve Corps March 15, 1862.

Nathan M. Tripp, *Private*, mustered out of service July 8, 1864.

Joseph J. Vincent, *Private*, promoted Hospital Steward March 20, 1863.

George B. Walker, *Private*, severely wounded at the second battle of Bull Run ; died at Washington of wounds September 24, 1862.

George F. Whitcomb, *Private*, discharged for disability September 1, 1861.

Thomas W. Wall, *Private*, wounded at the battle of Antietam ; discharged for disability November, 1862.

Lewis B. Wade, *Private*, wounded at Fredericksburg ; detached as Provost Marshal ; mustered out of service July 8, 1864.

Herbert O. Morse, *Private*, no report.

Webster Howard, *Private*, detached to provost guard ; discharged April 29, 1863.

Jerome R. Hodge, *Private*, killed in the battle of Fredericksburg, December 13, 1862.

Franklin M. Godfrey, *Musician*, discharged from the Twelfth Regiment ; re-enlisted in the Thirty-third Regiment ; mustered out of service July 8 1864.

Richard Packard, *Private*, killed in the battle of Frdericksburg, December 13, 1862.

Samuel E. Chandler, *Private*, promoted to Quartermaster Sergeant January 25, 1863.

Freeman R. Ranney, *Private*, transferred to the Veteran Reserve Corps September 17, 1863.

John Howard, *Private*, discharged for disability December 27, 1862.

William Woods, *Private*, discharged for disability January 11, 1863.

Lyman Allen, *Private*, was drafted in North Bridgewater July 15, 1863, and was detailed to do guard duty at Long Island, where, by strict integrity of character, he won the confidence of all with whom he had to do. With others, he was sent to the front, and attached to the Twelfth Regiment, and was killed in the first battle that he was engaged in, near Spottsylvania, May 10, 1864.

Rodney M. Leach, *Private*, was drafted July 15, 1863, transferred to the Thirty-ninth Massachusetts Regiment, June 25, 1864, wounded.

Henry L. Winter, *Private*, killed at the battle of the Wilderness, May 5, 1864.

Names of those having deserted from Company F, Twelfth Regiment, after being regularly enlisted : —

John L. Colter, *Private*, August 30, 1862, at the second battle of Bull Run.

Charles E. Reed, *Private*, March 16, 1863, at Winchester, Virginia.

John E. Ford, *Private*, July 22, 1861, from Fort Warren, Boston Harbor.

Arthur J. O'Keefe, *Private*, August 30, 1862, at the second battle of Bull Run.

Lawrence Burke, *Private*, July 1, 1862, at Manassas Junction.

On the 3d of May, 1861, the President called for 42,034

volunteers, to serve for three years, unless sooner discharged, to be mustered into infantry and cavalry service; also for an increase of the regular army of 22,714, making nearly 65,000.

The number required of Massachusetts was three regiments; this number was afterwards increased to six, and again, by the persuasion of Colonel Fletcher Webster, to seven regiments.

On the 17th of June, Massachusetts offered ten more regiments to the United States for three years, which were accepted. Under these calls, regiments were filled and sent to camp, or to the field, to fill up old regiments as they were needed.

The following lists will show the regiments in which the men from North Bridgewater have served : —

List of Company I, First Regiment Massachusetts Cavalry, Captain Lucius Richmond, under Colonel Robert Williams : —

Nathaniel Merchant, *First Lieutenant*, discharged December 26, 1861.

Freeman H. Shiverick, *First Lieutenant*, promoted from Second Lieutenant.

Lewis Cabot, *Second Lieutenant*.

George B. Mussey, *Commissary Sergeant*. Francis A. Richardson *Quartermaster Sergeant*.

SERGEANTS.

Robert S. Capen,	George W. Leach,
William S. Huntington,	Joseph E. Cole, .
George N. Holmes.	

CORPORALS.

Benjamin Knight, Jr.,	Augustine A. Colburn,	Joshua Turnbull,
Joseph T. Stevens,	Matthew W. Lincoln,	Roscoe Tucker,
John H. Walker,	Samuel C. Lovell.	

BUGLERS.

Henry T. Daggett,   John D. Darling.

FARRIERS.

A. J. Bailey,   Alfred Worthington.

PRIVATES.

Richard Adams,	Charles P. Farnsworth,	Andrew Morse,
Giles R. Alexander,	Edward T. George,	Wilson Orr,
Martin Argan,	Isaac P. Gayner,	Horace F. Pool,
Caleb Badger,	Francis O. Harlow,	Isaac R. Porter,
Andrew W. Bartlett,	Henry P. Holmes,	John T. Peterson,
Joseph Bisbee,	Hiram F. Howe,	Charles M. Packard,
Francis A. Bliss,	George W. Hunt,	Samuel Patterson,
James Baynes,	James H. Howland,	Amandus Richardson,
Ezekiel N. Brown,	Freeman P. Howland,	Gilbert R. Richardson,
Virgil F. Blaisdell,	Daniel W. Jacobs,	William W. Robinson,
Isaac W. Cox,	John Jewett,	George W. Reed,
Samuel A. Chandler,	Edward T. Jordan,	John A. Studley,
Richard Cunningham,	Caleb H. Joslyn,	Moody K. Stacy,
Thomas F. C. Dean,	Andrew J. Keene,	Joseph S. Stone,
Joel D. Dudley,	Noah M. Knight,	William A. Smith,
Edward Drury,	Thomas D. Knight,	John Sylvester,
George A. Edson,	William H. S. Kimball,	Edward Tilden,
Elihu T. Ellis,	John H. Leonard,	James H. Tucker,
Joseph C. Estes,	Ellis V. Lyon,	William A. Vining,
William H. French,	Edward A. Lunt,	Rufus H. Willis,
Ebenezer R. Faxon,	Jeremiah Leavitt,	Henry M. Wheeler,
James Fitzpatrick,	Daniel Linnehan,	Joseph Ware,
Tolman French,	Stephen C. Moulton,	Nathan C. Wood,

Frederick M. Wortman. Eugene W. Whitehouse.

This company was recruited in North Bridgewater by Captain Lucius Richmond. In 1853, a dragoon company was chartered in the town, and when the call was made for men, he enlisted as many of that company as he could, and offered their services to the Government, and was accepted.

The company left North Bridgewater in the morning train for Camp Brigham, Readville, on the 11th of September, 1861. Before leaving the town, the company partook of a collation at their armory, and then marched through the principal streets in the village to the music of drum and fife, escorted by a large concourse of citizens, with engine companies Nos. 2, 3, and 5. The streets were filled with an eager crowd to witness their departure, and bid them farewell.

The regiment left the State in battalions. The first battalion left on the 25th, the second on the 27th, the third on the

29th of December, 1861. The third battalion — consisting of Company I, of North Bridgewater, Captain Lucius Richmond, Company K, Captain James H. Case, of Middleboro', Company L, Captain William Gibbs, of Waltham, Company M, Captain Marcus A. Moore of Waltham — left Camp Brigham December 29, 1861, by the way of the "Shore Route" to New Haven and New York.

Upon their arrival in New York, they had a collation provided for them at Park Barracks, where they remained for fourteen days. Left New York for Port Royal in steamer "Marion," January 11, 1862, where they arrived after a passage of seventy-two hours. Camped at Hilton Head till about the 1st of August. From thence removed to Beaufort, South Carolina; was engaged in the battle of Pocataligo, South Carolina, during which three men were slightly wounded in Company I. Afterward remained in camp till April 1, 1863, when twenty-five men were detached for courier duty on Morris and Folly Islands. On the last of May, the remainder of the company was ordered from Beaufort to Hilton Head, and again, on the 7th of June, fifteen were ordered to James Island, under General Terry.

On the 7th of July, Captain Richmond was placed in command of fourteen infantry companies, forming the picket-line from Hilton Head to Cariboque Sound, near Fort Pulaski; removed to head-quarters at Hilton Head, January 4, 1864. Ordered to Jacksonville, Florida, February 5, where they arrived on the 8th of February. Here they joined Captain Elder's First United States Battery of four guns, and the Fortieth Massachusetts Regiment Mounted Infantry, under command of Colonel Guy V. Henry. These companies were brigaded and placed under the command of Colonel Henry, as acting brigadier-general.

These forces started on an expedition of one hundred and fifty miles into the country on the day of their arrival, and during the first night surprised and captured four picket-posts of five men each, and captured an artillery camp of eight guns, called "Camp Finnegan," after which they proceeded on to Baldwin Station, on the Jacksonville and Tallahassee Railroad, where they arrived at sunrise February 9, 1864, and captured four cars loaded with ammunition, cannon, and forage, and also a quantity of turpentine, rosin, and cotton. On the 10th, arrived at Barber's Ford, on the south fork of St. Mary's River; here the forces engaged in fight about noon. During this engagement, Thomas F. C. Dean, of Stoughton, was killed; he was a member of Company I, from North Bridgewater. Four men were slightly wounded. The Union forces captured forty-five prisoners. The next night they bivouacked at Sandersonville, after driving Finnegan's forces from there, which was his head-quarters at that time.

After destroying distilleries, corn, etc., started for Lake City, and arrived within one and a half miles of that place, when they engaged General Finnegan's force, in sight of the city. After a severe fight of about two hours, ammunition becoming short, and having no supply-train, they fell back to Barber's Ford, by order of General Seymour.

On the 15th of February, went to Callihan Station, on the Gainesville and Fernandina Railroad. At St. Mary's River destroyed three ferries, and returned to Barber's Ford on the 19th February. On the following day, General Seymour engaged the rebels at Olustee with 5,000 men, the enemy having 13,000 men. After a severe fight, both sides fell back. On their retreat, the Union forces destroyed Baldwin Village. Fought at Camp Finnegan February 23, Mile Run, February 25.

On the 30th of March, the battalion was ordered to Pilatka, Florida, where they remained fourteen days. While there, they lost four men, while on picket duty, — Matthew Lincoln, of Abington, H. F. Poole, of Easton, John Sylvester, of East

Bridgewater, Roscoe Tucker, — who were carried to Andersonville Prison; the last three have since died.   On the 14th of March, the battalion evacuated Pilatka.   At this time, part of the company having re-enlisted and gone on a furlough to the North, Captain Richmond was ordered to St. Augustine, Florida, with the remainder of the company; stopped there three days; from thence removed to Jacksonville, Florida. On the 22d of April, was ordered to Virginia; embarked for Hilton Head, and arrived there next day.   May 1st, started for Yorktown, Virginia; arrived May 3d; joined General Gilmore May 8th, at Bermuda Hundred.   The company was engaged in fights on the 8th and 9th of May at Swift Creek; was engaged in front of Fort Darling from the 11th to the 16th of May, and fell back to Bermuda Hundred the same day.   On the 9th of June, was engaged in front of Petersburg, Virginia; on the 28th of September, was in front of Richmond, and from that time to the middle of November was in several fights.   About the 15th of November, was ordered to the head-quarters of the Army of the James, under General Butler, and was employed on escort and courier duty.   Captain Richmond was honorably discharged December 17, 1864, after thirty-nine months' service, in which he proved himself a brave and good officer.   In the advance from Jacksonville to Lake City, it was Captain Richmond's company that led the advance, capturing and first engaging the forces of the enemy in front, and was in almost every instance successful.

In 1864, this company was consolidated into the Fourth Massachusetts Cavalry, so that the history of those from North Bridgewater, or belonging in Company I, may be found in that regiment.

List of men from North Bridgewater in Company K, First Massachusetts Cavalry, Captain James H. Case, of Bridgewater: —

Edmund Crockett,	Waldo Field,	Austin H. Snow,
Joseph Dam,	John Simonds,	Hiram Thayer,
	William Welsh.	

List of changes, casualties, deaths, etc., that have occurred in Company I, of the First Massachusetts Cavalry, under Captain Lucius Richmond : —

Freeman H. Shiverick, *First Lieutenant*, resigned July 28, 1862.

Lewis Cabot, *Second Lieutenant*, transferred to the Fourth Massachusetts Cavalry.

B. Knight Jr., *Corporal*, discharged for disability at Beaufort, May 12, 1863. He was engaged in the battle of Pocataligo, October 22, 1862.

George N. Holmes, *Sergeant*, discharged for disability April 23, 1864.

Joseph T. Stevens, *Corporal*, died at Hilton Head March 31, 1862.

A. J. Keene, *Private*, discharged for disability at Beaufort, April 22, 1863.

Joshua Turnbull, *Corporal*, discharged for disability January 19, 1863.

A. W. Bartlett, *Private*, died at Beaufort, from wounds received at Barber's Ford, Florida, February 10, 1864.

Joseph C. Stone, *Private*, discharged for disability at Bedloe's Island, New York Harbor, August 29, 1862.

Henry T. Daggett, *Bugler*, promoted chief Bugler of the regiment May 7, 1864.

Richard Adams, *Private*, discharged for disability April 20, 1862.

Virgil S. Blaisdell, *Private*, discharged for disability April 8, 1864.

Caleb Badger, *Private*, discharged for disability July 9, 1863, at Beaufort, North Carolina.

Joseph P. Bisbee, *Private*, died July 14, 1862, was in action at Pocataligo.

Thomas F. C. Dean, *Private*, killed at Barber's Ford February 12, 1864. He was in action on James and Morris Islands during the siege of Fort Wagner, and Pocataligo, East Florida.

Tolman French, *Private*, discharged for disability May 4, 1864.

James Fitzpatrick, *Private*, transferred to the Invalid Corps, July 9, 1863.

Eben R. Faxon, *Private*, discharged for disability at Beaufort, April 22, 1863.

James H. Howland, *Private*, discharged for disability at Hilton Head, April 8, 1862.

John Jewett, *Private*, transferred to Company K December 23, 1861.

Jeremiah Leavitt, *Private*, promoted to Hospital Steward 1862.

Edward A. Lunt, *Private*, discharged for disability at Beaufort, July 9, 1863.

George B. Mussey, *Commissary Sergeant*, transferred to the non-commissioned staff April 9, 1862 ; discharged December 10, 1862.

Francis A. Richardson, *Quartermaster Sergeant*, discharged for disability at Hilton Head, December, 1863.

34

Gilbert R. Richardson, *Private*, discharged February 7, 1862.

W. A. Smith, *Private*, discharged for disability at Hilton Head, April 8, 1862.

Frederic M. Wortman, *Private*, fell overboard from steamer "Rebecca Clyde," in Port Royal Harbor, February 6, 1864, in action at Pocataligo.

Hiram M. Wheeler, *Private*, discharged for disability at Boston, November, 1862.

R. S. Capen, *Private*, promoted to Sergeant-Major in the Fourth Massachusetts Cavalry.

S. C. Lovell, *Corporal*, transferred to Company K; promoted to Orderly Sergeant August 23, 1864.

F. A. Bliss, *Corporal*, transferred to Company F; promoted to Quartermaster Sergeant August 12, 1864.

J. E. Cole, *Private*, transferred to the non-commissioned staff as Saddler's Sergeant September 10, 1864.

John H. Walker, *Corporal*, promoted to Quartermaster Sergeant; discharged at the expiration of service, September 24, 1864.

Augustine A. Colburn, *Corporal*, promoted to Commissary Sergeant; discharged September 24, 1864.

J. H. Leonard, *Corporal*, honorably discharged September 24, 1864.

Isaac Cox, *Private*, discharged September 24, 1864.

William S. Huntington, *Sergeant*, discharged September 24, 1864.

George N. Hunt, *Sergeant*, discharged September 24, 1864.

F. O. Harlow, *Sergeant*, discharged September 24, 1864.

D. W. Jacobs, *Sergeant*, discharged September 24, 1864.

John T. Peterson, *Sergeant*, discharged September 24, 1864.

J. R. Porter, *Sergeant*, discharged September 24, 1864.

J. D. Darling, *Bugler*, promoted to the non-commissioned staff September 25, 1864.

H. P. Holmes, *Private*, discharged October 8, 1864.

George S. Richards, *Private*, discharged October 14, 1864.

H. F. Howard, *Private*, discharged October 30, 1864.

Ai. J. Bailey, *Farrier*, discharged October 30, 1864.

E. W. Whitehouse, *Private*, discharged November 13, 1864.

John Sylvester, *Private*, died at Andersonville, December, 1864.

Roscoe Tucker, *Private*, died at Florence, South Carolina, January 29, 1865.

Horace F. Poole, *Private*, died on the passage home from Florence, where he had been confined as a prisoner of war, March 9, 1865.

Matthew W. Lincoln, *Private*, was a prisoner at Florence, exchanged August 9, 1865.

R. H. Willis, *Private*, promoted to Second Lieutenant January, 1865.

George W. Leach, *Private*, promoted January, 1865.

H. S. Kimball, *Private*, promoted to Second Lieutenant in Colored Infantry, December, 1864.

Joel D. Dudley, *Corporal*, killed at High Bridge, Virginia, April 6, 1865.

Samuel Patterson, *Private*, captured in front of Jacksonville, March 16, 1864.

Ellis V. Lyon, *Private*, died September 24, 1864; funeral October 2, 1864.

First Massachusetts Regiment: —

Company E, Captain Clark B. Baldwin, John Donahue.

List of men in Captain Francis H. Tucker's company, Company H, of the Second Regiment of Massachusetts Volunteers, under command of Colonel George H. Gordon, for three years' service, as mustered May 25, 1861, from North Bridgewater: —

James P. Bell,	Benjamin N. Gardner,	Patrick Keenan,
John Cullen,	Charles M. Hall,	Patrick Murray,
Richard Casey,	Maurice Keating,	Linus B. Thomas,
	Jeremiah Merea, Hugh O. Donald.	

List of men in Captain Ward L. Foster's company, Company G, of the Seventh Regiment of Massachusetts Volunteers, under the command of Colonel Darius N. Couch, as mustered into three years' service June 11, 1861, from North Bridgewater: —

Charles W. George, *Corporal.*   James S. Newman, *Corporal.*

George L. Horr,	Morgan Jones,	Joseph Reynolds, Jr.,
Samuel F. Howard,	John B. Dean,	Horace M. Clark,
Alonzo S. Hamilton,	Albert D. Hunt,	Jacob Rotch,
Russell S. Higgins,	Edward B. Leach,	Alfred H. Tilden,
Oliver Horton,	Francis S. Packard,	David Thompson, Jr.,
	John Griffin.	

We also find the following names in the same regiment, as follows: —

Company A, Captain David H. Dyer, John B. Cobb.
Company K, Captain Franklin P. Harlow, Walter C. Churchill,
Company E, Captain Horace F. Fox, William Douglas.

List of men in Company K, Captain George W. Dutton's company, of the Ninth Regiment of Massachusetts Volunteers, Colonel Thomas Cass, as mustered into three years, service, June 15, 1861, from North Bridgewater: —

John Lanagan,	Charles O. Collins,	Dennis Wheelan,
William Linnehan,	Michael Clark,	James Webb,
David Maguire,	Patrick Cunningham,	Roger Cunningham,
William Mitchell,	John Sweeny,	William Farrell,
Michael Connell,	John Scannell,	James Gilbridge,
	James Harris.	

Also in Company B, Captain Christopher Plunkett, June 15, 1861: —

Thomas Hogan,	John Horan,	John Russell,
James Riley,	Michael Kelly,	Patrick Sheridan.

Company E, Captain John R. Teague, Michael Horan.
Company I, Captain James E. McCafferty, Jr., Owen Sweeney.

A list of men from North Bridgewater in the Eleventh Regiment of Massachusetts Volunteers, for three years, as mustered June 12, 1861: —

Company B, Captain John H. Davis, Thomas Donahue, William Walsh.
Company C, Captain Porter D. Tripp, George W. Wood.
Company E, Captain James R. Bigelow, Dennis Downey, Miletus Luther, Patrick O'Brien, Perley A. Doyle. .

In the Thirteenth Regiment of Massachusetts Volunteers, Company K, Captain William P. Blackmer, is

Charles Drayton, mustered June 26, 1861.

The muster-rolls of the Eighteenth Massachusetts Volunteers, Colonel James Barnes, contain the following names mustered in July and August, 1861.

Company A, Captain Lewis N. Tucker, James Mathison.
Company B, Captain George C. Ruby, William Flannagan
Company E, Captain Thomas Weston, Samuel Kimball, Ferdinand Robinson, David Sanford, Thomas W. Childs, Howard P. Keith.
Company F, Captain Henry Onion, Thomas P. Leyden.
Company H, Captain Joseph W. Collingwood, James F. Willis.
Company I, Captain Frederic D. Forrest, Ira Belcher.

Twentieth Regiment, Colonel W. Raymond Lee: —

Company H, Captain George M. Macy, George H. Howard.
Company I, Captain A. W. Beckwith, James Barney.

Twenty-second Regiment, under command of Colonel Henry Wilson and Colonel Jesse Gove : —

Company D, Captain John F. Dunning, Francis E. Allen, Edward Lathrop.

Twenty-third Regiment, Colonel John Kurtz : —

Company K, Captain Carlos A. Hart, Moses Paron.

Twenty-fourth Regiment, Colonel Thomas G. Stevenson : —

Company G, Captain Robert F. Clark, George A. Howard, Justin Howard, Paul W. Jackson.
Company F, Captain George F. Austin, Heman E. Packard,

List of men in the Twenty-eighth Regiment of Massachusetts Volunteers : —

Company B, Captain Lawrence P. Barrett, Philip Donahue.
Company C, Captain John Brennan, Timothy Connolly, Michael Casy, Edward Duyer, John Doherty, Edward Magrane, Thomas Maloney, Thomas Sullivan, Uriah Phillips, John Flannagan.
Company I, Captain G. F. McDonald, Timothy Regan, Hugh Riley, John Canara.

Twenty-ninth Massachusetts Regiment, under command of Colonel E. W. Peirce, three years' service, 1861 : —

Company B, Captain Israel N. Wilson, Anthony La Rochelle.
Company C, Captain Lebbeus Leach, Edward F. Drohan, David W. Harden, John S. Howard, William Keith.
Company G, Captain Charles D. Richardson, George W. Pope.

Thirtieth Regiment, Colonel N. A. M. Dudley : —

Company D, Captain Marsh A. Ferris, D. M. Rochester.

Thirty-second Regiment, Colonel Francis J. Parker : —

Company B, Captain George L. Prescott, Charles Augustus.
Company G, Captain Charles Bowers, Julius R. Churchill.
Company H, Captain Henry W. Moulton, Sylvester Russell, Daniel Shannahan.

Again the President, at the request of the various governors of the loyal States, issued a proclamation, July 1, 1862, calling for three hundred thousand more volunteers, to serve for three years, or during the war. The number of regiments sent from the State, up to this date, was twenty-seven, besides thirteen unattached companies, making in all 31,377 men.

The quota for Massachusetts was 15,000; the number called for from North Bridgewater was 52. In response to the above call, a legal meeting of the town was held at the new church vestry July 19, 1862, at which it was "voted to borrow $5,200 for a term of years; and to pay $100 each to any person that should volunteer into the service of the United States, under the late call of the President."

After remarks by several gentlemen present, the following resolutions were offered by D. C. Cowell, and adopted : —

Resolved, That earth has never seen a holier war than that now waged by the Government of the United States, to put down rebellion ; and that we should be derelict and criminal in the highest degree, if we failed to make every needful sacrifice, in order to transmit to our posterity the glorious heritage of popular government

Resolved, That we hail with satisfaction the recent legislation in Congress, as an evidence on the part of the government that treason and rebellion shall be promptly and effectually crushed.

Resolved, That there shall be paid from the town treasury to each volunteer from this town, who shall enlist on or before the 30th inst., until our quota is complete, the sum of one hundred dollars.

Resolved, That while the citizens of this town will endeavor to do, and will do, their duty, and their whole duty, they have a right to expect that those in authority, whether in Congress, the cabinet, or the field, will pursue a vigorous policy, and make war in earnest, until the last rebel has laid down his arms, and acknowledged paramount allegiance to the United States.

Resolved, That justice, which is the only sound policy and the best economy, demands that the government should call upon every loyal person, without distinction of complexion or race, within the rebel States, to rally around the flag of the Union, and should give freedom and protection to all who obey the call, and that the neglect in the future so to do will be a stupendous blunder, unparalleled in the history of the world.

Immediately after the above meeting, the business of recruiting and filling the town's quota was brisk, resulting in the following persons enlisting for the term of three years, or during the war.

In the Thirty-third Regiment of Massachusetts Volunteers for three years' service, Colonel Albert C. Maggi commander, we find : —

Enlisted in July and August, 1862.

Company B, Captain James Brown, Andrew Anderson, Alexander Turner.

Company H, Captain Edward B. Blasland, Thomas Drohan, Charles O. Flannagan, Arthur McIntee, Peter Donahue, Patrick McEstee.

Company I, Captain Elisha Doane, Caleb Athearns, Albert B. Dunbar, Matthew Grady, Gustavus Arfridson, Daniel Feeley, Oliver M. Holmberg, Joseph Beals, John Finnegan, John Maguire, Charles Strommet.

Company M, Captain B. Frank Rogers, William O'Brien, John H. T. Sanford, John Mason, Harrison L. Higgins, Charles F. Swanstrom.

List of men in the Thirty-fifth Regiment of Massachusetts Volunteers for three years' service, Colonel Edward A. Wild commander : —

Enlisted in July and August, 1862.

Company A, Captain Stephen H. Andrews, Thomas P. Barnfield, Albert G. Drake, Marcus E. Packard, Alden Cushing, Charles N. Packard, Edwin L. Snow, Dudley Wade, Henry C. Ames.

Company C, Captain Tracy P. Cheever, Preston Holbrook, Davis B. Reynolds, William P. Roberts, Elmer W. Holmes, Heman F. Stranger, John Kendall, James Ide, Horatio D. Snow, Edward F. Snow, George L. Robinson, Elisha A. Cushing, Henry A. Willis, William Deane.

List of men in Company K, Thirty-eighth Massachusetts Regiment of Volunteers, Colonel Timothy Ingraham : —

Captain James H. Slade,

George A. Jenks,	Gibbon Sharp, Jr.,	John Kendall,
Edmund A. Landers,	Samuel H. Sanford, Jr.,	William A. W. Averill,
	Thomas R. Broadhurst.	

Thirty-ninth Massachusetts Regiment, Colonel P. Stearns Davis : —

Company A, Captain George S. Nelson, Sylvanus E. Packard, George W. Cole, Samuel Dean.

Company F, Captain Joseph J. Cooper, Fernando C. Skinner.

Company H, Captain Charles N. Hunt, Francis J. Childs, Ephraim F. Howard.

List of men, in Company A, Captain James T. Lurvey, Fortieth Regiment of Massachusetts Volunteers, Colonel Burr Porter : —

Nelson Cushman,	A. G. Tinkham,	Lucius S. Perkins,
John D. Sanford,	John L. Mason,	Albert W. Hayden.

The following men enlisted in the Ninth Massachusetts Light Battery in July and August, 1862, for three years' service, under the command of Captain Achille De Vecchi : —

David Brett,	Richard Holland,	Henry Packard,
Bartlett C. Edson,	John H. Kelley,	Eleazer Cole,
Henry Fenn,	Henry F. Nash,	H. A. Packard,
	Reuben L. Willis,	Austin Packard.

List of men in Tenth Massachusetts Battery, under the command of Captain J. Henry Sleeper, for three years' service, mustered September 9, 1862 : —

John P. Apthorp,	Charles N. Packard,	Franklin Ward.

In the early part of the year 1862, permission was given to raise a company of Heavy Artillery for garrison duty at Fort Warren, Boston Harbor ; this company was raised by Stephen Cabot of Boston.

For this service we find the name of

John Geary, mustered March 6, 1862.

Again in August, came a call for 300,000 more troops as follows : —

Ordered, First, that a draft of 300,000 militia be immediately called into the service of the United States, to serve nine months, unless sooner discharged.

Ordered, Second, that if any State shall not, by the 15th of August, furnish its quota of the additional 300,000 authorized by law, the deficiency of volunteers for that State shall be made up by a special draft from the militia.

EDWIN M. STANTON,
Secretary of War.

The quota for Massachusetts, under this call, was 19,080. In response to this call, the people were, as in the previous calls, "wide awake." Early on Thursday morning, August 21, 1862, a large handbill was circulated with the following announcement: "*War meeting! Grand rally! Volunteering vs. drafting! Rally to your country's call!*" etc. The meeting which this bill called together was held on the afternoon of Thursday, the 21st, at two o'clock, in the new church vestry. Patriotic speeches were made by Hon. B. W. Harris, of East Bridgewater, J. C. Cluer, of Boston, and others of the town, the sentiment of the meeting being decidedly in favor of crushing the rebellion. This meeting closed at five o'clock P. M., to give way for a legal town meeting, to be held in the same place. At the close of this meeting, which had been adjourned to the Saturday following, after remarks by several persons present, the following resolutions were offered by David L. Cowell, which were adopted by the meeting: —

Resolved, That the citizens of North Bridgewater, in furnishing their quota of the 300,000 volunteers for *three years*, and the additional quota for *nine months*, have neither exhausted their means nor their patriotism, but that they are ready to respond to another call, and still another, if necessary, to put down *treason* and *rebellion*.

Resolved, That the present rebellion is an insurrection of political slaveholders against republican institutions, and therefore the power of slavery should henceforth be turned to the use of freedom; that the slaves of rebels should be liberated, and as many of them as are willing armed; and, while we have unwavering confidence in the honesty and patriotism of the President, we earnestly implore him to have faith in the people, and *go ahead*.

Resolved, That, without detracting from the merit of those who have gone before, the alacrity with which our young men come forward, in response to the call for nine months' men, eminently entitles them, under the peculiar circumstances of the case, to be called volunteers.

The number that had enlisted, up to the close of the meeting, was seventy, each of whom generously offered to relinquish fifty dollars on their bounty of one hundred and fifty dollars, as voted by the town to be paid to each volunteer.

From August 25 to December 9, 1862, the following persons enlisted in the nine months' service, as appears on the rolls of the various companies from North Bridgewater : —

List of men in Company K, from North Bridgewater, in the Third Massachusetts Regiment of Volunteers, for nine months' service, under Colonel Silas P. Richmond, from September 23, 1862 : —

Samuel Bates, *Captain.*

Augustus Davenport,	Albert L. Marshall,	Shepard B. Wilbur,
N. M. Davenport, Jr.,	Isaac P. Osborne,	Nathan F. Packard,
Luther M. Morse,	James H. Packard,	George Phelan,
Henry L. Manly,		Elisha Reynolds.

The above regiment served in the commencement of the war as three months' volunteers from the old militia organization. After their term of service at Fortress Monroe had expired, it returned to its old place in the militia of Massachusetts. When the call was made for a draft of nine months' men, the *Third Regiment,* Colonel Silas P. Richmond, volunteered at once, and was sent to Camp Joe Hooker, at Lakeville, where it filled up its ranks to the full requirement. The above company embarked on board the steamers " Merrimac " and " Mississippi," at Boston, October 22, 1862, and sailed for Beaufort, N. C., the same evening.*

List of men in Company E, Fourth Regiment of Massachusetts Volunteers, Colonel Henry Walker, for nine months' service, from September 26, 1862 : —

Lewis Soule, *Captain.*

Henry F. Dearborn,	Albert S. Peck,	Matthew T. Packard.

This regiment went into Camp Joe Hooker, at Lakeville ; afterwards in service, under General Banks, at New Orleans.

List of men in Company C, Forty-second Regiment of Massachusetts Volunteers, under Colonel Isaac S. Burrill, for nine months' service, mustered in October, 1862 : —

* See Colonel Richmond's Report for further items concerning their service.

Orville W. Leonard, *Captain.*

Frederick C. Blanchard,	William McGrane,	Cornelius Duffy,
Augustus Bowley,	Patrick McGrane,	Frank Langren,
Christopher Corcoran,	Andrew P. Olson,	Hugh McIntire,
Swan P. Colberg,	Willard F. Packard,	Robert Owens,
Josiah Edson,	Albert Thompson,	George F. Parker,
Leroy S. Hamilton,	Thomas M. Farrell,	Michael Reardon,
James Kenyon,	Hiram A. Freeman,	Thomas Kelly,
David Murphy,	Volney H. Dunbar,	James Corcoran.

This regiment was recruited at Camp Meigs, Readville, the necleus of which was the Second Regiment, afterwards changed to the Forty-second. It was ordered to General Banks's Department, in the Gulf, and was on duty at New Orleans, Galveston, and Carrollton, La.

List of men in Company K, Forty-third Regiment of Massachusetts Volunteers, under Colonel Charles L. Holbrook, mustered September 16, 1862, for nine months' service : —

J. Emory Rounds, *Captain.*

Cyrus F. Copeland,	Martin V. B. Dunham,	George H. Fullerton,
Aaron S. Harlow,	Daniel B. Lovell,	Sherman T. Merea.
	John S. Perry,	Charles Tillson.

This regiment was recruited through the influence of the Second Battalion, M. V. M., First Brigade, First Division, otherwise known as the " Tiger Regiment ; " was in camp at Readville ; left camp, and embarked on board transport, October 24, 1862, and sailed for Newbern, N. C., where it was in service in General Foster's Division.

In the Forty-fourth Regiment of Massachusetts Volunteers, Colonel Francis L. Lee, nine months' service : —

Company D, Captain Henry D. Sullivan, Howard Davis,

This regiment, otherwise known as the " New England Guard Regiment," encamped at Camp Meigs, Readville, embarked on board steamer " Merrimac," for Newbern, N. C., October 22, 1862.

List of men in the Forty-fifth Regiment of Volunteers, for nine months' service, under Colonel Charles R. Codman, Company G, Captain Joseph Murdock: —

George E. Allen,	Richard Field,	Charles E. Tribou,
William S. Brett,	Robert S. Maguire,	William H. Vose,
Sydney Chandler,	Moses A. Packard,	Charles A. Crocker,
Andrew C. Gibbs,	Warren Shaw,	William E. Bryant,
Augustus B. Loring,	George Thacher,	Davis H. Packard,
	Marcus H. Reynolds.	

This regiment was well known as the "Cadet Regiment," from the fact that many of the officers belong to that organization; embarked on board steamer for Newbern, N. C., October 24, 1862, where it joined General Foster's forces. They were engaged in the battles of Whitehall and Kinston.

In the Forty-eighth Regiment of Massachusetts Volunteers, for nine months' service, Colonel Eben F. Stone, Company K, Captain J. S. Todd, we find

Charles B. Shaw, mustered December 9, 1862.

This regiment was in the Department of the Gulf.

This completes the lists of those who were from North Bridgewater in the nine months' service. The foregoing exhibits all the regular enlistments in the various companies in Massachusetts regiments. We next find the scattering enlistments, as follows: —

Men in the Rhode Island Contingent, belonging in North Bridgewater, previous to January, 1863: —

George B. Bunker, Albert Mathison, Thomas O. Mera, Patrick Casey, in the Third Regiment.

John W. Curtis, in the Fourth Regiment.

Ninth Rhode Island Battery: —

Benjamin Packard,	John Pike,	Eben Luther,
Franklin Reynolds,	Edmund Reynolds,	William H. Wade.

List of men in the New York Contingent, from North Bridgewater, previous to January, 1863: —

Terrance Connell, Company K, Fourth Regiment.
William Fitzgerald, Sickles Brigade.
Rufus E. Matthews, Mounted Rifles.
Philip McDonald, Ninety-ninth Regiment.
Hugh Riley,   "   "   Company K.

MEN WHO ARE, OR HAVE BEEN, IN THE NAVAL SERVICE, FROM
NORTH BRIDGEWATER, PREVIOUS TO 1863.

Names.	Entered service.	Term.	Name vessel.	Remarks.
William W. Packard,	Feb. 10, 1861	3 years	Kingfisher	Promoted to Capt. Steward
Charles H. Packard,	Sept. 12, 1862	1 year	Dacotah	Discharged Sept. 12, 1863
Walter L. French,	Aug. 11, 1862	1 "	Hunchback	" Aug. 15, 1863
George F. Packard,	" 12, 1862	1 "	Daylight	" June 6, 1863
Samuel J. Wade,	" 11, 1862	1 "	Miami	" Sept. 6, 1863
Lorenzo J. Dam,	" 11, 1862	1 "	"	" " 6, 1863
Elijah Smith,	" 11, 1862	1 "	Colorado	" " 1863
S. S. Churchill,	" 12, 1862	1 "	Housatonic	" " 17, 1863

Names of persons drafted in North Bridgewater, Sub-District No. 27, July, 1863: —

Rufus E. Howard,
Rufus Copeland,
Ellison Hawes,
Charles H. Cary,
Levi Leach,
John D. Thayer,
Michael McSweeney,
Josiah E. Packard,
Henry Cross,
Lorenzo D. Bates,
Leonard C. Stetson,
Francis Brett,
Henry M. Jackson,
Charles H. Phillips,
Perez McFarland,
Nathaniel B. Blackstone,
John W. Hayward,
Samuel A. Holbrook,
James McGuire,
Sylvanus C. Stetson,

[The above persons paid a commutation fee of three hundred dollars each.]

Simeon W. Edson,
George W. Andrews,
William H. Searle,
Luther H. Hollis,
George M. Nash,
Lyman Allen,
Rodney M. Leach,

[The last named were sent to rendezvous]

Warren A. Howard,
John P. Bertman,
Joseph Bullard,
George E. Sturtevant,
Zina Hayward, 2d,
Edwin Howard,
Simeon D. Carr,
Lysander F. Gurney,
Francis L. Wilder,
Pelham Jones.

Lyman E. Tribou,
[Each furnished substitutes.]

A proclamation was issued, October 17, 1863, calling for

300,000 more soldiers, for three years, or during the war; and, "in all places where the quotas are not filled on or before January 5, 1864, on that day a draft will be enforced." In the enlistments under this call, they were for one, two, or three years, and in any company that was not full, and hailing from the same State that the recruit resided in.

In the First Regiment of Heavy Artillery from Massachusetts, mustered in November and December, 1863, for three years, are the following: —

David W. Graves,	Frank E. Drake,	John E. Hollis,
Luther Shepardson,	Daniel B. Eames,	Charles E. Jernegan.

List of persons from North Bridgewater in the Second Heavy Artillery, mustered into three years' service in August, October, and December, 1863: —

William E. Bryant,	Jonathan W. Shaw,	James Coffee,
William Kerrigan,	Philip Saxton,	Joseph Hurley,
Christopher Brannagan,	John M. Wentworth,	Dexter D. Keith,
William Murphy,	George T. Whitcomb,	Sumner A. Smith,

Veteran Reserve Corps: —

Nehemiah C. Ivers, three years; mustered October 21, 1863.
Patrick Powers, one year; mustered November 11, 1863.
Morris Glancy, three years; mustered November 24, 1863.

Fifty-sixth Regiment Massachusetts Volunteers: —

Company A, Captain George A. Fletcher, Warren S. Gurney, mustered for three years, December 26, 1863.
Company G, Samuel T. Packard, mustered January 19, 1864.

Second Massachusetts Cavalry, three years' service: —

Fisher Copeland, mustered December 29, 1863.
George H. Matthews, mustered January 1, 1864.
Patrick Donahue, mustered October 80, 1863.

March 14, 1864, an order was given to the various provost marshals throughout the State, by order of President Lincoln, to draft two hundred thousand men, as a reserve force, in addition to the five hundred thousand called for in February, 1864, to be used in the army, navy, and marine corps of the United States.

The different towns were allowed till April 15th to fill up their quota, under this call, by volunteering.

Under this call, the following persons were in service in the Veteran Reserve Corps of the United States : —

Patrick Powers,	Edward Creedan,	Daniel Donahue,
Daniel Delaney,	Thomas Havy,	Patrick Lynch,
Simeon Dowling,	Elbridge L. Leach,	Edward P. Packard,
Caleb Badger,	James Fadden,	Cyrus L. Williams,
	Turner Torrey.	

First Brigade, First Division, Twentieth Corps, United States troops : —

Orlando Dow,	A. M. Robinson,	Otis H. Hamilton,
Alden B. Winns,	George A. Stone,	George H. Stearns,
John L. Hibbard,	William Kearney,	Nathaniel McKinsley,

The following persons were obtained to fill up the town's quota under call of March 14, 1864 : —

Three Years' Recruits obtained at Washington.

James Wilson..............May	2, 1864, 1st Reg. Reserve Corps.		
James Rexss	"	"	"
Gerthref Wentgel	"	"	"
Charles Hammond	"	"	"
Henry A. Levick	"	"	"
Lyman A. Root	"	"	"
William Hunt..............	"	"	"
George J. Miller............	"	"	"
George Jordan ....May	3, 1864,	"	"
James R. Brown............	"	"	"
Michael F. Kelley	"	"	"
James D. Cole	"	"	"
Baptist Sawyer.............	"	"	"
Adolphus Richards..........May	2, 1864,	"	"
James S. Badger............April 30, 1864, 1st Battery.			
Nathaniel Colman ....May	1, 1864, 22d Reg., Co. H.		
Robert Eckhart..............	"	"	"
Henry Hughes	"	"	"
Michael Ryan	"	"	"
Andrew J. Covell...........May	3, 1864, 24th Reg., Co. B.		
Nicholas Paul..............	"	"	"

Michael Stanton ....May 3, 1864, 24th Reg., Co. **B**
Christian Alson ....   "   "   "
John F. Cunningham ....   "   2d Batt., 101st Co
David Martin ....   "   "   "
Michael Fony ....   "   "   123d Co
Charles Gall ....   "   "   "
Charles R. Goodwin...... ..   "   "   "
James Miller...............   "   "   "
David P. Shaw.............   "   "   "
Theodore Sheltz ....   "   "   "
John Lyons................   "   "   39th Co. **V. R. S.**
Thomas Hillman...........   "   1st Batt., 205th   "
John Darling ....   "   "   "
Albert Marquis.............   "   "   "
James H. Grew ....   "   "   "
Lewis Artemas ....   "   "   "
David White...............   "   "   "
Nathaniel Brown ....May 6, 1864.
Jacob Greely..............

Again in July, 1864, the enemy having marched to within
a few miles of the capital, and the governors of several
States feeling desirous to aid in the defence of the same, at
their earnest solicitation, they were permitted to call for
troops to serve for one hundred days. An order was issued
by General William Schouler, from the head-quarters at Boston, July 8, 1864, calling for four thousand men to do garrison duty in the forts in and around Washington, to be
raised immediately. In response to the above call, forty-
two companies were in camp at Readville in less than ten
days after the order was issued. Again did North Bridgewater come up nobly to the work of filling up the ranks.
A company of a hundred and one, rank and file, was recruited, and left the town under the command of Captain
Uriah Macoy, July 13, 1864. The company left town in
the morning train of cars for Readville. A large concourse of the friends of the company assembled at the
depot to witness their departure, and to bestow their parting
good wishes.

The following is a list of the company : —

One Hundred Days' Men, Company C, Sixtieth Regiment.

Mustered in July 14, 1864; *mustered out November* 30, 1864.

URIAH MACOY, appointed Captain July 11 ; promoted Major July 30.

CHARLES L. SPROUL,   1st Lt.   "   "   Captain   "

THOMAS P. BARNFIELD, 2d Lt.   "   "   1st Lt.   "

BERIAH T. HILLMAN,   "   2d Lt.   "

D. Perkins Reynolds, promoted 1st Sergeant, July 31.

John Ryan,	"	2d	"	"
Daniel L. Weymouth,	"	3d	"	"
Peter Dalton,	"	5th	"	"
Huron Wade,	"	3d Corporal,	"	
Emery Z. Stevens,	"	5th	"	"
Alfred W. Jones,	"	6th	"	"
Amos S. Perkiss,	"	7th	"	"
Seth L. French,	"	8th	"	"

F. D. Millet, *Musician,*
Geo. F. Hayward, "
Ethan Allen,
Elijah Bates,
Willard Bryant,
Ezekiel R. Bartlett,
Charles R. Beals,
George W. Barnfield,
James E. Ball,
George W. Barnard,
*Herbert C. Blood,
Frederick N. Bigelow,
Nathan B. Blood,
John A. Belcher,
James Corcoran,
John H. Cole,
George Churchill,
Charles R. Curtis,
Benjamin B. Curtis,
James Dwyer,
Willard Howard,
Andrew Johnson,
Flavel B. Keith,
Thomas Kenney,
Justin V. Keith,
Avory F. Keith,
Edward Luney,
Daniel Lawson,

Benjamin F. Lewis,
Benjamin E. Mitchell,
Frederick Mitchell,
Timothy McCarty,
Austin S. Macoy,
Albert W. Mowry,
William McGonnigle,
Augustus Melburg,
Joshua Morse,
Timothy Mullens,
Anthony Phillips,
Harrison Phillips,
Charles D. Packard,
John W. Porter,
Reuel W. Dunbar,
Barzillai Field,
Seth L. French,
Leonard Faunce,
Varanes Filoon,
Michael Fitzgerald,
Thomas Fitzpatrick,
William H. Foster,
Henry Gardner,
Charles E. Graves,
Spencer B. Glass,
Charles W. Gardner,
George A. Haven,
Robert Henderson,
George H. French.

Frederick M. Hathaway,
Samuel W. Holbrook,
Seth M. Hall,
Bela B. Hayward,
Frederick Hanson,
Roland Harris,
Edwin Holmes,
David Perkins,
Cyrus Reed,
Gardner W. Reynolds,
Howard W. Reynolds,
Josiah E. Reynolds,
Henry A. Soule,
Lewis D. Stinchfield,
George B. Smith,
William Stevens, *Clerk,*
James Sullivan,
Alexander Thrasher,
Charles H. Thompson,
David L. Tinkham,
Asa W. Tinkham,
John Towle,
Herbert M. Thompson
Albert E. Windship,
Edward M. Willis,
Dexter E. Wilbor,
Samuel J. Wade,
John Westgate,

This company was located at Indianapolis, Ind., and,

* Died October 25, at Indianapolis, Ind.

36

although not actively engaged in any battle, did valuable service in doing guard duty, and received the thanks of the commanding general.

The following persons enlisted in the service, in August and September, 1864, for one year, mostly in heavy artillery companies : —

Charles W. Bacon,	Otis Cobb,	Lucas W. Alden,
Joshua R. Bartlett,	Thomas Shean,	Stephen Davis,
John Gartland,	James Herrod,	George W. Stephens,
Thomas Moran,	John Donohue, 2d,	James Hoyt,
Galen E. Pratt,	Franklin M. Sturtevant,	Wilson Morse,
Patrick Diamond,	James Farrell,	Daniel D. Sanford,
Ira O. Severance,	Jacob Peacock,	Edward W. Spencer,
John Fury,	John Keegan,	George E. Peck,
John Diamond,	Charles H. Crosby,	St. Clair McLeod,
William Emerson,	Volney H. Dunbar,	Marcus W. Wheeler,

Alexander D. Washburn,   James H. Keenan,

List of men in Company B, Captain Robert Crossman, 2d, Fifty-eighth Massachusetts Regiment, under command of Colonel John C. Whiton, for three years' service : —

William A. Start, *Chaplain*,   Joseph Skinner,   Charles Bond.

Company D, Captain Charles E. Churchill : —

Charles D. Hunt,	Daniel Y. Soper,	Isaac A. Reynolds,
Osman J. Perkins,	Daniel W. Willis,	John R. Mills,
Charles W. Reynolds,	Joseph L. Bunker,	Clarence Caulkins,
Joseph G. Warren,	Francis I. Snow,	Samuel J. Caulkins,

William F. Willis,   Bradford Snell.

Company F, Captain Charles D. Copeland : —

George E. Holmes,	Levi B. Holbrook,	George M. Skinner,
George H. Thompson,	Nehemiah Thompson,	Henry M. Bartlett,
William Mackay,	Jerrie C. Vaughn,	Daniel C. Bird,
Albert G. Thompson,	John B. Parker,	Thomas Eagan,

Hiram A. Freeman,   Henry D. Peirce.

Company G, Captain Samuel B. Hinckley : —

Anthony P. Faunce.

Company H, Captain William H. Harley : —

James A. Smith,   Dennis Higgins.

Company I, Captain Nathan S. Oakman : —

Elijah Gay,   George B. Stevens,   Henry L. Thompson,
                         James F. Williams.

Company K, Captain Albion M. Dudley : —

William S. Brett,   John S. Perry,   Frank Benson,
                         Peter Johnson.

Fifty-ninth Massachusetts Regiment, Captain James Gibson : —

Harrison A. Hunt,   John E. Hunt.

United States Signal Corps : —

James M. Kimball,   Edwin T. Cowell,   Jeremiah S. Young.

Second Massachusetts Light Artillery, Captain William Moreland, for one year's service : —

Henry J. White,   Ziba H. Bryant,   Jeffrey A. Potter,
                         James Coffee.

Fourth Massachusetts Light Battery, Captain George G. Trull, three years' service : —

William Geary.

Fifth Massachusetts Light Battery, Captain Charles A. Phillips, one year's service : —

James Sheerin,   Francis E. Baxter.

Seventh Massachusetts Light Battery, Captain Newman W. Storer, three years' service : —

Patrick McCullough.

Tenth Massachusetts Light Battery, Captain J. Webb Adams, one year's service : —

Cornelius McAuliffe.

Eleventh Massachusetts Light Battery, Captain Edward J. Jones, three years' service : —

Josiah H. Foye.

Sixteenth Massachusetts Light Battery, Captain Henry D. Scott, three years' service : —

Rufus C. Bean.

Fourth United States Artillery, Company L : —

Nathaniel J. Huntress,　　　　Willis F. H. Fisher.

Fortieth United States Regiment Colored Troops, **three** years' service : —

George Bussey.

Third Massachusetts Cavalry, three years' service : —

Thomas P. Williams.

Fourth Massachusetts Cavalry, Captain Joseph W. Morton, three years' service : —

Charles M. Hathaway,　　　　Edward E. Holden,　　　　Philip Rochester.

For one year's service in same regiment : —

Lawrence Hogan,　　　John Farrell, Jr.,　　　James Donahue,
Philip II. King,　　　Alien F. Williams,　　　Cornelius Birmingham.

In the call of July, 1864, for 500,000 troops, a draft was to be made in all districts that were not filled within sixty days. To avoid a draft and the liability of serving, the following persons furnished substitutes : —

SUBSTITUTE.			PRINCIPAL.
James Davis	Aug. 29, 1864,	3 years.	George E. Bryant.
John Brown	Sept. 3,	"	Charles H. Curtis.
James Collins	" 5,	"	Horatio B. Thayer.
Emill Thompson	" 1,	"	William A. Osborn.
John H. Stevens	" 1,	"	Elmer L. Keith.
Peter Keenan	Aug. 15,	"	Charles P. Keith.
John Dobbins	" 25, 1864,	4 years.	Charles H. Cole.
John James	" 14, 1864,	3 years.	Nelson J. Foss.
John Roach	Sept. 1,	"	Francis A. Thayer.
Ambrose Dube	" 2,	"	George R. Thompson.
John Fitz Gibbons	" 7,	"	Luther Studley.
Alfred Grey	" 9,	"	Henry L. Bryant.
John Allen	Aug. 29,	"	Charles R. Ford.
Martin Hawkins	" 27,	"	George Sawyer.
Charles Auringer	" 24,	"	Simeon F. Packard.
John Nelligan	" 24, 1864,	4 years.	Barnabas H. Gray.
John Dyer	" 30,	"	Augustus T. Jones.
Jeremiah Maloney	" 23, 1864,	3 years.	Sylvanus Keith.
Charles Felman	Sept. 14,	"	Henry E. Lincoln.
Michael Martin	" 14,	"	Arza B. Keith.
Jonathan J. Thompson	" 15,	"	Charles Howard, Jr.

SUBSTITUTE.				PRINCIPAL.
John Pointon	Sept.	17, 1864, 3 years.		Jonas Reynolds.
Edwin R. Sice	"	21,	"	Eben G. Rhodes.
Benagah C. Boston	"	13,	"	L. Bradford Howard.
Charles Werner	"	22,	"	Elbridge W. Morse.
James Edwin	"	19,	"	Mitchell Willis.
Thomas McManus	Aug.	1, 1864, 1 year.		Jonas R. Perkins.
James Brown	Oct.	10, 1864, 3 years.		Cyrenus W. Blanchard.
Antone Robero	"	25,	"	Eliphalet L. Thayer.

Navy Recruits.

Alvan Howe, September 6, 1864, one year.
Stillman Billings, September 7, 1864, one year.
William C. N. Sanford, Acting Master's Mate.

List of casualties, promotions, changes, deaths, etc., in the foregoing companies : —

David W. Graves, First Heavy Artillery, wounded in the foot at the battle of Spottsylvania, May 19, 1864.

George W. Pope, enlisted October 28, 1861, in Company G, Twenty-ninth Massachusetts Regiment for three years' service, was soon promoted to Second Lieutenant, December 6, 1862; First Lieutenant, July 29, 1864; he died August 5, 1864, at the Seminary Hospital, Georgetown, D. C., from the effects of a wound received in one of the battles before Petersburg, Virginia, June 15, 1864.

John B. Cobb, Company A, Seventh Massachusetts Regiment, died of yellow fever at Mansfield, North Carolina, October 20, 1864. At the time of his death he was Quartermaster Sergeant of Company B, Second Massachusetts Heavy Artillery.

Preston Holbrook, Company C, Thirty-fifth Massachusetts Regiment, taken prisoner in the battle at Poplar Spring Church, carried to Libby Prison, and there remained one night; from thence to Salisbury, North Carolina, where he remained five months ; released from prison in March, 1865.

George E. Holmes, Company F, Fifty-eighth Massachusetts Regiment, was taken prisoner while on picket-duty near Petersburg, Virginia, June 7, 1864 ; was carried to Andersonville Prison, released in March, 1865 ; he died at Camp Parole Hospital, Annapolis, Maryland, May 28, 1865.

John E. Hunt, Company B, Fifty-ninth Massachusetts Regiment, Musician.

Harrison A. Hunt, taken prisoner at Petersburg, died November 22, 1864, at Danville, Virginia.

Alfred H. Tilden, Company G, Seventh Massachusetts Regiment, wounded in one of the battles in the Shenandoah Valley, 3d and 4th of June, 1864.

Samuel T. Packard, Company G, Fifty-sixth Massachusetts Regiment, severely wounded in the face ; died at his residence October 10, 1864.

Sylvanus C. Packard, Company A, Thirty-ninth Massachusetts Regiment, taken prisoner in one of the battles on the Weldon Railroad ; released in March, 1865.

Charles T. Packard enlisted in Company F, Twelfth Massachusetts Regiment ; promoted to Second Lieutenant June 26, 1861 ; Captain, August 20, 1862; he was wounded in the severe battle of Fredericksburg, Virginia, December 13, 1862, losing one eye.

Frank E. Drake, Company I, First Massachusetts Heavy Artillery, taken prisoner, and died at Andersonville, Georgia, November 18, 1864.

Daniel W. Willis, Company D, Fifty-eighth Massachusetts Regiment, killed in battle.

John R. Mills, Company D, Fifty-eighth Massachusetts Regiment, killed in battle.

Simeon W. Edson, Twenty-second Massachusetts Regiment, lost a leg in the battle of Spottsylvania, May 10, 1864.

Daniel W. Edson, Twenty-second Massachusetts Regiment, lost a leg in the battle of Spottsylvania, May 10, 1864.

Walter D. Allen, of the Third Massachusetts Cavalry, died at the Philadelphia hospital October 29, 1864, from the effect of wounds received in Sheridan's army, in the Shenandoah Valley.

Charles E. Johnson, Company C, Third Rhode Island Battery, wounded while skirmishing near Harper's Ferry.

John D. Sanford, Company K, Fortieth Massachusetts Regiment, died a prisoner at Andersonville, Georgia, July 16, 1864.

Heman F. Stranger, Company C, Thirty-fifth Massachusetts Regiment, wounded at the battle of Antietam.

Alonzo S. Hamilton, Company F, Seventh Massachusetts Regiment, also of Company C, Thirty-third Maine Regiment, wounded at the battle of Petersburg, Virginia, June 17, 1863.

George M. Nash was drafted and sent to join the Thirty-second Massachusetts Regiment ; was severely wounded at Spottsylvania, and died in an ambulance on the way to Fredericksburg, Virginia.

Jerrie C. Vaughn enlisted March 12, 1864, in Company F, Fifty-eighth Massachusetts Regiment ; promoted to Second Lieutenant March 25, 1864 ; wounded near one of his eyes, a bullet lodging behind one of them ; he was formerly Major of the Sixty-seventh New York Regiment.

Horace Baker lost an arm in one of the battles of May 12, 1864.

John A. Holmes, Twenty-ninth Massachusetts Regiment, severely wounded in both knees.

John B. Parker, Company F, Fifty-eighth Massachusetts Regiment, wounded in the leg in battle, June 3, 1864.

Andrew C. Gibbs, wounded in the leg June 1, 1864.

Daniel C. Bird, stunned by a shell in the head, May 12, 1864.

Frederic C. Blanchard, Company C, Forty-second Massachusetts Regiment, appointed one of the Louisiana Engineers ; also ordered on the staff of General Couch, as chief engineer of the Department of the Susquehanna.

Henry L. Thompson, Company I, Fifty-eighth Massachusetts Regiment, taken prisoner near Petersburg, July 30, 1864 ; sent to prison at Danville, where he remained one month ; paroled, and arrived at Annapolis, Maryland, September 3, 1864.

Samuel F. Howard, Company G. Seventh Massachusetts Regiment, was shot in the foot in the battle of Fredericksburg, during an assault on St. Mary's Hill.

Charles W. Reynolds enlisted April 2, 1864, in Company D, Fifty-eighth Massachusetts Regiment ; fell in the battle of Petersburg, a day or two before the final surrender.

John W. Burns, Bugler in Company H, Twelfth Massachusetts Regiment, taken prisoner October 11, 1863, and sent to Libby Prison, Richmond, Virginia, where he died February 24, 1864.

Caleb T. Athearn, Company F, Thirty-third Massachusetts Regiment, wounded in the leg.

Dr. Charles H. Mason, Surgeon on board the gunboat " Virginia," died at a station near New Orleans of yellow fever, Thursday, October 13, 1864 ; was medical examiner of recruits at New Orleans.

George W. Packard, Eleventh Massachusetts Battery, wounded by a bullet in the neck.

William Mackey, Albert Fisher, D. Y. Fisher, B. C. Allen, of North Bridgewater, were removed from prison at Salisbury, North Carolina, December 15, 1864.

Daniel P. Sherman, Company B, First Massachusetts Cavalry, killed at the battle of Aldie, June 17, 1863.

Enos W. Thayer, enlisted in the volunteer service September 10, 1861 ; commissioned as Captain of Company C, Twenty-sixth Regiment Massachusetts Volunteers. September 25, 1861 ; he sailed with the regiment from Boston, November 21, 1861, on the steamer " Constitution," and arrived at Ship Island December 3, where they remained till May 30, 1862 ; was in the attack on Sabine Pass ; also in the battle of Winchester, where he fell, wounded in a charge upon the rebels, September 19 ; he was a prisoner within the rebel lines five hours, when the Union cavalry made a charge, and rescued him. He died October 10, at Winchester Hospital ; his remains were buried at Mansfield, Massachusetts, with military honors, November 11, 1864. He was very much respected as an officer by his superiors, and was a brave, noble, and generous man.

Albert M. Smith, son of Albert Smith, of Charlestown, Massachusetts, formerly of North Bridgewater, was a member of Company C, Forty-second Massachusetts Regiment ; was in the " Banks Expedition," at New Orleans, Louisiana, 1862-3. At the expiration of that service, re-enlisted, and was engaged in the battle of Coal Harbor, since clerk in the hospital department.

Joseph Scott Packard, Jr., formerly of North Bridgewater, was color-bearer in the Second Massachusetts Regiment ; wounded at Gettysburg, Virginia.

Acting Master Frederic Crocker, promoted to Lieutenant for bravery at Sabine Pass ; afterward commanded an expedition that captured one thousand prisoners, with their arms and ammunition ; he was attached to the gunboat " Kensington," on the Florida coast, under the command of Commodore Farragut ; his promotion is said to have been richly deserved.

Lucius F. Kingman, son of Davis Kingman, formerly of North Bridgewater, lately of Northboro', Massachusetts, was killed in battle 1863.

George H. Thompson, Company F, Fifty-eighth Massachusetts Regiment, taken prisoner June 7, 1864; died at Andersonville, Georgia.

Sumner A. Smith, Company H, Second Massachusetts Heavy Artillery, died on the Mississippi River.

Edwin E. Faunce was in the Seventy-fifth Illinois Regiment.

Ambrose Henry Hayward was in Company D, Twenty-eighth Pennsylvania Regiment of Veterans; he enlisted May 24, 1860; he died in the hospital at Chattanooga, Tennessee, June 15, 1864, from the effects of wounds received at the battle of Pine Knob, Georgia. He was a noble, true-hearted soldier; at the time of his being wounded, he was in command of his company, and had been in several engagements. He was endeared to all his companions by his courteous and manly deportment.

Charles N. Packard, *Corporal*, was in the Thirty-fifth Massachusetts Regiment. Mr. Packard was one of the one thousand that were inspected by the regimental, brigade, and division commanders, and pronounced in every respect the most efficient soldier. He has participated in no less than fifteen battles; was at the siege of Vicksburg, and marched through Virginia, Kentucky, Tennessee, and Mississippi, with great credit to himself, and much respected by his comrades.

Austin Packard enlisted July, 1862, in the Ninth Massachusetts Battery; wounded in the arm at the battle of Gettysburg; he was conveyed to Philadelphia in the cars, where his arm was amputated. A prostrating fever was caused by the operation, in consequence of which he died September 21, 1864. Funeral honors were paid to his remains at the grave by a detachment under Captain A. K. Harmon.

George W. Cole, William Mackey, Fernando Skinner, and Ellis Howard were released from rebel prisons in March, 1865.

Samuel Kimball enlisted in Company E, Eighteenth Massachusetts Regiment, August 26, 1861, and was killed at the battle of Bull Run, August 30, 1862.

William Flennagan enlisted June 26, 1861; killed at the battle of Bull Run, August 30, 1861.

Ferdinand Robinson enlisted August 26, 1861; killed at the battle of Bull Run.

Joseph Beals enlisted July 30, 1862; died July 30, 1863, of wounds received at Gettysburg.

Edward F. Drohan, Company C, Twenty-ninth Massachusetts Regiment, enlisted May 22, 1861; died January 12, 1862.

Charles F. Swanstrom, Thirty-third Massachusetts Regiment, died December 23, 1862.

Henry Fenn, Ninth Massachusetts Battery, killed in the battle of Gettysburg.

Andrew P. Olson, enlisted in Company C, Forty-second Massachusetts Regiment; died at the Massachusetts Hospital, New York City.

Orrin D. Holmes, son of Nathan Holmes, of North Bridgewater, enlisted from Plymouth; fell in the battle before Petersburg, Va., March 25, 1864.

NARRATIVE OF THE TWELFTH MASSACHUSETTS REGIMENT.*

WE have inserted the following account, thinking it would be of great interest to those who have taken a part in subduing the rebellion.

" On the 23d of July, 1861, this regiment left Boston, and arrived at Sandy Hook, Maryland, on the 27th inst., and went into camp. They marched twenty-one miles to the Monocacy River, and encamped, remaining there several days; from that place they marched to Hyattstown, a distance of six miles; to Darnestown, eighteen miles; to Muddy Branch, seven miles; to Edward's Ferry, fifteen miles; and to Seneca Mills, by the way of Poolesville, fifteen miles. They went into winter quarters at Frederick, Maryland, having arrived through Darnestown and Barnestown, a distance of thirty miles. Upon the 27th of February, 1862, they broke camp at Frederick, and went into camp at Shenandoah City, Virginia, distant twenty-five miles from Frederick. March 1st, they went to Charlestown, Virginia, by the way of Bolivar Heights, a distance of seven miles; they left Charlestown March 10th, for Winchester, Virginia, by the way of Berryville, twenty-four miles; marched from Winchester to Snicker's Gap, by the way of Berryville, on the 21st of March, eighteen miles; March 23d went to Aldie, distant eighteen miles; they returned to Snicker's Gap on the 24th, from whence they marched to Goose Creek, distant eleven miles; on the 28th they left for Cub Run, and on the 29th marched to Bull Run, five miles. They were almost continually on the march from place to place, through the Shenandoah Valley between the 1st of April and August 1st, seldom remaining long in one camp; August 9th they were engaged in the battle of Cedar Mountain, in which they lost Captain N. B. Shurtleff, Jr., and ten men wounded; after this they made several marches and counter-marches, and on the 20th of August were engaged in the battle of the Rappahannock, in which they suffered no loss; from this to the 30th, they were almost constantly on the march, and on the day last mentioned, in an engagement at Grovetown, near Bull Run, Colonel Webster, Captain Kimball, and ten men were killed, and one hundred and thirty-five men were wounded and missing. After this battle, the regiment retreated to Centreville, arriving there the next day; on the 14th of September, they marched to South Mountain, and were engaged in that battle, in which one man was killed, and five wounded; from that place they went to Keedysville, and on the afternoon of the 16th, formed in line of battle and bivouacked for the night; they engaged the enemy at five o'clock in the morning, but were ordered to leave the field at nine A. M., and withdrew in good order. They went into this fight with three hundred and twenty-five men, and lost forty-seven men killed, and one hundred and sixty-six wounded, several of whom subsequently died of their wounds. On leaving the field, bringing off their regimental colors, four officers, and thirty-two men, they volunteered to support a battery; after which they rejoined their brigade,

* For a further and very interesting account of this regiment, see the Adjutant General's Report for 1863-4.

and participated in the pursuit of the flying enemy, who withdrew across the river.

"The regiment was at this time under the command of Captain B. F. Cook, of Company E. On the 23d of September, Colonel James L. Bates took command of this regiment. From this time, until November 10th, they were mostly on the march in Maryland and Virginia, and arrived at the Rappahannock Station November 8th, near which they encamped.

"At the battle of Fredericksburg, fought on the 13th of December, 1862, the Twelfth Regiment was in General Gibbons's Division. The division was formed in three brigade lines, and the third, commanded by General Taylor, had the advance, the Thirteenth Massachusetts Regiment acting as skirmishers for the division. Colonel Lyle's Brigade, composed of the Twelfth Massachusetts, the Twenty-sixth New York, and the Nineteenth and One Hundred Thirty-sixth Regiments of Pennsylvania Volunteers, formed the second line, this regiment having the right. The third line was Colonel Root's Brigade, the Sixteenth Maine Regiment having the right. The position of the Twelfth Regiment was taken nine o'clock A. M.; the enemy were hidden from view by a thick wood. Our men remained lying down until one o'clock P. M. under a brisk fire of shot and shell, the skirmishers being hotly engaged, and the balls of the enemy passing over us. During these four hours there was but one man of this regiment injured. At one o'clock the signal to advance was given to the whole division, and immediately obeyed. A heavy fire of musketry broke from the whole line of woods in our front. General Taylor's brigade stood the fire some thirty minutes, when the brigade in which was this regiment was ordered to relieve them. As they advanced, they became separated from the brigade by the retiring regiments of the Third Brigade, and continued to advance independently, taking a position and firing until their ammunition began to fail. Their brigade had fallen to the rear, and they were alone until the third line came forward; their solid ranks broke the right of this line, which opened to the right and left to get to the front, where it was quickly formed. The Twelfth Regiment followed the one in their front, the Sixteenth Maine, a short distance, and being out of ammunition, were about to join their brigade in the rear, when they were ordered by General Taylor to prepare for a charge. The colonel thereupon gave the command to fix bayonets, and filed to the right of the brigade, and charged with them into the woods in their front. About two hundred of the enemy rushed through our lines, and gave themselves up as prisoners of war. We carried the position and remained some twenty minutes, expecting support; but none was in sight, and the men were constantly falling before the fatal fire of an unseen enemy. Captains Ripley, Reed, Packard, and Clark, and a hundred of the men had fallen. After consulting with the officers, the colonel gave orders to about face, and they fell back slowly and reluctantly, and in very good order, bearing their tattered banners with them to their brigade. After reaching the place, they were ordered to fall back to where they were supplied with ammunition and rations. They remained under arms all night, and early on the morning of the 14th, they were ordered to another position, where they remained till the night of the 15th, when they recrossed the river to Falmouth with their corps. During the battle, the Twelfth was under fire six hours, and their loss was chiefly sustained during the last two hours. During that time they had five officers wounded, and fifteen men killed, eighty-seven wounded, and three missing, making an aggregate of one hundred and five out of two hundred and fifty-eight, with which they went into the fight.''

We have now brought the chapter of the great rebellion of 1861 down to the close of enlistment of troops in September, 1864. From this time to the close of the war, there was one continuous line of successful victories over the Confederates.

The year 1865 opened with bright prospects before us, by the capture of Fort Fisher, January 15th; of Columbia, S. C., February 17th; Charleston, S. C., February 18th; Wilmington, N. C., February 21st; of Richmond, April 3d; flight of the Confederate officers of State from Richmond, April 4th; surrender of Lee's army, April 9th; surrender of Johnston's army, April 26th; capture of Jeff Davis, May 10th. But that which gave the greatest joy to the Union people was the surrender of Lee. Then we began to see through the clouds that had been so long over us. And, in the middle of May, 1865, the greatest armed rebellion of the world was at an end, so far as fighting was concerned; and the nation now appears to be as prosperous as ever. Business is good; mechanics have returned to their occupations, the farmers to their long-neglected fields: and everything wears the appearance of a peaceful and prosperous hereafter. We are, as a people, stronger than before the war. We have stood up against everything that any people has ever been called to bear; and now the "star-spangled banner in triumph still waves over the land of the free and the home of the brave."

CHAPTER XV.

MILITIA HISTORY.

First Militia Company. — Officers. — Military Division of the Parish. — North and South Companies. — Plymouth County Brigade. — First Cavalry Company 1787. — North Bridgewater Dragoon Company 1853. — Militia Districts. — Active and Reserve Companies. — District Number Sixty. — District Number Sixty-one.

THE first military company formed in the ancient town of Bridgewater was formed October 2, 1689 : Thomas Hayward was chosen First Captain, John Hayward, Lieutenant, and Samuel Packard, Ensign. At that time, the militia of the counties of Barnstable, Plymouth, and Bristol, constituted one regiment, and Josiah Winslow, of Marshfield, was the Colonel.

In 1762, the population of the town had become numerous enough to increase the number of companies to six. The one in the North Parish of Bridgewater (now North Bridgewater) was called the Sixth Company. Daniel Howard was First Captain in the Parish, Robert Howard, Lieutenant, and Abiel Packard, Ensign. These were succeeded by Robert Howard, promoted to Captain, Abiel Packard, promoted to Lieutenant, and Henry Kingman, Ensign. Afterwards, Lieutenant Abiel Packard was promoted to Captain, and Ensign Henry Kingman, promoted to Lieutenant, and Constant Southworth, Ensign.

These continued in office till about 1765, at which time the Sixth Company in the town was divided into two distinct and separate companies, known as the North and South. The line of division was across the Parish from East to West, near the Centre Village. The officers of the North Company were Barnabas Howard, Captain, John Howard, Lieutenant, and Abiel Packard, Ensign. The officers of the South Com-

292

pany were Isaac Packard, Captain, Josiah Packard, Lieutenant, and Issachar Snell, Ensign. These officers held their commissions till the Revolutionary War.

In 1773, the military companies of ancient Bridgewater had been increased to nine, and these, with two companies from Abington, constituted the Third Regiment, of which Josiah Edson was Colonel. This regiment was honored with a review by Governor Hutchinson on the 13th of October of that year. Josiah Hayden was appointed Colonel of this regiment, July 1, 1781; Daniel Cary, Major, September 6, 1792.

In 1810, the Plymouth County Brigade was placed under the command of Colonel Sylvanus Lazell, promoted to Brigadier-General. The brigade then consisted of four regiments of infantry, a battalion of cavalry, and a battalion of artillery. Among the field and staff officers of the Third Regiment, were : —

Caleb Howard, Lieutenant-colonel,		appointed	April 19, 1817.	
Nathan Jones,	"	"	"	October 3, 1829.
Martin Cary,	"	"	"	October 1, 1832.
Benjamin Keith,	"	"	"	November 17, 1838.
Edward Southworth, Major,			"	August 22, 1815,
Martin Cary,	"			"	September 22, 1831.

This regiment disbanded April 24, 1840.

April 7, 1787, a cavalry company was organized in the town, and Isaac Lazell was appointed First Captain.

The following are the names of commanders from the North Parish : —

Gideon Howard, Captain,	....	May 25, 1803.
Noah Chesman, "	....	September 23, 1811.
Jeremiah Beals, Jr., "	....	September 9, 1819.
Nathan Hayward, "	....	September 20, 1823.

This company was disbanded April 10, 1828.

In June, 1853, a charter was granted to Nahum Reynolds and fifty others, to form a cavalry company, which was organized June 27, 1853, under the name of " North Bridgewater Dragoon Company." The first meeting for the choice of officers, was held in Tyler Cobb's Hall, General Eliab Ward presiding over the meeting, at which time the following officers were chosen: —

Nahum Reynolds, *Captain.*

Robert A. Stoddard, *First Lieut.*   J. Freeman Ellis, *Second Lieut.*
H. A. Raymond, *Third Lieut.*   Jonas R. Perkins, *Fourth Lieut.*

SERGEANTS.

Freeman Bicknell, 1st,   Charles T. Packard, 2d,   Samuel S. Brett, 3d,
             E. C. Mayhew, 4th.   James H. Case 5th.

CORPORALS.

Lucius Richmond,   George N. Holmes,   Welcome White,
                         Daniel Hayward.

MUSICIANS.

J. H. Smith,   Samuel Parsons,   Henry Kitman,   William Upton.

PRIVATES.

Cyrus B. Kingman,	James C. Snell,	Frederic Perkins,
Ephraim Noyes,	Manly Packard,	Julius Thompson,
James E. Lyon,	F. P. Hartwell,	Bela T. Brown,
Peter Dalton,	Mitchell Willis,	Charles J. F. Packard,
E. A. Packard,	Horace Bryant,	Rufus S. Noyes,
George L. Howard,	James S. Sherman,	Leander Waterman,
Richard M. Fullerton,	Edward B. Packard,	Charles E. Smith,
Willard Packard,	Shubael P. Mears,	Isaac Kingman,
Oliver Jackson,	Horatio G. Macomber,	William Poole,
David F. Tribou,	George W. Leach,	H. T. Sanford,
E. M. Dunbar,	Charles Woodward,	Harrison Packard.

In consequence of the various calls upon the commonwealth for troops for the United States service, during the rebellion of 1861, the volunteer militia of Massachusetts, as it existed previous to the beginning of the war, was nearly broken up, by the enlistment of its members individually, and as companies and regiments, for three months', nine months', one year's, three years', and one hundred days' service; and the law establishing the volunteer militia being no longer

in conformity with the system of organization prescribed by
the laws of the United States, it was found impossible to
recruit this militia as the law then stood.   To remedy this
evil, the Legislature of Massachusetts passed a law, in 1864,
for the reorganization of the entire militia of the commonwealth.

This act was approved May 14, 1864, and all laws in existence previous to that date, for the regulation of the militia,
were repealed.

The new law provided for a new enrolment, to be made by
the several assessors of the towns throughout the State, of
all persons between the ages of eighteen and forty-five, the
same to be returned to the adjutant general.

The commander-in-chief then proceeded to divide the
commonwealth into military districts of companies.   Under
this arrangement there were two hundred and forty-nine districts established.   North Bridgewater and West Bridgewater constituted two districts, and was divided as follows : —

District Number Sixty includes the whole of North Bridgewater except the School Districts Four, Five, Six, and Seven,
otherwise known as "Marshall," "Ames," "Campello," and
"Copeland" Districts.

District Number Sixty-one comprises the southerly school
districts, numbered four, five, six, and seven, in North
Bridgewater, and the whole of West Bridgewater.

An order was next issued to some justice of the peace within the district, to call a meeting for the election of captains
of the several companies.   After the election of the captain,
it became his duty to enroll all persons liable to enrolment,
within their respective limits.   "And all persons under the
age of twenty-four years, liable to do military duty, shall be
enrolled in one roll, and constitute the 'Active Militia.'   And
all such persons as shall be above the age of twenty-four
years, together with all persons that shall be exempt from

duty, excepting in cases of riot, invasion, insurrection, war, etc., shall be enrolled in another roll, and constitute the 'Reserve Militia.'"

The Active Militia was to have been formed into regiments, brigades, and divisions, by the commander-in-chief, and organized in conformity with the laws of the United States, subject to such changes as the commander-in-chief might make from time to time.

The Reserve Militia was to have been organized into companies, regiments, brigades, and divisions, and attached to such brigades in the Active Militia as the commander-in-chief should deem expedient, when ordered out for actual service.

Orders were received by George W. Bryant, Esq., to notify a meeting to be held January 30, 1865, for the choice of a captain for District Sixty. The meeting was held at the armory on Chapel Street, at one o'clock P. M., when Samuel F. Howard was elected captain, who was commissioned January 30, 1865. A meeting was subsequently held for the choice of lieutenants April 1, 1865, when George Southworth was elected First Lieutenant, and Bradford Wild, Second Lieutenant, both of whom were commissioned April 1, 1865.

The choice of captains for District Sixty-one was made at a meeting held at West Bridgewater on Friday, January 27, 1865, at which Austin Packard, Esq., was called to preside. Mr. Thomas P. Ripley was elected captain, and received a commission dated January 27, 1865.

At a meeting of the company soon after, in April, Nathaniel M. Davenport, Jr., was elected First Lieutenant, and Ziba C. Keith, Second Lieutenant, both of Campello.

Agreeably to instructions from head-quarters an enrolment was made by the captains of the above-named districts, and placed in the adjutant general's office, in which we find the number of persons enrolled in District Number Sixty, Captain Samuel F. Howard, for Active Service, was one hundred and thirty men; Reserve Militia, five hundred and nineteen men. The number of persons in District Number Sixty-one, Captain Thomas P. Ripley, for Active Service, was seventy-eight men; Reserve Militia, three hundred and nine men.

We have given the foregoing account of the militia organization up to May, 1865. The companies had hardly been formed, and officers chosen, when the Legislature passed a law, approved May 16, 1865, disbanding the "Active Militia," allowing them to volunteer in the service for five years. "All companies that do not volunteer within sixty days, from May 16, 1865, shall be discharged," thus leaving a militia force of volunteers only, of which there are but few old companies. Neither of the above companies has volunteered to do duty, and hence in a short time will be disbanded, according to law.

CHAPTER XVI.

MISCELLANEOUS HISTORY.

Public Roads. — Streets. — Turnpike. — Railroads — Stages. — Post-Offices.— Post-masters. — Town Maps. — Newspapers. — Publications by the North Bridge-water People. — Libraries. — North Bridgewater Library Association.

THE laying out of public roads has but little interest to the stranger, having merely a local value which may serve to locate some of the early residents of the town. The prominent thoroughfare through this town was what was termed the "Old Bay Path," reaching far out towards the shore towns. This was also called, in the records of early date, the "Country Road," and which extended the entire length of the town, and at first was very crooked. Many of the earliest roads were but the foot-paths of Indians, and it was common to build roads in the tracks that were used by them in their travels.

The following are published, hoping they may be of some interest to the people of the town in which they are lo-cated: —

PUBLIC ROADS.

1673. Thomas Snell was to make and maintain two horse Bridges, one at the hither end of Salisbury Plain over the Brook, and another over the River.

1741. A Road from Ames's Land by Downey's house, and so on, between Abiel Packard's and Daniel Richards's Land, to the Country Road.

1742, September. Layed out a way from Bay Path or Country Road to William Packard's house, past David Packard, Jr.'s, house.

1744, March 30. Road from Daniel Ames's, running between Daniel Richards's and Downey's house.

1781, March 10. Road from Abram Packard's, by land of Benjamin Kingman and Lieutenant Henry Kingman, to Simeon Packard's.

1785, March 14. From Widow Mary Howard's at the head of the way easterly of Mrs. Howard's, continuing the same point to the south-west corner of Abington.

1786, March 28. A Road one hundred Rods long on westerly side of Bay Road, northerly side of Rev. John Porter's land, and adjoining Benjamin Packard's land, to Thomas Macomber's house.

1789, March 24. Road beginning at road leading from Joseph Snell's and Joseph, Jr.'s, at Nathan Keith's line, to the south-east corner of Akerman Pettingill's land, by Ephraim Jackson's and Anna and Keziah Keith's land, to the road leading to Jacob Dunbar's.

1790, March 19. Road beginning at south-west corner of Jacob Rickard's land, and then running west in the two mile grant, to Easton.

1790, March 19. Another road a little south from Mark Ford's, running east to Jonas Packard's house.

1791, March 14. From North Boundary of Asa Keith's land, then to the Bridge north of Salisbury Plain, called Drift Road.

1793, March 11. Road beginning where the road through the West Shares (so called) in the North Precinct strikes the four mile line, running easterly on said line to road leading by Dr. Philip Bryant's.

1799, May 13. Road beginning at Colony line, between Edward Faxon's and John Hunt's, then running south, then east to Abington line.

1801, April 6. Road from Ridge, near John Bisbee's on Beaver Brook, to Dea. David Edson's, to where a gate lately stood.

1801, October 12. Road beginning at the intersecting of two Roads at westerly end of Mill Dam, at Howard's Saw-Mill so called, east and north over said dam, and called the Mill Dam Road.

1803, April 25. Road beginning at middle of road opposite south-west corner of Nathaniel Snell's woodland, Lying on Road leading from Shepard Snell's to Samuel V. Turner's.

1803, April 25. Also a Road beginning East side of Road leading from Lieutenant Samuel Brett's to Deacon Josiah Eames's house at South-east corner of Land of Josiah Packard's heirs East to Abington Line.

1818, October 29. Drift Road Laid out at Campello, from the Burying Ground to "Sprague's Factory."

1821, October 29. Road from John Smith's near School House, to Bridge west of Abel Kingman's.

1822, November 4. Road from Galen Packard's to —— Street leading by Ephraim Cole's.

1823, May 12. Road from near Samuel Ford's, to Jonas Reynolds's.

1823, September 22. Road leading from near Jacob Packard's, to where it intersects the road west of Jacob Fuller's, now known as "Town Farm."

1831, December 19. Road leading from nearly front of Williams Cary's Dwelling House, running northerly till it intersects the old Road leading from Williams Cary's to Mike's Brook.

1834, November 1. Road from Captain Asa Jones's to Joseph Brett's, built by John Packard.

1836, July 11. Road leading from Captain Ziba Keith's, to West Bridgewater line and East Bridgewater.

1837, April 4. Road from Caleb Copeland's to Jesse Packard's, widened and straightened.

1841. Road from Sidney Howard's to Willard Snell's.

1841, July 21.   Road from North Corner of Tyler Cobb's to A. K. Borden's.

1842, March 14.   Road from Captain David Ames's to Benjamin Ames's.

1844, April 22.   Road from John Ide's house to Warren Goddard's.

1846, March 4.   Road south portion of Pond Street and Elm Street.

1846, June 15.   Montello Street, from Lincoln to Centre Streets.

1847, March 29.   Road from Main Street in Campello, to Campello Depot.

1850, April 19.   Eliot Street, from Asa B. Jones's to Montello Street, and across Railroad, east.

1851, October 6.   Pond Street, from Warren Goddard's to Spring Street.

1852, March 22.   Road from corner Rockland Street, near Austin Snow's dwelling-house, running west to Turnpike Street.

1852, February 27.   Road from Sidney Packard's house, east to Curtis's land.

1853, February 28.   Road from Hotel to Crescent Street.

1853, March 28.   Road from Spring Street, north to Apolos Packard's.

1854, February 14.   Road from the late Caleb Howard's farm to the Turnpike.

1854, February 14.   North Side of Elm Street widened.

1854, December 7.   Road from westerly side of Montello Street, near William Snell's house, to Main Street in Campello.

1856, June 15.   Road from north-east corner of Lyman Clark's land, past Railroad Depot, to Azel Packard's.*

1860, February 15.   Grove Street, from Main Street to Railroad.

1861.   Green Street, across Parish Green, from Colonel E. Southworth's store, to Pond Street.

The following list comprises the different streets in the town, as named, and on record: —

STREETS.

Main Street, from Old Colony line, East Stoughton, to West Bridgewater line.

Albion Street, from John May's corner to Howard Street.

Howard Street, from Main, near William C. Leonard's, to East Randolph line.

Winter Street, from Howard Street, near Willard Snell's, to the corner near Widow Martin Cary's.

Quincy Street, from Randolph line, at Sassafras Stake, to the corner near Samuel Packard's.

* When the commissioners — John B. Turner, of Scituate, Thomas Savory, of Wareham, and Joshua Smith, of Hanson — were called to lay out Centre Street, that leads from Robinson's store to railroad depot, and so on to Abington Road, passing the cemetery, they thought it could not be called a public thoroughfare. The road was finally built through the generosity of public-spirited individuals, among whom were Colonel Edward Southworth, Franklin Ames, Esq., Charles Packard, and others interested.

Chestnut Street, from Randolph line, near Daniel Faxon's, to Quincy Street, near Simeon Warren's.

Ashland Street, from Main, near the burying-ground, to Abington line.

Cary Street, from Crescent, near F. Sylvester's, crossing Ashland, by Edward B. Packard's, to Quincy Street.

Ames Avenue, from Main, near David Ames's, to Cary Street.

Montello Street, from Ashland, near the burying-ground, to Plain Street.

Court Street, from Main, near D. Cobb's, crossing Montello, Cary, and Quincy Streets, to Abington line.

Centre Street, from Main, near Lyman Clark's, crossing Montello, Cary, and Quincy Streets, to Abington line.

Short Street from Centre, near Alvah Noyes's, to Court Street, near Widow Reliance Ames's.

Crescent Street, from Main, near Micah Faxon's, to Centre Street.

School Street, from Main to Crescent.

Pine Street, from Crescent, near Sprague's Factory, to South Abington line.

Plain Street, from Main, near Ziba Keith's, to West Bridgewater line, near Josiah Dunbar's.

Summer Street, from Pine to Plain Street.

East Street, from Summer, near Jesse Packard's, 2d, to West Bridgewater line, by Enos Thayer's.

Hammond Street, from Pine to East Street.

South Street, from Main, near Josiah W. Kingman's, to Liberty Street, at G. and S. Manly's.

Belmont Street, from Main, near John Wales's, to Easton line.

Manly Street, from Belmont, near Martin Dunbar's, to Liberty, near Galen Manly's.

Mill Street, from Manly to Liberty Street.

Linwood Street, from Belmont, near Fiske Ames's, to West Bridgewater line.

Ash Street, from Belmont, by Perez Crocker's, to South Street.

Grove Street, from Main to Sprague's Factory.

Pond Street, from Belmont, near Josiah Packard's, to the corner near Freeman Dexter's.

Elm Street, from Main, near W. F. Brett's, to Pond Street.

High Street, from Main to Pond Street, near Rev. Warren Goddard's.

Pleasant Street, from Main, near First Congregational Church, to Easton line.

Spring Street, from Main, near John Battles's, to Pleasant Street.

Prospect Street, from Main, near Asa D. Jones's, to Pleasant Street.

Oak Street, from Main, near William C. Leonard's, to Turnpike Street.

Battles Street, from Main, near Thomas Wales's, to Oak Street.

Eaton Street, from Prospect to Battles Street, near Nahum Battles's.

Cross Street, from Prospect to Battles Streets, near Zibeon Brett's.

Turnpike Street, from Stoughton line to West Bridgewater line.

Sumner Street, from Pleasant, near Meritt French's, to Stoughton line

West Street, from Pleasant, near Eliphalet Thayer's, to Belmont Street.

Rockland Street, from Belmont, near Fiske Ames's, crossing Turnpike Street, to Easton line.

Church Street, from Rockland, near Silas Snow's, to Turnpike Street.

Liberty Street, from Turnpike, at Tilden's Corner, to West Bridgewater line.

Stone Hill Street, from Turnpike, near M. L. Reynolds's, to Easton line.

Chapel Street, from Main to Montello, near David Howard's.

TURNPIKE.

The road known as the old " Taunton Turnpike " extended from South Boston to Taunton, passing through the towns of Raynham, Easton, West Bridgewater, North Bridgewater, Stoughton, Randolph, and Milton. Its location was like most other roads of that day, — it was laid out in as near a straight line as could conveniently be done without regard to hills or valleys, believing the shortest way to be the most expeditious.

This road was chartered as a turnpike corporation to Messrs. John Gilmore, Joshua Gilmore, Samuel Bass, and William P. Whiting, and constituted the " Taunton and South Boston Turnpike Corporation " in June, 1806, and was built during the years 1806 and 1807.

This road ran through the westerly portion of the town, or what is well known as the " West Shares " or North-west Bridgewater. At one time there was a large amount of travel upon this route, both by stages, and heavy baggage teams.

It is, however, of very little account as a toll-road at present, the counties through which it passes having taken it into their own hands to repair, and use for the public good.

> " The old Turnpike is a pike no more,
>   Wide open stands the gate ;
> We have made us a road for our horse to stride,
>   Which we ride at a flying rate.
>
> " We have filled the valleys and levelled the hills,
>   And tunnelled the mountain side ;
> And 'round the rough crag's dizzy verge,
>   Fearlessly now we ride."

RAILROADS.

March 25, 1845, the Legislature of Massachusetts granted a charter to Messrs. Artemas Hale, Nahum Stetson, Aaron Hobart, Solomon Ager, Benjamin B. Howard, Dwelly Fobes, Edward Southworth, Benjamin Kingman, Henry Blanchard, Ebenezer Alden, Royal Turner, and David Blanchard, and their associates and successors to build a railroad from the Old Colony Railroad at South Braintree, running through Randolph, Stoughton, and North Bridgewater, to Bridgewater, to connect with the Middleboro' and Bridgewater Railroad, under the name of the " Randolph and Bridgewater Railroad Corporation." The road was finished, and commenced running cars to North Bridgewater in 1846. Previous to this, the " Fall River Branch Railroad " had been in existence for some time, from Myrick's Station on the " Taunton Branch Railroad " to Fall River. Another short road was chartered, to run from Bridgewater to Myrick's Station, to connect with the " Fall River Branch Railroad," thus making a continuous route from the Old Colony Road at South Braintree to Fall River, and three different corporations. These were united in one, under the name of the " Fall River Railroad Corporation," by which it was known until, by an act of the Legislature March 25, 1854, the " Old Colony Railroad Company " and the " Fall River Railroad Company " were made into one corporation, under the name of the " Old Colony and Fall River Railroad Corporation." The road has since changed its name, upon the completion of the road to Newport, to " Old Colony and Newport Railway Company." The town has now direct communication with Boston, Fall River, Newport, Middleboro', and towns on Cape Cod, and also to Fairhaven. Mr. Joseph O. Bennett was the first station agent at the centre village, succeeded by George W. Bryant, Calvin Keith, and the present agent is J. Hermon French. There is another depot at Campello Village,

one and a half miles south of the centre. Varanes Wales
was the first station agent, and was succeeded by Isaac T.
Packard and Nelson J. Foss, the present incumbent.   During
the year 1845, a charter was applied for, to build a branch
road from Stoughton to North Bridgewater Village, with a
capital of $200,000 ; but for some reasons, to the writer un-
known, nothing was done.   Such a project, if ever accomplished, would result to the great advantage of a thrifty town
like North Bridgewater, and we hope to see it accomplished
ere many years.

STAGES.

Who is there in the town that does not recollect how the
old mail-coach sounded, as it rattled over the stone roads
from this town to Boston, first tri-weekly, then daily, carrying the mails.   How the people gathered around the driver,
to catch the latest news on the route; for a stage-driver was
the greatest man of the age.   Hear the crack of his whip, as
he reins the horses up to every person's door, and piles on
the trunks and bandboxes.   Now the iron horse takes the
place of horse-flesh, and steam the place of oats and hay.

The first public stage that ran through or from North
Bridgewater was about 1820 ; it was a joint-stock company,
of whom Silas Packard, Esq., of North Bridgewater, Seth
Allen, of Halifax, Captain Nathaniel H. Cross, of East Bridgewater, and Captain Asa Pratt, of South Bridgewater, were
part owners.   It consisted of a two-horse carriage, that was
formerly used by Governor Phillips as a private carriage.
Colonel Nathan Jones, of North Bridgewater, was a driver for
one year.   It started from Bridgewater three times a week.
After running about two years, the company sold their interest to Messrs. A. M. Withington and Burr, who afterward sold
to Nathaniel Blake, and Wheeler.   Soon after Mr. Wheeler
sold his interest to Jacob Churchill, and he to Newton
Hodges, who continued to conduct the line with Mr. Blake.

At the time Mr. Withington bought of the company, Colonel Jones left the line, and started a two-horse coach from North Bridgewater, running from that place on Mondays, Wednesdays, and Saturdays, in and out from Boston the same day. While Colonel Jones was running his coach, Mr. John Madden, of Randolph, put on a coach to run from that place to Boston. Mr. Madden and Colonel Jones soon put their teams together, and ran from North Bridgewater for two years. At the end of that time they ran their coach to Bridgewater. Messrs. Hodge and Blake continued to own and run the line carrying the mails from Bridgewater through North Bridgewater, they running one day, and Messrs. Jones and Madden running opposite days. Mr. Blake then sold his interest to Colonel Jones, and he to John Long, who continued till the opening of the railroad.

An opposition coach was started in 1837 or 1838 by Jabez Gould, and ran to Boston daily from North Bridgewater Village till the "Stoughton Branch Railroad" was built, when he ran in connection with the cars : he ceased to run when the "Fall River Railroad" began to run their cars, in 1846. Another line of coaches passed through the "West Shares" in the west part of the town, on the old turnpike from Taunton to Boston. The line was owned for many years by Jesse Smith, of Taunton.

S. D. Butler commenced running a line of coaches, in connection with the Stoughton cars, from the Salisbury House, Campello, October 2, 1854, but continued for a short time only. May 13, 1857, A. S. Porter commenced a line to Boston three times a week, and in the middle of next month commenced to run a daily line. I. Tisdale, of Stoughton, and John O. Hudson, of East Bridgewater, ran a coach from Stoughton to Plymouth for a year or more, about twelve years since. There was also a line of stages connecting at Bridgewater with a coach for New Bedford, owned by

39

Pelatiah Gould, that ran through the town to Boston tri-weekly, about the same time.

POST-OFFICES.

The first post-office established in North Bridgewater was in 1816. The following are the names of the postmasters, with the dates of their appointments : —

Charles Packard...................November 2, 1816.
Nathaniel H. Cross................July 1, 1829.
Edward Southworth. Jr.............September 16, 1836.
Aaron B. Drake...................July 20, 1853.
Abel W. Kingman.................December 11, 1855.
Henry French....................1861.

A post-office was established in the west part of the town in 1828, called North-west Bridgewater, with the following appointments : —

Heman Packard.................November 13, 1828.
Nathaniel H. Cross.............July 1, 1829.
George Clark...................February 11, 1831.
Levi French...................September 5, 1840.

Previous to 1850, the people of the south part of the town known as Campello had for some time hired the mail for that village brought down to them by a messenger, for distribution at the store ; but finding the business increasing to such an extensive amount daily, a few public-spirited individuals of that place petitioned for the establishment of a separate post-office. This was granted to them February 12, 1850, at which time Mr. Nelson J. Foss the present incumbent, was appointed postmaster. Previous to the establishment of a post-office in the North Parish, and the running of a mail-coach, the letters and what few newspapers people had in those days were brought to town by post-riders,* market-wagons, and other private conveyance from Boston.

About the time of the incorporation of the town of North

* Major Hartwell, of West Bridgewater, was one.

Bridgewater in 1821, a regular established line of mail communication having been provided by the government, the people had one mail per day from the city ; and since the mail has been carried by railroad they have two mails each way daily.

TOWN MAPS.

March 1, 1830, the Legislature of Massachusetts passed a resolve requiring the several towns in the commonwealth to " make a survey of their territory, and deposit a copy in the office of the Secretary of the Commonwealth." In conformity to this resolve, and by a vote of the town, passed May 10, 1830, Jesse Perkins, Esq., made a survey of the town, and a map was published, a copy of which may be found, as above ordered, at the State House.

April 5, 1853, at a legal meeting of the town, George W. Bryant, Chandler Sprague, Edward Southworth, Jr., Benjamin Kingman, and Frederic Howard were chosen a committee to cause the town to be resurveyed, and a new map to be published. The contract for publishing the same was given to Messrs. H. F. Walling and E. Whiting. The map contained names of residences, views of churches, manufactories, roads, wood, streets, ponds, rivers, and divisions of the various school districts. The first map was about twenty inches square, of which a few copies only are in existence. The last map was thirty by thirty-nine inches.*

NEWSPAPERS.

The first newspaper published in North Bridgewater was commenced by George H. Brown, Esq., of East Bridgewater, August 22, 1835, under the name of " Bridgewater Patriot and Old Colony Gazette," in the hall over Major Nathan Hayward's store.

* The first map of the ancient town of Bridgewater, including what is now North Bridgewater, was drawn with a pen by Beza Hayward, at that time one of the Selectmen, June 16, 1795.

Mr. William H. Burleigh and Rev. E. Porter Dyer assisted Mr. Brown in the publication of the paper till its removal to East Bridgewater.

The next paper in the town was entitled the " Old Colony Reporter," and was published by Messrs. F. W. Bartlett and Thomas D. Stetson, of Kingston, Massachusetts, under the firm of " Bartlett and Stetson," commenced in November, 1848. Mr. Bartlett left the firm after a term of one year, after which Mr. Stetson and Rev. William Whiting continued the paper, in Colonel Edward Southworth's hall, till 1851.

During the latter part of the winter of 1850 and 1851, one Dr. Cawdell (*celebrated for having stepped out on sundry individuals for various small bills*) commenced the publication of a paper called the " Bay State Clipper; " a few numbers were printed, and the paper, press, types, and one form of the paper were left in the hands of Colonel Southworth, the owner of the premises occupied by the doctor, for expenses.

The " Adelphian," a literary paper, was published for two years from October 11, 1850, by the Messrs. Loomis, which was edited by the young ladies of the Academy, and was especially devoted to the interests of the young.

About the same time, there was a small sheet published at the office of the "Reporter," devoted to the temperance cause, edited by young persons. May 16, 1851, the " North Bridgewater Gazette" was commenced in the hall over Colonel E. Southworth's store, by George Phinney, who continued to publish the same till July 25, 1855, when he removed his office to a new building on Franklin Street. Mr. Phinney continued to edit and publish the paper till 1863, when he sold his interest in the paper and printing-office to Mr. Augustus T. Jones, who has recently removed to the old stand in Southworth's Hall, opposite the First Congregational Church, and continues to publish a weekly paper, second to none in the county for general intelligence, and local news.

PUBLICATIONS.

List of publications by the people of North Bridgewater: —

Rev. John Porter.

" Evangelical Plan ; " or, an Attempt to form Right Notions in the Minds of the Common People, and to establish them in the Minds of the People. Republished by Dr. E. Alden, of Randolph.

Rev. Asa Meech.

Ordination Sermon, delivered by Rev. Lemuel Tyler, A. M., October 15, 1800. Colleague Pastor with Rev. John Porter.

Oration by Rev. Asa Meech, delivered in North Bridgewater July 4, 1805, in commemoration of the Anniversary of American Independence.

Valedictory Sermon. By Rev. Asa Meech, A. M., December 1, 1811. Preached at the North Church, in Bridgewater.

Rev. Daniel Huntington.

Sermon at the Funeral of Alpheus Packard, delivered in the North Meeting-House in Bridgewater, May 12, 1812.

Discourse delivered in the North Meeting-House in Bridgewater, December 22, 1820. Being the Second Centennial Anniversary of the Landing of the Pilgrims at Plymouth. Published by Ezra Lincoln, Boston.

Sermon on the Occasion of the Death of Rev. R. S. Storrs's Wife, April 9, 1818.

Discourse delivered before the Society for Promoting Christian Knowledge. May 26, 1824.

A Memoir of Mary Hallam Huntington, his Daughter. Published by the American Sunday School Union, Philadelphia.

A full Account of the Great Revival in 1816 was published by him in the " Boston Recorder " of June 10, 1818.

Address before the Pilgrim Society, at Plymouth, Massachusetts.

Discourse delivered in the South Church in Campello, October 31, 1852, it being the Fortieth Anniversary of his Ordination.

A Poem on the Pleasures and Advantages of True Religion, delivered before the United Brothers' Society in Brown University, on their Anniversary, August 31, 1819.

Rev. Eliphalet Porter, D. D.

Thanksgiving Sermon. 1783.
Sermon before the Roxbury Charitable Society. 1794.
Sermon on the Occasion of the National Fast. 1798.
Sermon on the Death of Gov. Increase Sumner. 1799.
Eulogy on the Death of Washington. 1800.
Sermon, New Year's. 1801.
Sermon before the Humane Society. 1802.
Sermon at Ordination of Rev. Charles Lowell. 1806.

Sermon before the Society for Propagating the Gospel among the Indians in North America, 1807.

Sermon before the Convention of Congregational Ministers.* 1810.

Sermon on the Occasion of Artillery Election. 1812.

Sermon at the Ordination of Rev. John G. Palfrey. 1818.

Rev. Huntington Porter.

A Discourse on " Sympathy with the Afflicted." Occasioned by the Death of his wife, Susannah Porter. Delivered February 27, 1794, the Sabbath following her death, which took place February 24. Text, Job xix. 21 : " Have pity upon me, have pity upon me, O ye my friends ; for the hand of God hath touched me."

A Discourse delivered to his people, at Rye, New Hampshire, Thursday, January 1, 1801, being the Commencement of a New Year, and a New Century. Text, Psalms lxxvii. 10–12.

A Eulogy on Washington. 1800.

A Discourse delivered June 5, 1803, occasioned by the late remarkable sickness and mortality in the town of Rye, New Hampshire. Text, Psalms ci. : "I will sing of mercy and judgment ; unto thee, O Lord, will I sing."

Two Discourses delivered at Rye, New Hampshire, January, 1825, on the Occasion of the Closing of the Fortieth Year of his Ministry in that place, and the Commencement of a New Year. Text, 1 Peter i. 12–14.

A Funeral Discourse. August, 1800.

Two Discourses delivered on First Lord's Day after President Madison's Declaration of War. Upon Peace, and War. Another on the Present Unhappy and Perilous Situation of the Country, and the Duties of Ministers and People in such a Time as this. Delivered on the National Fast. Text, Ecclesiastes iii. 8. August 20, 1812.

A New Year's Address to the People of Rye, New Hampshire. January, 1836.

Rev. Theophilus Packard, D. D.

Sermon at the Ordination of Rev. Josiah W. Cannon.

Sermon before the Hampshire Missionary Society. 1821.

Sermon on the Death of Elisha M. Case, at Williamstown, Massachusetts. 1831.

Two Sermons on the Divinity of Christ. 1808.

Sermon before the Hampshire Missionary Society. 1813.

Sermon on the Evil of Slander. 1815.

Sermon on the Life and Death of his Son, Isaac T. Packard. 1820.

Rev. Joshua Cushman.

Sermon Thanksgiving Day, November 24, 1804.

Oration July 4, 1807, at Augusta, Maine. Pp. 23.

Oration at Wiscasset, Maine, July 4, 1808.

Oration at Waterville, Maine, July 4, 1814.

Discourse delivered before the citizens of Winslow, Maine, on National

* This sermon is spoken of as being of singular merit.

Thanksgiving Day, April 13, 1815. Dedicated to James Madison, then President of the United States. Published at Hallowell, Maine.

Rev. D. Temple Packard.

Sermon Preached at Somerville, Massachusetts, on the National Fast, entitled " The Dawn of the Morning." December 28, 1862. Published by Rand & Avery.

Rev. Edward L. Clark.

Daleth ; or, the Homestead of the Nations. Egypt Illustrated. Published by Ticknor & Fields, 1864.

Rev. James Andem.

The Rise and Progress of the First Baptist Church, North Bridgewater, Massachusetts. Being the first Annual Sermon. Preached on Sunday, January 26, 1851. Published by J. M. Hewes & Co., 1851.

Rev. Jonas Perkins, D. D.

Sermon before the Palestine Missionary Society, on the " Constraining Love of Christ," June 20, 1828.

Sermon before the Norfolk Educational Society, on the " Treasure in Earthly Vessels," June 8, 1831.

Sermon preached to his own people, on the " Condition of a Happy Life," December 9, 1838.

Thanksgiving Sermon, on " God's Blessing on his People," November 30, 1843.

Sermon, published in the " National Preacher," Vol. 23, No. 11. " This Life Man's Season of Probation for Eternity."

Two Tracts, published by the Congregational Board of Publication. No. 10, on the " Personality and Offices of the Holy Spirit." No. 22, " Immortality of God."

Reports of the Doctrinal Tract Society, from the commencement, June 24, 1829. Published by them. (Secretary of the same twenty years.)

Farewell Sermon, October 21, 1860. " Christ's Design in the Institution of the Ministry."

Rev. Paul Couch.

Two Sermons, preached December 23, 1849. Published by Damrell & Moore, Boston. 1849.

Temperance Sermons, on Different Occasions.

Sermon preached at the Funeral of Rev. Daniel Thomas, former Pastor of the Second Congregational Church, in Abington, on Friday, January 8, 1847. Published by T. R. Marvin, 1847.

Sermon preached in the First Congregational Church of Stonington, Connecticut, August 6, 1863, on National Thanksgiving.

B. Winslow Packard.

Honesty. A Poem delivered before the Phi Beta Society of the Adelphian Academy, North Bridgewater, February 8, 1853. Published by J. B. Chisholm, 1853.

D. Hudson Howard.*

Journey of the Israelites in the Wilderness, Considered in its Spiritual Meaning. Published by T. H. Carter & Co., 1864.

Rev. Austin Cary.

Prize Tract, on Dancing, by the American Tract Society.

Rev. Warren Goddard.†

An Address delivered before the County Lyceum of Worcester County, at their annual meeting in Worcester, October, 1831.

A Sermon. Text, Luke ix. 24. Delivered before the Convention of the New Church in America, at its meeting in Boston, June, 1836.

Two Discourses on the Commandments respecting the Sabbath, from Exodus xx. 8–11. Published May, 1837.

A Discourse from Zechariah ix. 9. Published May, 1839.

A Discourse from John xxi. 6. Published November, 1839.

A Discourse from Matthew xviii. 1–4. Published May, 1840.

An Address to the Receivers of the Doctrines of the New Jerusalem in the United States. Written at the request of the General Convention. Published September, 1840.

A Discourse from John xiv. 2. Published February, 1844.

A Discourse from Matthew xvi. 24. Published December, 1845.

A Discourse from Matthew xiii. 45, 46. Published October, 1846.

A Discourse from Matthew vii. 13. 14. Published June, 1847.

A Discourse preached before the Maine Association of the New Jerusalem at the meeting in August, 1851. Published April, 1852.

A Discourse, in Two Parts, from Psalms cxxxvi. 1–3, cviii. 4, and xxxvi. 5, 7, 9. Published April, 1853.

A Discourse preached at the Dedication of the Temple of the Society of the New Church, in Gardiner, Maine, August, 1855, from Revelation xxi. 9–17.

A Discourse preached at the Dedication of the Temple of the New Church Society in North Bridgewater, January 22, 1857, from John i. 1, 3, 4, 11–14.

A Discourse from Psalms xxxvii. 5. Published October, 1858.

A Discourse preached before the Massachusetts Association of the New Church, at its meeting, October 7, 1858, from John xvii. 3.

An Address to the General Conference of the New Church in Great Britain. Written at the appointment and in behalf of the General Convention of the New Church in America, June, 1860.

A Discourse from John xvii. 24. Published September, 1860.

---

* Mr. Howard has contributed a large number of articles for the " New Jerusalem Magazine," to which the reader is referred. There are but a few numbers of that magazine that do not contain something from his pen, either poetry or prose, since 1845. He has also contributed poems for various public gatherings.

† In addition to the foregoing, Mr. Goddard has contributed to various journals, magazines, and newspapers, upon the doctrines of the New Church.

A Discourse from Isaiah lxiv. 4. Published November, 1861.

A Discourse from Kings v. 9–14. Published March, 1862.

An Address delivered before the Massachusetts Association of the New Church, at its meeting in October, 1863.

Response of the Ministers of the Massachusetts Association of the New Jerusalem to a Resolution requesting their consideration of what is usually known as "Modern Spiritualism." Published by George Phinney, 1858. Pp. 50.

Bradford Kingman.

Kingman Memorial.

History of North Bridgewater.

Contributions to Different Magazines.

LIBRARIES.

The first public or social library in North Bridgewater was raised by subscription about 1781, and was kept for most of the time in private houses. The last librarian was Colonel Edward Southworth, and the library was given up.

In 1842, the Legislature appropriated fifteen dollars for the use of every school district in the commonwealth that should raise an equal amount for the purchase of a School District Library. With this encouragement, many of the districts raised the requisite amount, and purchased libraries. They are now, however, nearly laid by.

At a regular town meeting, held March 30, 1857, the town " voted to purchase a town library, the amount not to exceed $1,400, or one dollar on every poll paid in the town." For this purpose the following committee were chosen ; namely, Edward Southworth, Jr., C. C. Bixby, Dr. Alexander Hichborn, David L. Cowell, Ellis Packard, Jonas R. Perkins, Lucius Gurney, 2d, Jonathan White, and M. L. Keith, who proceeded in the selection and purchase of such books as were thought suitable to the wants of the community. The library was well selected, and consisted of many of the best works extant. Many persons, not wishing that the town should have any library, raised an opposition to the plan, and as the result, the town " voted, May 1, 1857, that all books, effects, and appurtenances of the Town Library be placed in the hands of the Selectmen, to be disposed of in the best manner for the interest of the town." And in accordance with these instructions, the Selectmen sold the library of books that cost $1,183, to an association called the "North Bridgewater Library Association." The price for the entire lot was $600, being only three months old, which, we should judge, was a heavy discount.

NORTH BRIDGEWATER LIBRARY ASSOCIATION.

This association was formed by a few individuals for the purpose of holding a library. It was organized under a statute made for such purposes, July 11, 1858. Each member paying five dollars becomes a stockholder, and an additional one dollar annually entitles him to all the rights and privileges of a member of the association. It has over two thousand volumes, and is in a flourishing condition. The officers at the organization of the association were, David L. Cowell, *President;* Rufus L. Thatcher, *Vice-President;* Augustus Hayward, *Secretary;* David F. Studley, *Treasurer.* Henry A. Ford, John L. Hunt, Alpheus Holmes, Charles B. Crocker, Darius Howard, Edward Southworth, Jr., Lorenzo D. Hervey, Charles Curtis, Jr., Washburn Packard, *Directors.*

CHAPTER XVII.

MISCELLANEOUS HISTORY — CONTINUED.

Indians. — Slavery. — Colored Persons. — Temperance. — Sinclair Band of Hope. — North Star Division No. 88. — Fraternal Lodge No. 24. — Old Colony Temperance Union. — Sabbath-Schools. — Music. — Band. — Thespian Society. — Union Musical Association. — Bank. — Savings-Bank. — Fire Department.

INDIANS.

> " There was a time when red men climbed these hills,
> And wandered by these plains and rills ;
> Or rowed the light canoe along yon river,
> Or rushed to conflict armed with bow and quiver,
> Or, 'neath the forest leaves that o'er them hung,
> They council held, or loud their war-notes sung."

THE war of the colonists with King Philip proved very disastrous to the Indian race. Many obstacles were thrown in their way, which so far discouraged them that they were forced to give up their possessions, and seek other localities away from the new-comers, who were gradually extending their territory westward.

To what extent Indians occupied the North Parish we are unable to learn. We have no doubt however, that they were quite numerous, as the plough frequently brings to light some relic of past days, and of an uncivilized people. Spear-points, arrow-heads, mortars, pestles, gouges, and stone hatchets are often found in different sections of the town.

In the north part of the town are found hearthstones of ancient Indian wigwams. There was one directly under the house of the late Oliver Howard, which was taken down a few years since. Judging from the number of relics found in the northerly section of the town, we should judge they frequented that part of the parish to a considerable extent.

The author has a clay pipe found by Mr. Willard Howard,

near his residence; also specimens of arrow-heads of stone, found by Bela Keith, Esq., on his land at Campello, which are splendid specimens of natives' work, besides many other relics of barbarous days.

There is another evidence of the town having been the residence of the red man. In the west part of the town, on what is called " Stone House Hill," a natural cave is found in the solid stone, from which the hill derives its name, which is said to have been the dwelling of some tribe of Indians. It is situated on or near the old road leading from North Bridgewater to Easton, and near the residence of Timothy Remick.

It is also traditionary that Indians had their huts in the valley of Salisbury River opposite Campello, and so on north as far as the bridge at " Sprague's Factory." There was an Indian family named Hammond, who lived on the land now owned by Benjamin Kingman, west of his barn, in a lot formerly known as the " Old Pasture," and nearly opposite the residence of Lucius Keith. The native Indian tribes living upon " maize " and fish principally, as well as game, we are inclined to the opinion that they generally sought for dwelling spots near some stream, where fish could be found, as it made no difference about their game; that they could find all over the forests.

It is impossible at the present time for us to realize to ourselves the situation of the first white settlers of the town. They lived in constant fear of a sudden attack. Exposed at all times, they were haunted in their imaginations by death with torture, or of a hopeless captivity. The principal companion of the white man, whether in the field or at his dwelling, was his gun. While at his daily labor in the cultivation of his lands, if he had not his gun, he was likely at any time to be carried away.

Even down to a late period, when people assembled for

public worship, a guard was the first thing to establish, in order that they might not be suddenly captured.

We do not learn that the people of the North Parish were so much molested as in some other portions of the ancient town, for the reason the white people did not settle that portion to any extent till after 1700.

Mitchell, in his excellent " History of Bridgewater," says, " that the people displayed great courage and intrepidity during Philip's War, and were often advised to desert their dwellings, and repair to the sea-shore towns." They, however, resolutely kept their ground, and helped other towns to do the same. Whatever others may think, there is something sad in the reflection that the natives of these hills and valleys have disappeared, while at the same time we cannot regret that a Christian and enlightened people have taken the places of a barbarous and heathen race. The last vestige of the tribe that once travelled over the soil of Bridgewater has long ago disappeared.

> " Alas for them ! their day is o'er ;
> Their fires are out on hill and shore."

SLAVERY.

It is difficult to fix the number of slaves that have been owned in the North Parish ; but however disagreeable it may seem to many, we have to record the fact that the "peculiar institution" did exist in the town previous to the Revolutionary War. It was not thought improper for the clergy, deacons, or physicians to hold slaves. Colonel Simeon Cary had a slave named " King Ring," of whom it is said "he whipped the apple-trees, to make them grow." He had children, — " Patience," " Jenny," " Mary," and " Fanny." Many persons are now living who can remember " Patience Ring," who always lived in the family of Colonel Cary, and his descendants.

Another colored man lived nearly opposite the residence of the late Oliver Dike, who is said to have been a slave by the name of " Toby Tarbet."

We find in the records of the parish the names of several colored persons, who undoubtedly were servants in families, if not " slaves," as it was quite common for slaves to be known by one name only, like those we find in the list of marriages, as " Plato," " Pompey," " Nero," " Tobias " " Violet," and the like; and for a surname they usually took the name of their owner.

In 1780 the adoption of the State Constitution forbade traffic or ownership of colored people, and from that time all have been alike free. Those who were slaves generally remained with their former masters as a matter of choice, and many of them had large families.

Among the colored people in the town, we find the names of several persons whose descendants are not in the town, many of them having removed to other localities, as Calvin and Luther Jotham who removed to Maine, Thomas Mitchell, Amos Cordner, Moses Sash, Cuff Robin, Bennett O. Batton, Henry Traveller, Elias Sewell, Boston Foye, Cæsar Easton, Cuffee Wright, Susannah Huggins, and Oxford, who were married while servants in the family of Daniel Howard, Esq., Segmo Scott, and Primus Freeman.

The number of colored persons in the town at different periods were as follows: in 1820, 23; in 1830, 40; in 1840, 22; in 1850, 30; in 1860, 32.

There is one family of these people who have become quite numerous, — the descendants of James Easton, who came from Middleboro' previous to the incorporation of the town. He had seven children, three of whom settled in this vicinity. Caleb married, and had six children, some of whom are now residents of the town.*

* See Genealogy of Families.

The anti-slavery movement in this town did not meet with that favor which it received in many other places. It began by the circulation of tracts upon that subject, and with lectures by various persons, among whom were W. L. Garrison, Parker Pillsbury, S. S. Foster, C. C. Burleigh, and, later, Wendell Phillips and Frederic Douglas. These persons were the champions of the cause, and their efforts have, no doubt, produced some good results.

Political parties have changed from time to time, till, in the election of Gov. Andrew and Abraham Lincoln, the town has shown, by their votes, that they were in earnest in the cause of freedom.

TEMPERANCE.

Previous to 1800, it was a common custom to use liquors as a beverage ; and even till about 1830 it was the practice to have it at public gatherings, weddings, ministerial associations, auctions, raisings, military parades, and such occasions were not complete without their punch.

It was also indispensable that those who acted the part of bearers at funerals should have something to stimulate or keep up their spirits. All the grocery stores in the country kept liquor for sale as much as they did molasses. Upon an examination of some of the old account-books of those that kept groceries, we found about one half the charges were for rum, gin, brandy, etc., which were included in the list of necessaries of life.

The first item we find recorded in regard to restricting the open sale of intoxicating liquors, was " to post the names of those who were reputed as ' drunkards,' or ' common tipplers,' in the houses of those that held licenses for retailing liquor," which duty devolved upon the selectmen, as well as to forbid their selling to such persons.

Previous to 1820, licenses were granted by the " Court of

Sessions " in each county to a certain number in each town to sell liquor, subject to the approval of the " Fathers of the Town." After that date, they were granted by the county commissioners.

The first effort we find recorded of an effort to stop the peddling of " ardent sperit," was October 8, 1800, when the parish, at a meeting held on that day, " voted that there be no sellers of liquor, and carts on the green, and that the parish committee see that the above order is complied with." This vote was passed for a special occasion, — that of the ordination of Rev. Asa Meech, October 15, 1800.

Again, September 23, 1812, the parish " voted that the parish committee keep the green clear of carts and sellers of lickers," etc.

February 5, 1813, a society was formed in Boston, under the name of " Massachusetts Society for the Suppression of Intemperance," the object of which was to discontinue and suppress the too free use of ardent spirit, and its kindred vices, profaneness and gaming, and to promote temperance and general morality. This society labored hard against the tide of public opinion till 1825, when the subject began to be discussed so freely that a still more efficient method was proposed, and new means were taken to spread the fearful effects of intoxication before the people.

A meeting was held by a few individuals during the year, which resulted in the foundation of the American Temperance Society, whose grand principle was abstinence from strong drink, and its object, by light and love, to change the habits of the nation, with regard to the use of intoxicating liquors. On the 13th of February, 1826, the society was regularly organized, officers chosen, and a constitution prepared.

This society employed agents to travel through the country, preaching and delivering temperance lectures, arousing the people to the evil effects of liquor. Among those engaged in that calling, were Rev. Nathaniel Hewett, Rev. Joshua Leavitt, and Daniel C. Axtell. These men came to this town, and gave lectures, to arouse the people of the town to a sense of their responsibility, and which had its effect.

In 1829 we find the following on the records of the town, in answer to a call for a town meeting, "to see what measures the town will take to prevent the too frequent use of ardent spirit."

March 9, 1829 "voted to raise a committee of twenty persons, to prevent the improper use of ardent spirit." The following persons were chosen as that committee: —

Joseph Sylvester, Esq.,	Dea. Jonathan Perkins,	Perez Crocker,
Darius Howard,	Lieut. Ephraim Cole,	Jesse Perkins, Esq.,
Isaac Keith,	Micah Shaw,	Benjamin Ames,
Eliphalet Kingman,	Nathaniel Ames,	Edward Southworth,
Deacon Jacob Fuller,	Ensign Mark Perkins,	David Cobb,
Lieut. Isaac Packard,	Capt. Abel Kingman,	Caleb Howard, Esq.,
	Silas Packard, Esq.,	Joseph Packard.

Again, Monday, April 6, 1829, "voted to direct the select-men to post up the names of such persons as, in their judgment, drink too much ardent spirit."

Also, made choice of the following persons, to constitute a committee, to give the selectmen information of such persons as above named; namely, —

Edward Southworth,	Micah Shaw,	Capt. Ziba Keith,
Thomas Wales,	Isaac Curtis,	Turner Torrey,
Martin Cary,	Capt. Thomas Thompson,	Mark Perkins,
	Lieut. Isaac Packard,	Lieut. Ephraim Cole.

Again, February 26, 1830, an attempt was made to reduce the number of persons licensed to sell liquor. The town "voted to leave the subject of licenses to the selectmen."

In 1840, the "Washingtonian Movement" commenced, which was started in Baltimore by a few individuals. At

41

this time, there was a complete overhauling of the temperance question. Speeches were made, picnics were frequent,
and every effort made to induce people to join in the enterprise. Societies were formed among the children, " cold
water armies " were organized, who held meetings for mutual
benefit and social intercourse.

Next came the " Maine Law," that originated in Portland,
Maine, by Neal Dow. This caused a new movement among
the temperance people. Votes were passed at nearly every
town meeting to prosecute and bring to the law those who
violated the same, by using or selling liquor.

March 15, 1847, the town " voted that the selectmen be
instructed to take effectual measures to suppress the sale of
ardent spirits, within the town."

March 10, 1848, " voted, to choose seven persons to prosecute to conviction, if practicable, those that deal in intoxicating drinks."

April 10, 1848, in town meeting, Messrs. George W. Bryant, Esq., George B. Dunbar, and Alpheus Holmes were
chosen a committee to draft a set of by-laws for the action
of that meeting, and who submitted the following report :
namely, —

" Whereas it appears to the inhabitants, in town meeting assembled, that,
in order to preserve the peace, good order, and internal police of the town,
it has become necessary to avail ourselves of the advantage of making Town
By-Laws for the suppression of intemperance, agreeably to authority vested
by the Legislature of Massachusetts ;

" Therefore be it enacted by the town of North Bridgewater, in legal
meeting assembled, Sec. 1. That no person within said town shall presume
to be a retailer or seller of Cider, Strong Beer, Ale, Porter, or any other
fermented liquors, in less quantities than twenty-eight gallons, and that
delivered and carried away all at one time, under pain of forfeiting the sum
of Twenty-Five Dollars for each offence. Sec. 2. All forfeitures incurred
under the foregoing shall be put to such use as the town shall from time to
time direct."

March 19, 1849, a committee of seven were chosen to

prosecute all violations of the liquor law, with unlimited authority.

March 11, 1850, at a meeting held this day, it was " voted that any person guilty of the violation of any law regulating the sale of spirituous or fermented liquors shall receive from the treasurer of the town the sum of twenty-five dollars for the expense attending said prosecutions, the same to be paid on application, after having been approved by the selectmen."

During the month of May, 1851, Rev. Henry Morgan came into town, and created no little enthusiasm throughout the town on the subject of temperance. His cause was the theme of conversation in the parlor, work-shop, and by the way. Parents, cousins, and friends joined in the work with children and youth. The clergymen, also, rendered valuable aid; so that, when Mr. Morgan left town, it was with a cheerful heart, and a list of seventeen hundred signers to the pledge, which was more names, in proportion to the population, than he had obtained in any other town.

Among those who were especially entitled. to credit for being active in the labor of procuring signers to the pledge, were Gardner J. Kingman, Joseph Vincent, Ellis V. Lyon, Frederic Packard, Lucretia A. Drake, Alma F. Leach, Bradford E. Jones, Ellen A. Howard, Martha A. Packard, and Bethia Hayward.

The citizens of the town held a public meeting at Satucket Hall September 10, 1851. The meeting was called to order by George B. Dunbar, and Dr. Henry Eddy chosen president, and the following resolution was passed: —

" *Resolved*, That the friends of Temperance in this town are in favor of enforcing the law for the suppression of the sale and use of intoxicating drinks, now and always, by every means in their power, both legal and moral, and that, too, against the whims and moans of a conscienceless class of persons, who are willing for a few dollars to scatter destruction amongst their fellow-citizens."

January 21, 1852, a mammoth petition, containing 120,000

names in favor of the "Maine Law," was presented to the Legislature of Massachusetts. Many friends (one hundred and twenty-six) of the temperance movement, repaired to Boston, to join in a procession that was formed at Tremont Temple, to accompany the roll to the State House.

March 1, 1852, "voted to instruct our town representative to vote for the bill to prohibit the manufacture and sale of intoxicating drinks, as originally reported to the Senate by the committee; and that he also be instructed to oppose the sending of the bill to the people for their ratification.

A public temperance meeting was held at the vestry of the Methodist church August 9, 1852, Dr. Henry Eddy president, at which a committee of forty-two were chosen to inform of, and furnish evidence of, violations of the new and stringent law for the suppression of the sale of intoxicating liquors.

March 20, 1854, "voted to exclude alcoholic drinks from the fire department." Also, "voted that any member of the same that shall become intoxicated while on duty at a fire shall be excluded from the department."

SINCLAIR BAND OF HOPE.

Established in 1858.

This association was under the direction of the superintendent of the Porter Church Sabbath-school, the object of which was to encourage the young to abstain from the use of intoxicating liquors, tobacco, and profanity.

NORTH STAR DIVISION NO. 88, SONS OF TEMPERANCE.

This division was instituted February 23, 1859, and was known by the above name. "The design of this association is to shield all classes from the evils of intemperance, afford mutual assistance in case of sickness, and elevate their characters as men." The charter of this association was surrendered December 4, 1863.

FRATERNAL LODGE NO. 24, I. O. OF GRAND TEMPLARS.

This organization was instituted September 28, 1860, under the above name, the object of which was similar to the North Star Division.

There was another Division of the Sons of Temperance in the town, called the Crystal Fount Division, in 1847, which is not in existence at the present time.

Another organization, known as the Eagle Wing Division No. 109, was instituted at Campello, January 1, 1861, which lived only a short time.

August 14, 1863, the State of Massachusetts was divided into thirty districts, and in each was formed a District Temperance Union. Such a one was formed, including North Bridgewater, East and West Bridgewater, Lakeville, and Carver, and was known as the Old Colony District Temperance Union. George B. Dunbar was Vice-President, Rev. William A. Start, Secretary and Treasurer.

We have thus far seen that the movements of the temperance cause in North Bridgewater are not unlike those in most country towns. There have, at different times, been various temperance organizations, both among the adult population and the children, but the particulars of which are not at hand. It is to be hoped that the efforts to restrain the free use of intoxicating liquors may still continue as in times past, that the baneful effects of intoxication may not increase, but grow beautifully less.

SABBATH-SCHOOLS.

The first Sabbath-school in the North Parish commenced in May, 1818, through the efforts of Mrs. Huntington, the wife of the pastor. The school consisted of one hundred and seven girls and seventy-eight boys. These were divided into classes of from four to eight persons, according to their ages, the males under the care of teachers of their own sex, and the females under teachers of their sex, the whole number under the direction of the superintendent. The time allotted for the school was during the intermission between the morning and afternoon services on the Sabbath, and was usually one hour long.

The books in use during the early part of its existence were the New Testament, "Emerson's Evangelical Primer," and "Hymns for Infant Minds." Most of the scholars, during the first term, were well versed in the Primer, and in addition to that, for the first sixteen Sabbaths, they had committed 32,674 verses of Scripture, and 27,300 verses of hymns, which were recited.

As further specimens of individual diligence on the part of the younger members of the school, we publish the following : —

A girl eight years of age, recited 402 verses of Scripture, and 236 verses of hymns. Another girl, ten years of age, recited 1,408 verses of Scripture, and 1,464 verses of hymns. Another, eleven years of age, recited 995 verses of Scripture, and 1,558 verses of hymns Another, thirteen years of age, recited 1,885 verses of Scripture, and 1,000 verses of hymns. Another girl, seven years of age, recited 2,191 verses of Scripture, comprising the Gospels of Matthew and Mark, and nine chapters of Luke, besides 287 verses of hymns. It is with pleasure we record of this little girl that, when a pecuniary reward was presented her by a relative for her exemplary diligence, she generously sent the amount, by the hand of her pastor, to the treasurer of the American Board of Commissioners for Foreign Missions, for the education of heathen children. Another girl, five years of age, recited the whole of "Assembly's Catechism," with proofs, 12 verses of Scripture, and 100 hymns.

The first term of the Sabbath-school closed with public religious exercises on the day of the annual meeting of the

Bridgewater Evangelical Society. The sacred music on the occasion was performed principally by the scholars.

There are at the present time schools connected with all the churches in the town, together with extensive libraries of well-selected books.

MUSIC.

According to a universal custom in early times, there was nothing but congregational singing. Tunes were few, and for want of books the exercises were read a line at a time, and then all would join in singing; then the good deacon would read another line, and thus the service was "deaconed" through the whole of the verses.

The first music-book in the country was brought by the Pilgrims, and entitled "Ainsworth Version of the Psalms." This gave way to the "Bay Psalm Book," the first book printed in America, which went through seventy editions, and, in 1758, was revised and republished by Rev. Thomas Prince, of Boston.*

Previous to 1765 or 1770, there were no choirs in the churches, and as these were formed, the custom of lining or "deaconing" the hymns grew into disuse, but not till after a great deal of determined opposition. The custom had been introduced by the Westminster Assembly of Divines, and hence could not easily be surrendered.

The first choir in the North Parish was established about 1801, under the leadership of Major Daniel Cary, a noted singer of that day. Previous to that time there were no seats specially provided for singers. Those persons who had thought of forming a choir in 1801 asked that seats might be provided for them.

* In 1690 there were but six tunes known in the province; namely, "Oxford," "Litchfield," "York," "Windsor," "St. David's," and "Martyr's," and no new tunes could be introduced without a vote of the church. The first tune-book, especially devoted to music, was published by Rev. William Walter, in 1721, and was the first music with bars printed in America.

January 12, 1801, we find an article in the parish records for meetings as follows : —

" To see if the parish will erect, or suffer to be erected, seats for the singers, in the front of pews in the front gallery." January 19, 1801, " voted to erect seats in the front gallery for the singers, in front of the front pews." Also, " voted that the above seats for the singers, be erected in a ' *surkerler forme.*' "

Major Daniel Cary, Moses Cary, and Colonel Caleb Howard were " chosen a committee to git the above seats built." The above seats were specially set apart for the use of those who had become " *larned* " in the rules of " *musick.*"

Oliver Bryant, Josiah Brett, Isaac Packard, John Field, John Cobb, and Luke Lincoln were " choristers " in the parish until the town was incorporated. Since that time, Thomas J. Gurney, then living in Abington, was invited to lead the choir and teach them to sing, in 1829, who was the first person that received any compensation for services in singing. Commencing in 1829, Mr. Gurney continued to lead the choir and teach singing-schools until 1840, when he removed to Abington. From that time the choir of the First Church has been led by Mr. Seth Sumner, who became celebrated for his success in teaching singing-schools in the immediate vicinity, and Messrs. Isaac T. Packard, of this town, Whiting, Brown, and Appleton, of Boston, and Edmund Packard.

When the Porter Church was formed in the town, in 1850, Mr. Gurney was invited to take charge of their choir, which he continued to do till April 1, 1864, when he resigned. Mr. T. Emerson Gurney was organist at the Porter Church from 1850 to 1855 ; Mr. Joshua V. Gurney, from 1855 to 1858.

The First Congregational Church had the first organ, in their old church, which was exchanged for a new one in

1854, for their new house. At the present time there are
four organs in the churches; namely, in the First Congregational Church, Porter Evangelical Church, Second Methodist, and the Catholic Church.

There was a musical society formed in the county of Plymouth, called the Old Colony Musical Society, which was for
the benefit of singers throughout the county. Bartholomew
Brown, Esq., was leader; Rev. Daniel Huntington was president. This society fell through for want of support. Mr.
Huntington was a man of fine musical talent, and did much
to elevate the standard of church music in the first part of
his ministry, when so little attention had been paid to rula-
ble music.

The next musical club formed for the purpose of improving the singing was the Calcott Singing Society, which
was about 1827 or 1828, and included the four Bridgewaters. Rev. Daniel Huntington was their first president;
Nathan Lazell, of Bridgewater, was leader.

Next in order was the Union Harmonic Society, that
was in existence about 1835. From that time to the present,
it would be impossible to give a full detail of the various
singing-schools, rehearsals, clubs, etc. But probably no town
in the county has given more attention to music, or been
more successful in the production of talented singers and
highly-entertaining performances, than North Bridgewater.
The church music in this town is of the highest order, and
much time is devoted to the improvement of the singing
throughout all the societies.

This town has sent forth some excellent teachers of music
and performers of instrumental music, among whom are
Thomas J. Gurney, T. Emerson Gurney, George T. Ather-
ton, and William Faxon, who have made music a profession.

42

BAND MUSIC.

About the year 1840, a few individuals met together for the purpose of drill and practice in music upon various brass instruments, drums, etc., under the lead of Samuel M. Holmes, under the name of the North Bridgewater Brass Band. They met every week or oftener for practice, and were very successful; so that after a time they were engaged in all the surrounding places to play upon public occasions, and their fame soon spread abroad, and it is at present one of the best bands of the kind in that section. A large delegation of this band joined the Twelfth Massachusetts Regiment in the rebellion of 1861.

Soon after this band was formed, another was organized at Campello, under the lead of Martin L. Keith. The following persons were among the members of that band; namely, Charles P. Keith, Theodore Lilley, Sylvanus Keith, Albert Keith, Bela B. Hayward, Jarvis W. Reynolds, James C. Snell, Thomas French, Lucius Hayward, and Harrison Bryant. This company continued only about six months, when some of the number joined the Centre Band.

About the same period there was another band at the "West Shares," under the leadership of Ellis Packard, which continued about a year, and was then given up, some of its members joining the Centre Band. At the present time the united musical talent of the town is engaged in the original Brass Band.

The members of this band that joined the Twelfth Massachusetts Regiment received the highest praise from General Sherman; and it is said that this was his favorite band, and was conducted under the leadership of William J. Martland.

THESPIAN SOCIETY.

In February, 1836, a company of gentlemen and ladies were organized into a society under the above name, for the purpose of giving dramatic performances. The orchestra consisted of fifteen members, and was under the leadership of Sihon Packard. The songs, duets, and choruses were of a high order, and were performed before crowded assemblies. A slight fee was asked, to pay expenses of scenery, and expenses only.

UNION MUSICAL ASSOCIATION.

About the first of May, 1864, a new musical association was formed under the above title, for the purpose of improvement in singing, practising choruses, oratorios, etc. It was regularly organized with a constitution and by-laws. The following were the officers: Henry W. Robinson, *President;* Charles R. Ford, *Vice-President;* F. A. Thayer, *Secretary;* Sumner A. Hayward, *Treasurer;* James Porter, *Librarian;* Charles J. F. Packard, William H. Faxon, Samuel McLauthlin, Thomas Leonard, S. Franklin Packard, D. B. Lovell, *Trustees;* William H. Faxon, *Musical Director.*

BANK.

The business of the town of North Bridgewater had increased to such an extent, and the wants of the people were such, as to induce a few public-spirited individuals to petition the Legislature for a charter to do banking business, which was granted to Messrs. Bela Keith, Benjamin Kingman, and Jesse Perkins, March 28, 1854, with a capital of $100,000, divided into shares of $100 each. The bank was organized under the name of the North Bridgewater Bank, with the following officers; namely, Martin Wales, of Stoughton, *President;* Rufus P. Kingman, *Cashier;* Benjamin Kingman, Frederick Howard, Chandler Sprague, William F. Brett, Ebenezer Tucker, and Pardon Copeland, *Directors.* In 1857 Mr. Brett resigned his office, and in 1860 Elijah Howard, of Easton, was elected to fill the vacancy.

The first bills issued from this institution was September

4, 1854, since which time it has been in successful operation, and has proved a valuable addition to the business facilities of the town, and a mark of the enterprise of her citizens. Previous to the establishment of this bank, the business people, wishing banking accommodations, were obliged to go out of town for the same.

At the time of writing this, most other banks in the country are being changed into " National Banks," and the stockholders of this institution are not in favor of changing; hence there is a prospect of its discontinuing business.

SAVINGS-BANK.

The beneficent spirit of the present age is in nothing more remarkably displayed than in the combined energy with which individuals of the highest rank in society are laboring to promote the welfare of the lower order.   The advantages that have arisen, both to the individual contributors and the public, by these institutions have been great.   The first attempt made to give effect to a plan for enabling the laboring poor to provide support for themselves in sickness, as well as old age, was in 1789.   Again, in 1808, a bill was introduced in the " House of Commons," for promoting industry among the laboring classes, and for the relief of the poor, which was as follows, —

" *Whereas*, such of the laboring poor as are desirous of making out of their earnings some savings, as a future provision for themselves or their families, are discouraged from so doing by the difficulty of placing out securely the small sums which they are able to save ; and believing it would tend to promote habits of industry and frugality, and encourage the poor to make a provision for themselves and their families, if an establishment was formed in which they might invest their money with security and advantage."

These institutions are in general intended for that class of poor but industrious persons who deserve help by endeavoring to help themselves, the primary object not being for gain, but benevolence, and are for the benefit of the widow, the orphan, and the aged.

Many a penny that is now safely deposited in the vaults of these savings institutions in the country might have gone where the possessor would never have seen them again ; for this reason savings-banks are a great blessing to the community.

In the town of North Bridgewater, there are individuals that look to the interests of others as well as themselves, and having at the same time an eye to the interests of the community generally, they petitioned for an act of incorporation as a savings-bank, which was granted to Messrs. Franklin Ames, Edward Southworth, and George B. Dunbar, April 24, 1851, under the name of the North Bridgewater Savings-Bank. The following were the officers of the institution at the time of its organization in 1851 ; namely, Colonel Edward Southworth, *President ;* Franklin Ames, George B. Dunbar, *Vice-Presidents ;* Edward Southworth, Jr., *Secretary* and *Treasurer ;* Edward Southworth, Lorenzo D. Hervey. Henry V. French, Franklin Ames, Algernon S. Sylvester, Oakes S. Soule, George B. Dunbar, Edward Southworth, Jr., *Trustees.*

This institution under able management has been very successful, and productive of a great amount of good to the community. The amount of deposits for the year 1865 were about $160,000, which was invested in bank stock, real estate, public funds, and personal security.

FIRE DEPARTMENT.

Water is the grand agent that nature has provided for the extinguishment of flames, and the different ways and means for applying it with effect have been sought for in every civilized country. In the absence of more suitable implements, buckets and other portable vessels of capacity at hand have always been seized to throw water upon fire, and when used with celerity and presence of mind in the early commence-

ment of a fire, have often been sufficient; but when a confla-
gration extends beyond their reach, the fate of the burning
pile too often resembles that of the ships of " Æneas."

> " Nor buckets poured, nor strength of human hand,
>   Can the victorious element withstand."

Hence the necessity of some device by which a stream of
water may be forced from a distance on flames. Ingenious
men of former days were stimulated to an unusual degree to
invent machines for that purpose. The first machine used
for throwing water upon fire was the common syringe. Fire
was the most destructive agent employed in ancient wars;
hence every effort that could be made by ingenuity for protection from the assaults of pitch, oil, and fire, that were
thrown from the ramparts, was made.

The introduction of " fire-engines " was an important
event in the country, and indicates a certain degree of refinement in civilization and an advanced state of the mechanic arts. If we review the progress of fire-engines in
modern times, from the syringe to the splendid engine of to-
day, we cannot fail to observe that progress marks the age.
At first was used the single cylinder, then a double cylinder
and air-chamber, which was first used in 1825.*

FIRE-ENGINES.

The first fire-engine in North Bridgewater was purchased
by subscription in 1827, and was owned by a private company. The following is a copy of the original subscription
paper: —

   " This proposes a method for obtaining a fire-engine, to be kept near the
road betwixt the Old Meeting House and Mr. Whitman's office, for the use
of the inhabitants of North Bridgewater who are liable to suffer loss by fire.
And to accomplish said object, twenty-three shares, valued at twenty dollars
each, are offered to those who may feel interested to become proprietors

---

* The first fire-engine in use in this country was imported from Holland for the
city of New York, in December, 1731.

thereof. Each subscriber will annex to his name how many shares he takes, and if less than one, what part. And we, the subscribers, do severally feel under obligations to pay, agreeably to our subscription, to the proprietors, treasurer, or agent duly authorized by a majority of proprietors to receive their money, and procure their engine.

" North Bridgewater, February 10, 1827."

Subscribers' Names.	No. of Shares.	Subscribers' Names.	No. of Shares.
Eliab Whitman	One.	Eliphalet Kingman	One half.
Nathan Perry	"	Bela Keith	"
Edward Southworth	"	Ephraim Howard	"
Silas Packard	"	William Faxon	"
Jabez Field	"	Nathan Jones	"
Benjamin Kingman	"	David Packard	"
John Wales	"	John Packard	"
David Ames	"	Nathaniel H. Cross	"
Rosseter Jones	"	Charles Packard	"
Micah Faxon	"	Hiram Atherton	"
Nathan Hayward	"	Azor Packard	One quarter.
Arza Leonard	"	Josiah W. Kingman	"
Azel Wood	"	Benjamin Stoddard	"
Lemuel French	"	John Crafts	"
Zibeon French	"	Thomas Wales	Three quarters.
Perez Crocker	"	Nathaniel B. Harlow	One quarter.
John Battles	"	Sidney Perkins	"

This engine was called the "Union No. 1," and was a bucket-tub to be filled by hand. The machine passed out of the proprietors' hands to the town, on condition that the town would put the engine in perfect order, and keep it in order for use at fires. They also furnished a hook-and-ladder carriage, with fire-hooks, ladders, chains, etc.

The above constituted all the facilities for extinguishing fires previous to 1845. At that date, the town, finding the alarms of fire growing more numerous as new buildings were erected, and were so near together, " voted to procure two new and improved suction fire-engines." This vote passed February 9, 1846. The town appropriated $1,000, provided the citizens would subscribe $1,000 more. The subscription was promptly raised, and Benjamin Kingman and Amasa Edson appointed a committee to purchase the machines.

Previous to this time, the management at fires was under the direction of " fire wards " appointed by the town.

The two new engines were manufactured by Messrs. T. and E. Thayer, costing seven hundred and fifty dollars each, and were completed and received February 6, 1847. One of them was called " Protector," and was kept in the Centre Village; the other, called " Enterprise," was located at Campello.

The present " fire department " was organized by an act of incorporation by the Legislature of Massachusetts, March 18, 1846, and at the time of the receipt of the two new engines, consisted of the following: one old engine, the " Union," Captain Henry L. Bryant; " Protector No. 3," Captain B. P. Lucas, — motto, " We will endeavor; " " Enterprise No. 2." Captain Aaron B. Drake, — motto, " Always ready; " one hook-and-ladder carriage with the fixtures, and one old and two new engine-houses.

In 1850 the town purchased a large engine of John Agnew, of Philadelphia, Pennsylvania, costing $1,700, which was called the " Protector No. 3." The old engine of that name was changed to " Relief No. 4," — motto, " Our aim, the public good." In May, 1853, a new machine was purchased by private subscription, by the name of " Independence No. 5," — motto, " Still live." About the same time, the " Relief Engine No. 4 " was sold to the town of Randolph, and located at South Randolph. In the fall of 1853, a new engine was purchased of L. Button & Co., of Waterford, New York, named " Mayflower No. 4," which name was changed to " Columbian No. 5," — motto, " On the alert."

In the spring of 1861, the town voted to sell " Protector No. 3," which was done during the year, by exchange with William Jeffers, of Pawtucket, for one of his engines, using the same name and number. In 1854 " Enterprise Engine No. 2 " was transferred to the " West Shares," or North-West

FIRE ENGINE HOUSE (Campello).
"Enterprise" Co. No. 2.

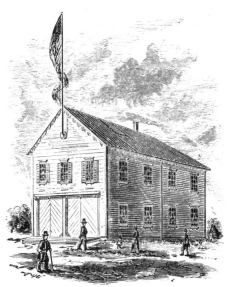

FIRE ENGINE HOUSE (Centre Village).
"Protector" Co. No. 3.

Bridgewater, and the name changed to "Niagara No. 6." During that year a new engine was purchased of L. Button & Co., of Waterford, New York, to take the place of the old engine, adopting the same name, and was located at Campello. In 1865 the "Niagara Engine" was sold to go to South Easton, and a new engine was purchased at Charlestown, named "Hancock No. 1."

At the time of writing the above, in 1865, the fire department of North Bridgewater consists of "Hancock Engine No. 1," Captain Isaac H. Hartwell, located at the "West Shares," — motto, "Our aim, the public good;" "Enterprise Engine No. 2," Captain William Stevens, located at Campello, — motto, "Always ready;" "Protector Engine No. 3," Captain Henry B. Packard, located in the Centre Village, — motto, "We will endeavor;" "Columbian Engine No. 5," Captain E. Z. Stevens, also located in the Centre Village, — motto, "On the alert;" and one hook-and-ladder carriage and three engine-houses.*

* On Saturday the 21st of October, 1865, the fire companies made a trial of fire-engines for a silver trumpet. "Protector" took the prize, playing horizontally 220 feet.

43

CHAPTER XVIII.

MISCELLANEOUS HISTORY — CONTINUED.

Burying-grounds. — Melrose Cemetery. — Hearse. — Town Pound. — Lock-up. — Poor. — Town House. — Telegraph. — North Bridgewater Gas Light Company. — Franklin Debating Association. — Pi Beta Society. — Library Association. — Agricultural Library Association. — Soldiers' Aid Society. — Freedmen's Relief Association. — Industrial Association. — Philomathian Association. — Massasoit Lodge of I. O. of O. F. No. 69. — Paul Revere Lodge of Freemasons. — Fires, Casualties, and Miscellaneous Events.

BURYING-GROUNDS.

THE custom of burying the dead in public places prevailed among the most ancient nations. The Romans observed this custom in the earliest days, and in the more flourishing periods of the republic they burnt their dead, and only buried their ashes in urns. The ancient Germans deposited their dead in groves, consecrated by their priests, and with the introduction of the Christian religion consecrated places of burial have been appropriated for that purpose, all over the world. Christians of all denominations are beginning to regard the burial-places of their friends with that reverence due to the departed.

Few evidences of a more refined sentiment can be found more marked than the selection of beautiful and choice grounds for the final resting-place of their friends. The once cheerless and gloomy aspect of our old burying-grounds has become attractive, by the removal of all noxious weeds, thistles, and briers, and the yards neatly laid out with walks " round about."

In the early settlement of the country, burying-lots were selected more with regard to convenience than for looks. Now beautiful spots of ground are selected in retired localities, in some shaded grove, or in some rural locality. Costly

monuments are erected without regard to expense. Formerly after the bodies were buried, the care of the grave
ceased. Now neat headstones are erected and beautiful
flowers are kept in bloom over the remains of loved ones.

Probably the first burial-place in North Bridgewater was
that situated on the westerly side of the main street, leading
from the Centre Village to Campello, and but a short distance
from the residence of the late William Tribou. These
grounds are of small size, and contain one tomb, and that of
ancient date. In this yard many of the headstones are broken, or rough and irregularly placed, and some covered with
moss, rendering the names quite illegible. This yard shows
how little regard so many in the community pay to the final
resting-place of their friends. It would seem as though the
friends and posterity of those buried there would try to improve a spot so exposed as that, on one of the public
streets of the town. A few trees set out would change the
appearance very much, and a trifling expense in rearranging
might make it quite attractive. We hope ere long to see
some improvements in that direction.

Another yard is situated nearly opposite the Salisbury
House, Campello, which is a very small family yard belonging to a few individuals. The first person buried there was
Jonas Keith, the former owner of the land, who died of the
small-pox. A long time since many of the occupants or proprietors of this lot have removed the remains of their friends
to the new Union Cemetery, leaving but few now buried in
the yard. There is a family tomb in the yard, belonging to
the heirs of the late Simeon Keith. This lot is situated quite
near many houses and is in so exposed a condition that it
will probably be given up as a burial-place ere long.

There is still another quite large burying-ground at the
north end of the Centre Village, forming the corner of Main
and Ashland Streets. This is an old yard, and is well

filled with graves. How long this yard has been used for the purpose of burial, we have no means of knowing. It is, however, one of the oldest in the town, and, like the first-mentioned, needs care and some expense to make it attractive. There is one tomb in this yard erected by Col. Caleb Howard.

There is also another yard near the residence of the late Ezekiel Merritt. This is probably quite an old spot, and is not much used of late, very few families being interested in the lot.

Following Belmont Street to the west till we come near the mill, at Tilden's Corner, on Liberty Street, we find a neat little yard, fenced with a substantial stone wall, with but a few graves in it, and those that are there seem to exhibit some care.

We find another small burying-ground on Pleasant Street, near the residence of Charles T. Reynolds, in which are but a few graves.

There is also a yard in the easterly part of the town, on Pine Street, and near the residence of the late Samuel Packard, in very good order.

On Summer Street, near the residence of John Thompson, is another small yard, enclosed with a substantial stone fence, in which are several graves of comparatively recent date.

MELROSE CEMETERY.

Travelling on the road from North Bridgewater to Stoughton, on the Taunton Turnpike, we find a moderate size spot of ground set apart for burial purposes, under the above name. In the yard is one tomb belonging to the heirs of the late Capt. Lemuel Packard. This yard has the appearance of neatness, and is a very desirable location for a cemetery,

In 1848 Messrs. Chandler Sprague, Esq., and William F. Brett purchased a lot of land, containing about fifteen acres, of Azel Packard, extending from Centre Street, on the north, to Crescent Street, on the south, and bordering upon Sprague's Pond on the west, for the purpose of a cemetery. The land was divided into lots, walks, and avenues, and sold to various individuals for burial purposes.

The following persons were organized into a corporation under the name of Union Cemetery, Oak Grove, of North Bridgewater, April 27, 1849; namely, Benjamin Kingman, George B. Dunbar, Abel Kingman, George W. Bryant, David Howard, Chandler Sprague, Francis M. French, Robert Smith, Lorenzo D. Hervey, William P. Howard, Edward Southworth, Jr., Charles S. Johnson, and William F. Brett.

The cemetery was consecrated by appropriate exercises, May 21, 1849, at which Rev. Daniel Huntington, of Campello, delivered an able address appropriate to the occasion.

There is also another cemetery on the north side of Court Street, near Perez Southworth's, containing about three acres, which is occupied by the friends of the Catholic persuasion, under care of Rev. T. B. McNulty, called St. Patrick's Cemetery.

HEARSE.

In the early history of towns, we find it was customary to carry the remains of departed friends to the grave upon a bier made for that purpose. It was usually carried upon the shoulders of men selected for that service, who were called bearers. Upon the introduction of carriages, an effort was made to procure a hearse to take the place of the bier.

In a warrant calling a meeting of the North Parish in April, 1818, we find an article " to see if the parish would build, or cause to be built, a hearse or decent carriage to carry the dead to the place of interment, and a building to keep the same in." " Voted not to act upon the article."

Judging by a vote passed in November, 1828, we should

suppose that a hearse and house were built by private enterprise.   The vote is as follows : " Voted to accept of the
hearse and house as presented by the proprietors to the town
of North Bridgewater, and that said town will pay the balance due to Captain David Ames for building said house,
amounting to fifty-two dollars."

The house stood on the old church green, until August 10,
1835, when the parish voted to have it removed, on account
of building the parsonage house.

November 4, 1850, a committee was chosen to-day, to repair the old or build a new hearse. Franklin Ames, Eliphalet Kingman, and Ruel Richmond were the committee. A
new hearse was procured during the year, and is the one now
owned by the town.

March 18, 1788, at a meeting held this day in the North
Parish, " to see if the parish will vote to purchis a burying
cloath, and choose a man or men to purchis the same," it
was " voted that the precinct cormittee purchis a burying
cloath, and they use their Discresion in that afair."

TOWN POUND.

In the early settlement of the towns throughout the province, swine were allowed to run at large, upon their being
properly yoked, between April 1st and October 15th, and
" ringed in the nose all the rest of the year," under a penalty
of sixpence each.   Also all sheep running at large and not
under a shepherd between May 1st and October 31st, to a fine
of threepence each.   The several towns could, by vote of a
majority, allow them to run at large ; but when they voted not
to have them run, there was need of a place to put those who
should violate the law, and break into cornfields or private
enclosures.   In 1698 a law was passed requiring towns to
make and keep a pound, as follows : —

." That there shall be a sufficient pound or pounds made and maintained, from time to time, in every town and precinct within this province, in such part or places thereof as the selectmen shall direct and appoint, at the cost and charge of such town and precinct, for the impounding or restraining of any swine, neat cattle, horses, or sheep, as shall be found damage-feasant in any cornfield or other enclosures ; or swine, unyoked or unringed, neat cattle, horses, or sheep, going upon the common, not allowed to feed there by the major part of the Propriety,'' etc.

In accordance with the above requirement, the town of Bridgewater maintained a town pound from its first settlement, and when it was divided into precincts, each precinct was required to erect one within their limits. The North Parish, being a law-loving and law-abiding people, erected one upon or near the meeting-house green, which remained till 1828, when, by vote of the town of North Bridgewater, it was removed. April 7, 1828, the following record appears on the town books: "Voted to accept the offer of Benjamin Kingman, which is to furnish the town with a pound for forty years, and remove the stone of the pound for his own use as a compensation."

Since that time Mr. Kingman has furnished the same according to agreement.

When the lands of our fathers were wild and unfenced, the "cattell," "hoggs," "sheap," and "hosses" were allowed to run at large in the fields and roads, and then the cattle were usually marked in some way, generally by a slit in one or both of the ears, and the marks were recorded upon the records of the town, and a bell was also attached to their necks. The hogs were either "yoaked" or had "wrings" in their noses to prevent their doing damage, and the sheep wore yokes also ; the horses were fettered with a chain passing from one ankle to another, that they might be taken at pleasure.

As the country became settled, people began to fence their lots and farms, and swine were placed in small pens, the sheep placed in folds, and the cattle enclosed in lots used as pastures.

LOCK-UP.

The next thing in order should be the lock-up. Provision having been made for penning cattle and other animals, there was also a need of some place in which persons committing crimes, and who could not take care of themselves, could be placed for safe-keeping, or be kept until they could have a trial.

The number of such persons was very few previous to about 1852, when the town voted to provide a place for the safe-keeping of criminals. The first place provided was the building that had previously been used as a hearse-house, which was fitted for that purpose, and used till 1857, when the town voted to dispose of the lock-up, and provide a suitable place for the safe-keeping of criminals upon the town-farm.

Again, November 30, 1857, the town "voted to choose a committee of three to build a lock-up for the detention of criminals, and that said committee be and are hereby authorized to purchase or lease a lot of land within the limits of the Watch District." George B. Dunbar, Elisha H. Joslyn, and Lyman Clark were the committee, who proceeded to erect the same upon a lot of land purchased of W. Holliston Whitman, a short distance south of Crescent Street. The building is built of brick, with cells fitted with iron bedsteads, bars, and bolts, in a durable form. The building is enclosed by a board fence, several feet high.

POOR.

"Rob not the poor because he is poor."

Until within a few years, it was the custom of the different towns of Massachusetts to "vendue the poor;" that is, to sell the support of the poor to the one who would do it the cheapest. The last vote we find on record in relation to selling the poor in the town of North Bridgewater was April 1,

1822, as follows: "Voted that all paupers who cannot by themselves or friends procure a home, to be put out at public auction or private sale, for one year from the 15th inst., the remainder to be provided for by the selectmen."

In 1830 the propriety of building a house for the use of the town, and to provide a place for the poor, was brought to the attention of the citizens in town-meeting April 1, 1822, and a committee appointed to examine and report concerning the expediency of purchasing a poorhouse. Mark Perkins, Caleb Howard, Esq., Eliphalet Kingman, Jonathan Cary, and Bela Keith, Esq., were the committee, who reported that the subject of purchasing a town-farm was worthy the attention of the town. Accordingly, April 4, 1834, Benjamin Kingman, Micah Packard, and Abel Kingman were appointed a committee with full power to purchase a house and land for the use of the town's poor. April 25, 1831, a farm was purchased of Benjamin King, Esq., in the easterly part of the town, consisting of ninety-four and three quarters acres of land and buildings thereon, formerly known as the Deacon Jacob Fuller farm, for the sum of $2,625. A superintendent was appointed yearly to manage the farm, and take proper care of the poor. Deacon Jacob Fuller was the first person placed in charge. Theron Ames, Josiah Dunbar, Weston Simmons, Colwell, Jones, and the present superintendent, Howard, have had the management since the first. A board of faithful and trusty Overseers of the Poor are annually elected by the town, who have the general oversight of the poor and provide for their wants, and upon inquiry we are satisfied that the poor of the town are well cared for.

WARNING OUT OF TOWN.

The people in ancient days resorted to various means to prevent immigrants coming into town from becoming chargeable upon the public. A custom much in use in the town of

Bridgewater was to notify or warn the parties moving into the town " to depart hence." We insert a copy of one handed to us, as a specimen of early notions : —

" *Plymouth SS.*

To John Tilden, Joiner :

" By virtue of a warrant from the selectmen of the town of Bridgewater, you are requested to depart the limits of said town within fifteen days, you not having obtained leave of inhabiting the same.

" JONATHAN KEITH, *Constable.*

" November 25, 1789."

TOWN HOUSE.

The first town meeting in the town of North Bridgewater was held in the meeting-house of the First Congregational Church, in 1821. Since that time the meeting has been holden in the various public halls in the village. Several attempts have been made to see if the town would build a house suitable for holding town meetings. The first move in that direction was in 1843, as appears by vote of the town, December 16, 1843. At a meeting held on that day to see if the town would purchase the Second Congregational Meeting-house, it was voted to choose a committee of three to consider of the matter, and report at a future meeting. Benjamin Kingman, Jesse Perkins, and Eliphalet Kingman were the committee. In 1847 the subject was brought before the town at a meeting held in May, at which it was voted to postpone building a town-house at present. Again, March 11, 1850, Bela Keith, Esq., Jesse Perkins, Esq., Col. Edward Southworth, Caleb Copeland, Marcus Packard, Isaac Hartwell, and Capt. Henry French were chosen a committee to procure a plan of a building, and the probable cost of the same, also the subject of purchasing a lot of land, and report at a future meeting. A report was made, and, September 6, 1850, the committee were instructed to purchase a lot of land of William P. Howard, which was done. The lot situated opposite H. W. Robinson's store, corner of Main and Centre Streets, was purchased of Mr. Howard for the sum of $1,500. April 30, 1855, the town voted to authorize the selectmen to sell the town-house lot at public auction within thirty days. The lot was sold to Mr. David F. Studley and others for $3,050.

The above is the last we have heard in reference to erecting a town-house. A town of the size of North Bridgewater certainly ought to have a house of her own, and we doubt not the time is near at hand when she will have an edifice that shall be an ornament to the town.

TELEGRAPH.

The first electric current that passed through the town of North Bridgewater, on wires, was in 1856. The line was run from Boston to Myrick's Station, on the line of the Fall River Railroad. The proprietors were Messrs. Brewer & Baldwin. At first the nearest office to this town was at Bridgewater. A short time had elapsed after the completion of the wires when an effort was made to have an office established nearer to this town, and through the efforts of Franklin Ames, Esq., one was opened to the public May 6, 1856. The following is the first message to the citizens of the town, and was from the editor of the " Barnstable Patriot," to the editor of the " North Bridgewater Gazette."

" To GEORGE PHINNEY :

" We congratulate you, and others of North Bridgewater, on the opening of a telegraph office at your place. I am happy to shake hands with you this P. M. God bless and prosper you.   S. B. PHINNEY."

REPLY.

" To MAJOR PHINNEY :

"We receive your congratulations upon the occasion of opening a telegraph office here with heartfelt pleasure. May the connection this day effected between North Bridgewater and Cape Cod never be severed. With the hope that the Union may be preserved,

" I remain yours truly,
" GEORGE PHINNEY."

NORTH BRIDGEWATER GAS LIGHT COMPANY.

During the year 1858 several of the citizens in the thick-
est settled portions of the town began to discuss the subject
of a better means of lighting their stores, factories, and
dwelling-houses; or, in other words, the people wanted "more
light," and as is always the case, when people wish for light,
it can be had.   For this purpose a few public-spirited individuals were called together July 22, 1859, to see what measures it was thought best to adopt.   Subscription papers were
opened, and stock taken to the amount of $12,000, divided in-
to shares of $100 each.   A company was organized Septem-
ber 5, 1859, with the following officers: William F. Brett,
President; David F. Studley, *Treasurer;* Noah Chesman, H.
W. Robinson, and Jonas R. Perkins, Esq., *Directors.*

FRANKLIN DEBATING ASSOCIATION.

A society was organized during the winter of 1836, with
the above name, for the promotion of useful knowledge and
debating.

The last question for discussion was, " Are dancing-schools,
balls, cotillon-parties, etc., worthy the support and encouragement of the community?"   The decision has not as yet
come to the writer's notice.

PI BETA SOCIETY.

This society was established September 17, 1844, and was
in active operation eight years.   Its object was the mental
improvement of its members, for the accomplishment of which,
beside the literary exercises of its regular meetings, it had a
reading-room, and a cabinet of natural history of nearly two
thousand specimens, and a library of two hundred volumes,
most of which were presented the first six months of its existence.   The society held weekly meetings, and had addresses from distinguished speakers from time to time.   During

the active term this society was in existence, it had gathered one thousand volumes, and ten thousand specimens of cabinet curiosities of various kinds.

The Messrs. Loomis, of the Academy, had the care of the society, it being connected with the Adelphian Academy.

The officers of the institution, in 1851, were Charles R. Ford, *President;* Jacob Emerson, Jr., of Methuen, *Recording Secretary;* John H. Bourne, of Marshfield, *Corresponding Secretary;* Caleb Howard, *Treasurer;* Silas L. Loomis, *Librarian;* L. F. C. Loomis, *Superintendent of Cabinet;* Jacob Emerson, Charles R. Weeden, Lavoice N. Guild, *Prudential Committee;* besides many honorary members.

LIBRARY ASSOCIATION.

Prior to the year 1847, the town of North Bridgewater had not enjoyed the privilege of many literary or scientific lectures or social gatherings. During the winter of that year, the principals of the Adelphian Academy, feeling an interest in the matter, and the want of some elevated and improving intercourse for the multitude of young people in the town, proposed and finally arranged a series of social levees or gatherings, composed mostly of members of the school. The exercises consisted of brief essays and addresses, interspersed with music and a season of social conversation.

This association was reorganized in October, 1851, or a new one formed under the above name; and a series of useful lectures was given by able lecturers, together with excellent musical entertainments.

NORTH BRIDGEWATER AGRICULTURAL LIBRARY ASSOCIATION.

An association under the above name was formed April 3, 1859, the object of which was to obtain a library of agricultural books, papers, etc., such as would tend to the improvement of agricultural pursuits. The following persons were

its officers: Chandler Sprague, Esq., *President;* Isaac
Kingman, *Vice-President;* Alpheus Holmes, *Treasurer* and
Librarian; H. W. Robinson, *Secretary.*

NORTH BRIDGEWATER SOLDIERS' AID SOCIETY.

Agreeably to a notice previously given, the ladies of the
town, feeling a deep interest in the welfare of those who
had gone forth to fight the battles of our country, met at the
chapel of the First Congregational Church, and organized
themselves into a society under the name of Soldiers' Aid
Society, and made choice of the following officers: Mrs.
George Wilbour, *President;* Mrs. H. W. Robinson, *Vice-President;* Mrs. —— Wheldon, *Secretary* and *Treasurer;* Mrs.
Henry Howard, Mrs. A. Harris, Mrs. —— Snow, Mrs. Elijah
Tolman, Mrs. Darius Howard, Mrs. M. J. Clark, Mrs. Russell
Alden, *Directors.*

The society held its meetings every Tuesday, in the Engine Hall on Elm Street, for the transaction of business. The
object of the society was the collection of clothing and
packages, such as are needed by the soldiers, and forwarding
them to their proper places. Much good has been already
accomplished. During the first year of this society's existence, the amount contributed in cash by the different societies was $278.43. The amount of clothing and other
goods sent to the Sanitary Commission at Boston amounted
to $800, making a total of $1,078.43. During the year
ending October, 1863, the amount of goods, clothing, supplies, etc., sent to the Sanitary Commission at Boston, was
$827.45. The amount of cash contributed was $176.05,
making a total of $1,003.50. During the year ending
October, 1864, the amount sent to the Sanitary Commission at Boston was $1,327.11. The amount of cash con-
tributed in various ways, including the proceeds of the
Sanitary Fair for Soldiers of $800, was $1,034, making

a total of $2,361.11, making the handsome sum of $4,-443.04 contributed for the benefit and relief of the soldiers up to October, 1864.

FREEDMEN'S RELIEF ASSOCIATION OF NORTH BRIDGEWATER.

July 8, 1864, an association was formed under the above name, as an auxiliary to the National Freedmen's Relief Association of New York City, having for its object the improvement of the Freedmen of the colored race, by raising money, clothing, and necessary material for their relief, and teaching them civilization and Christianity, to imbue their minds with correct ideas of order, industry, economy, self-reliance, and to elevate them in the scale of humanity by inspiring them with self-respect. The following is a list of the officers: Augustus T. Jones, *President;* A. B. Keith, *Vice-President;* Mrs. E. L. Clark, *Secretary;* Frances French, *Treasurer;* J. R. Perkins, George Copeland, Capt. Henry French, Thaddeus E. Gifford, A. T. Jones, and A. B. Keith, *Executive Committee.*

NORTH BRIDGEWATER INDUSTRIAL ASSOCIATION.

This association was organized in 1860, with the following officers: Chandler Sprague, Esq., *President;* Isaac T. Packard, *Secretary;* Lyman Clark, *Treasurer;* Charles Gurney and David L. Cowell, *Vice-Presidents.*

The object of this association is for the encouragement of the mechanic arts, agriculture, and horticulture. On account of the rebellion of 1861, this association has not made rapid progress, and their plans were suspended for a while. In October, 1863, a new board of officers was chosen, and we hope they may meet with all the encouragement that is needed to make it a valuable addition to the town. The following are the present board of officers: John S. Eldredge, *President;* H. W. Robinson and Dr. L. W. Puffer, *Vice-Pres-*

idents; David L. Cowell, *Secretary;* Charles Sprague, Esq.,
Treasurer.

PHILOMATHIAN ASSOCIATION.

The above is the name of an association connected with
Mr. S. D. Hunt's Academy, the object of which was mutual
improvement.   It was formed in 1855, soon after he opened
his school, and was in existence till the close.   Weekly meetings were held by the members, at which exercises, consisting
of debates, declamations, lectures, essays, critiques, and the
reading of a paper published monthly by the association,
was read.

MASSASOIT LODGE OF I. O. OF O. F. NO. 69.

This Lodge was instituted in June, 1846.   Of this organization we have no particulars from which to write.   Among
the members of the society were the following persons, who
held some office at its beginning: Robert Smith, Waldo
Bradford, James F. Packard, Cephas W. Drake, Ellis Packard, Samuel Webster, Lorenzo D. Hervey, Lorenzo Dilling-
ham, T. S. Mitchell, and Aaron B. Drake.

PAUL REVERE LODGE OF FREEMASONS.

This Lodge was instituted February 4, 1856, and is in a
flourishing condition, with a prospect of extended usefulness
under its excellent officers.   The original petitioners were
Lucien B. Keith, George Clark, Lorenzo D. Hervey, Robert
Smith, Alexander Hichborn, Jonas R. Perkins, Esq., Augustus
Mitchell, David Cobb, Thomas May, Samuel Howard, and
Hiram Packard.

The following were the officers at the formation of the
society : —

Lucien B. Keith, *Worshipful Master*.   Alexander Hichborn, *Junior Deacon*.
George Clark, *Senior Warden*.   Robert Smith, *Treasurer*.
Lorenzo D. Hervey, *Junior Warden*.   Jonas R. Perkins, *Secretary*.
Augustus Mitchell, *Senior Deacon*.   Hiram Packard, *Senior Steward*.
Thomas Mayhew, *Tyler*.

The foregoing comprise all of the prominent benevolent and literary associations or organizations, which we have published somewhat at length, that the reader may see what kind of material the town is made of, and to what extent the tastes of her citizens have been led in literary enterprises. There have been at different times various other societies in existence for a shorter or longer term that have not been mentioned, as they did not make great progress, nor continue any length of time. We are happy to notice that, as the population increases and new-comers settle in the town, there has been somewhat of an increase in literary pursuits, and greater attention paid to educational matters.

FIRES.

1804. Dwelling-house of Issachar Snell destroyed by fire.

1816. Dwelling-house of Arza Keith partially burned, caused while making varnish in one of the rooms. Mr. Keith was injured by inhaling smoke, from the effects of which he never recovered.

1818. Barn belonging to Charles Keith destroyed by fire.

1819. Barn belonging to Oliver Leach struck by lightning and destroyed by fire.

1836, March 6. Dwelling-house formerly belonging to Rev. Daniel Huntington, and occupied by Dr. A. K. Borden and George H. Brown, destroyed by fire.

1846. Cabinet shop belonging to Howard & Clark destroyed by fire.

1847, January 30. Dwelling-house belonging to Freeman Dexter destroyed by fire at half-past five o'clock A. M. (a very cold morning).

1847, March 11. Shoe manufactory of William French partially destroyed by fire, about five o'clock A. M.

1847, March 19. Store owned by George Clark destroyed by fire at eleven o'clock P. M. Also, a dwelling-house belonging to Micah Packard nearly consumed at the same time.

1847, September 26. Dwelling-house belonging to Nathan Hayward, slightly damaged by fire at four o'clock A. M.

1848, March 1. Edward E. Bennett's dwelling-house slightly damaged.

1848, March 23. House of Edward J. Snow slightly damaged.

1848, March 30. Woods near Benjamin Eaton's burned.

1848, May 1. Woods near Thomas Wales's burned.

1849, July 28. A carpenter-shop owned by Charles S. Johnson, about three o'clock P. M.; his dwelling adjoining narrowly escaped destruction.

1850, February 6. Ruel Richmond's wheelright shop consumed by fire

45

at three o'clock A. M. Weather severely cold ; engines could not work well ; thermometer 6° below zero.

1850, April 2. Barn belonging to Silas Packard burned at three o'clock A. M.

1850, April 15. Building owned by S. & G. Manly, at eleven o'clock P. M., was totally destroyed.

1850, August 6. David Ford's barn struck by lightning and destroyed about three o'clock P. M.

1850, October 11. Lucius Keith's periodical depot damaged by fire.

1850, October 11. Tailor shop owned by W. F. Brett nearly destroyed, about four o'clock A. M. Also a building occupied by W. E. Skinner.

1851, June 29. Store of Messrs. Brett & Kingman, in Kingman Block, badly damaged by fire about three o'clock A. M.

1852, April 9. Barn on the John Tilden farm consumed about eight o'clock A. M.

1852, May 30. Pine Grove, a short distance south of the Centre Village, was burned. Buildings were saved with difficulty.

1852, May 30. Baptist Chapel damaged by fire, about $1,000, at half-past eight o'clock P. M.

1853, March 30. Dwelling-house near " Keith's Mill " partly burned ; formerly occupied by Zenas Packard.

1853, March 31. The last and boot manufactory owned by Chandler Sprague, Esq., and formerly known as the " Old Cotton Factory," was totally destroyed by fire at half-past three o'clock A. M. Loss, $4,000.

1853, May 23. Stable belonging to Nathaniel Snow, in the Pine Grove, was destroyed about four o'clock A. M.

1853, May 23. The steam mill connected with the furniture manufacturing establishment of Josiah W. Kingman, at Campello, took fire about a quarter to one o'clock P. M., communicating with the lumber yard and buildings around, destroying the dwelling-house of Mr. Kingman, stable, warehouse, and finishing shop, three workshops belonging to the same, also the dwelling-house owned and occupied by Anson Morse, dwelling of David Allen, meeting-house, and fire engine-house belonging to Enterprise Engine Company No. 2. Many other buildings took fire from these, but, by the prompt and energetic working of seven different engines, were saved from the devouring element. The loss by this fire was estimated at about $50,000, with a very small insurance, a severe loss to the village, besides throwing a large number of workmen out of employment.

1853, May 24. Barn belonging to Turner Torrey, in the west part of the town, was burned in the evening.

1853, June 9. Barn belonging to John Thompson, together with fifteen tons of hay. Loss, $1,000.

1853, September 29. The building owned by Rev. A. B. Wheeler, and occupied by C. C. Bixby, F. & H. Baylies, and S. W. S. Howard, partially burned.

1854, May 22. House owned and occupied by Jarvis W. Reynolds slightly burned.

1856, January 4. The dwelling-house of Dwight E. Hale was partially burned.

1856, September 8. The building known as the Unitarian Church, owned by Major Nathan Hayward, totally destroyed about one o'clock P. M.

1856, September 9. Barn and shop of Daniel McIntee, with two horses, were destroyed.

1856, October 5. The grocery store near the depot in the village, occupied by William H. Pierce, partly destroyed between two and three o'clock A. M.

1856, December 22. Ara Snow's house slightly burned.

1857, January 8. Dwelling-house owned by C. J. F. Packard partially burned. Loss, $300.

1857, November 26. Shoe manufactory of Martin L. Keith & Co., at Campello, slightly damaged by fire. Damage, $100.

1857, December 17. A small building owned by the heirs of Maj. Nathan Hayward, situated in the Tilden District. Loss was small.

1857, December 21. Railroad depot took fire from the telegraph. Damage was slight.

1857, December 30. The saw-mill belonging to Messrs. Thomas & Welcome Howard nearly consumed.

1859, January 22. House on Ashland Street, belonging to heirs of Maj. Nathan Hayward. Damage, $200.

1859, September 8. Dwelling-house and stable of Marcus Packard, on Mount Ashland, about eleven o'clock A. M. Loss, $9,000. Also, a lot of wood near by, caused by sparks from the same.

1859, September 2. The musical instrument manufactory owned by Caleb H. Packard, at Campello, occupied by A. B. Marston, destroyed.

1859, December 12. House owned by Henry Baylies. Loss, $800.

1860, January 11. Varnish factory near Ephraim Brett's house. Loss, $500.

1860, January 25. Barn belonging to John Reardon, at one o'clock P. M.

1860, April 2. An old building on Pond Street. Loss, $100.

1860, April 8. An old building corner Centre Street. Loss was small.

1860, October 19. Barn belonging to William F. Brett, containing thirty-two tons of hay and one cow, destroyed at twelve o'clock at night. Loss, $700.

1860, October 27. House belonging to Orren Bartlett partially burned. Loss, $500.

1860, November 7. Hall belonging to Baker & Kingman destroyed at half-past eleven o'clock P. M. Loss, $9,000. Insured for $6,000.

1860, November 8. Steam-mill of Howard & Clark slightly damaged by fire.

1860, November 29. Small dwelling-house owned by Benjamin Kingman, near "Keith's Mill," destroyed by fire.

1860, December 30. Tailor shop occupied by Daniel Logue, and owned by Tyler Cobb, partially destroyed by fire.

1861, March 2. Barn belonging to Galen Packard, together with one

horse and three cows, destroyed by fire about five o'clock A. M.   Loss, $600.
No insurance.

1861, March 11.   Shop occupied by Alexander Chaplin slightly damaged.

1861, May 8.   Store belonging to Col. E. Southworth partially burned.
Loss, $300.

1861, June 21.   House of John McCullough.   Loss, $300.

1861, July 6.   House belonging to Franklin Keith partially destroyed.
Loss, $600.

1861, November 29.   House belonging to Moses W. Hancock slightly
damaged by fire.

1862, January 2.   Store belonging to Daniel Hayward partially burned.
Loss, $450.

1862, February 1.   Store belonging to Charles Curtis partially destroyed.

1862, May 14.   Barn, shop, and wood-house, together with three cows
and a calf, belonging to Galen Warren, destroyed by fire.   Loss, $1,000.

1862, June 14.   Barn, three cows, and two tons of hay belonging to
Edward E. Bennett destroyed.

1862, June 16.   House of Sylvester Cotter partially destroyed.   Loss,
$500.

1862, August 17.   House belonging to Clark Paul.   Loss, $200.

1863, September 30.   Barn and shop of William Gegin destroyed.
Loss, $700.

1863, November 26 (Thanksgiving morning).   House and barn belonging to the heirs of Jesse Perkins, together with two cows.   Loss, $1,500.

1863, December 4.   House of Davis S. Packard slightly damaged by fire.

1864, July 8.   Barn belonging to Henry Edson destroyed.

1864, July 31.   Barn belonging to Alvin P. Kingman destroyed at
eight o'clock A. M.

1864, August 11.   Barn belonging to Dea. John W. Hunt destroyed
at half-past four o'clock P. M.   Loss, $200.

1864, August 14.   Barn belonging to Marcus Holmes destroyed at
half-past eight o'clock P. M.   Loss, $500.

1864, August 16.   House belonging to Hugh Burke destroyed at eleven
o'clock P. M.   Loss, $600.

1864, September 3.   Lot of wood owned by Rufus S. Noyes.   Loss, $200.

1864, September 15.   House in the north-east part of the town destroyed
by fire.   Also a barn.

1864, October 10.   House owned by S. & G. Manly, on Cottage Street,
destroyed by fire.   Loss, $400.

1864, November 6.   House owned by William Perry partially burned.
Loss, $200.

1864, December 1.   Car-load of straw took fire at the railroad station
and burned.   Also, freight-house partially burned.

1865, March 29.   Shoe manufactory owned by George Stevens, at Campello, partially burned at three o'clock A. M.

1865, April 3.   House on Pleasant Street slightly damaged.

1865, April 18.   Shoe manufactory belonging to Peleg S. Leach, on
Pine Street, entirely consumed by fire, at eleven o'clock.

1865, August 5. Barn belonging to Reuben Drake struck by lightning, and destroyed by fire, with from five to six tons of hay.

1865, August 24. Barn and slaughter-house belonging to Mr. Sanford Winter destroyed by fire.

CASUALTIES AND MISCELLANEOUS EVENTS.

In or about the year 1725, Henry Kingman came from the West Parish (now West Bridgewater) and settled on the spot where the late Seth Kingman lived and died. He was about twenty-one years of age, and unmarried. Soon after his arrival at his new home, he proceeded to the woods for the purpose of cutting fencing, about ten or eleven o'clock A. M. While in the act of splitting a large oak log, it split prematurely, and the axe entered the calf of his leg, nearly severing it, only a small portion of flesh remaining on each side to connect the parts; the bone was cut off entirely. It was a bitter cold day, and all he had to bandage with was his small handkerchief, in which was his luncheon. This he used as best he could; tied up the wound, and dragged himself to a small bridge, where he remained till evening, when, by the merest accident, some one heard him cry out for help, and even then passers-by supposed it was only the wild animals in the woods, which in that day were quite common. At last some person found him; a litter was made on which to carry him home; and when he reached his boarding-place, a messenger was despatched four miles or more to West Bridgewater for a physician. A long time must have elapsed before one could reach him, as the snow was deep and very bad travelling. But, strange as it may appear to the reader, the parts grew together, and he afterwards became an efficient officer in the army.

1727, October 29. The shock of a violent earthquake was severely felt throughout New England, which lasted for several days.

1739, February 5. The first meeting of the North Parish was held to-day. Timothy Keith, *Moderator;* Robert Howard, *Clerk,* who continued to hold that office thirty-two years in succession.

1748. Indian corn sold for thirty-two shillings per bushel; rye, forty-six shillings per bushel; wheat, three pounds per bushel; flour, ten pounds per hundred.

1749. This summer the most severe drought ever experienced by the oldest person then living. In the last of May the grass was all burnt by the sun; the ground looked white; the earth was dried to a powder at a great depth, and many wells, springs, brooks, and rivers were dried, so that fish lay dead on the bottom. The pastures were so scorched that cattle grew poor. Hay had to be brought from England to supply their wants, which sold for three pounds ten shillings per cwt. Barley and oats were so much injured they scarcely saved enough for seed. Flax was a total failure. Corn rolled and wilted. Herbs of all sorts were destroyed. During all these troubles Government ordered a day of fasting and prayer; and on the 6th of July, copious showers of rain fell to refresh them, and things looked brighter; and what was fortunate for the people, the next winter was very mild. After the plentiful rains, a day of public thanksgiving was ordered

1751, June 17.   Severe hail-storm.   Hailstones large as English walnuts were in abundance, breaking glass and doing other damage to a large amount.

1755.   Summer very hot and dry.   Hay scarce and high.

1755, November 18.   Shock of an earthquake, shaking down chimneys. In Boston and vicinity buildings were prostrated by the shock.

1762-3.   Very cold winter.   Snow of great depth.

1762, September 10.   Wild pigeons flew in abundance.

1763, June 8.   Wild pigeons flew in abundance.

"In the year 1769, when the disputes between England and America had begun, and the importation of foreign goods was stopped, it became customary for people to manufacture their own clothing; and, in many places, the young ladies had spinning matches at their ministers, for the benefit of their families.   On the 15th of August, 1769, at two o'clock, P. M., ninety-seven young ladies met at the house of their pastor, the Rev. John **Porter,** and generously gave his lady, for the use of her family, 3,322 knots of linen, tow, cotton, and woollen yarn, which they had spun for that purpose.   At three o'clock something, of American produce only, was set before them for their refreshment, which was more agreeable to them than any foreign dainties, considering the situation of the country at that time.   At four o'clock the ladies walked in procession to the meeting-house, where a discourse was delivered by their pastor, from Acts ix. 36: 'This woman was full of good works,' in which piety, industry, frugality, and benevolence were recommended and encouraged.   The closing prayer being made, the following lines, composed by their pastor, were sung: —

> ' Ye rubies bright, ye orient pearls,
>   How coveted by men !
> And yet the virtuous woman's price
>   Excels the precious gem.

> ' How kind and generous her heart !
>   How diligent her hand !
> How frugal in economy,
>   To save her sinking land !

> ' Foreign productions she rejects,
>   With nobleness of mind,
> For home commodities; to which
>   She's prudently inclined.

> ' She works, she lends, she gives away,
>   The labors of her hand ;
> The priest, the poor, the people all,
>   Do find in her their friend.

> ' She clothes herself and family,
>   And all the sons of need.
> Were all thus virtuous, soon we'd find
>   Our land from slavery freed.'

After which, anthems were sung; and, the assembly being dismissed, they retired to their respective homes."

David, son of Rev. John Porter, was riding in a chaise when about ten years of age; the horse took fright, ran, and threw him out, breaking one of his legs, which was soon after amputated. He survived but a short time. Died May, 1767.

1769, October 20. Violent storm, doing great damage.

1771. Very mild winter; not over four inches of snow fell during the season.

1772, March 9, 11, 13, and 20. Very severe snow-storm.

1772, April 3. Snow six to ten feet deep. People were obliged to dig themselves out of their houses. Many sheep and cattle lost.

1778, November 10. Hay sold for six dollars per cwt.

1779, February 16. Hay sold for nine dollars per cwt.

1779, November 12. Hay sold for twenty dollars per cwt.

1780, November 19. Hay sold for thirty-three pounds per cwt.

1780. Winter very severe. Great depth of snow.

1780, May 19. Remarkably dark day. Between twelve and one o'clock people could not work; were obliged to light candles to see to eat dinner; looked very melancholy indeed; but little rain. The evening was very dark.

1781, August 5. Wild pigeons flew very thick.

1782. Very dry season.

1785, April 1. Severe snow-storm. Snow three to five feet deep.

1785, April 15. Very cold. Ground frozen hard. Rivers crossed on the ice, with excellent skating on ponds.

1785, May 20. Severe snow-storm. Snow several inches deep.

1785, November 25. Severe snow-storm. Snow very deep.

1786, May 21. Wind east for eight weeks in succession.

1791, July 18. Rev. John Porter's horse killed by lightning in a severe thunder-storm.

1804, October. Severe gale; large trees blown down, and torn up by the roots.

1805, February. Snowed five days in succession. The road between North Bridgewater and Randolph was even with the top of the walls.

1806, June. Total eclipse of the sun.

1806. Winter of 1806-7 very mild; ground not frozen over four inches deep all winter.

1806. Summer of 1806 very cold.

1808. Very heavy frosts in August.

1811, May 5. Severe snow-storm.

1811, July. Great freshet, doing great damage,

1815, September 23. Severe gale, Monday. Some verses published soon after, were as follows:—

"It chanced to be our washing-day;
The clothes were all a-drying;
The stormy winds came through the lines
And set 'em all a-flying.

> " I saw the shirts and petticoats
>   Go riding off like witches ;
>   That day I lost — ah, how I wept ! —
>   I lost my Sunday breeches.''

The air became filled with limbs, shrubs, old pieces of timber, etc., roofs blown off from buildings, and great damage generally.

1815, September 25. Very powerful wind, unroofing many buildings, and doing considerable damage to other property.

1816. This year was remarkable for its severe cold weather.

1816, February. Arza Keith was severely burned while making varnish in his house, from the effects of which he never recovered.

1817, February 20. Remarkably severe snow-storm.

1818. Great freshet, doing great damage.

1820, December 22. Rev. Daniel Huntington delivered a discourse in the meeting-house of the North Parish, it being the Second Centennial Anniversary of the landing of the Pilgrims at Plymouth. Text, Psalms xliv. 1–3.

1821, July 4. The first town meeting was held in North Bridgewater this day. The meeting was opened by prayer by Rev. Daniel Huntington. Over two hundred were present, and the first yearly town officers were chosen. Joseph Sylvester was Moderator. Col. Edward Southworth was chosen Town Clerk.

1821, October 31. Messrs. Daniel Temple, of Reading, Mass., and Isaac Bird were ordained as missionaries to the heathen, in the old meeting-house. Rev. Richard S. Storrs, D. D., of Braintree, preached the sermon ; Rev. Daniel Thomas, of Abington, gave the charge ; and Rev. S. Green, the right hand of fellowship. Mr. Temple married Miss Rachel B. Dix, of Boscowen, N. H., and sailed for Malta January 2, 1822, on the brig " Cypress " from Boston. In 1823 Rev. Isaac Bird sailed for Beyroot as missionary. Mr. Temple has since died, August 9, 1850.

1823, November 13. David Brown, a native of the Cherokee tribe of Indians, delivered an address in the meeting-house of the First Church, after which a collection was taken for supporting schools in his nation.

1835, November 6. Miss Susan Hersey, a young miss of sixteen, who resided in the family of Dea. John Crafts, was drowned in Howard's Pond.

1837, July 15. David Lincoln drowned in Sprague's Pond.

1845, August 23. Daniel Brett's house struck by lightning, and Mr. Brett instantly killed.

1845, November 22. Joseph Brett killed by an ox.

1844, November 6. Hon. John Quincy Adams delivered a discourse to the citizens of North Bridgewater, in the meeting-house of the First Congregational Church.

1847, August 14. Lorenzo D. Hervey had his left arm fractured by coming in contact with another train at South Boston, which was standing on a side track, his arm resting at the time on the side window.

1849, May 21. North Bridgewater Union Cemetery consecrated.

1849, May 22. Ethan and Henry Leach (brothers) were thrown from a chaise while crossing the railroad at the burying-gound crossing, and instantly killed.

1849, March 22. Howard's mill-dam washed away ; also railroad bridge near Lewis Keith's mill, damaging so much as to stop the cars.

1851, October 30. Timothy Sullivan was killed by coming in contact with a bridge at the north end of the village, known as " Harlow's Bridge."

1852, May 12. David I. Gray had thumb sawed off in Howard's mill.

1852, May 27. Michael O'Leary drowned.

1852, July 22. " Enterprise" Engine Company, accompanied by the North Bridgewater Brass Band, visited New York.

1852, July 26. Eugene Marshall was a passenger on board the steamer " Atlantic," that sunk on Lake Erie. The steamer came in contact with the " Ogdensburg " near Longport, two o'clock Friday morning. Three hundred lives lost. One hundred and fifty men and women were drowned in the cabin. Mr. Marshall narrowly escaped drowning.

1852, August 15. Salmon Manly died from injuries to his spinal column to-day.

1852, September 18. Galen Edson died from wounds received by a fall that fractured his skull.

1853, November 24. Frederick A. Babcock injured on railroad.

1853, February 5. George Washington, son of Levi French, was badly scalded, injuring him so much that he died the next day (Sunday). Age, two years and ten months.

1853, February 26. Edward Elmer, son of Perez Marshall, was drowned while attempting to cross a pond near his father's house. Age, six years and five months.

1853, February. Ellridge G. Cobb, and one hundred and seven others, sent a petition to the Legislature opposing the passage of a law restricting the sale of intoxicating liquors.

1853, November 21. A collision took place between two trains of cars on the railroad, one of which was the steamboat train ; four persons severely injured. One died soon after.

1853, December 29. Severe snow-storm. The cars on the railroad were stopped, for the first time since the road was opened.

1853. Alonzo S. Drisko, a workman engaged in building the new house of worship for the First Congregational Church, had an arm broken by a board falling from aloft.

1854, March 18. Severe gale. Railroad-crossing sign, at Court Street, blown down. The steeple of the Porter Church was somewhat damaged by the force of wind, which was pretty general throughout this section of country.

1854, June 14. Severe hail-storm about noon. Thermometer stood at ninety in the shade. Hailstones as large as cherries fell in abundance. Zophar Field's house struck. Cow belonging to Chandler Sprague, Esq., instantly killed.

1854, June 19. The house of Weston Simmons, known as the " Poor Farm," was struck by lightning, instantly killing Lemuel Reynolds, who had just stepped into the house for protection from the storm.

46

1854, July 27. The new meeting-house of the First Congregational Church was dedicated to-day.

1854, September 18. Michael Coleman and Michael Keho were run into by a steamboat train that came in contact with chaise.

1855, September 20. To-day was observed as a holiday, for the purpose of holding a fair, to obtain means for erecting a fence around the new cemetery. A large and brilliant procession, consisting of the various fire engine companies in full uniform, drawing their engines, handsomely decorated, preceded by a band of music; also, the North Bridgewater Light Dragoons, under the command of Captain J. Freeman Ellis, together with a representation of the various trades, in large numbers. The procession was formed at one o'clock, when, after marching about the various streets, they proceeded to Yale's mammoth tent, which had been erected for the purpose of serving the dinner, in a lot owned by Frederick Perkins, and opposite the residence of Franklin Ames, Esq. The procession was under the care of Francis M. French, Esq., as chief marshal.

1856, January 5. Severe snow-storm. No trains passed for two days. No meeting on the next day (Sabbath). Roads badly blocked.

By an Act of the Legislature, passed April 19, 1856, a Probate Court was established at North Bridgewater, to be held the last Tuesday of July in each year.

1856, June 3. The centennial celebration of the four Bridgewaters was held to-day, and the bells of all the four towns were rung half an hour before sunrise, and cannon fired on Trooper's Hill.

1856, June 4. A meeting was held to show the feeling in regard to the assault on Charles Sumner at Washington, at which resolutions were passed condemning the act in the strongest terms.

1857, January 18. Very severe snow-storm. Trains on the railroad were blocked for several days. The thermometer during the day was sixteen degrees below zero. The sky was obscured by a dense cloud of snow, that extended in every direction. At night the weather moderated; but the wind increased to a gale, piling the snow in huge drifts. The storm in the night was of unexampled severity. The force of the wind caused the spire of the church at Campello, which had been erected but a short time, to break just below the clock, and the bell to break through the roof and lodge in the vestry below. The damage to the house by this fall was about $3,000.

1857, April 6. Some fiend placed some iron rails upon the railroad track about one mile north of the village, causing the locomotive called the " Pilgrim " to run off the track and injure the train, breaking Alden Reed's jaw-bone, an employee of the road in charge of the train.

1857, May 17. Ice formed one-sixteenth of an inch thick to-day.

1857, May 31. Terrible hailstorm, doing great damage to crops and fruit-trees in the town. Hailstones, as large as robin's eggs, fell to the depth of an inch, continuing about one half-hour.

1858, March 30. Emma Olivia, daughter of F. B. Washburn, was so severely burned while at play that she died in fifteen hours after. Age, seven years and eight months.

1858, May 14.   Bela Keith, Esq., fell and broke his collar-bone while at work repairing a shed belonging to the Satucket House.

1858, May 14.   Elisha Hall had his hand badly injured at Howard & Clark's steam-mill.

1858, July 21.   Charles W., a son of Rev. J. Cooper, was drowned in Howard's Pond.

1858, September 21.   Frank Richmond, son of Philo W. Richmond, broke his leg by falling from a ladder while at work painting on the east side of Kingman's brick block.

1859, January 22.   John B., son of Charles Wentworth, was drowned. Body found Sunday noon following.

1859, June 3.   Gershom I. Sylvester, son of F. M. Sylvester, seven years of age, was run over by cars near Keith's mills, and injured so that he died soon after.

1859, July 30.   Mrs. Harriet Everson and Thacher Everson, wife and daughter of Joseph H. Everson, of Hanson, were killed by a locomotive near Keith's mills.   George W. Monroe and Miss Sarah F. Stetson were in the covered wagon at the time, and severely injured.

1859, August 25.   Herbert, son of Albert Keith, choked to death by a piece of apple, which he was eating while running.

1859, September 9.   Mr. Henry Volney French, who had just arrived at the depot in the Centre Village, from New York, in the steamboat train, attempted to jump from the cars while the train was in motion, was thrown upon the track and run over by the train, and lived but two hours after the accident.   Mr. French was of the firm of French & Howard, shoe manufacturers.   He was a man of excellent habits, smart, active, and very exemplary in all the walks of life.   A deep feeling of sadness pervaded the entire community upon learning of the sad affair.   His wife and children were absent from home at the time of the accident, in Maine.

1859, November 26.   When the four o'clock train was approaching Campello, and near the brick factory, from Boston, a woman named Joanna Barrett, in attempting to cross the track, was struck by the locomotive, and injured so that she died in a few moments.

1860, June 16.   Severe hail-storm.   Hailstones plenty, as large as bullets, doing much damage to fruit.

1860, July 11.   C. Adelbert, son of T. M. Packard, came to his death by falling into a tub set in the ground to catch water.

1860, August 2.   A young child of Daniel Hayward, eighteen months old, fell from an attic of a two-story house to the ground, a distance of thirty feet, through the carelessness of a domestic ; taken up apparently uninjured.

1861, February 25.   Bridget O'Brien was killed by violence.

1861.   Mr. G. E. Wilbor and Thaddeus Keith made a bet on the election of Abraham Lincoln, Wilbor betting he would be elected and Keith that he would not.; the condition was, that the one that lost was to walk to Boston.

Mr. Keith, having lost the bet, started for Boston March 6, and walked the entire distance to the city in five hours. He was accompanied through the village by fife and drum.

1861, March 24. Severe storm, — snow. Trains delayed twenty-four hours.

1861, April 8. As Mrs. John Ellis and another lady were riding from North Bridgewater Village to Campello, they were robbed of their pocket-books. The rogue was caught soon after, and punished.

1861, October 3. M. W. Dwight jumped from a car when in motion near Campello Station, and was killed.

1862, May 26. Michael Larry, a lad of eight years, was drowned in a sawmill flume, at Sprague's Factory Pond.

1863, June 15. Malcolm Howard died of injuries received by the kick of a horse owned by Dr. Baldwin, in the north part of the town.

1863, September 24. William Tolman, son of Elijah Tolman, engineer at Ellis Packard & Co.'s steam-mill, had an arm broken and otherwise severely injured.

1863, October 20. Leroy Hamilton, a driver in the employ of Hancock's express, was struck by a locomotive while crossing the track at Elliot Street crossing. The wagon was made a complete wreck. Mr. Hamilton escaped with a few bruises only.

1863, November. Nahum Perkins, a man over seventy years of age, shot a goose from a flock that was passing over his home.

1864, February. Moses Packard fell and broke his leg in his barn.

1864, February 12. Michael Murphy and Patrick Early were burned to death in the town lock-up.

1864, February 13. Herbert Eaton broke his collar-bone while at play.

1864, April 29. A child of Cornelius McAuliffe was so badly burned while playing with fire in the Pine Grove that she died next day.

1864, July 14. Jennie, daughter of Patrick McCullough, was drowned in a tub of water.

1864, September 26. A boy in the employ of Harrison Rogers was dragged about by a horse till life was extinct, by incautiously fastening the rope-halter around his arms. The horse became unmanageable, so the boy could not release himself.

1864, October 12. Eliza J., wife of James S. Bond, of North Bridgewater, committed suicide by drowning, at Mansfield, Mass.

1864. The drought of 1864 has had no parallel for years. For June and July only 2.38 inches of rain fell; May previous, only two inches; July, 1.32 inches; June, 1.06 inches. In 1854, ten years in August previous, there was no rain.

1864, January 3. The body of an unknown man was found on the railroad track, about a half-mile south of Campello depot; supposed to have fallen from the New York train. The body was terribly mangled, so that it could hardly be identified.

1864, October 27. Five cattle were killed by a Fall River train at Howard's crossing, in the north part of the town, and others badly injured.

1864.   Adeline Harris was appointed teacher by the Freedman's Relief Association, stationed at Newbern, N. C., and sailed from New York December 8.

1865, July 4.   Charles Hayward, son of the late B. F. Hayward, was badly burned in the face by powder.

1865, July 4.   Daniel Huntington, son of Joseph Vincent, had a thumb blown off by the discharge of a pistol.

1865, August 23.   Mrs. Sanford Winter committed suicide.   Cause, temporary insanity.

1865.   This summer season has been very dry.   Wells throughout the State dried up.   Fall feed very light, or none at all.   Mills stopped running for want of water.

CHAPTER XIX.

EARLY HABITS AND CUSTOMS.

Social Life. — Parties. — Spinning Matches. — Raising Flax. — Process of Manufacture. — Dress of Men and Women. — Amusements. — Raisings. — Style of Architecture. — Use of Cranes. — Tinder-Boxes. — Food of the Early Inhabitants. — Drinks. — Well-Sweep. — Rising and Retiring Early. — Attendance on Church Worship.

THE people of the North Parish, in its early settlement, were on a footing of remarkable equality. Their social manners and customs were very simple, friendly, and unceremonious. Visiting was common and frequent among neighbors, and without the formalities of invitation. When a company of neighbors were invited, the women went early, taking their knitting and babies with them, and spent the afternoon; and the men went in season to take supper and return in the evening. Many of the social gatherings partook of the useful as well as the agreeable. They joined together to help their neighbor husk their corn, or to raise a building; and occasionally some neighboring housewife had a quilting party, in which all the good housewives gave an afternoon to make a covering for a bed. In the social gatherings of the young people, dancing was a favorite amusement, and generally using a fiddle. If that could not be had, they used to dance by whistling and singing the tune. Spinning matches, at one time, were quite common, and the people made their own cloth and yarn, and hence were obliged to raise their flax. Nearly every farmer in town owned and cultivated a patch of ground devoted to that purpose. We here give an account of the method of preparing it for use. The quantity of seed required for an acre varied from one half to three bushels. The stalk, or stem, when grown, was of a pea-green, and from two to three feet in height,

366

bearing a blue blossom, which ripened into a ball that contained the flax-seed. When the flax was ripe, it was pulled carefully by the roots, tied into small handfuls, left to dry on the ground a day or two, then set up in small stooks, and, after becoming well dried, was stacked in the field a fortnight or more. Then the seed was threshed out, and sometimes dipped in water for a week or more, and evenly and thinly spread out on the grass to be rotted. This being sufficiently done, it was packed away for the winter; and, as soon as the fair days appeared in spring, there was a general turn-out of men for dressing flax, which consisted of separating the fibrous thread from the stalk. This had to be done by several implements, called the brake, the hatchel, the swingling board and knife. A smart man dresses nearly forty pounds a day. After the process of dressing and twisting it into bunches, it was handed over to the good woman and her daughters to spin, weave, whiten, and convert into thread, cloth, and neat, beautiful garments. We shall describe the process of manufacture, as follows: first, the hatchel was brought and fastened into a chair with a string or stick, and the mother, with her checked apron, and a handkerchief pinned about her neck, and another handkerchief tied about her head to keep off the dust, sat in another chair. Winding one end of the flax tightly around the fingers of the right hand, and holding it, she drew the flax through the hatchel till it was thoroughly combed; then, changing, she combed in a similar manner the other end. Next, it was snarled or wound on the distaff, and spun into *thread* or yarn upon the *foot* or linen-wheel. That drawn out by *hatcheling* was called *tow*, which was carded by hand, with hand-cards, and spun upon the large wheel. That was called *tow-yarn*. From the wheel it went to the *reel*; from the reel to the *loom*, which nearly every family had, and every woman knew how to use, although some families let out their flax to be made into cloth and yarn.

Thus we see our ancestors were independent of foreign looms and spindles for their ordinary dress; and for mere decorations, such as are common at the present day, they had but little regard; and, indeed, a showy costume would have excited contempt rather than emulation. Their attire on the Sabbath, as well as on working-days, was plain. The father's common dress consisted of a woollen coat, a striped woollen frock, tow frock, and woollen, velvet, tow, or leather breeches. These, with long stockings, were fastened at the knee by a buckle; in winter they wore woollen or leather buskins, and thick cowhide shoes, fastened with buckles on the instep. Their best hats were what are now called "cocked-up hats," turned up with three corners; and the more noted men wore wigs.

The ordinary outer dress of the women, in summer, was tow and linen *gowns, checked "tyers,"* or "aprons," and in winter, woollen *gowns* and aprons, thick woollen stockings, and cowhide shoes. The clothing was all of their own manufacture, and every house might properly be called a "home factory." They not only spun their own flax and wool, but wove their cloth in a hand-loom. They also made garments for fathers, sons, and brothers with their own hands. They disdained no kind of domestic labor; they needed no help. Contentment and happiness reigned in their abodes, and amid all their laborious toil, personal wants were few; and, even with their limited means of supply, few remained unsatisfied. Boys and girls (for such they were till married) were early taught to work, and as soon as they acquired muscular power, were taught to make the most of life, and apply it to some useful purpose; and none were allowed to waste it in idleness and dissipation. There was no distinction between the laborer and employer, no difference between the kitchen and the parlor; for that was almost unknown, and generally shut up, except on public days, as Thanksgiving-days, fasts, and

the like, most of the year. Balls, concerts, and places of
amusement, scenic exhibitions, and the long list of modern
devices for killing time were unknown. A *sing*, a *bee*, a
raising, a *husking* party, or a domestic circle, a sleigh-ride in
the winter, or a cherry ride in the summer, were sufficient
for all the purposes of recreation and social intercourse ; and
for those that wished for enjoyment of a more questionable
character, the means and associates were to be found in other
localities.   The amusements and recreation of young men
were mostly of the athletic kind, as "playing ball," which
was always practised, and is now kept up in spring and fall.
Wrestling was very common, especially at raisings and social
and public gatherings.   When at the raising of buildings the
labor was over, and the men stimulated by the treat all had
received, they usually commenced *raising* or *lowering* one
another.   This sport commenced by two young persons
getting inside of a ring formed by spectators, then older
persons joined in the same exercise.   Wagers would be laid,
and a little more stimulant taken to give elasticity and
strength to the parties.   In course of time parties would
get in earnest ; angry words and defiant gestures would be
made, and it generally ended in a fight.   These wrestling-
matches, we are happy to say, are nearly gone by.   It may
be said here that, at the raising of buildings, it was customary to call the men of the town together, and the owner was
expected to furnish the drinks and lunch, and, as soon as the
ridgepole was fairly in place, for the master workman to dedi-
cate the whole by dashing a bottle of *rum* upon the frame,
followed by three hearty cheers from the company present.

We will now give the reader some idea of the early customs in regard to living, the dwellings, and other ancient
matters.   First in order are the

47

DWELLING-HOUSES.

The first was built of logs, and called log-cabins, erected
on land which was usually laid out in lots and ranges.   Next,
after the introduction of saw-mills, came the frame house, of
one story in height, and about sixteen by twenty-four or five
feet on the ground, and containing from one to three rooms.
The next in order of architecture was a two-story house,
with gambrel roof; and some were two story in front, with a
roof slanting back to one story at the back part.   The third
order of houses was the "*hip-roof*," and was introduced
soon after the Revolutionary War, and consisted of a two-story
house, with two front-rooms, a door in the middle, with a
hall running through the centre, and generally a one-story L,
on the back side, for a kitchen, such as the house of Benjamin
Kingman, the late Eliab Whitman, David Cobb, in the village,
and Josiah W. Kingman at Campello, that was burned in
1853.   The windows in the earliest dwellings were either of
mica or diamond-shaped glass, set in tin or lead.   The chimneys were first built of stone, with mammoth fireplaces, and
an oven on one side running back, which, with the chimney, occupied nearly as much room as a modern bedroom.
In the chimney, running from end to end, was a lug-pole,
usually made of oak, from two to four inches in diameter, on
which were hung hooks and trammels of wrought iron,
so constructed as to be raised and lowered at pleasure to suit
the various sized kettles, which were hung over the fire for
culinary uses.   In the course of time these lug-poles gave
way to the old iron crane, on account of their liability to
burn, which was made to swing into the room, or to hang
over the fire.   Cranes were first used in this town about
1750.   The fire was made of large logs, one large one,
called a back-log, being placed on the back side of the fireplace, usually from two to four feet in length; two stones
were used for *andirons*, and a large *fore-stick* resting on the

stones to keep up the fire, beside a *back-stick* or the *back-log* ;
then a sufficiency of smaller fire-wood was piled up ; a
pitch-pine knot being placed under the fore-stick, and lighted,
made a rousing fire. At each end of the fireplaces were
small benches or stools, on which the children usually sat,
warming one side and then the other till they were thoroughly warmed through, while the old folks were seated in
front upon a "settle," enjoying the full blaze. With this
they needed no modern gas-light, no oil, nor candles ; for in
the evening, pitch-pine knots were used, which gave a strong
and brilliant light. Splinters were used to carry about house,
or into the cellar for cider and apples, instead of lamps and
candles. Previous to the introduction of friction matches,
which are of a recent date, every family was supposed to
have a "tinder-box," which consisted of a round tin box,
about six inches in diameter, two inches deep, with a flat
cover of tin, on the outside of which could be inserted a
candle. The box contained tinder, made of burnt linen
cloth, or pieces of punk. By the use of a piece of flint upon
the corners of a file or steel, a spark would catch in the punk ;
and then a stick, with brimstone on the end, coming in contact with the spark, set the stick on fire, from whence the
kindling in the fireplace was lighted. Another method in
general practice was, to cover live coals in the fireplace with
ashes, so as to keep the fire alive on the hearth till morning.
When this failed, the tinder-box was resorted to.

FOOD.

The morning and evening meal usually consisted of bean
or pea porridge, dipped out with a wooden spoon into a
wooden bowl, with bread and butter. Coffee and chocolate
were added upon extra occasions. Tea was seldom used,
especially by the children. The bread consisted of rye and
Indian meal ; occasionally wheat bread. The dinner con-

sisted of salt beef or pork, with vegetables boiled. Fresh
meat was a rarity.   Potatoes are an article of comparatively
recent culture.*   For pudding, they had baked or boiled Indian meal.   The dishes used in early days were mostly of
wood.   The plates were called trenchers.   These wooden
utensils were the first used ; they gradually gave way to
pewter, and still later to crockery and earthen ware.

DRINKS.

Malt beer was a very common drink in the early settlement
of the country, which was made from barley, and was raised
by nearly every farmer.   Next came *cider*, which soon sup-
planted beer.   This was a universal drink, morning, noon,
and night, each family laying in from ten to thirty barrels
for a year's stock.   So common was the use of cider, that it
was considered a mark of disrespect not to pass it round when
a neighbor or traveller called.   Another very common drink
was *flip*, which was made of beer sweetened with sugar, with
a "loggerhead," or red-hot iron, thrust into it ; a little new
rum was then poured in, and nutmeg sprinkled into it.
Toddy was another favorite beverage, made of rum and
water, well sweetened.   A stick, flattened on the end, for
crushing the sugar and stirring it up, was called the "toddy-
stick."   The ring of the tumblers, as it hit the sides in mix-
ing, had its peculiar music, with which nearly every one was
familiar.

Skilful men made graceful flourishes in making another
excellent drink, called "egg-nog," otherwise known as "Tom
and Jerry," which was composed of sugar, milk, and
spirits, mixed with a beaten egg, stirred in rapidly till the
whole was made into froth, and drank hot.   There are many
now who have not forgotten how it tastes, and relish it quite
well.

---

* Introduced into this country in 1732.

Having mentioned many of the drinks that were stimulating, we will now describe another kind, — *cold water*. This is obtained from the earth, and is a natural production. Various means have been in use for obtaining this liquid. The most ancient is the " *well-sweep*." A well was usually dug at a distance of from ten to fifty or more feet from the house ; and but a few feet from the same a post was erected, having a crotch on the top end, in which a long pole was so nearly balanced and swung upon an iron or wooden pin, that when a bucket suspended upon the end of another smaller pole that descended into the water was filled, it could be easily drawn out. There are but few of this kind of apparatus for drawing water now to be found, only here and there a solitary one. Another means of obtaining water is by a windlass erected directly over a well, turned by a crank, the bucket being fastened to the end of a rope that passes over the windlass, and even this has given place to the *pump* and pipe. Here and there is a natural spring, from which water is conducted by pipes to houses, supplying pure, unadulterated liquid.

The custom of *retiring* and *rising* early was universal. The time of retiring was eight to nine o'clock ; that of rising, at dawn of day.

The attendance on church worship was also a custom which nearly all practised. Elderly people that owned horses rode *double*. The wife was seated behind her husband upon the pillion, with her arm around him. In summer the young men went barefoot, or with shoes in hand ; the young women wore coarse shoes, carrying a better pair in hand, with stockings, to change before entering the meeting-house. Going to meeting on foot was not confined to young people ; many women walked three to five miles to attend church. In winter it was customary for the women to carry small foot-stoves, which were usually made of perforated tin, fastened in a

wooden frame, about eight or nine inches square, in which
were placed hot coals. These stoves were all the warm.
ing allowed in church. The usual time for church service
was one and a half hours, — from half-past ten to twelve
o'clock, or one glass and a half long, as hour-glasses were
their time-pieces in the absence of clocks. The intermissions
were short, being one hour in winter and one hour and a half
in summer. The interval was generally spent in the nearest
neighbors' houses, who always had a good blazing fire in
winter, and plenty of coals with which to replenish their
foot-stoves. This intermission was a grand opportunity for
the people of the remote portions of the parish to meet every
week and become acquainted, as it promoted social union and
good feeling throughout the society. Every new and interesting event was discussed ; and while partaking of their
lunch they had brought with them, the father would request
the boys to bring in and pass round the cider. The afternoon
services being over, people might have been seen gathering
around the horse-block that stood a short distance south of the
church, on the green, which was a large flat-topped stone for
the use of women in mounting and alighting from their horses.
The means of locomotion in the days of our fathers consisted
of an ox-cart, or the back of a horse. A chaise or wagon
was a curiosity. A journey of forty or fifty miles was a great
undertaking, requiring much preparation; while now, many
travel by steam hundreds of miles in a day, and think it
nothing compared to that in early days.

A journey from the North Parish to Boston was the labor
of two days with oxen and cart. The same journey is now
performed in one day, and nothing thought of its being hard.
It is one hour's ride in a steam train, and the trains run in
such a manner that a person can leave home after dinner, go
to the city, and return in the evening train, and have several
hours for business.